ROTHMANS JUBILEE HISTORY
OF CRICKET

Rothmans
Jubilee History of Cricket
1890–1965

JOHN ARLOTT

with a foreword by Neville Cardus

ARTHUR BARKER LIMITED
20 *New Bond Street London W*1

PRINTED BY W. S. COWELL LTD, AT THE BUTTER MARKET, IPSWICH

James
1944 –1965

Contents

Foreword

The writer of lapidary inscriptions, Doctor Johnson wisely remembered, is not on oath. The same could be said of the writer of an introduction to a book written by a friend. The fact is that the more closely one knows, likes and admires an author, the more one is determined to be objective about him when it comes to a critical appreciation of his work. I have known, liked and admired John Arlott, in all his capacities, for many years; and as he himself spends much of his time professionally as a critic he will be the first to read what I am now about to say hoping for the best, and apprehensive of the worst.

His book sets out to record historically and biographically the beginning and development of cricket since 1890 – it is, in a word, a history of what might be called 'modern cricket'. There are other excellent volumes treating the same subject comprehensively – the Altham–Swanton classic, for instance. But John Arlott has composed his history in a fresh and fascinating way. He unfolds the historical canvas, relates sequence of events, the games played, the facts and the figures, the changing, growing and widening scene, but all the time he gives us insights into the cricketers who, summer after summer, in all parts of the world, have shaped and are shaping cricket's course and constitution. The book is alternatively a history and a cricketer's 'Who's Who' and 'Who was Who'. Most important and engrossing, John Arlott relates changes of technique and changes in the game's laws and procedure to the pressure of national life, economy, and so on. The book consequently is much more than a history of cricket since 1890; indirectly it tells us of changes in the outlook and mentality of the players and of the times in which they have lived and have been nurtured. If I may use a term borrowed from the music-critic's vocabulary, I describe this history as symphonically shaped and developed. 'If we are to maintain perspective,' writes John Arlott, 'we must realize that all these changes have taken place within an unbroken tradition. They are like eddies, swirls, dimples, calms and rushes within a single stream, as it twists, turns, widens or narrows. Cricket assimilates its changes because of its continuity.' This passage is a sort of leading-motive or governing theme of the book; also it is a fine example of our author's use of the English language. Arlott writes clear easy illuminating English; he is nearly the only Cardus disciple who doesn't, as he writes, slightly embarrass me.

J. R. Green, one of the first truly evolutionary writers of English history proper, argued that modern history of our isles began at least three times. In my own view, the vital and truly germinal periods in cricket's history were the coming and maturing of W. G. Grace, the passing of the rule permitting a new ball during a long innings, and the abolition of Mondays and Thursdays as days on which first-class matches were legally authorized to begin in this country. Every cricketer, hoping to understand cricket and its historical background with any sense of values, must constantly remember that when Tom Richardson, Surrey and England fast bowler, took 1,000 wickets within four seasons he did so using the same ball most of the time. Not until round about 1906 was the 'new ball' concession introduced by MCC.

We are astonished nowadays – in fact staggered – to recall that less than sixty years ago the great cricket grounds of England might often be silent and vacant on Saturdays. Even a Test match, beginning on a Thursday, could come to an end on a Friday, or, as at Lords in 1899, just after lunch on the Saturday. Obviously the public 'gates' and assistance was loftily regarded in the 'Golden Age' as of secondary significance. Here is one of the reasons why cricket in the 'amateur' period of governance and example was so opulent and masterful of gesture and performance.

All or nearly all the clues are to be found in this book. It is a valuable contribution to the library of cricket – and, I think – a permanent contribution. Such a volume, with its many photographs, couldn't possibly be printed and published at what Mr Montague Tigg in Dickens would not doubt have called the 'ridiculous sum' of a guinea. Thanks to the munificence of Rothmans – another of this establishment's services to the game – this history is brought within the reach of the most, in these times, modest pocket. It – and the author – have my blessings.

Neville Cardus

Acknowledgements

Like everyone who attempts a history of any branch of first-class cricket, I must – and most gratefully do – acknowledge recourse to *Wisden*, which provides not only the basic reference to the game but also a mirror of contemporary cricketing thought of each year. Almost equally helpful, in respect of the two earlier sections, was Vol XV of *MCC Cricket Scores and Biographies*, compiled from Haygarth's notes by F. S. Ashley-Cooper.

Invaluable guidance has come, too, from *The History of Cricket* by H. S. Altham and E. W. Swanton, *Australian Cricket* by A. G. Moyes, *West Indian Cricket* by Christopher Nicole, the three volumes of *The History of South African Cricket* by W. M. Luckin and Louis Duffus; *New Zealand Cricket* by T. W. Reese, *Great Days in New Zealand Cricket* by R. T. Brittenden, *Indian Cricket* (v.y.) by S. K. Gurunathan, *Test Cricket* by Roy Webber; *Cricket Records* by Roy Webber, revised by Michael Fordham.

For half the years covered by this book it was possible to write from some degree of personal observation. But, for that period and to an even greater extent on pre-1914 play and players, I am deeply grateful for talks with cricketers who spoke from first-hand knowledge. Those conversations were a delight which I enjoyed with no thought that their content would ever be set down here. A sad number of those men, alas, are now dead so that my thanks here are also a valediction. In his eighties, Charles Kortright, the legendary 'fastest bowler of all' still talked with crystal clear recollection, and often vivid imagery, of the great players of his day. Sir Pelham Warner, too, was so immersed in the subject that a question on a particular player or event would elicit an instant and precise answer. Len Braund, Sir Jack Hobbs, C. B. Fry, Maurice Tate, Philip Mead, J. N. Crawford, Alec Kennedy, George Brown and Harry Altham, through many happy and absorbing hours, brought to life great players I had never seen in action. This book remembers them affectionately as well as gratefully.

On the play of later years I am indebted for much wisdom to Herbert Strudwick, Bill Bowes, Walter Robins, Arthur Mailey, Ian Peebles, Tony Lock, Douglas Insole, Willie Watson, Wilfred Wooller and countless others who have talked so freely and well about their game. Something of all of them is in this book – though they are responsible for none of its deficiencies.

Finally, my thanks go to Walter Robins and Jack Price for reading the proofs and giving me much encouragement: but for them there would have been more errors than now remain – and are mine, not theirs.

Note. In the biographical notes on players, it may be assumed that they are right-handed batsmen or right-arm bowlers except where left-handed or left-arm is specified.

The Ever-Changing Game

The story of cricket is a record of change, never more so than in the modern game. The transformation from ancient to modern, though occasionally violent – as in the two bowling 'revolutions' – was, in general, slow. As in many other fields of British life, the eighteen-nineties were the years of modernization. Even a decade earlier, no cricket of any quality existed outside England and Australia and, even in those countries, and at what was regarded as first-class level, standards were erratic. Many players regarded as outstanding were limited in technique, and too much cricket was played on unreliable pitches.

By 1890, however, the game was firmly rooted in a number of countries, the standard of grounds had been improved and, especially in England, the collieries and the mills, village greens and common lands, as well as the public schools and Universities, were turning out the heaviest spate of gifted, and basically sound, players ever known.

The shape of cricket was now broadly established, and it aroused public interest and enthusiasm, partly because its outstanding players' performances were exciting in their own right. That alone would not have been enough; it would have tended to monotony. Cricket retains its air of freshness because its great players do not only adorn the game; in varying measure, directly or indirectly, they change it and give it its essential qualities of development and variety. They do not simply win matches in their own day; they create the methods of the next generation.

Thus, for thirty years, W. G. Grace outstripped every other batsman. He was so masterly and so versatile that he lifted the whole standard of batting to a fresh level. In his effect, he went much further. He changed batting by his own performance, and he changed bowling, too. He became the great problem for bowlers. First, by his cool power, he routed a whole generation of slinging, erratic, physically dangerous fast-bowlers. Soon he posed a major problem not merely of getting him out, but even of checking the rate and size of his scores. So a whole race of bowlers grew up who knew that the true trial of their skill was in contest with W.G. In the fixture lists of those days, with so many matches like Gentlemen v Players, so many more by MCC at first-class level than now, North v South – and even Smokers v Non-smokers – as well as County Championship games, the better bowlers had to encounter 'The Champion' perhaps a dozen times a season. Trial, error and punishment produced the school of the 'length' bowler. Nottingham, with its flawless batsmen's wicket, was the home of the craft, but it had its practitioners throughout the top level of the game.

Sixty years afterwards, when Sir Donald Bradman established a similar position of dominance, the process was reversed and D. R. Jardine worked out the fast leg-theory known as 'Body-line' to check his scoring.

In the period between, the dominance of the batsmen of the 'Golden Age', on their immaculate lawns,

Dr W. G. Grace, the creator of modern cricket, the eminent Victorian of the game and, for almost half a century, its symbol

bred high pace, sharp leg-spin and slow left-arm bowlers who, denied any turn by perfect wickets, became utter masters of the subtleties of flight. Soon, too, came the googly bowlers, who turned the ball back through the flowing off-side strokes of that elegant race of batsmen. Bosanquet, the googly's exploiter if not its inventor, won a rubber for England with it; the South African experts, Vogler, Faulkner, White, and Schwarz, turned the tables and beat England; and Dr Hordern won at least one Test for Australia before batsmen began to 'read' the 'wrong 'un' or to find counters to it.

The faster bowlers, too, set out to stop batsmen butchering them through the covers. George Hirst with his sharp left-arm inswing, and others, like W. T. Greswell, J. T. Rawlin and T. A. Jaques who were right-armed, moved the ball through the air towards the leg stump. The lovely play through the off-side was more and more curtailed.

Batsmen, keeping pace with history and led by Jack Hobbs, mastered the googly, turned more and more to back-play, learnt to place the ball to the inch on the leg side. O'Reilly bowled his rolled leg-breaks, and sharper googlies, at a pace almost medium, never putting the ball up to drivable length, and hemming in the batsman with short-leg fieldsmen. In England, B. H. Lyon threw his close catchers up on the leg side for Tom Goddard's off-breaks, and a new type of attack was begun, constrictive on good pitches, deadly when the ball would turn: soon every county had a stock off-break bowler. In reply came Denis Compton, quick to use his feet as soon as the ball was given air but, when the bowler 'dug it in', as fast to sweep through a wide leg-side arc, with such placing as pierced even the most tightly set field. In Australia, the cult never took root, with the consequence that, when the perfect off-spinner, Laker, emerged – as it was an historical certainty he would – he routed the Australians of 1953 and won a Test rubber.

These are major examples of the development of cricket, instances clearly apparent to us, looking back from 1965. There have been countless others. Faced by the truly great opponent, both batsmen and bowlers have formulated fresh techniques in the attempt to contain or repulse them. There were bowlers who forsook all attempt to attack against the batting of Ranjitsinhji, Jessop or Bradman: batsmen who resolved that when a ball from S. F. Barnes or Maurice Tate pitched outside the line of the stumps they would play it (before the day of the 'new' lbw

Robert Peel (Yorkshire) second in the line of the famous Yorkshire and England slow left-arm bowlers: successor to Peate, predecessor of Rhodes

law) with their pads. We see the figures and the performances of the great players; but their full significance and effect are not always apparent at the time. It is certain, nevertheless, that, groundsmen apart, the *great* players have created virtually all the changes which make cricket the absorbing game it is.

There is little doubt that we are in another state of change, even if we are so close to it that we cannot distinguish its pattern. Dismayed by the killer onslaught of post-war Australian and West Indian batsmen, the opposition adopted two different methods. Where great pace has been available – Miller and Lindwall, Tyson and Statham, Trueman and Statham, Davidson and MacKenzie, Hall and Griffith – it has been thrown in ruthlessly, with the bouncer as its trademark, and Test rubbers have been decided in a series of high-speed opening bursts. Lacking such pace, captains have employed short-of-a-length bowling, to stranglehold fields placed, with rare cunning, to the inch. On most levels, and certainly on the plane of Test cricket, a majority of batsmen have answered with almost strokeless resistance so that, side by side with the brilliant stroke-play of Weekes, Worrell, Harvey, Sobers, Kanhai or Dexter, some of the longest and slowest innings in Test history have been played by batsmen of undoubted ability who still had no answer to restrictive field-settings.

Let us not be too impatient. Batsmen have always found the answer to bowlers' tactics in the past: they will do so again – at least to restriction, if not in every case to the bouncer. Then it will be the bowlers' turn to think again. Otherwise cricket will become static – which, as this story shows, has never happened before.

If we are to maintain perspective, however, we must realize that all these changes have taken place within an unbroken tradition. They are like the eddies, swirls, dimples, calms and rushes within a single stream, as it twists, turns, widens or narrows. Cricket assimilates its changes because of its continuity, which often makes itself apparent in the most unexpected ways. Thus, the succession of the mighty Yorkshire slow left-arm bowlers was uninterrupted from Peate, who began to play in 1879, through Peel and Rhodes to Verity, who continued as a Test bowler to the beginning of the 1939-45 War, in which he lost his life. Sometimes the links are even more startling. When Jim Cornford came to Sussex for a trial as a fast-medium bowler, his action was so much like Maurice Tate's that everyone who saw him assumed that he

The Lord's Test – England v Australia – of 1896: Australia in the field

had simply imitated Tate – but he had never even seen Maurice Tate bowl. Tom Graveney was said to reproduce Hammond's cover drive before he had ever seen Hammond lift a bat. Again and again a young slow left-arm bowler will appear in Yorkshire with an action exactly like that of Wilfred Rhodes – who had ceased to play before the younger man was born.

Account for it, if you will, by the fact that they have instinctively copied a perfect action or style from an earlier imitator.

Whatever the explanation, the continuity is beyond doubt – and it is the quality which makes possible the constant pattern of change on the endless stream of cricket.

The Shaping of Modern Cricket: 1890–1899

Seventy-five years ago, in 1890, cricket began to take its modern shape. When that season began, cricket in England was the most firmly and healthily established game in the world. Dr W. G. Grace had given it the stamp of respectability – the idea of a country doctor was *so* healthy and reassuring – and now it ran from top to bottom of society. Its champion, W. G. Grace, was unmistakably an eminent Victorian; and, in true Victorian fashion, its empire was expanding. It was less obvious that W.G. had completed the foundations of modern cricket and that, within a single generation, his successors would build the edifice.

The nation saw – or thought it saw – more importantly, that W.G. could hardly hope to retain his sovereignty. Already, surely, his powers were on the wane. He was forty-one, and no one could foresee that, a full five years hence, he was to surprise everyone with what may well have been the most amazing season of even his mighty career. At least he was still there: the world of cricket was secure. There were still the two classical master batsmen of Nottingham – Arthur Shrewsbury (regarded by W.G. as second only to his mighty self) and William Gunn: Attewell was there to preach, by example, his unfailing sermon of length, length – always length: George Ulyett – the 'Happy Jack' of Yorkshire – merry Johnny Briggs, the subtle George Lohmann, and tiny Bobby Abel, were established stars, and Peel had already inherited Peate's place as Yorkshire's – and England's – slow left-arm bowler.

Those who had been long in the game knew it was changing. Many changes had been wrought by great players, but one immense factor was purely mechanical – the grass mower. Not long before, the grass at Lord's had been kept level by grazing sheep, a tradition so firmly established that Robert Grimston, seeing a mower on the ground, summoned some navvies from St John's Wood Road to break up the 'contraption' with their pickaxes! In a perceptive article entitled 'The Development of Cricket' for the 1892 *Wisden*, the Hon. R. H. Lyttelton wrote – 'On Lord's Ground thirty years ago Jackson, Willsher and Tarrant had merely to bowl their fastest and straightest, and the batsman might, any ball, expect a dead shooter or a body blow'. This was the menace W. G. Grace had faced and mastered. But now that groundsmen, up and down the country, could, and did, make true wickets, he could almost fancy that batting had become a simple matter. The ball now did only what the bowler could *make* it do. It was the turn of the out-cricketers to make good the disadvantage.

Dr Grace and good pitches had transformed the game of the village green to a pursuit which was about to enter into realms of comparative sophistication.

All this was clear in the crystallization of fresh techniques. Over-arm bowling had been legalized in 1864, but the round-arm tradition had persisted in many quarters for some years afterwards. Now, however, slow bowlers with straight-over actions were setting problems of flight such as the lower-arm men had never been able to do. Indeed, 1890 saw the final appearance for Yorkshire of Edmund Peate, the last of the great round-arm slow bowlers. The new type of fast bowler, high-armed and controlled, had replaced the slingers, and there were clear signs of the imminent flowering of accurate pace in which virtually every county had a genuinely fast bowler fit to play for England. More important, perhaps, George Lohmann was demonstrating the immense resources of medium-pace bowling in terms of movement from the pitch, concealment of length and deception in pace. Fielding, though far short of the post-1945 standard, was improving by leaps and bounds, especially in the Universities.

Pilling, MacGregor and the Australian Blackham, for all the scanty nature of the protection available, had demonstrated that it was possible to take even bowling of some pace much closer to the stumps than the wicket-keepers of previous eras ever contemplated: and they had scorned the post of long-stop out of cricket.

In face of this heightened challenge, batsmen were relatively fortunate. They had as their model the batting of W. G. Grace which the increased invention and fresh methods of outcricket were designed to combat. He had swept away the concept of a man as a forward player or a back player: according to the state of the pitch, type of bowler – or even the separate deliveries from the same bowler – a batsman needed to be sound, whether he went forward or back. The on side was becoming – though less than in later years – almost as important as the off: sometimes a batsman must concentrate on defence, sometimes on attack. There was a defensive stroke for every good ball, an attacking one for every bad ball.

If this represented development of the game in depth, it was also growing in extent. In the spring of 1890 G. F. Vernon's side had returned from the first tour of India: a year before, Test Matches had been played for the first time in South Africa.

The Currie Cup competition had just been completed in South Africa where a Board of Control had lately been formed. The first Triangular Tournament – between Barbados, Trinidad and Demerara (British Guiana) – was being arranged in the West Indies: and, though no one yet knew it, the competition between the Australian states for the Sheffield Shield lay only two years ahead, the formation of the New Zealand Cricket Council two beyond that. The cricket world was taking shape.

Although the game was spreading, it is important to appreciate that there were restrictive influences in places of power. When it was proposed to the county secretaries' meeting in 1895 that the Australians, on their tour of England during the following season, should play five Tests instead of three, only one county representative supported the proposal. The remainder regarded Test Matches as an interference with the more important County Championship.

This was not solely an official attitude. In 1890, A. E. Stoddart chose to play for Middlesex rather than in two Tests against Australia, while Yorkshire refused to release Ulyett and Peel for the Oval Test on the grounds that it was more important for them to play in the county match against Middlesex – and Stoddart. So, again in this crucial decade, the Board of Control was formed to take over the organization of Test Matches. An important piece of legislation, allowing a declaration – though only on the third day – had been introduced in 1889.

1890 was a significant year for the extension of the first-class game in England. Since Derbyshire withdrew from the County Championship after the 1887 season, the accepted Championship had involved eight counties – Gloucestershire, Kent, Lancashire, Middlesex, Notts, Surrey, Sussex and Yorkshire. In 1887 the County Cricket Council had been formed to deal with administrative details of the competition such as qualification and methods of scoring. At its meeting in August 1890 it categorized the cricketing counties in first, second and third classes, and was asked to approve a scheme which amounted to promotion and relegation through the three levels. This was more than the traditionalists could stomach. The Council dissolved itself *sine die*. That meeting marked the end of the isolation of the eight senior counties. In the next season Somerset were admitted to the first-class competition, and their immediate success opened the gates so that, by 1900, Derbyshire, Essex, Hampshire, Leicester, Warwickshire and Worcestershire were also of the number. In 1890 the Second-class County Championship began, to be replaced by the Minor Counties competition in 1895.

There is no doubt that to the cricketers of the day and their steadily growing army of followers, these events of long-term historic importance seemed less important than the outcome of the various Tests and competitions, the results of which may be listed here.

1890–1899

Test Matches

1890 in England, England beat Australia 2–0: one match abandoned

1891–92 in Australia, Australia beat England 2–1

1891–92 in South Africa, England beat South Africa 1–0

1893 in England, England beat Australia 1–0: two matches drawn

1894–95 in Australia, England beat Australia 3–2

1895–96 in South Africa, England beat South Africa 3–0

1896 in England, England beat Australia 2–1

1897–98 in Australia, Australia beat England 4–1

1898–99 in South Africa, England beat South Africa 2–0

1899 in England, Australia beat England 1–0: four matches drawn

County Champions

1890 Surrey
1891 Surrey
1892 Surrey
1893 Yorkshire
1894 Surrey
1895 Surrey
1896 Yorkshire
1897 Lancashire
1898 Yorkshire
1899 Surrey

Sheffield Shield Winners

1892–93 Victoria
1893–94 South Australia
1894–95 Victoria
1895–96 New South Wales
1896–97 New South Wales
1897–98 Victoria
1898–99 Victoria
1899–1900 New South Wales

Currie Cup Winners

1889–90 Transvaal
1890–91 Griqualand West
1892–93 Western Province
1893–94 Western Province
1894–95 Transvaal
1896–97 Western Province
1897–98 Western Province

West Indies, Inter-Colonial or Triangular Tournament

1892–93 Barbados beat Trinidad
1895–96 British Guiana beat Barbados
1897–98 Barbados beat British Guiana
1899–1900 Barbados beat British Guiana

The Scene in 1890

The summer of 1890 was wet, and a particularly rainy spell in late August completely washed out the third – Manchester – Test against W. L. Murdoch's Australian team and interfered with a number of county matches.

It is difficult, in 1965, to realize the importance of county cricket matches to people, often with limited resources, who, before the days of the motor car, lived in the great cities of England and to many of whom the Bank Holiday match was the event of the year. *Wisden* commented 'The presence of an Australian team had, of course, some little effect upon the interest taken in county matches, but the contests did not suffer to any extent, the attendance all round being very good and in some cases – notably at the Oval and Old Trafford – enormous.'

Public interest in the county competition was maintained all the summer, though the runners-up, Lancashire, never really looked like overhauling Surrey, who won seven of their first eight Championship matches. Surrey were in the middle of a run that gave them the Championship in eight of nine consecutive seasons. They were the most powerful bowling side in the country, although their attack was confined almost entirely to pace: only F. Smith (slow left-arm) and D. L. A. Jephson (lobs) contributed any spin of faintly comparable effect. Between Lohmann's first

George Lohmann (Surrey) The first of the 'modern' medium-pace technicians, accurate, subtle and, when the pitch suited him, almost unplayable

bowler whose quality is indicated by his figures in Tests against Australia of 77 wickets at 13·01: against South Africa, 35 at 5·8. Lohmann took a hundred wickets in a season for the eighth time in 1892 when he was twenty-seven years old and an utter master of his craft. For all his fine appearance and physique, he was not truly well. He went to live in South Africa in hope of improving his health and, though he returned and took a fair share of wickets for Surrey in 1895 and 1896, and was quite deadly on the 1895–96 tour of South Africa, he was a sick man. He died of tuberculosis in South Africa in 1901, only 36 years old.

Tom Richardson

Tom Richardson was the classical fast bowler. He had a fine, honest face and black curly hair. Six feet tall, he weighed twelve stone at peak fitness and, as one who frequently walked from his home at Mitcham to the Oval with his cricket bag on his shoulder, he *was* fit. In his younger days there was doubt as to the fairness of his delivery, but he straightened his arm to the satisfaction of his critics and, in his brief but glorious prime, his action was tall and flowing – perhaps 'noble' is the best word for it – and his pace extremely high. He was a fine, loyal character, incapable of bowling at less than his utmost. He was not so subtle as Lohmann or Lockwood, and on dangerous wickets, so far from attempting to intimidate batsmen, he often bowled wide of the off stump, but he had the classic body-action break-back of the old fast bowlers. Herbert Strudwick, who kept wicket to him in practice matches while Richardson was still near his peak, has said that, on true hard turf and at full speed, he would pitch six inches outside the off stump and 'do' so much that he – 'Struddy' – would take it standing back, a yard or more wide of the line of the leg stump.

Richardson played for Surrey from 1892 to 1904 and took 2,105 wickets: but, so prodigal was his effort, that he took 1,005 of those wickets in the four English seasons between 1894 and 1897 – despite tours to Australia in two of the intervening winters. No other fast bowler had ever produced remotely comparable figures. If ever a man bowled his heart out it was Tom Richardson, and he was only 42 when, alone and depressed, he took his own life.

W. H. Lockwood

The third of the great Surrey bowlers was Bill Lockwood, who could be as fast as Richardson and as subtle

county match in 1884 and Lockwood's retirement in 1904, Surrey had three of the finest medium-to-fast bowlers in the history of cricket. Yet, through a series of odd coincidences, they were never all at their best at the same time.

George Lohmann

They were George Lohmann, Bill Lockwood and Tom Richardson: all England bowlers and each indisputably a master. Lohmann was the least of them in pace: though he had a faster ball, his normal rate was about medium. He was the first accepted master of what is nowadays called 'cut' and he moved the ball both ways off the pitch: but some batsmen found themselves in greater difficulty from his masking of length. Tall, wide-shouldered and handsome, Lohmann was a useful batsman and one of the finest slip-catchers of his time. But, above all, he was a match-winning

Tom Richardson (Surrey) The classical fast-bowler: honest, mighty, loyal and tireless

W. H. Lockwood (Surrey) Uncertain in performance, dubious in action but, on his day, one of the most effective bowlers in the history of cricket

as Lohmann. He bowled brilliantly in 1891 and 1892, before Richardson found his feet, and again through 1893 and 1894 while Lohmann was ill. Then, when Lohmann returned, Lockwood went into eclipse because, *Wisden* said plainly enough, he did not keep himself fit. Ironically, yet perhaps characteristically, after he had been discounted as burnt out, he played his way back so effectively that he was top of the Test bowling averages against Australia as late as 1902.

Lockwood was strongly built, a useful field and a free batsman, good enough to be ranked as an all-rounder. But it is as a bowler that he is entitled to a place in cricket history. For the two seasons of 1893 and 1894, and to only slightly less degree between

1898 and 1900, he and Richardson were the finest pair of opening bowlers ever to play for any county. Lockwood was notably less firm in character and less consistent than Richardson, but his bowling had greater variety. His slow ball was famous throughout the cricket of his day; he held it back so cleverly that the best of players found themselves drawn forward too soon. On difficult wickets, his lift made him almost unplayable. He was, though, one of the bowlers named by the county captains at their meeting of 1900 as having a doubtful action.

Surrey were amazingly lucky through the nineties to make good the absences and deficiencies of Lohmann and Lockwood by a series of briefly successful bowlers. The first, and most remarkable, was the one-

Bobby Abel (Surrey) The myopic little man, known as 'The Guv'nor', who, for more than a dozen years, was one of the heaviest scorers in the game

eyed J. W. Sharpe who, negligible in 1889, emerged to take 100 wickets and play against Australia in 1890 and 1891, and then lapsed again into obscurity. For odd seasons Brockwell, Smith, Hayward, and finally Walter Lees, gave the three masters support.

This penetration gave Surrey their fine Championship run from 1887 to 1889. Their slip catching was good. Wood was a Test wicket keeper. The two Reads – W.W. and J.M. – and then Brockwell and Hayward played for England as batsmen but, through the nineties, Bobby Abel was their heaviest run-scorer.

R. Abel

In an age devoted to nicknames for its heroes, Abel was known as 'The Guv'nor'. He was a wry little man, only five-feet-five tall, frailly built and with eyesight so defective that, in 1893, it ruined his batting; and he played in glasses through some of his most success-

ful seasons. Small wonder that, though he grew up on rough pitches, he was said to back away from fast bowling. Abel was essentially a good-wicket player, for his bat was crooked, but he was one of the steadiest run-scorers of his day and he had some decisive successes on wet pitches.

J. Briggs

Though they had not the great weight and superb blend of the Surrey team, Lancashire, in 1890, could be highly effective. Johnnie Briggs was top of both their batting and bowling averages in that season. He was a lively little man, full of jokes but of precarious nervous balance, a popular figure with a quick cricket brain. He bowled left-arm off a short, perky run, turned the ball appreciably, and used many variations including a much faster ball which he could direct on yorker length. As a batsman he was less important than impetuous, with a fondness for cutting and slashing; but he scored many runs quickly and his brilliant fielding at cover-point completed his equipment as an England all-rounder for many seasons.

The other two main Lancashire bowlers were Watson, a slow off-spinner of the old type, and Mold, one of the fastest of his time and effective at Test level, but an arrant thrower. Albert Ward and Frank Sugg were the two established batsmen but, in 1890, an eighteen-year-old Harrovian, A. C. MacLaren, in his first match for the county, scored 108 against Sussex: one of the characteristic figures of the age to come had made his initial impact.

Kent, third in the table of 1890, relied largely on the contrasting left-arm bowling of Martin and Wright: their batting never realized its attractive promise, partly because W. H. Patterson could play only in August. The Hearnes worked loyally through this 'trough' period between one group of the county's major players and the next.

Yorkshire were in a transition stage between the old eleven and the side Lord Hawke was building to take the place of Surrey at the undisputed head of English cricket. Meanwhile, their successes were so few that the team came in for savage criticism in their own county. Peel took the main weight of the bowling with some support from Wainwright, an off-break bowler of sharp spin but inadequate control. Ulyett, Hall and Lord Hawke batted serviceably and with David Hunter, the wicket-keeper, bore the main weight of the 1890 season in which, significantly, 37 different players appeared in county matches.

George Ulyett (Yorkshire) 'Happy Jack' from Sheffield: bluff, brave, cheerful, reliable all-rounder and a fine Yorkshireman

G. Ulyett

George Ulyett's day was almost done, but he had been an automatic selection for England since the start of Test Matches a dozen years before. Broad, cheerful, honest and humorous – he was known as 'Happy Jack' – he was still one of the most popular players of any age. A genuine all-rounder, his round-arm fast bowling was marked by straightness and endurance rather than any inspired quality or great resource: but he had been valuable in years of shortage of true pace. The strength and quality of the man were reflected in his batting which was resolute, but never dull: on the bad wickets of his early days he took some terrible batterings without flinching and his bat was very straight in defence. His major gift was his savage but correct and well-judged hitting, and he was at his best in a difficult situation. In 1890 he played his last Test when England collapsed, and Ulyett's innings of 74 out of 173 effectively won the match.

R. Peel

In Yorkshire's lean years about 1890, Bobby Peel had to become an all-rounder and his left-handed batting was more than merely serviceable. His distinction, however, is as the second in the historic line of the Yorkshire slow left-arm bowlers. With an easy action and an almost automatic accuracy, he spun the natural break more sharply than many of his kind. Peel was short and tubby but active in the field and capable of long bowling spells without loss of accuracy or turn. In fifteen years from 1882 to 1897 he took 1,554 wickets for Yorkshire and 102 for England against Australia alone. He was still a capable bowler when, in 1897, he was accused of going on to the field when 'not in a fit condition to play' and he never appeared in first-class cricket again.

A. Shrewsbury

Notts made a good start to the season though, with Barnes's best days over, they were virtually a three-man side: those three, though no longer young, were among the finest cricketers in the world. Arthur Shrewsbury, a dumpy, sloping-shouldered man, was for years second only to W. G. Grace as a batsman. An impeccably straight player with neat footwork, a preference for the back-foot and on-side strokes, he was the model for the subsequent generation of north country professional batsmen, a master of the dead bat, quick to drop his wrists to the lifting ball, unperturbed on bad wickets and, though never physically strong, a consistently heavy scorer for thirty years. His 164 at Lord's in 1886 against Australia, with Spofforth bowling on a helpful wicket, was described by Lord Harris as the finest innings he had ever seen in his life. Shrewsbury began his career on rough country pitches and perfected his technique there. He was often ill, and his eyesight was so bad that he found it difficult to read more than a few lines. Yet, in 1902, when he was forty-six, he ended his last season for Notts at the top of their batting averages. He, too, made a sad end; but he was pleasant in manner and is remembered for his frequent remark to Kirk, the pavilion attendant at Trent Bridge, when he went out to bat after lunch – 'Send me out a cup of tea at half-past-four, please'.

W. Gunn

His partner, William Gunn, who played for England at soccer as well as cricket, made a strong contrast with Shrewsbury. He is remembered as the epitome of

Arthur Shrewsbury (Notts) A master of bad wicket play, cool and certain. When W. G. Grace was asked to name the next batsman to himself, he said 'Give me Arthur'

William Gunn (Notts) The typical Victorian batsman; a patient, correct forward player. A double international for England, at cricket and football

forward play. Six-feet-three tall and stringily built, he was extremely correct, strong on the off side and with the gifts of an extremely punishing driver but generally regarded as being over-concerned with defence. Though Gunn came into cricket relatively late, he played valuably for Notts for more than twenty seasons.

W. Attewell

The third of the Nottingham mainstays was William – 'Dick' – Attewell, a stockily-built slow-medium stock bowler and Alfred Shaw's heir as the arch disciple of length. On responsive wickets he could turn the ball from the off: but in general he contented himself with perfect length and line. His great gift lay in his untiring accuracy and control; it was almost impossible to collar him.

Gloucestershire were no more than an average county side and would have been less than that without 'W.G.'. Cranston and Painter gave him some assistance in batting; Woof and Roberts in bowling. 'The Old Man' scored more runs than anyone else in the side, was second in the bowling averages and had the best all-round assistance from his elder brother, E.M. who, though rising forty-nine, had a batting average of 20·12 and took 18 wickets.

The Middlesex batting, apart from Webbe, Stoddart and O'Brien was unreliable and only Burton took more than fifty wickets (53): neither E. A. Nepean nor F. J. G. Ford, who would have added considerable strength, was regularly available, while A. E. Stoddart and J. T. Hearne were only on the brink of their careers.

Sussex had, in C. A. Smith – later better known as Sir Aubrey Smith, the actor – an immensely enthusiastic captain, but his side was simply lacking in real ability. Walter Quaife batted well early in the season and he had some assistance from Newham and the experienced Jesse Hide, but no bowler took even as many as thirty wickets.

This, then, was the state of the counties in 1890, with Surrey in a class almost by themselves, setting such a pace that only Lancashire could pretend to pursue them. A generation of great players was ageing. On the other hand, in the University Match, there were at least nine players of future eminence in Francis Ford, Gregor MacGregor, D. L. A. Jephson, A. J. L. Hill, S. M. J. Woods, F. S. Jackson, Ernest Smith, M. R. Jardine and L. C. H. Palairet – six of whom were to play for England.

G. MacGregor

Gregor MacGregor, now in his third year at Cambridge, was a superb natural wicket-keeper, and though he had played no Championship cricket, he was chosen for England in both Tests of 1890. He was born and brought up in Scotland against no strong cricketing background yet, as a nineteen-year-old Freshman, he was considered second only to Pilling amongst English wicket-keepers and had played for the Gentlemen and England before he was twenty-one. A Scottish international rugby full back, MacGregor was lean, wiry, well balanced, a neat mover. His keeping was simple, quick and completely without flourish or extravagance, but he stood crucially closer to the stumps than the men of the earlier generation had done, and his balance and timing allowed him to take erratic fast bowling with an air of ease. His taking of S. M. J. Woods's fast bowling over the stumps in Cambridge matches was considered one of the sights of cricket in 1890. He went on to play for, and later to captain, Middlesex and, with the exception of an unhappy tour of Australia in 1891–92, he remained one of the best English wicket-keepers for twenty years.

The 1890 Australians

W. L. Murdoch

The Australian touring team captained by W. L. Murdoch, though beaten in the two Tests that could be played, was a strong one. Though his best period was 1880 to 1884, Murdoch was still, to the end of the century, considered the best batsman Australia had ever produced. He was a relaxed but astute captain with a genuine sense of humour. His experience in England – he played for Sussex for some years

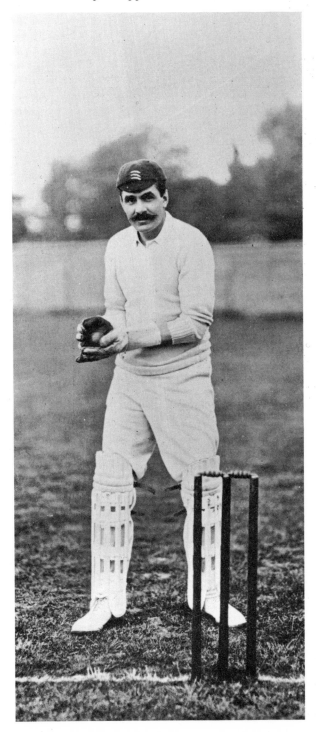

Gregor Macgregor (Middlesex) with Pilling and Blackham, founded the school of wicket-keepers who dispensed with a long-stop and stood up to the stumps to most bowlers. Played cricket for England, Rugby for Scotland

25

John McC. Blackham (Victoria) Member of each of the first eight Australian teams to tour England, the greatest of the early wicket-keepers and one of the creators of modern wicket-keeping technique

– gave him greater command on turning wickets than most Australians. He was cool, orthodox and patient, with strong defence at need, but an aggressive bent. His strongest strokes were the off drive and the cut and he lifted the ball less than most batsmen of his day. Until he became a major batsman he kept wicket, and once did so for Australia.

Turner and Ferris

The tour of 1890 was the last made by the remarkable bowling pair C. T. B. Turner and J. J. Ferris – popularly known as 'The Terror' and 'The Fiend' – who proved such an effective and tireless combination in the wet English summer of 1888 as to take 534 wickets between them – almost five times as many as all the other bowlers of the party put together. Turner was reckoned the better and, over a long period, was

the more successful. Strongly built with a rather low delivery, varying between medium-fast and fast (an early experiment timed a ball from him at 55 miles an hour), he turned the off-break extremely sharply for one of his speed and had unusual pace from the pitch. Ferris made a good foil for Turner: and in 1890 some English batsmen thought him the more difficult. Short and stocky, a little slower than Turner, he bowled left arm with a high action, considerable natural spin and some subtlety of arc. In 1891 he settled in Bristol and played for Gloucestershire but, though he occasionally made runs, he completely lost his bowling skill.

J. M. Blackham

John McCarthy Blackham, Australia's first choice wicket-keeper, played 35 times against England from the beginning of Test Matches in 1877 until he was seriously injured against Stoddart's 1894–95 side. Said to be the first man to dispense with a long-stop to fast-bowling, Blackham was the finest wicket-keeper of the nineteenth century and a creator, with Pilling and MacGregor, of modern wicket-keeping technique. In skintight gloves and meagre pads, he stood close to bowlers of more than medium pace and, though he was over average height and had a gangling stance, he was remarkably clean handed, so quick in stumping and so sure that he set fresh standards of consistency in his position. He made eight consecutive tours of England and, on the last of them, in 1893, captained the team: but, though cool enough on the field, he was too tense and anxious in the pavilion to be either happy or successful in charge of a team.

H. Trumble

The rising young bowler of the party was Hugh Trumble, an orthodox medium pacer who was to be the sharpest edge of Australian attack in many future series. He bowled well within himself and kept a precise length. His most dangerous characteristic – a steep and awkward rise from the pitch – derived from his considerable height – six-feet-three-and-a-half – and a very straight arm. In the next fourteen years he took 141 wickets in Tests against England, including two hat tricks. Trumble was a good slip but, to the disappointment of his colleagues, neglected his natural gifts as a batsman.

G. H. S. Trott

G. H. S. – Harry – Trott was the outstanding all-

Hugh Trumble (Victoria) one of the finest Australian all-rounders: a highly skilful bowler on any pitch, deadly on a difficult one. He twice did the hat trick in Tests against England

rounder in Victorian sides of the period. An upstanding and stylish batsman, he played some extremely slow defensive innings, but in the Lord's Test of 1896 he took an attacking century off Richardson, who was then at his fastest and best. Trott bowled slow leg-breaks, and, given a dusty pitch, he was difficult to play, though at times expensive.

S. E. Gregory

Syd Gregory, of the famous cricketing family, was making his first tour and made few runs in the Tests. He was to become one of the most brilliant of all Australian batsmen. Although he was less than five-feet-five tall, he was a powerful and wristy hitter with all the strokes. He cut, drove and glanced well, and relished the defiance of hooking or pulling a ball off the stumps. He had a truly combative streak and played many of his best innings in difficult situations. A brilliant field at cover and a quick-witted captain with an amazingly fast, long throw for so short a man, Gregory went on to play in 58 Tests, a remarkable figure in his period.

J. J. Lyons

J. J. Lyons was a tall, powerful, firm-footed hitter, exceptionally strong in the drive and with a cool head in a crisis. He turned the course of at least two Test Matches with quickly-scored innings.

England v Australia 1890

England won two Tests, and the third was abandoned. There was heavy rain before the game at Lord's, where Australia batted first and, after Lyons had scored 55 of 66 for the first wicket in three quarters of an hour, collapsed against Peel and Attewell. Lyons – 33 in 25 minutes – and Barrett, who went in first and carried his bat for 67, set England 137 to win. Against the bowling of Ferris and Turner, the first four English batsmen – Grace, Shrewsbury, Gunn and W. W. Read – were out for 20. Then J. M. Read hung on while Ulyett, with a characteristically strong 74, half-rebuilt the innings, only for Lyons to destroy it with five for thirty. Grace decided the match with a militant 75 not out. Gunn batted carefully with him, and England won by seven wickets. Neither the seasoned Blackham nor the young MacGregor allowed a single bye in the entire match.

At The Oval, the wicket was again affected by rain

and the highest of the four innings was Australia's second – 102. Martin of Kent, in his only Test against Australia, virtually won it by taking twelve wickets: Lohmann had six. Harry Trott with 39 and 25 was top scorer in each Australian innings. Gunn cautiously steered England to a lead of eight: but Turner (five wickets in the match) and Ferris (nine) harried them all the way through. England needed 95 to win and Grace, out for 0 in the first innings, was dropped from his first ball in the second. Maurice Read, whose 35 was the highest English score, was also missed and, when England, with eight wickets down, wanted two to win, MacGregor and Sharpe played out five maiden overs in an atmosphere of acute tension, before Barrett, who could have run out either batsman, lost his nerve and gave away the two runs with an overthrow.

At Test, county and University level the new decade had started impressively.

The Season of 1891

Another wet summer gave bowlers an advantage, and a result was achieved in all but fifteen of the sixty-eight Championship matches.

Surrey again won the Championship with an almost uninterrupted run of wins to mid-August. Lohmann, Lockwood and Sharpe took 262 wickets between them: the other bowlers only twenty: meanwhile the batting was even stronger than in 1890.

The most important matter of the domestic season – and it was purely domestic, for there was no touring side – was the 'break-through' by the first of the 'lesser' counties – Somerset. Their progress was watched with much interest and when, in August, they beat Surrey with only minutes to spare, the 'class barrier' in county cricket was broken.

Somerset's achievement consisted not only of winning five matches and removing the idea from the public mind of an exclusive group of eight counties: they also created an image which has endured over the years of a happy team with a knack for bringing off surprise results. Their first county side consisted mainly of amateurs, chief among them Lionel Palairet, S. M. J. Woods, H. T. Hewett and R. C. N. Palairet, supported by the two experienced professional bowlers, Edwin Tyler, slow left-arm (one of the men named in the throwing purge of 1900) and George Nichols, a steady fast bowler.

L. C. H. Palairet

Lionel Palairet, perhaps more than any other player, reflects the impression of the so-called 'Golden Age' of cricket which lay only a short way ahead. Tall, slim, elegant, with a lean, long, rather patrician face, he batted with an unhurried air, a model for the forward stroke and a fine, graceful hitter on the off side, whose timing invested apparently languid strokes with immense power. The best bowlers could tie down Palairet on the line of his leg stump, but that development came later.

S. M. J. Woods

S. M. J. Woods – the bluff, hearty, 'Sammy' – was an Australian, and he played for Australia (three Tests in England, 1888, while he was still at Cambridge) as well as England (three Tests v South Africa, 1895–96). He came to England as a schoolboy in 1884, and went on from Brighton College to Cambridge, where he was four years a blue, and captain in 1890.

He played for Somerset from 1886 until 1907 – as captain for the last thirteen years – was secretary of the club until 1923, and spent the rest of his life in Somerset. In his earlier days, Woods, a tall, burly, rugged and ruddy-looking man, was primarily a fast bowler, accurate, with a fine yorker, and – apparently out of character – a well hidden slower ball. As the years passed and his bowling slowed, he turned more to his batting. Basically correct in defence, his great strength made him a menacing firm-footed hitter, and his long reach enabled him to hit some of the most accurate bowlers off their length. His square cutting of the short ball was murderous. A fearless and safe catcher of the ball, Sammy was the rare combination of a good, and well-liked, captain; a man of great gusto who adopted the county of Somerset with as great enthusiasm as it adopted him.

The two Notts batsmen, Shrewsbury and Gunn, were top of the batting with averages, remarkable in so wet a summer, of 48 and 41: Abel was next with 33. W. G. Grace (19·3) as Wisden said 'had for him a singularly unsuccessful season'.

The surprise of the Championship season, apart from the success of Somerset, was the rise of Middlesex to third position, substantially as a result of the bowling of J. T. Hearne and J. T. Rawlin – first and third in the first-class bowling averages. Rawlin, who had not previously looked more than steady, though with some ability to swing the ball, proved a useful foil to Hearne who, in the space of a few weeks, established himself as a world-class fast medium bowler.

J. T. Hearne

Except when summoned for representative games, J. T. Hearne missed only two matches – through an arm injury – for Middlesex, from 1890 until his retirement in 1914. Only three bowlers – Rhodes, Freeman and Parker – have taken more than his 3,061 wickets. Tall and well proportioned, Hearne bowled off a fairly long, easy run with a high, full swing. His off-break turned on all but the most perfect wickets and he bowled a good late outswinger. He was, more than anything else, an accurate bowler, in both length and line, and even in good batting conditions he could pin down the best batsmen. The intense competition among many fast-medium and fast bowlers in his time explains the fact that he played in only twelve Tests. He was a superb craftsman, and a model professional.

Yorkshire finished last but one in the table. Ulyett and Hall as batsmen, Wainwright and Harrison as bowlers, and the invaluable Peel as an all-rounder, kept the side going while the younger players matured: but the county's supporters continued, to say the least, impatient.

England in Australia and England in South Africa, 1891–92

A strong England team under W. G. Grace lost a three-Test rubber in Australia while a substantially weaker party won the only representative game of its tour in South Africa.

Grace's team lost the first two Tests to the bowling of Turner and George Giffen, in support of the batting of Bruce and the amazingly contrasted opening pair, Lyons and A. C. Bannerman – one of the first Australian professionals. In the first match of this series Bannerman's two innings – 45 and 41 – occupied altogether seven-and-a-quarter hours. In the first Test Sharpe took eight wickets in the match and Peel five: and when Grace and Shrewsbury put on 60 for the first wicket on a still good pitch, England seemed to face no great difficulty in making 213. Then Turner and Harry Trott cut through to 98 for seven and Attewell and MacGregor could make only a fighting gesture before Australia won by 54 runs.

In the second match, Lohmann took eight for 58 in the first Australian innings and Abel carried his bat for 132. England had a first innings lead of 163. In face of that disadvantage, Bannerman – 91 in seven-and-a-half hours – Lyons, who hit a fast 134, Giffen and Bruce all made runs. Then there was rain; Briggs finished off the Australian innings with a hat trick and, on a damaged wicket, England were put out for 156. Only Stoddart – 69 – made more than 22 against Giffen. Australia won the match by 72 runs and, with it, the rubber.

A. E. Stoddart

A. E. Stoddart had now started on the high plateau of his career as a forcing batsman. He was athletically built, and had marked stamina and concentration. He batted with his right hand much lower on the handle than was general at the time, but drove with great power and, quite fearless on the most fiery wickets, was at his best against fast bowling. An English international rugby three-quarter, a superb outfield and a useful medium pace change bowler, he played until 1900, when, in his last innings for Middlesex, he made the highest score of his first-class career – 221. In club cricket for Hampstead his performances were prodigious, and included one innings of 485 and a batting average, over twenty-two years, of 70.

G. Giffen

George Giffen who made five Test tours of England – and refused two more – was the elder of early Australian cricket, an all-rounder who was an automatic Test choice from 1881 to 1896. If he was, on the whole, most successful on the good wickets of his own country, his performance in England during 1886, when he was top of both batting and bowling averages for the touring side, won him the reputation of the best all-rounder in the world. His responsibilities in the South Australian and Australian sides changed his batting from the free and aggressive style of his early days to a more mature and measured method, based on careful defence. He was a slow-medium bowler of accurate length, some off-spin, and an effective slower ball which dipped sharply and brought him many wickets. Giffen was what the old cricketers called a 'head' bowler, who learnt his stratagems on perfect batting wickets. In a match for South Australia against Victoria in 1891–92, he scored 271 runs and took sixteen wickets for 166.

The third Test, also decided by the weather, was won by England. Stoddart made 134, Peel 83, Grace 58, J. M. Read 57 in a total of 499. Then, after rain,

George Giffen (South Australia) The major figure of nineteenth century Australian cricket and, during the mid-eighteen-nineties, probably the finest all-rounder in the world

Briggs and Lohmann, unchanged in the first innings, and with the assistance of Attewell in the second, bowled Australia out for 100 and 169.

The one Test Match in South Africa was an all too easy innings win for England. Harry Wood, the Surrey wicket-keeper, made 134 not out – his only century in first-class cricket – and the bowling of the Australian, Ferris (13 wickets), was too much for the improving, but still inexperienced, South African batsmen.

The Season of 1892

A drier summer meant more runs in the County Championship which was followed eagerly all over the country. Surrey won for the sixth consecutive season, but this time almost by default. Notts, unbeaten until the 10th August, seemed to have a

winning lead, only to lose two and draw two of their remaining four matches; meanwhile Surrey, winning five out of five, came through and passed them. Happily, though without seriously threatening either of the sides ahead of them, Somerset finished third.

Surrey were fortunate to have Richardson making his first mark, for, though Lohmann took a hundred wickets, his illness sadly reduced the quality of his bowling. In the decisive days of August, however, Lockwood carved out the final shape of the competition. On a series of rough Oval wickets, his constantly short-pitched bowling was dangerous and almost unplayable, while some of the least timid batsmen who played against him declared flatly that his action was illegal. W. W. Read returned to his old position as Surrey's leading batsman. A regular England player from the early eighties, he had shown only ordinary form since 1889; but now, when the ball came through quickly, his pleasant style and forcing strokes brought him many runs. An occasional lob bowler, at one time a useful stop-gap wicket-keeper and a competent field at point, he had a pleasing personality and was one of the most popular players of the day. Abel, Henderson, Lockwood, Shuter, J. M. Read and Lohmann all made enough good scores to keep the Surrey batting a daunting force.

The Notts batting was again almost all Shrewsbury – once more top of the first-class averages – and Gunn: but Attewell now had useful bowling support from Flowers, Shacklock and Barnes. For years afterwards it was argued in Nottingham that if, on the second day of the Gloucestershire match at Cheltenham, the latter batsmen had thrown their wickets away – the laws forbade a declaration until the third day – the result would have been a win for Notts, instead of a draw, and the whole position would have been changed.

Somerset were well behind the two leading counties, but they won eight matches and, against Yorkshire, Lionel Palairet and H. T. Hewitt set up a new record for the first wicket with a partnership of 346. Hewitt, who captained Somerset for their first three seasons in the Championship, was thought the best left-hand bat in English cricket in 1892. An unorthodox player, he had none of the elegance of Palairet. His chief assets were huge physical strength and a sharp eye, while his invariable tactical approach – of getting at the opposition before they could get at him – reduced some of the best bowlers of the age to the confession that they found it almost impossible to bowl to him.

No county had a better attacking balance than Lancashire, in Mold, Briggs and Watson, but the batting was too thin to give them adequate elbow-room.

The Season of 1893

In one of the sunniest summers within living memory, England won, albeit narrowly, their fifth consecutive home rubber against Australia; and Yorkshire, to general surprise but on merit, were County Champions.

It will seem incredible to any follower of cricket in the twentieth century that this was Yorkshire's first Championship in the twenty years of the competition – or that, during the eighties, they had a reputation for being 'too polite to run out an opponent'. It is an enduringly imposing monument to Lord Hawke that, in ten apparently discouraging years from 1883, he created not only a match-winning team but a tradition and an atmosphere which, for generation after generation, was to carry his county to almost monotonous success. He now had a young team which he kept on its toes, and most of its members were to go on to further heights. J. T. Brown, 'Long John' Tunnicliffe of Pudsey, and Arthur Sellers were the specialist batsmen. Peel, at last, could concentrate on bowling – he was second in the English averages – and there, too, work became easier for him through the great advance of Ted Wainwright – whose sharp spin so outweighed the vagaries of his length that he played for England against Australia – and the young, but as yet raw, George Hirst. Moreover, Wainwright scored enough runs this year to rank as an all-rounder. The fielding was keen; David Hunter was a sage and efficient wicket-keeper and, after the University match, the side was further strengthened by F. S. Jackson, whose assured steps to the centre of the stage of world cricket were the most dramatic feature of the season.

Yorkshire's pleasure was reduced by the fact that they were twice beaten by Lancashire, who chased them hard until the latter part of August. At that point their lack of a third bowler – in the absence of Watson who had retired – proved too great a strain on Briggs and Mold, and they cracked. Middlesex, carried by Stoddart, Hearne, F. J. Ford and Rawlin, were third. Surrey, without Lohmann, fell to fifth and Notts, with a team of ageing players, to sixth.

In the Test series with Australia, England won the Oval match and were never in danger of losing the other two drawn games. The English batting was massive – Shrewsbury averaged 71, Jackson, Gunn and Grace over fifty. The bowling – in which Lockwood, Briggs and Richardson all took their wickets more cheaply than any Australian – was equally powerful.

Grace, back to good, if not gigantic, form, was kept out of the Lord's match by a hand injury and Stoddart took over the captaincy of England. Long innings by Stoddart, Shrewsbury, Gunn and Jackson meant that, despite Graham's 107, England could declare their second innings with Australia needing 300 to win: at that juncture, rain ended the game.

At The Oval, the English batting was so long and strong that Jackson, at number seven, made 103 in a total of 483, and only Giffen (seven for 128) could check the scoring. To the sorrow of some idealists, England's bowling was opened by the highly suspect pair of Mold and Lockwood. Australia were surprisingly put out for 91 and, though they emphasized their first failure by batting steadily down the second innings, Lockwood took eight wickets and Briggs ten in the match, and England won by an innings and 43.

Yorkshire refused to release any of their players for the Third Test and Lockwood, injured, could not play, so Richardson appeared in his first Test and took five wickets in each innings. England never tried to score 198 to win in two and a quarter hours: they contented themselves with a draw.

F. S. Jackson

F. S. Jackson – known as Stanley Jackson in his playing days, later as Sir Francis Stanley Jackson – was one of the rare, true all-rounders, good enough to be a Test player as either batsman or bowler and, improving his catching by constant practice, a fine cover-point. All his playing life, at preparatory school, for Harrow, Cambridge, Yorkshire, the Gentlemen, and England, Jackson was a match-winner. Six feet tall, well-proportioned and never seeming to carry any unnecessary weight, Jackson had a strikingly distinguished appearance. His cricket was a reflection of his character. He was undemonstratively but completely self-confident, and a man of considerable courage. As Governor of Bombay, he behaved with amazing coolness when, in an attempted assassination, he looked coolly into the revolver while five shots were fired at him from close range.

Unlike many of his somewhat dashing contem-

poraries, Jackson was a completely equipped batsman, an assured forward player on fast pitches, poised
on the back foot when the ball turned: and, if his
cover driving was more spectacular, he probably was
the safest attacking on-side player of his day. He is
memorably portrayed in one of George Beldham's
action photographs leaping out to slow bowling, and
he was a highly efficient cutter.

He bowled fast-medium, from a relaxed approach,
with a high arm and an athletic body swing which
gave him his characteristic pace from the ground.

In 1893, Jackson's fourth season as a Blue and
second as captain of Cambridge, he was chosen for
England against Australia. His business and professional duties prevented him from ever touring
Australia or South Africa, whilst the long reign of
Lord Hawke precluded him from the captaincy of
Yorkshire – a post he could have filled admirably – in
any but occasional matches. Nevertheless, his batting
average of 49 in Tests against Australia ranks him
unquestionably as a great player. In his one full season
of county cricket – 1898 – his record was 1,566 runs
and 104 wickets.

The Season of 1894

This was virtually a domestic season. In fact, the first
South African touring side came to England, but no
preparations were made for them and their fixtures
were not regarded as first-class. In the last Championship before it 'opened out' only a brief challenge by
Middlesex interrupted a struggle between Yorkshire
and Surrey which continued desperately close until
the last match. At the end, Surrey won through the
mighty bowling of Richardson and the luck of the
weather. Yorkshire, in their last fixture of the season,
had bowled out Somerset for 99 when rain came and
washed out the game. Had they won – and they had
beaten Somerset by an innings at home – they would
have shared first place.

Had Surrey not won it would have seemed a slight
on the prodigious performance of Richardson who,
in only fourteen Championship matches, took 120
wickets, at 11·3. Lockwood (92 at 14·1) completed the
most terrifying opening bowling in county cricket.
The slow left-arm Smith gave them just enough relief
while Brockwell, the infinitely impressive young Tom
Hayward, W. W. Read, Lockwood and Abel made
the runs.

Yorkshire's bowling – Wainwright, Jackson, Hirst
and Peel – made an ideal blend for all conditions: but
Tunnicliffe had a bad year and Sellers could not play
regularly, so, in the last analysis, Yorkshire were short
of one more class batsman to stand with Jackson and
J. T. Brown.

All season there was unease at the growing number
of bowlers whose actions were regarded as unfair.
There was wide agreement that an insoluble position
was created by umpires, even those accounted good,
who would not, in any circumstances, 'call' the men
whose bowling was illegal. It was to be ten years
before the matter came to a head.

England in Australia, 1894–95

This was a convincing example of the argument that
two good and evenly matched sides should produce a
stirring series. Both countries have had greater teams,
but the rich variety of natural talents on the two sides
looked so levelly balanced that either could reasonably
believe itself the better. In the event, it is probable
that a single night of rain – during the first Test –
tilted the balance in England's favour. Giffen's 161,
and the innings of 201 with which S. E. Gregory
announced himself as a major Test player, took
Australia to a total of 586. Only Ward of the early
English batsmen played firmly, and later resistance
by Brockwell and Briggs could not prevent Blackham,
with a lead of 261, enforcing the follow-on. Again the
English batting hinged on Albert Ward of Lancashire,
a powerfully-built man with the ability to play strokes
but whose county, in his time, often needed a defensive approach. He made 117, and every other batsman
except Gay, the wicket-keeper, made double figures.
Still Australia needed only 177 to win and, at the end
of the fifth day, they had 113 for two. There was heavy
rain in the night and, after a few more runs, the wicket
began to dry out so awkwardly that Peel, true to his
confident morning prophecy, cut down Australia from
130 for two to 160 all out. Giffen's all-round figures –
161 and 41: four for 75 and four for 164 – can rarely
have been approached by a man who finished on the
losing side.

At Melbourne, the rain came before the match. For
the first time in Tests, a captain – Giffen – won the
toss and put the other side in. Coningham, Turner
and Trumble bowled England out for 75. Before the
wicket could ease completely, Richardson, in two

killing stints which were eventually decisive, took five for 57 and confined the Australian lead to 48. The second English innings, on a mild pitch, was fought out between the two captains – Stoddart, who made 173, and Giffen, who bowled a third of the Australian overs and took six for 155. No England batsman failed: a total of 475 left Australia 428 to win. A vastly changed Australian batting order tilted the game their way until Stoddart, in a flash of imaginative captaincy, put on Brockwell who took three crucial wickets in a single brief spell: England won by 94.

At Adelaide, in heat which some of the English players recalled with distress many years afterwards, the bowling of Giffen, Callaway and Albert Trott, coupled with the runs of Giffen, Bruce, Iredale and Trott, took Australia to a towering win. Only Richardson – 52 overs and eight wickets – matched their efforts in such sapping heat.

There was rain again at Sydney, and Stoddart put Australia in. Graham and Albert Trott between them made 191 out of Australia's first innings of 284. That was enough. The pitch never improved: only J. T. Brown scored as many as 20 for England. Harry Trott, Turner and Giffen bowled them out for 65 and 72. Albert Trott, who had taken eight for 43 in the last innings at Adelaide, did not even turn his arm.

So to Melbourne, with the rubber depending on the issue: the two teams remained evenly balanced until the end. Only two batsmen failed in Australia's 414. MacLaren (120), Peel (73) and Stoddart (68) played England to 385 – only 29 behind. In another prodigal outpouring of effort, Richardson took six for 104 in 45 overs to put an English win inside the bounds of possibility. Brockwell and Stoddart were out early, and then, at the pinch, J. T. Brown played the innings of his life and he and Albert Ward as sheet-anchor put on 210 for the third wicket. England, winners by six wickets, took the rubber.

J. T. Brown was an opening batsman in the 'new' Yorkshire team built by Lord Hawke. He was, by inclination and aptitude, a quick scorer, confident but shrewd, capable of most of the strokes, but a murderer of short-pitched bowling on the off, a fine square-cutter, even better in the late-cut. At one period he adopted the pull stroke to a grotesque extent but, after constantly losing his wicket through the obsession, he completely abandoned it. Brown was safe in the field: as an occasional bowler of 'donkey-drops', he was flattered by a hat trick against Derbyshire in 1896.

During the same English winter, R. S. Lucas took a team of University and club cricketers to the West Indies to play matches not only in Jamaica, Barbados, Trinidad and British Guiana, but also in Antigua, St Kitts, St Lucia and St Vincent. In the same year, C. H. King of British Guiana made the first century in an inter-colonial tournament: Caribbean cricket was growing up gaily.

A stronger team of amateurs under Frank Mitchell visited the United States and Canada but the heyday of American cricket already lay in the past: it had no place in the growing future of the game.

The Season of 1895

English cricket has known no more historic summer than that of 1895. It was the first in the modern pattern of the wider County Championship; it saw the setting up of remarkable records, the rise of players who were to make history in the succeeding generation and, to balance the picture, it held a moving and majestic echo of the older time.

Let us deal with the last event first for, framed in day after day of early summer sun, it gave a gloriously exciting start to a season in which, at Derby, Leyton, Leicester, Southampton, Portsmouth and Birmingham, fresh crowds and players were sharing in the first-class game.

When W. G. Grace began this, his thirty-first season in first-class cricket, he was forty-six years and ten months old. For several years he had been troubled by hand injuries and knee trouble, but he took great pains, during the spring, to put himself in condition. He still carried far more weight than was comfortable but that was part of his image. Huge, high-shouldered, mightily bearded, humorous, autocratic, he was the best known sportsman in the history of England and, if the public were reluctantly reconciled to the fact that his powers were now in decline, they still crowded to see him with greater enthusiasm and admiration than they felt for any of his young successors.

Now, in a splendid Indian summer – perhaps, all things considered, the greatest performance of even his mighty career – he gave them reason to cheer. He limbered up with a century in the Gloucestershire practice match before he started his first-class season with two matches for MCC – at Lord's – against Sussex, when he made 13 and 103, and Yorkshire, 18 and 25. Then to Taunton where, with a few jitters in the nineties, he reached his hundredth hundred, celebrated it in champagne and went on for, altogether, five-and-a-half hours without an error, to 288. It is a just indication of his supremacy that the next player in the tally of centuries was Arthur Shrewsbury with 41. Next, Cambridge: 52 in his only innings against the University. On to Gravesend and the match with Kent: another chanceless innings, 257 out of 443: a draw seemed certain, but Kent collapsed on the third day, leaving Gloucester 104 to win. They made them in an hour – W.G. 73 not out – and he was on the field for every ball of the match. For England against Surrey – W. W. Read's Testimonial – he batted only once and had started confidently when Richardson bowled him with a superb break-back.

So to Lord's, for Gloucester against Middlesex, beginning on 30th May, and wanting 153 to achieve the hitherto unimagined feat of 1,000 runs in May.

The crowds flocked to Lord's to see if 'The Old Man' could set up yet another record. Surely enough, he won the toss, and went in first against a strong Middlesex attack of J. T. Hearne, Nepean, Rawlin, Stoddart and Dr Thornton. Was he nervous? To close watchers he seemed simply determined, playing firmly within himself. He scored only 58 in the hour-and-a-half before lunch and, in the early afternoon, was at less than his ease with Nepean's leg-breaks. Then, all at once, he settled down: at 149 he swept what may well have been a friendly leg-side ball down to long leg, and he had done it – and again he had not given a chance. Between the 9th and the 30th of the month he had scored 1,016 runs at an average of 112 – still no one has done it in shorter time.

W.G. did not find runs so easy to make on the difficult wickets of July, but his eventual 2,346 was the highest aggregate of the season and his form lifted Gloucester from a decade of poor positions – bottom in 1893 and 1894 – to fourth. Once more, Surrey were Champions: Lancashire were second and Yorkshire third. Again Richardson effectively decided the Championship. In 25 matches he bowled 1,354 overs and took 237 wickets at 13·21, setting a standard of stamina and penetration never paralleled by any fast bowler before or since.

Lancashire partly made good the deficiency of 1894 in providing some relief for Mold – highly penetrative on hard wickets – and the industrious Briggs, from Hallam and Lancaster. Their chief access of strength, however, lay in the advance of A. C. MacLaren as a batsman. Only one match was lost when he was in the side and, against Somerset at Taunton on 15th and 16th July, he played an innings of 424, in under eight hours, with a six and 62 fours: it remains the highest individual innings for a three-day match.

A. C. MacLaren

Archie MacLaren was an outstanding and controversial figure in cricket from his first impressive batting for Harrow in 1887 until, in 1922, at the age of fifty-one, he played an innings of 200 not out for MCC against New Zealand at Wellington. There was no doubt of the quality of his batting, which was based on careful study and practice. An upstanding player with a high back-lift, he built on strong defence in which he inclined to the back foot. He had most of the orthodox attacking strokes and drove through the covers and mid-off in the classical manner; but he was also adroit in placing the ball on the leg side and, in form, would hit straight balls to leg imperiously and with far greater safety than could be expected. He was essentially a combative player and many of his best innings saved or won games which seemed lost.

MacLaren captained Harrow, Lancashire (for twelve seasons) and England (in 22 Tests), yet opinions remain divided as to his quality as a captain. He had strong ideas; some of them – like taking the unknown S. F. Barnes to Australia in 1901 – were brilliant beyond dispute, and, in the crucial match of 1904, his decision to send in Yorkshire gave Lancashire the Championship. Yet he made some amazing blunders, like the misplacing of Fred Tate at Manchester in 1902, the omission of Buckenham and then the over-bowling of D. W. Carr at The Oval in 1909 which, in each case, probably cost England a Test rubber. It may appear conclusive that England never won a series with Australia under his captaincy. On the other hand, in 1921, when Armstrong's Australians crushed England, MacLaren declared he could pick a side to beat them. Characteristically, though he was almost fifty, he captained his side on the field – and made good his boast. It was MacLaren's tragedy that all his virtues bred their own faults. He was strong, but inflexible: intelligent, but intolerant: single-minded, but humourless: impressive on the field, but often disappointingly petty off it: a courageous leader who lacked the tact to encourage the best from his men. Yet he remains one of the epic figures of cricket.

C. L. Townsend

The season was also remarkable for the performance

of C. L. Townsend, an eighteen-year-old from Clifton who, in only 12 Championship matches, took 124 wickets at 12·73. Charles Townsend had first played for Gloucestershire when he was only fifteen, but he came to the cricket of 1895 as a revelation, spinning his leg-breaks so sharply that he completely routed such strong batting sides as Notts (twice), Yorkshire, Sussex and Surrey. In August he was unquestionably the finest slow bowler in England. Four years later he was picked against Australia as a left-hand batsman. Slight in physique, he may have found the strain of both batting and bowling too great for him; certainly, like many other young leg-spinners, he lost some of his control. But he did the 'double' in 1898 and, in 1899, took a hundred wickets and scored over two thousand runs. He might have been an England cricketer for many years, but his profession as a solicitor prevented him from playing more than six full seasons in his career. He performed a unique hat trick against Somerset at Cheltenham in 1893 – all three stumped by W. H. Brain.

What of the 'new' counties? Derbyshire, who had withdrawn at the end of 1887, returned; and Essex, Hampshire, Leicester and Warwickshire all now came into the Championship. Derbyshire finished fifth, Warwick sixth, Essex ninth, Hampshire tenth and Leicester twelfth among the fourteen competitors: Notts and Kent filled the last two places.

Derbyshire was a strong, professional team. George Davidson, pace bowler and sound batsman, performed the feat, rare in those days, of the 'double' in first-class matches, and William Storer was the best wicket-keeper batsman of the time. Four more professionals, Bagshaw and Chatterton as batsmen, Porter and Bennett as bowlers, balanced the team admirably.

Though the leading Essex batsman was Harry Carpenter, he had useful assistance from the amateurs, A. P. Lucas, who had played for England as long before as 1878, and Charles McGahey. The bowling lay largely in the hands of Walter Mead, a seasoned slow-medium bowler who turned the ball both ways, who is usually credited with being the first man to bowl the googly (however inadvertently) with any frequency; and Charles Kortright, by general consent the fastest of the remarkable crop of fast bowlers which was springing up throughout the counties.

Warwickshire's successes stemmed largely from the batting of Walter Quaife, the captain, H. W. Bainbridge, A. A. Lilley and W. G. Quaife. Both Quaifes

Charles Kortright (Essex) 'Korty' the legendary 'fastest of them all' was the doyen of the old-fashioned, straightforward school of fast-bowlers

had previously played for Sussex. Walter was a jaunty batsman with plenty of strokes and a fluent style. His brother, Willie, only five-feet-four-and-a-half inches tall, was one of the safest batsmen in England for thirty years. He sometimes scored at crawling pace: but there was a delicate, almost scholarly, air about his utterly correct play which made him absorbing to watch.

A. A. Lilley

In 1896, Dick Lilley became England's wicket-keeper and, with one break, held the position for thirteen years. He was a student of cricket who learnt much from Blackham and the South African, Halliwell. He could stand up to fast bowling but in some conditions or to more erratic bowlers he considered it more economic, and no loss of face, to stand back. He worked hard to develop understanding with his bowlers and

The Players XI at Lord's, 1895. Back row, left to right: Abel, Mold, Attewell, Peel. Middle row: A. Ward, Richardson, W. Gunn, Sugg, Hayward. On ground: Davidson, Storer (wicket-keeper)

used to 'offer them his hands' to aim at, a tactic he brought to a high degree of perfection with Arnold of Worcester. It was some measure of his ability that, relatively late in his career, he encountered the problem of the googly as bowled by Bosanquet but 'read' it and handled it well at Test level. By application, Lilley became a capable batsman at number eight for England, often a rock of reliability in a crisis. The best type of professional cricketer, his standards were high, and he was a wise counsellor to more than one captain.

Hampshire cricket consisted in the main of amateur batting, professional bowling, and an unusually high standard of fielding, especially in the slips. A. J. L. Hill and Capt. E. G. Wynyard both played for England as batsmen. R. A. Studd and Captain Quinton

held the first two places in the county's 1895 batting averages and only Victor Barton and Webb, of the professionals, made many runs. Three professionals, however, took all but 32 of the wickets that fell to Hampshire in county matches. Harry Baldwin, tubby and shrewd, from a Berkshire cricketing family, bowled slow off-breaks steadily on good wickets, viciously on 'turners'. Tom Soar, fairly fast with steep lift from the pitch, was Baldwin's partner for many years. The third bowler was James Wootton, already thirty-five, who had left Kent after a serious injury and was now coach at Winchester: he gave the side added experience during this settling-in period.

Leicestershire ended lowest of the new counties in the final table, after a most impressive start. They beat Surrey in their first match, Notts in the second and Essex in the fourth. They did not win another game for the rest of the season and *Wisden* was outspoken about lack of discipline among the professionals. William Tomlin, best of the early Leicester batsmen, led their averages with a figure of only 20·22, A. D. – Dick – Pougher, fast-medium with a high delivery, an occasionally sharp break-back, and some variation of pace, was one of the best county bowlers of his day, and a serviceable bat. His main support over these early seasons was Arthur Woodcock, in pace reckoned second only to Kortright and, on his day and pitch, a difficult bowler, though by no means consistent.

In the new Second-class Counties Competition, Norfolk, Durham and Worcester tied for first place. A change in the Laws made the follow-on compulsory for a side 120 behind on first innings.

The whole vista of English cricket had become wider and bright with new promise.

In 1895–96 Lord Hawke took a medium-strength side to South Africa. Its arrival, unhappily, coincided with the Jameson Raid and it only narrowly escaped a financial loss: but it won the three Tests easily. George Lohmann, who had now made a home in South Africa, was far too much for the South African batsmen: he took eight wickets (including a hat trick) for seven runs in the second innings at Port Elizabeth, 35 at 5·8 in the series, and Halliwell's 41 at Johannesburg was the highest score made against him in a Test.

The Season of 1896

Fine weather in May, June and July gave way to rain in August. In a stirring series, England beat Harry Trott's Australian side by two Tests to one, and Yorkshire won the Championship after a hard struggle through the early months with Surrey, who then fell away to fourth, behind Lancashire and Middlesex.

In the first Test, played at Lord's, Australia inexplicably collapsed for 53 on a good wicket before Richardson (six for 39) and Lohmann (three for 13). Grace, Abel and Jackson built an England lead of 239 and, though Trott and Gregory scored aggressive centuries – they put on 221 in two-and-a-half hours – in the second Australian innings, England, with only 111 to make, won by six wickets.

At Old Trafford Australia again batted first: Iredale opened the innings with 108 and almost everyone scored runs in a total of 412, while, apart from Richard-

son (seven for 168), the England bowlers were so powerless that Lilley took off his pads and bowled. Only Ranjitsinhji and Lilley scored over fifty for England, who followed on. Then Ranjitsinhji, in his first Test, scored 154 not out in 190 minutes; an historic innings in which he so dominated the bowling that members of both sides subsequently said that, if only anyone could have stayed with him, he might well have won the game. In the event, no one else except Stoddart (41) made as many as twenty, and Australia needed 125 to win. The task seemed easy enough, for the wicket was friendly: but Richardson rose to yet another of his staggering peaks of sustained endeavour. He bowled unchanged for three hours, took six of the seven wickets that fell, and then, with Kelly and Trumble together, nine runs still wanted and only the tail-enders to come, Kelly edged Richardson to Lilley who made one of the few important mistakes of his Test career. He dropped the catch and an Australian win by three wickets left the rubber depending on the Oval match.

Of the England team chosen for the decisive game, Abel, Hayward, Richardson, Gunn and Lohmann wrote demanding £20, instead of the usual £10, as match fee. The Surrey club did not reply and the first three climbed down: but Gunn and Lohmann did not play. Rain prevented a start until after five on the first day, when Grace, Jackson, Ranjitsinhji and Abel took England to 114 for three on a mudheap. All the second day the pitch was drying and difficult: Trumble and McKibbin took the remaining seven English wickets for only another 31 runs. Darling and Iredale made an impressive 75 for the first Australian wicket, but then two run-outs, and the bowling of Hearne and Peel, toppled the innings to 119. By the end of the day, however, Trumble and McKibbin had regained the advantage and reduced England to 60 for five which, in less than an hour next morning, became 84 all out: Australia needed 110 to win. Richardson bowled the first over of their innings – a maiden. In the next, Hearne bowled Darling for 0. At once, W.G. took off Richardson and put on Peel, whose pairing with Hearne – fast-medium off-breaks at one end, slow left-arm breakaways at the other – won the match by 66 runs, and the rubber with it.

F. Iredale

Frank Iredale had matured slowly in the New South Wales team but at this period he was considered the best batsman in Australia. Once described as an

A contemporary artist's impressions at the Test Match, England v Australia, at The Oval, 1896. Albert Craig – bottom right – 'The Cricket Poet' wrote topical doggerel about cricket and printed it on broadsheets which he hawked round the ground

'apostle of pessimism' he was a lanky, solemn-looking man. Often hesitant at the beginning of an innings, he was usually a forward player, a strong driver who rarely lifted the ball, and a graceful cutter. He was one of the long line of great Australian deep fieldsmen, a fast runner, strong thrower and safe catch.

J. Darling

Joe Darling was making his first tour to England: he was to return as captain of the 1899, 1902 and 1905 Australian teams. Brilliant as a schoolboy, he did not begin to play state cricket – for South Australia – until he was 23. He soon became a competent, somewhat rugged, left-handed batsman. He had a good cricket mind and, as at Old Trafford in 1902, was a capable judge of the occasion to take risks – and a good executant of the decision. Athletically built, a safe and fearless mid-off, he became an astute and well-liked captain.

E. Jones

Ernest Jones, the powerful and extremely fast Australian bowler, is remembered chiefly for the story of his bowling a ball through W. G. Grace's beard and exclaiming 'Sorry Doc, she slipped'.

Wisden declared quite boldly that two Australian bowlers who took a hundred wickets on the tour, Jones and McKibbin – the latter somewhat slower in pace with a sharp off-break – threw.

A. E. Trott

One Australian cricketer who was not chosen for the tour travelled over to England. Albert Trott was affronted at his omission from the side his brother captained to England. So, when it was suggested that he should go to England and qualify for Middlesex, he agreed. He began to play for the county in 1898 and, often spectacular and always popular, was a successful all-rounder until he became seriously ill in 1905. Even then he continued, though with decreasing frequency and effect, in the first-class game, until 1914. In both 1899 and 1900 he scored over 1,000 runs and took more than two hundred wickets.

Strongly built and extremely active, Trott was a cricketer of infinite zest and a bowler of vast variety. His arm was rather low, though his action was undoubtedly fair, and he often bowled medium paced off-breaks: but he could also flight the ball and turn it from leg or, without apparent change of approach, bowl a faster one. He attributed to his early baseball

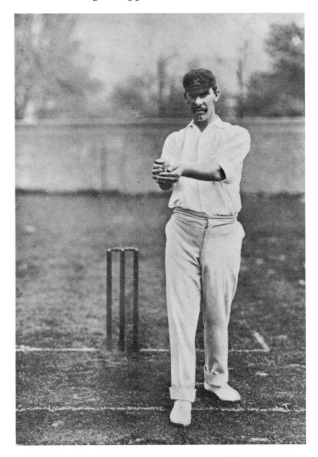

Albert Trott (Victoria and Middlesex) Shrewd and lively bowler, the only batsman to hit a ball over the Lord's pavilion and one of the most popular cricketers of his time

experience the swinging delivery he called his 'curly' ball. As *Wisden* said, he commanded 'every pace and device'. It was suggested that, as a batsman, 'Alberto' suffered from the fact that he was the only man ever to hit a ball over the Lord's pavilion – a straight drive off M. A. Noble for MCC against the Australians in 1899. If he reduced the total of his runs by trying to repeat the feat, he nevertheless played a number of brilliant innings. His huge hands helped to make him a superb short leg fieldsman, and a safe catcher anywhere.

After he became ill, Trott's cricket fell away tragically but, in his benefit match, against Somerset at Lord's in 1907, he rose to the last great peak of his career when he took four wickets with four consecutive balls and then finished off the same innings with a hat trick. Trott had always been a gay man and

39

cricketer but, at the age of 42, hopeless of ever recovering from his illness, he took his own life.

K. S. Ranjitsinhji

In 1896, Kumar Shri Ranjitsinhji scored 2,780 runs, more than anyone had ever made in a season. This was only his second full season, yet already responsible judges spoke of him as a genius. The evidence of his contemporaries – particularly those who bowled at him – places him among the first half-dozen batsmen in the history of the game.

Ranjitsinhji – 'Ranji' – had been coached, and had made some good scores, as a schoolboy in India. When he came to Cambridge he could not even get a game with his college side, and was not given his Blue until his fourth year – 1893. In the three preceding summers he had applied himself to batting with remarkable assiduity. He engaged the best professionals to bowl at him in the nets – sometimes Lockwood, Richardson, Hayward and J. T. Hearne, all at the height of their careers and under instructions to bowl their fastest, in the same afternoon. His nets often went on for so long that C. M. Wells once asked him if he was not taking too much practice. 'I must now learn endurance' was the reply.

Ranji, was, by race, a Rajput; of average height, neatly but not strongly built. He brought to batting four unusually rich natural attributes: his sharp eye saw and assessed the ball extremely early: his balance and speed of movement were such that he could leave his stroke almost impossibly late: he had steely wrists: and his concentration was unwavering. At first he tended to score largely behind the wicket, especially on the leg side, but through intense practice and his innate sense of timing, he became a strong driver. He was famous for the leg glance he seemed to spirit off the line of the stumps so late that the bowler thought the ball was through – but he had all the other strokes as well.

Ordinary cricket followers were turning out in appreciable numbers to watch Ranji bat before his University captain ever recognized him, and all his playing life he attracted the Victorian and Edwardian crowds for whom he represented a compelling blend of the strangely contrasting concepts of Empire, the mysterious East and cricket. For season after season he scored well over two thousand runs – twice more than three thousand. On fast wickets, even against the tightest bowling, his cutting, glancing, pulling and driving kept his scoring rate at rarely less than 50 an hour. It was said, first critically and later admiringly, that he was an unorthodox batsman and, certainly, his magnificent eye and speed enabled him to take startling liberties with the most accurate bowling. On the other hand, with experience, he became a sound defensive player on slow and turning wickets. His last appearance for Sussex, in 1920, was a sad occasion: he had lost an eye (in a shooting accident) and put on much weight and, though he played a few exciting strokes, even he could not overcome that dual disadvantage.

Through his great years – from 1896 to 1904 – Ranji knew only one spell of failure. In the Test series against Australia his scores were 13, 0, 2, 0: nevertheless, his average in fourteen Tests with Australia is almost 45.

Ranji was also a brilliant slip field, but the true measure of his eminence is that he became the successor to W. G. Grace in the esteem of the cricket public.

G. H. Hirst

This season, too, another of those who were to make cricket history for years to come stood up high and clear above the ordinary run of county cricketers. George Hirst performed the double for the first time. His potential was clear so early that he played for Yorkshire in 1889, when he was only seventeen years old. At first, his bowling was lively but straightforward fast left-arm: but in 1901 he suddenly acquired the savage, late inswing which would have been deadly in any period but which, in his time, was also a novelty. Hirst was thickly powerful: he stood only five-feet-six but as a young man weighed fourteen stone; later, while still quite active, far more. He bowled round the wicket with a full body swing and, in a vintage period of fast bowling, his top pace was rated unequivocally as fast. Granted a little turn, however, he bowled the left-armer's breakaway, spun with the first two fingers at more than medium pace.

Hirst was a right-handed batsman with the thick man's characteristic speed of foot, so that, though he could bat soundly in orthodox manner, he could hook bowling not truly short of a length. He also employed the pull profitably and, in normal circumstances, he was a fast scorer. He was one of the men who moulded modern Yorkshire cricket in character as well as method, and his defence could be unwinkingly correct.

He was reckoned the best mid-off of his day, safe-handed and unflinching against a generation of the hardest off-drivers there has ever been. Add to this one of the keenest of cricket minds, unfailing determination and a broad sense of humour, and you have the picture of a great all-rounder and an outstanding Test player even in a splendid period.

From start to finish, George Hirst's first-class cricket career spanned thirty-eight years, from 1891 to 1929; and from 1895 to 1914 he was a major power in the game. Fourteen times he performed the all-rounder's double and, in 1906, the unique double-double – 2,385 runs and 208 wickets. This, someone once said to him, was a feat no one else would ever equal. Hirst's characteristic reply was 'I wouldn't say that, but if anyone ever does he will be very tired'.

F. R. Spofforth, the famous early Australian bowler, now playing occasionally for Derbyshire, was top of the first-class bowling averages, but with only 28 wickets: J. T. Hearne took 257 – 56 of them Australian. In the first innings of their game with Warwickshire, Yorkshire scored 887 – still the record for county cricket.

It was an historic season.

The Season of 1897

In a summer of fairly frequent turning wickets, a dramatic, five-cornered fight for the county Championship quite overshadowed the visit of the Gentlemen of Philadelphia. Notts were not beaten until late July, when they lost five of their last six matches: next, Yorkshire took up the running, only to lose four out of seven. Essex led briefly until they lost to Surrey who looked set to retain the title until, at the very end of August, they were bowled out by Tyler on a sticky wicket, and beaten by Somerset. So Lancashire became Champions – deservedly, because they had made good their long-standing deficiency of bowling support for Mold and Briggs. Willis Cuttell, a former Yorkshire player who varied slow-medium off-breaks with a leg-break bowled through a low arc, took 102 wickets in Championship matches, and the steady and improving Hallam, 90. Mold had already 88 wickets to his name when he broke down in August, but by then Briggs (140) and his new reinforcements could see the business through in support of the batting of MacLaren, Ward, Baker, Sugg and J. T. Tyldesley.

J. T. Tyldesley
At one point in the season, J. T. Tyldesley scored three centuries in consecutive innings, two of them against Warwickshire on what must surely have been his favourite ground, Edgbaston. John Thomas Tyldesley was one of the finest of all Lancashire batsmen and, for ten years, even in the 'Golden Age', an almost automatic choice for England. Short and quick, he was a neat back-foot player on turning wickets and, at need, he could close up a game. But his natural style was aggressive; fast on his feet, he drove hard, his cut – square or fine – was a fiercely positive stroke, and he was one of the earliest masters of the hook. A nimble runner, reliable catch and strong thrower, he maintained a high standard in the outfield even into his late years.

Surrey once more made plenty of runs – twelve men averaged over twenty, Abel, fifty. But Lohmann had gone and Lockwood took only one wicket. So the bowling was all Richardson, with 238 wickets in Championship matches – the remaining thirteen Surrey bowlers took 239 between them.

Essex could attribute their rise to the batting of Peter Perrin – a master of fast bowling and often described as the best batsman who never played for England, but whose fielding explained that fact – the attractive young-stroke maker, A. J. Turner, Charles McGahey and Carpenter as batsmen and Bull, slow left-arm with considerable spin, who proved highly effective on dry wickets in support of Kortright and Mead.

G. L. Jessop
For Gloucestershire against Yorkshire at Harrogate, G. L. Jessop scored 101 in forty minutes. Yet another of the leading figures of the great period had made his mark. Jessop was an all-rounder: in this season of 1897 he took 116 wickets as well as making 1,219 runs: indeed, at his clinking pace, he opened the bowling for England against Australia, and he was as fine a cover point as any in his time, with a phenomenally long and low throw. Gilbert Jessop's unique place in cricket, however, is as the most consistent attacking batsman the game has ever known. From the age of nineteen, when he was raw, until he was forty, which is an advanced age for a hitter, he scored 26,698 runs at an average of 32. There have been men who hit the ball farther – Hewett, Albert Trott, Lyons, Sinclair and Ted Alletson in his own time – but no one has ever made so many runs so quickly. Four of Jessop's five scores of over 200 were made at over 80 an hour, the fifth at more than 70: at other times he scored centuries at nearer 100 runs an hour. Yet Jessop was not a slogger. He had the whole range of strokes and

the quick eye and catlike footwork to move into position to play a forcing stroke to an 'impossibly' good ball. From his low stance – hence his nickname 'The Croucher' – he would leap down the pitch to drive savagely off the front foot, or close on to his stumps to cut or hook off the back. Some of the best bowlers of his time – from the fastest (Jessop used to run down the wicket to Mold) through the most accurate to the sharp spinners – have told me that when Jessop was on the kill it was impossible to keep him in check, utterly disheartening to bowl to him. He would cut a ball for four and then step out and drive another, identical in pace, length and line, through mid-on. For the Gentlemen of the South against the Players of the South, at Hastings in 1907, he made 191 in 90 minutes and gave only one chance. After W. G. Grace left, he took over the captaincy of Gloucestershire from 1900 to 1913, and retired in 1914. Jessop's batting was one of the spectacles of cricket and it seems doubtful that there can ever be another who will so combine strength – of wrists and forearms – speed and a completely attacking approach with such timing and cold, quick calculation of risk.

1897 was an historic hinge-year within the pattern of the game. England had won 25 and Australia only 15 of the 46 Test Matches so far played between the two countries. Now, however, Australian techniques and tactics had grown to match the natural ability of their players and the balance of power was about to shift. The English teams of the next fifteen years were probably as good as any before or since, but, on results, the Australians were better.

England in Australia, 1897–98

This series, between two ponderously strong batting sides, went to Australia because their bowling was more steady, varied and, on good wickets, the more penetrative.

At Sydney, where England won, MacLaren and Ranjitsinhji made centuries and Hearne, with Richardson as his assistant, twice bowled out Australia. Australia won the remaining four Tests predominantly through the batting of Darling – who averaged 67 – the all-round cricket of Trumble, and the powers of three men who now stepped up to full Test class, M. A. Noble, Clem Hill and C. E. McLeod.

M. A. Noble

Monty – or Alf – Noble was recognized, quickly and rightly, as the successor to George Giffen as Australia's leading all-rounder. We can now see his greater historic importance as Australia's first player in the truly modern mould. He had pronounced aptitude as a player but it was more significant for the trend of technique in his country that he had an acute and original mind. His medium pace right-arm bowling was based on the old tradition of the off-break, but he added diversity of arc, not only through changing the point of release but by bending or straightening the left leg to deceive the batsman in pitch. He was, more importantly, one of the first controlled swing bowlers.

The salient quality of Noble's batting was absence of weakness. On hard true wickets he was mainly a forward player, using his reach to smother the good ball or drive the bad one. When the pitch was slow he would employ back play as if to the Yorkshire manner born. He usually fielded at point, where he caught safely. Yet Noble is remembered as much for his captaincy as for his playing ability: certainly no England captain of his time could outwit him.

Clem Hill

Australian opinion still ranks Clem Hill as the best of all left-handed batsmen. He was inherently sound with a fighting streak, thickly built and, out of his crouching stance, capable of forcing the pace or saving a game; powerful in driving and, when bowlers tried to check his scoring, strong off his legs: a safe cutter and amazingly certain in pulling the straight ball. Despite his five dismissals in the nineties against England, he was a player of firm temperament, a sound captain, for years the central pillar of the South Australian state side.

Jones was 'called' twice for throwing by the English umpire, James Phillips, in matches against Stoddart's team – once when playing for South Australia, again in the second Test: but he went on to take 22 wickets in the series while Trumble and Noble each had 19 and McLeod ten. For England the series was summarized in the bowling averages: Hearne 20 wickets at 26·9, Richardson 22 at 35·2. Five Australian batsmen – Darling, McLeod, Hill, Gregory, and Iredale – averaged over 40, but only two Englishmen – MacLaren and Ranjitsinhji – were as successful. Strong at every point, Australia won the second and third Tests by an innings, and the other two by comfortable margins.

The Season of 1898

The weather, especially in May and June, produced a series of bowlers' wickets for a domestic season in which Yorkshire, who faltered only once, took the Championship decisively from Middlesex and Gloucestershire.

Lord Hawke had now completed his plan. Yorkshire were firmly moulded as a regular eleven, which has remained the basic shape of their cricket ever since. The eleven of 1898, in usual batting order, was: J. T. Brown, J. Tunnicliffe, F. S. Jackson, D. Denton, E. Wainwright, Lord Hawke, G. H. Hirst, F. W. Milligan, S. Haigh, W. Rhodes and D. Hunter. Eight of that side played for England. In the match with Derbyshire at Chesterfield, J. T. Brown and Tunnicliffe scored 554, which remained the record first-wicket partnership until 1932. The most important facet of the Yorkshire season, however, was the appearance of Wilfred Rhodes – to replace Peel who had been 'disciplined' in the previous season.

Wilfred Rhodes

In May 1898, Wilfred Rhodes was an unknown, twenty-year-old, country cricketer in (by cherished coincidence) George Hirst's native village of Kirkheaton. Beginning with nineteen wickets in his first two matches for Yorkshire, he was the most successful slow bowler in the country and ended the season second to J. T. Hearne in the national averages with 154 wickets at 14·6. The critics could not recall such an impressive entry into the game since A. G. Steel in 1878. Over the next thirty-two years he was to make a prodigious mark on the history of the game, taking more wickets – 4,187 – than anyone else, scoring nearly 40,000 runs, performing the double the record number of sixteen times, taking part in 58 Tests, and becoming the shrewdest of tactical thinkers.

Rhodes made his first impact as a slow, left-arm bowler with a perfect sideways-on action which, far into his fifties, was as smoothly easy an employment of body swing as can be imagined. In this first season he had the fortune to play many of his early matches on turning wickets, where his spin and length brought good returns. Soon, however, he showed that, on pitches so perfect that the ball would not turn at all, his flight was so subtle that the finest batsmen in the world could not judge his length with certainty.

He went in at number ten or eleven in his early matches for both Yorkshire and England. By study over the years he developed his right-handed batting, fundamentally stubborn, with enough strokes from front and back foot to punish the bad ball until, on the 1911–12 tour, he and Jack Hobbs set up the record – 323 – for a first-wicket stand in Test cricket. His fielding was steady and, in the early nineteen-hundreds, he and George Hirst were beyond all compare the finest pair of all-rounders ever to play together in any team. When F. S. Jackson was with them – as well as Schofield Haigh – Yorkshire were equipped beyond any captain's reasonable hopes.

Schofield Haigh

Schofield Haigh was primarily a bowler. Stockily built and full of enthusiasm, with a long, rather ugly, delivery stride, he was steady fast-medium in good batting conditions, a deadly bowler of the off-break where the pitch granted any degree of turn. A presentable number eight batsman, he was never successful in Tests, but for sixteen seasons he was invaluable to Yorkshire.

The power of Middlesex lay in amateur batting and professional bowling. The first nine places in their batting averages were filled by amateurs, including, of course, Stoddart and also the strong and competent James Douglas, F. J. G. Ford, tall left-hander of long, flowing and ranging strokes, and the young P. F. Warner. Sir Timothy O'Brien, a highly gifted attacking bat, made all too few appearances, though for more than a dozen years it was apparent that, as a regular player, he might have reached appreciable heights. So far as the county's bowling was concerned, Hearne and Trott took 227 wickets in Championship matches while the other ten bowlers divided the remaining 64 between them.

Gloucester's strength lay primarily in the all-round cricket of Grace, Townsend and Jessop but they were reinforced by the steady defensive batting of Walter Troup and the superb off-side fielding of Jessop, Sewell, Champain and Hemingway.

C. B. Fry

Ranji was away in India and did not play for Sussex, who finished only eleventh in the table. The most heartening aspect of their season was the batting of C. B. Fry, second in the first-class averages. Fry was without doubt the greatest of all all-round athletes. A triple Blue at Oxford, for athletics (in the 100 yards, in which he did 'evens'; the long jump, at which he set a world record which stood for twenty-one years; and the high jump), Association football, and cricket, he missed a rugby Blue only through injury. At soccer he played right-back for the full England side and for Southampton in the F.A. Cup Final. He was a fine golfer and useful at swimming, tennis, rowing and throwing the javelin. After a First in 'Mods' at Oxford, original thinking as an editor and journalist, work at the League of Nations, and years of outstanding service in running the training ship *Mercury*, occupied him off the field of sport.

More than any other cricketer, C. B. Fry personified the change from ancient to modern in batting. At Repton and Oxford he was a heavy scorer primarily by forward play and driving. Later, as he admitted and many critics over-stressed, he was influenced by playing with, and watching, Ranji, so that he tended more and more to back-play. In the Oval Test of 1905 it was the Australian tactic to contain Fry by bowling short to restrict his front foot play: thereupon he scored 144 in an innings outstanding for the brilliance of his cutting. A superbly proportioned, handsome man with an upstanding method, he was at his most dashing and splendid as an off-driver, but he had immense power of defence and a closely controlled range of leg-side strokes. He was a safe slip catcher and a fast, graceful mover in the outfield and, until he was 'named' by the county captains in 1900 for throwing, an occasionally successful change-bowler at fast-medium pace. Ranji and Fry batting at Hove is one of the most memorable images of the Golden Age of cricket. Contrasted in appearance and method, they were the most prolific run-scoring combination of their time.

England did not lose one of the six Tests – those of the 1912 Triangular tournament – in which Fry was captain. One of the game's most profound thinkers, he wrote a masterly technical treatise called *Batsmanship*, was a superb conversationalist, and one of the most remarkable characters of his age.

Gentlemen *v* Players at Lord's began on W. G. Grace's fiftieth birthday and was played between two strong sides. The batting of Gunn and Storer plus the bowling of Hearne and Lockwood put the Players in a strong position, but W. G. Grace – coming in late because of a bruised hand – and Charles Kortright held out over an hour for the last wicket, until Kortright, who had Lockwood's deadly slower ball much in mind, received it – and saw it – but still played too soon and was caught at cover. So the Players won

by 137 runs with less than three minutes to spare.

The year's most far reaching – and belated – administrative decision stemmed from a suggestion by Lord Hawke, when a meeting of county representatives decided that all future Tests played by England should be organized, and teams selected, by a Board of Control: then, reversing the decision of the 1895 meeting, it was decided that in future Australian touring sides in England would be allotted five Test Matches.

In 1898–99, Lord Hawke took his second team to South Africa where, despite the fine all-round cricket of the best player so far produced there – J. H. Sinclair, a tall, fine, right-handed striker of the ball and fast-medium bowler – England won both Tests. A side with Albert Trott, Haigh and Cuttell to bowl, and J. T. Tyldesley and P. F. Warner as the leading batsmen, was always too strong for the rather unsophisticated opposition.

At about this time, news came from Australia that a young batsman, Victor Trumper, had scored 292 not-out for New South Wales against Tasmania.

The Season of 1899

This was one of the three great batting summers of cricket, though in the Tests, Australia, under Darling, won the rubber on rain-damaged pitches far removed in character from their own.

In a County Championship overshadowed for the first time by the visit of a touring side, Surrey marked the last of their run of wins which now stretched back to nine – one of them shared – in thirteen seasons. Richardson was at last beginning to flag – Lockwood, Hayward, Jephson and Brockwell all had better averages – but the five of them shared the burden and Abel, Hayward, Lockwood, Brockwell, Jephson and Hayes made enough runs, so that they needed only to avoid defeat by Warwickshire in the last match to fend off Middlesex. For the runners-up, Wells, Rawlin and Roche took a little of the weight of the bowling off Hearne – who had, for him, a poor season – and Trott. Among the batsmen, P. F. – later Sir Pelham – Warner scored most runs: against Kent at Lord's R. W. Nicholls and W. Roche made a last wicket stand of 230.

P. F. Warner

From 1890, when he was 'chaired' off at Lord's after making top score for Rugby against Marlborough,

'Plum' Warner was deeply involved in cricket – as batsman, captain, selector, critic, historian, administrator, elder statesman and perpetual enthusiast – until his death in 1963. Until he underwent an operation, long after his playing days, he was never truly fit nor free from pain, and he was quite slightly built. Thus his batting never had quite such strength or fluency on slow pitches as on fast, where his wristy driving and neat cutting brought him runs at a good pace, especially against the fastest bowlers, from whom he never flinched.

He was a constantly sanguine and encouraging captain, deeply concerned with humanity as well as with cricket, an idealist with as wide a first-hand knowledge of the game as anyone has ever had. His keen memory made him a human reference book to the players of seventy years. No cricketer ever travelled quite so far or so often and, for Middlesex, he was the captain who led them through many happy years to the Championship in 1920, his last county season.

In his entire playing career, which stretched from 1894, through isolated matches in his later years to 1929, he scored 29,028 runs with 60 centuries and an average of 36·28, and played in fifteen Tests.

The Tests proved amazingly absorbing for a series in which only one match was brought to a decision. At Nottingham W. G. Grace played his last game for England. A week earlier he had retired, after a dispute, from the captaincy of Gloucestershire which he had held since 1871 and now, though he could still bat well, he was – rising fifty-one – a sad handicap in the field. It was as if history had affronted itself.

Australia batted no more than steadily against Rhodes – in his first Test – and Hearne; but against Howell, Jones and Noble, only Fry and Ranji made more than 40 and Australia led on the first innings by 59. Their second innings was built round 80 by Clem Hill, and Darling's declaration left England 290 to win. The first four wickets fell for 19 and Hayward and Ranji were left to save the match – which they did, the latter rather unorthodoxly with a superb display of stroke-making for 93 not out.

The Lord's Test proved decisive. England probably erred in playing Jessop as the only fast bowler. The batting failed; only Jackson and Jessop, in the first innings, MacLaren and Hayward in the second, lifted them to 206 and 240. Against seven bowlers who were never more than steady, Clem Hill scored 135 and Trumper 135 not-out in a total of 421: Australia won by ten wickets.

V. T. Trumper

Nothing about Victor Trumper is more impressive than the warmth of feeling felt for him not only in his lifetime, but for long after his death at only 37. Even after the success of Bradman, there were still many in Australia who declared Victor Trumper the greatest batsman their country ever produced.

Of more than average height and finely built, he moved with an arresting, innate grace. As a batsman, he had all the strokes and rare skill in placing the ball through gaps in the field. But the utter gallantry of his cricket captured the imagination. He had such speed of divination that he could change his mind halfway through a stroke yet still hit a four. His timing was so instinctively perfect that, without apparent effort, he struck the ball vast distances. Whilst he could play quite correctly, he rose to supreme heights when, on bad wickets where other batsmen were helpless, he played innings of glorious improvisation. He would leap down the wicket to drive – as George Beldam caught him in the finest of all cricket action photographs – or move back close to his stumps and hook or pull a straight or lifting ball with fierce certainty. His Test batting average of 39 is surprisingly high for one who seemed to take so many risks and who, on two English tours, encountered a high proportion of rain-damaged wickets.

Occasionally he bowled at sprightly pace and he was a fine and fast outfielder. Above all, he must have been the gayest and most handsome of batsmen.

At Leeds, on a rain-affected wicket, in spite of good all-round play by Hugh Trumble, England held the advantage when rain washed out the last day. A bold hitting innings by Worrall brought him 76, the highest score of the match: J. T. Hearne performed one of the rare hat tricks in the series with three good wickets – of M. A. Noble, Syd Gregory and Clem Hill. Poor Johnny Briggs had an epileptic fit at the end of the first day and took no further part in the match. 'Sailor' Young, a fairly fast, left-arm bowler from Essex, took six wickets in this match and again in the next – twelve altogether, in his only two Tests.

At Old Trafford England made a bad start, recovered through Hayward's sound 130, and took a first innings lead of 176 when Bradley (the tall, strong, Kent fast-bowler) and Young put out Australia for 196; MacLaren asked Australia to follow on. With no hope of winning, Worrall, Noble, Trumper, Darling and Iredale made sure that Australia did not lose, and safely engineered a draw.

45

Tom Hayward

This was Tom Hayward's first century against Australia. His father and grandfather both played for Surrey, and his uncle and namesake was a prominent mid-nineteenth century batsman for Cambridge. Tom Hayward might be called the last great exponent of the old school of batting. He was next after W. G. Grace to reach a hundred centuries and, for twenty consecutive seasons, scored over a thousand runs, in eight of them more than two thousand, twice over three thousand.

He had the upright, somewhat open stance of the eighteen-eighties and, though back play was to some extent forced on him, he was primarily a forward player whose main scoring strokes were the off-drive and the cut. He never feared to lift the ball in driving and, both hands near the top of the handle, with a high back-lift and a long follow-through, he was a stylish, even dignified, batsman. Until 1904 his medium-pace bowling was so valuable to Surrey – more than once, when Lohmann was absent or Lockwood out of condition, it brought them the Championship – that he could be ranked as an all-rounder. In later years, however, he was purely a batsman, moving up the order to open the innings with the young Jack Hobbs. Towards the end of his career, inswing and the googly bothered him, but he was for several years the soundest professional batsman in England.

England needed to win the Oval Test to level the series. Hayward, opening the innings for the first time, and Jackson both scored centuries. Ranji, Fry, MacLaren and Townsend all made runs towards a total of 576, and the Australian bowlers were mastered for the first time in the series. Only Gregory (117), Darling (71) and Worrall (55), offered serious opposition to Lockwood who, in one of his great days, took seven for 71, and Australia followed on. Worrall, making his only tour since 1888 (when he was regarded as a crude player), had now become a strong front-of-the-wicket batsman and his 75, McLeod's 77, and Noble's 69 not-out, drew the match and gave Australia the rubber.

The remarkable Major – later General – R. M. Poore burst quite dramatically on the cricket world of 1899, at the age of thirty-three. On leave from his military duties, he could play for only half the season but scored 1,551 runs, with seven centuries, and was top of the batting averages with a figures of 91·23. This – W. A. Johnston's freak figures of 1953 apart – has been exceeded only three times, by Bradman (twice) and Sutcliffe. In Championship matches for Hampshire he averaged 116·58. Poore's previous cricket had been played largely in India and South Africa, where he was stationed. When Lord Hawke's side was in South Africa in 1895–96 he was invited to appear for both sides in Tests, but his commanding officer would only allow him to play for South Africa. Very strong and tall, Poore used his great reach to smother in defence, drive in attack, and, though thus limited and unprepossessing in style, he made some of his best scores in conditions where more experienced batsmen were routed.

These few matches were – tantalizingly – by far his longest experience of first-class cricket though, in 1906, when he was forty years old, in his last two matches for Hampshire he scored 232 runs at 58 an innings – and then retired to concentrate on his promotion to the rank of general and to relax in occasional club cricket.

This season Worcestershire entered the County Championship with three of the Foster brothers – R.E., W.L., and H.K. – buoying their batting; Wilson and Burrows – both fast right-arm – the most successful bowlers; and Arnold, somewhat reduced in stature by illness, the all-rounder of the side. They were twelfth in the final table.

Outside the first-class game, A. E. J. Collins, playing for Clark's against North Town in a Clifton College house match, scored 628 not-out, still the highest score ever made in any match anywhere.

So ended the epic, formative cricket of the eighteen-nineties.

The Edwardian Heyday: 1900 to 1914

Twentieth century cricket opened with an air of sparkling confidence. Its years down to the outbreak of the first World War were subsequently to be described as 'The Golden Age' and the whole game exuded consciousness of a great destiny. A sporting Prince – soon to be king – was replacing the widowed Queen-Empress, Victoria, in public imagination. Everywhere, too, increasing prosperity was having its effect on cricket, more and better facilities were becoming available for more players. More people had money and leisure to watch the game, and a rapidly growing press was disseminating more news of it to more readers. Cricket, though no one dreamt it, was entering on its last era as the undisputed summer game of England. Cricket could even be undisturbed – though nostalgically sad – that the pilot had been dropped. W. G. Grace might still be seen – as one of the 'sights' like Buckingham Palace and the Houses of Parliament – captaining his semi-serious London County XI, but his dominance was ended.

Some important changes in the Laws had now become necessary. Either umpire might call 'no ball' if not satisfied of the fairness of a delivery, and feeling about unfair bowling was drawing to a head. The number of balls to the over was increased from five to six. Declaration, previously confined to the third day, was now allowed at any time after lunch on the second day; and the follow-on, hitherto compulsory upon a deficit of 120 runs, became optionally enforceable on a side 150 behind.

Except in South Africa, the majority of the players who were to create a new high level of cricket had already been blooded in their appointed roles. The stage, too, was set for them in a whole series of superb fast wickets on virtually all the first-class grounds in England and Australia.

When this era is called 'The Golden Age' it means the Golden Age *of batsmen* and it should not be thought that bowlers or fielding captains wished it so. If this was the vintage period of batting, it was also the time of such technical advances in bowling and strategy as ensured that batsmen should never enjoy such prosperity again.

These were the chief results of the period 1900–14.

1900–1914

Test Matches

1901–02 in Australia, Australia beat England 4–1

1902 in England, Australia beat England 2–1: two matches drawn

1902–03 in South Africa, Australia beat South Africa 2–0: one match drawn

1903–04 in Australia, England beat Australia 3–2

1905 in England, England beat Australia 2–0: three matches drawn

1905–06 in South Africa, South Africa beat England 4–1

47

'The Opening of the Cricket Season' Ralph Cleaver's drawings in the first week of the historic summer of 1902: Surrey v Worcestershire (in the centre), and impressions of the Australians at practice at Lord's

1907 in England, England beat South Africa 1–0: two matches drawn

1907–08 in Australia, Australia beat England 4–1

1909 in England, Australia beat England 2–1: two matches drawn

1909–10 in South Africa, South Africa beat England 3–2

1910–11 in Australia, Australia beat South Africa 4–1

1911–12 in Australia, England beat Australia 4–1

1912 in England, England beat Australia 1–0: two matches drawn

in England, England beat South Africa 3–0

in England, Australia beat South Africa 2–0: one match drawn

1913–14 in South Africa, England beat South Africa 4–0: one match drawn

County Champions

1900 Yorkshire
1901 Yorkshire
1902 Yorkshire
1903 Middlesex
1904 Lancashire
1905 Yorkshire
1906 Kent
1907 Nottinghamshire
1908 Yorkshire
1909 Kent
1910 Kent
1911 Warwickshire
1912 Yorkshire
1913 Kent
1914 Surrey

Sheffield Shield Winners

1900–01 Victoria
1901–02 New South Wales
1902–03 New South Wales
1903–04 New South Wales
1904–05 New South Wales
1905–06 New South Wales
1906–07 New South Wales
1907–08 Victoria
1908–09 New South Wales
1909–10 South Australia
1910–11 New South Wales

1911–12 New South Wales
1912–13 South Australia
1913–14 New South Wales
1914–15 Victoria

Currie Cup Winners

1902–03 Transvaal
1903–04 Transvaal
1904–05 Transvaal
1906–07 Transvaal
1908–09 Western Province
1910–11 Natal
1912–13 Natal

West Indies, Inter-Colonial or Triangular Tournament

1901–02 Trinidad beat Barbados
1903–04 Trinidad beat Barbados
1905–06 Barbados beat Trinidad
1907–08 Trinidad beat Barbados
1908–09 Barbados beat Trinidad
1909–10 Trinidad beat Barbados
1910–11 Barbados beat Trinidad
1911–12 Barbados beat Trinidad

Plunket Shield Winners
(at this period held under a challenge system)

1906–07 Canterbury
1907–11 Auckland
1911–12 Canterbury
1912–13 Auckland
1913–18 Canterbury

The shape of twentieth century English cricket was sharply defined in 1900 when, in another rain-punctuated summer, Yorkshire, shaking off their only serious challengers, Lancashire, as early as July, won the Championship without losing a single match. Yorkshire's power still resided in Tunnicliffe, Brown and Denton as batsmen, Rhodes and Haigh as bowlers, Whitehead and Hirst as all-rounders. In this year they had assistance from T. L. Taylor – a powerful bats-man, at his valuable best on slow wickets – and Ernest Smith, the Oxford Blue and all-rounder.

For Lancashire, Briggs, apparently recovered in

health, returned to take 120 wickets – including an all-ten against Worcester – but this was his last season: he died less than two years later.

Kent and Sussex shared third place, Kent with a whole harvest of new talent – J. R. Mason, dashing bat, lively fast medium bowler and fine field; E. W. Dillon, C. J. Burnup and S. H. Day as batsmen; Alec Hearne, still a sturdy and steady county all-rounder; Bradley as fast bowler; and Colin Blythe.

Colin Blythe

The best indication of Colin Blythe's stature as a slow left-arm bowler is that, despite being a contemporary of Wilfred Rhodes, who had far greater batting ability to offer, he played in nineteen Tests for England. Slightly built and sensitive, Blythe had a lower arc of flight than Rhodes, which, in Ranji's opinion made him the more difficult of the two, and possibly spun more sharply, while the ball that went with his arm was surprisingly fast. An imaginative cricketer, he rarely shortened his length under punishment but backed his spin and changes of pace against the bat.

Like Briggs, Blythe was subject to epileptic fits and, highly strung, he found cricket an intense nervous strain. When, in 1907, he took seventeen Northants wickets in a day – all ten for 30 in the first innings, seven for 18 in the second – he came off the field in a state of near-collapse. Yet it should not be thought that he was a weakling. True, nine bowlers have exceeded Blythe's 2,506 wickets, but none of them had so short a career as his sixteen seasons. He was the key bowler in Kent's considerable run of success in the nine years up to 1914, when he announced his retirement. He was killed in the Great War.

For Sussex alone, Ranjitsinhji and Fry scored 4,393 runs with eighteen centuries between them, and an average of 74·44 *each*.

A West Indian side toured England, but since its matches were not rated as first-class, it was fortunate to gain so much experience for an eventual loss of only £291 1s. 3d.

The Season of 1901

Yorkshire this time ran away from the other counties to win the Championship in quite hollow fashion. Their bowling was carried by Rhodes and Hirst who, together, took 331 wickets in Championship matches. Haigh had, on the whole, a poor season but, on a

sticky wicket at Trent Bridge, he (four for eight) and Rhodes (six for four) bowled out Notts for 13. Some of the established batsmen fell away but, in compensation, the former Cambridge Blue, Frank Mitchell, a vastly improved, patient bat, strong in driving, came into the side and ended with the best aggregate and average. Yorkshire were beaten only once – in one of the most remarkable matches of the season. At Bradford they bowled out Somerset for 87 and, to their satisfaction, scored 325. In the second Somerset innings, however, L. C. H. Palairet (173), Braund (107) and Philips (122) mounted an onslaught which ended with a total of 630, made at over eighty an hour. Thrown out of their stride, Yorkshire collapsed before the spin bowling of Cranfield – slow left-arm – and Braund, and were beaten by 279.

L. C. Braund

Though Len Braund was for several years on the Surrey staff, he never played a full first-class season until 1901, when he had qualified for Somerset and was 24. He was an immediate success in that year – performed the 'double', was picked for the Players at Lord's, and for MacLaren's side to Australia in the winter. Len Braund was a well set-up, lively, athletic man whom *Wisden* for 1902 described as 'one of the very best of the new leg-break bowlers'. He was new in the standard of his accuracy and he spun the leg-break sharply, with consistently steady length and line. A strong batsman on all kinds of wickets and in any situation, and the finest slip fielder of his time, Braund had an unruffable temperament. C. B. Fry described him as 'a big match player' and few others can so often have changed the outcome of matches by outstanding feats in all three departments of the game. He was later an umpire, a fine raconteur and, even after both his legs were amputated, a merry, expansive man.

Three Sussex batsmen – C. B. Fry, George Brann and Ranjitsinhji – finished in the first three places in the averages and Fry ended the season by scoring six centuries in successive innings.

There were two developments of historic importance during the year. In December 1900 a meeting of the county captains had voted to bar certain named players from county games for unfair bowling. MCC refused to support the motion but, though only Mold was actually 'called' for throwing (sixteen times) in 1901, the captains' nominations had the effect of finishing the careers of not only Mold, but Tyler and

Len Braund (Somerset) One of the few true all-rounders at Test level: worth his place either as batsman or bowler and the finest slip field of his day

Geeson, putting a virtual end to the bowling of C. B. Fry, and causing W. G. Quaife to change his style.

In the first clear sign of the technical development which was to change the whole concept of pace bowling, George Hirst, in the words of *Wisden*, 'at times made the ball swerve in the air in a way that was nothing less than bewildering'. Albert Trott was still bowling his 'curly ball'; Ted Arnold, at Worcester, was developing his outswinger, and Albert Relf of Sussex, given some assistance from the wind, could make the ball move either way in the air. Perhaps most significant of all, M. A. Noble, after some advice from a baseball player, had practised until he could bowl the outswinger at will. Swing had been regarded as an occasional accident; now it was gradually being brought under control.

The method of the fast bowlers until now can best be summarized in the words of Charles Kortright – 'I never made the ball swing and neither did any of the people I played with, except the American J. B. King, until George Hirst. We bowled fast outside the off stump and challenged the batsmen to cut us – and they would all *try* to cut. When I took the new ball, I rubbed it in the dirt to get purchase for my fingers because I tried, every ball, to bowl an off-break. Sometimes it broke, more often not: and occasionally, when you spun it a lot, it would run away a bit in the air, but we never called that swing'.

In a time when there were already complaints about wickets – notably at Leyton – being too good for matches to be finished in three days, bowlers were being forced to new methods.

England in Australia, 1901–02

This should have been the first team sent overseas by MCC but, when that body found that Hirst, Rhodes, Mason, R. E. Foster, Jackson, Fry and Ranjitsinhji were all unavailable, they handed the problem on to MacLaren. He at once produced something of a sensation by inviting an 'unknown' league bowler – S. F. Barnes – to play for Lancashire in their last match of the season, against Leicester. In the preceding five years Barnes had played five Championship matches, three for Warwickshire and two for Lancashire and had taken, altogether, five wickets at an average of 55. In the Leicester match he took six for 70 before rain closed play, and MacLaren put him in his side for Australia. He was to prove the only truly penetrative bowler in a side of talent rather than weight in batting, but – characteristic of MacLaren – superb in the field.

It was significant of the strength of English cricket that even with so many distinguished absentees, MacLaren's side was still strong enough to win the first Test. MacLaren himself made the highest score – 116 – of the English 464. Then, on a true pitch, Braund and Blythe, with seven wickets apiece, and Barnes with six, twice ran through the Australian batting so commandingly that no one scored a fifty.

In the four remaining Tests, Noble (seven for 17 in the first innings of the second Test) and Trumble (who did the hat trick in the same match) took 58 wickets between them and won them all for Australia. Barnes took thirteen wickets for 163 runs in the second Test but broke down with a knee injury early in the third, and did not bowl again on the tour. England, nevertheless, took the third Test to as close a decision as four wickets and the fifth to 32 runs, but without Barnes they lacked a true cutting edge and Braund (21 wickets in the series), Blythe (18) and John Gunn (17) could not quite make good the deficiency.

S. F. Barnes

On his first – 1901–02 – visit to Australia, Sydney Francis Barnes was considered by stern judges in that country to be the best bowler England had ever sent there. He was to rise to higher levels of performance in later years. He has been described as the greatest of all bowlers, and no one has ever adequately refuted that claim.

Barnes had a most unusual career. He played his first first-class match – for Warwickshire – in 1895, when he was twenty-two, and his last – for Wales – in 1930, at the age of 57. Yet, because he spent most of his playing life in the northern leagues and Minor Counties cricket, he played only two full county seasons – both for Lancashire – and in only 44 Championship matches: yet he appeared in 27 Tests for England. In those matches – against Australia and South Africa – he took 189 wickets, at a striking-rate of one every seven overs and at an average of 16·43. In lesser cricket he was a complete killer. At Minor Counties level, in twenty-three seasons of play with his native Staffordshire, he took 1,437 wickets at 8·04. In League cricket his power is best illustrated by the fact that every club he played for won its competition.

Syd Barnes was a tall, bony, strong man who never, even in his erect nineties, carried any excess weight. His pace varied, with age and pitch-condition, between genuinely fast and medium. He has said that, at his peak – which he described as from 1901 to 1924 – he spun – *positively spun* – almost every ball he bowled. Though he admits his bowling often deviated through the air, that was due, he asserts – with good technical reason – to spin, and not to swing technique. From his high arm and full-flowing action, he made the ball lift sharply from any wicket, and almost vertically from the matting in South Africa. A solitary student of his craft, essentially aggressive, a hater of batsmen, and one who cared deeply for his professional reputation, Barnes maintained a remarkably high standard of performance for an amazing number of years. It might be extravagant to say that he was consistently

A. C. MacLaren (Lancashire) Imperious, brave, record-breaking batsman: strong but tactless captain

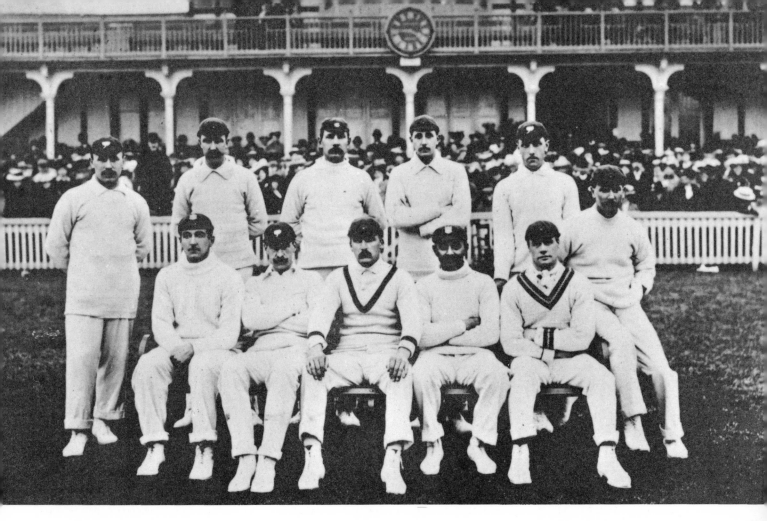

The England XI v Australia at Edgbaston, 1902 – the finest England team ever to take the field? Back row (left to right) G. H. Hirst, A. A. Lilley, W. H. Lockwood, L. C. Braund, W. Rhodes, J. T. Tyldesley. Front row: C. B. Fry, F. S. Jackson, A. C. MacLaren, K. S. Ranjitsinhji, G. L. Jessop

unplayable. It would be true to say that he took the wickets of the best batsmen of cricket's greatest period and took them cheaply. It would be true, too, to say that he was never collared.

R. A. Duff

In this series, Reg Duff made a hundred in his first Test: less than four years later, at The Oval, he scored another century in his last. Duff's was a short career and it may well be that he received less than his due of credit because, for New South Wales and Australia, he batted so often with Victor Trumper, who would have overshadowed any partner. Like Trumper, Duff was a forcing batsman, especially strong in driving and cutting: and, like Trumper, he died in his thirties.

This season a side of young amateurs, mainly undergraduates, under R. A. Bennett, was playing in the West Indies, where it lost two of its three games against combined West Indian teams.

In the Australian season of 1901–02 at Hobart, C. J. Eady, playing for Break-o'-Day against Wellington – not a first-class match – scored 566.

The Season of 1902

One of the finest of all Test series rose above a rain-harried summer to produce some of the epic matches of cricket history.

Darling captained Australia, and MacLaren England, in the rubber which began with the first Test ever played at Edgbaston. It has often been argued, and never convincingly disputed, that the team for this match was the strongest ever to take the field for England. In batting order it was – A. C. MacLaren, C. B. Fry, K. S. Ranjitsinhji, F. S. Jackson, J. T. Tyldesley, A. A. Lilley, G. H. Hirst, G. L. Jessop, L. C. Braund, W. H. Lockwood and W. Rhodes. The bowling consisted of two fast right, one fast left, one fast-medium right, one leg-spinner and one slow left: but neither Lockwood nor Jessop – both of whom had opened England's bowling in Tests – so much as turned his arm in the match. All eleven players scored centuries in first-class play, eight of them in Tests. The fielding included three superb slip catchers, two fine outfields, the best mid-off of the time, one of the most consistent of all wicket-keepers, and no one who needed to be 'hidden'. It is impressive that Barnes, Abel and Hayward were left out.

Australia won the series with an eleven unchanged for the last three Tests, a side long regarded as the best *they* ever produced. When Jones was dropped after the second Test, however, it lacked a truly fast bowler. Thus it was less ideally balanced than Bradman's side of 1948. On the other hand, it is difficult to believe that any other touring side could have been more successful in conditions so suddenly 'English' as to be completely foreign to their cricketing background and style. The basic 1902 eleven was – R. A. Duff, V. T. Trumper, C. Hill, J. Darling, M. A. Noble, S. E. Gregory, W. W. Armstrong, A. J. Hopkins, H. Trumble, J. J. Kelly and J. V. Saunders. Apart from Armstrong's leg-breaks, the attack was largely – if not monotonously – within the medium-pace bracket, but it was tight and, on the wickets of 1902, highly effective. The batting order was long, powerful and perhaps the most gifted ever listed by either country. The side had, too, notable spirit; bowled out for 36 in the first Test and immediately after by Yorkshire for 23, they recovered and overcame the depressing 'English' summer to retain The Ashes.

MacLaren won the toss at Edgbaston. England batted and slid to 35 for three before, out of the batting in depth, Jackson, Tyldesley – a century on his happy ground – Hirst, Lockwood and Rhodes built the score to 376. 146 runs had come for the last two wickets when MacLaren declared. There was rain in the night but the wicket was not bad – though the light was poor – when Rhodes (seven for 17) and Hirst (three for 15) put out Australia for an abject 36 (Trumper 18), and they followed on, only for more rain to stop their second innings at 46 for two, and grant them a draw.

The Lord's Test was flooded out after England had made 102 for two. So to the only Test ever played at Sheffield, where Australia batted first and Barnes, with six for 49, contained them to 194. MacLaren and Abel made 61 for England's first wicket but, in

bad light (the appeal was made too late), Noble and Saunders broke through to 102 for five by the end of the first day and finished off the innings for 145 next morning. Trumper – a memorable 62 in under the hour – and Hill – 119 in two-and-a-half hours – were the core of the Australian 289. England, set 339 to win, opened with Jessop and Abel, reached 75 before the second wicket fell and then, while MacLaren made a typically defiant 63, the others went down around him to Noble (eleven wickets in the match) and Trumble, and Australia won by 143.

On July 24th, 25th and 26th of 1902, at Old Trafford, England and Australia played the most dramatic of all Test Matches. All but a few of the major figures of a mighty era were there, though controversy continued for years over the omission of Barnes – surely an obvious choice after his figures at Sheffield – and of Hirst and Jessop, and over the inclusion of Fred Tate – his only Test – Palairet and Abel.

There had been rain for several days before the start. The wicket was soft and the outfield muddily sluggish, yet with the conditions against him, and faced by the bowling of Rhodes, Lockwood, Jackson, Braund and the monumentally steady Tate, Victor Trumper scored the first century before lunch in Test cricket – 103 out of 173. Australia had reached 179 when their third wicket fell but then as the pitch dried, only Darling, whose 51 was the solitary double figure score among the last eight batsmen, could check Lockwood and Rhodes, who ended the innings at 299. Quick to retaliate, Saunders and Trumble, lifting and turning, had England in apparent rout at 44 for five. Now, in a partnership alone sufficient to justify their reputations, Jackson and Braund came together, saw out the day and, on the Friday, made their stand worth 141 before Braund played on to Noble. As the late batting crumbled away, Jackson hit his way to 128 and England – 262 – were only 37 behind on the first innings.

The game was now again in the balance. Braund, falling at slip, half dropped and then caught Trumper; and Lockwood, in one of his savage bursts, had Australia 10 for three. Darling shrewdly countered by putting himself and Syd Gregory in ahead of Noble, and both began to hit.

Now came the decisive moment of the match and the rubber, and it may be best recounted in the words of the bowler, Len Braund. 'I was bowling to Syd Gregory and, off the fifth ball of an over, he played

Victor Trumper (NSW) One of the truly great batsmen; a gracious and exciting player, one of the happiest and best loved of all cricketers

me wide of mid-off for a single and brought Joe Darling, the left-hander, down for the last ball. I said to Mr MacLaren 'Can I have Mr Palairet across to square leg?' (He always fielded there for me in the Somerset side and he knew how that leg-break of mine curved when a left-hander hit it.) Mr MacLaren said 'What, do you want me to ask Lionel Palairet to run right across Old Trafford for one ball? – Send Fred Tate out there' and he did. Surely enough Joe Darling carted me, next ball, with the spin, high out to leg and it curved, as it always does when the left hander hits a leg-break with the spin. Poor Fred Tate moved to his right and then, as it boomeranged away, tried to get back, got his left hand to it but dropped it and there it was – I had to come off'.

At that point, Darling had made 16: he went on to 37, the only double figure score, apart from Gregory's

24, in Australia's 86 all out.

So England, on the last day, wanted 124 to win and Palairet, Abel, Tyldesley and MacLaren, hurrying under threatening storm clouds, carried them to 92 – only 32 short – before the fourth wicket fell. A shower livened the wicket and Trumble and Saunders – perfectly contrasted – sliced through the middle order. Lilley, hitting out, fell to a spectacular running catch by Clem Hill at square-leg, and England – 116 for nine – needed eight to win when Fred Tate (that dropped catch still on his mind) walked down the pavilion steps to join Rhodes. Before he could reach the wicket, rain drove the players in, and Tate sat in the pavilion under an unnerving barrage of advice for three-quarters of an hour before he took guard. Saunders was bowling: Tate stabbed down on his first ball and edged it to fine leg for four. Four wanted. He

55

lived through two more balls, then the fourth came faster and went straight on. It bowled Fred Tate before he could bring his bat down. Australia had won by three runs and retained The Ashes.

J. V. Saunders

The Victorian John Saunders, who caused the English batting considerable trouble whenever the ball would turn in three Test series, bowled left-arm round the wicket. He was a tall man with a high action – which was regarded as suspect – and his pace was nearer medium than slow. He was a natural spinner, with a sharp turn on drying or dusty pitches, a faster ball which went with his arm, and a dangerous yorker.

After such a match, and with the rubber decided, the final Test – at The Oval – could easily have been an anti-climax. It must, in fact, rank close to the previous game in the epics of Test cricket.

England brought back Jessop, Hirst and Hayward. MacLaren lost the toss and Australia batted on a fair day and a good wicket. They lost seven wickets to Hirst and Jackson for 175 then (after Trumble was dropped by Lilley), a typical Australian fight-back took them to 324.

Rain in the night left Trumble a wicket on which he made the ball lift to unmanageable heights and Hirst, with 43, was the highest scorer for England who, all out for 183, were 141 behind on the first innings and even at that, grateful to have avoided following-on. The pitch remained fairly difficult and against Lockwood, Braund – astutely introduced to deal with Noble and Gregory – and Hirst, Australia made only 121. England by the end of the second day, had played themselves back into the game.

Jessop has recalled how, as they heard the rain pelting down that night, their hopes faded. Surely enough, next morning, the last two Australians were hustled out and England, needing 263 to win, lost their first four wickets – MacLaren, Palairet, Tyldesley and Hayward – to viciously turning balls from Saunders. Trumble had Braund caught at the wicket by Kelly, and with the score 48 for five the game seemed as good as over, when Jessop came in to join Jackson. Jackson, was content – and wise – to hold on; by doing so he watched at close quarters one of the most exciting innings of Test cricket. Missed twice early on, Jessop set out to 'kill' Saunders. In a series of vivid strokes he made 104 (of 139) in an hour and a quarter. He and Jackson, however, were both out with 76 still wanted and, in an atmosphere of agoniz-

Gilbert Jessop (Gloucestershire) The finest consistent attacking batsman: a spectacular match-winner; an England fast-bowler, superb cover-point and phenomenal thrower

ing tension, Hirst batted with sturdy courage and unfailing judgement. Lilley stayed with him to put on 34, but the ninth wicket fell at 248 – fifteen still needed. Legend has it – but the players concerned have denied the story – that Hirst greeted Rhodes with the words 'We'll get 'em in singles'. In fact they scored thirteen singles and a two: but they got them.

After losing the rubber, England had gained a not inconsiderable victory and Jessop, in a single innings, had placed himself among the heroic figures of cricket. Jessop, Hirst and Rhodes are usually remembered as the history makers of the 1902 Oval Test. But if either of two catches had been held, it would have been Hugh Trumble's match: he bowled unchanged from the pavilion end throughout the two English innings and took twelve wickets for 173.

If the Edwardian cricketers of England and Australia had never taken the field again, their eminence, their high skill on bad wickets as well as good, and the stirring gallantry of their play, would be fixed beyond challenge by the Test series of 1902.

The domestic season was thrust into the background of public imagination by the Tests, but in it, too, the standard was high and, while the bowlers exploited the damaged wickets, there were many batsmen of the skill and temper to attack them with good results. There were three aggregates of over 2,000, led by Trumper – now, by common consent, the finest batsman in the world.

Yorkshire won their third consecutive Championship by a very long way from Sussex and Notts. Although Hirst fell away after June, their bowling was a highly destructive force – Haigh, Rhodes, and Jackson all had averages of less than 15 in Championship matches. Mitchell was not available but, in his place, T. L. Taylor showed similar strength on slow pitches, and the young left-hander, Irving Washington, revealed stylish promise in his only full season before ill health ended his cricket career. In these three Championship seasons, Yorkshire were beaten only twice, on both occasions by Somerset.

For Sussex the batting of Fry and Ranjitsinhji was given added point by the 153 Championship wickets of Fred Tate, the solid, steady medium-pace bowler who, making his off-breaks turn quickly on the responsive wickets of 1902, had, statistically, his best season.

At Trent Bridge, Shrewsbury was top of the averages in his last season – and Wass gave the bowling new force.

On their way home, the Australians stopped in South Africa to play six matches, including the first Tests between the two countries, of which Australia won two, and one was left drawn.

The Australian batting proved as powerful as had been expected, and the scores were driven home by the bowling of Saunders and W. P. Howell. Howell bowled right-arm medium and, with abnormally strong fingers, spun the ball abruptly. On his day an aggressive left-hand bat, he was a valuable all-rounder whose reputation has been dimmed by the unusual quality of his contemporaries.

South Africa, though beaten, were rapidly growing up. To Sinclair's immense natural all-round ability they could now add the batting of Tancred and Dave Nourse – who was to become the father-figure of South African cricket – the bowling of Kotze – genuinely fast; and the all-round power of Charles Llewellyn. Llewellyn had experience of county cricket with Hampshire, and his records show him as an

accomplished all-rounder, for his left-hand batting was basically sound and at times aggressive. At this time, however, his chief importance was as an orthodox slow left-arm bowler. He took more wickets – 25 – than anyone else on either side in the series, and subsequently became one of the first effective bowlers of the Chinaman – the left-arm bowler's off-break.

The batting of Trumper and Duff on this brief tour made a deep impression on the game in South Africa.

The Season of 1903

This was the wettest of the series of bad summers which would, surely, have depressed the cricket of any other period. Walter Mead, Colin Blythe, Wilfred Rhodes and Schofield Haigh, of course, flourished. So did Sam Hargreave of Warwickshire, whose flight and control spin must have made him an England slow left-arm bowler in any age but this, when Rhodes and Blythe vied with one another for the position. Not far behind the spinners – in a season when J. B. King on tour with the Gentlemen of Philadelphia, could be observed making the ball cut outlandish curves in the air – were the advance guard of the new school of swingers, not only George Hirst, but Ted Arnold, and Arthur Fielder – of Kent – both practitioners of abrupt outswing, and Albert Relf.

C. B. Fry – with the staggering average, in so wet a summer, of 81 – and Ranjitsinhji were again at the top of their batting, but close on their heels came George Hirst, and John Iremonger, who had succeeded to Shrewsbury's place as an opening bat for Notts.

Middlesex, with P. F. Warner deputizing for Gregor MacGregor as captain in the majority of their matches, won the Championship by a remarkably well-spread team effort: eight batsmen averaged more than twenty, and six bowlers shared most of the wickets. Sussex took second place through the capacity of Albert Relf, George Cox – steady medium-left – and Ted Killick – leg-breaks – to make good Fred Tate's poor season. Yorkshire wavered in June and July and their recovery, though strong, came too late.

This season saw John Gunn of Notts establish himself as an all-rounder. Left handed as batsman and bowler, he had now advanced from preoccupation with defence to stroke-making, and had reduced his bowling pace so that, while he did not turn the ball so much as Rhodes, Blythe or Hargreave, he 'did' enough on weathered wickets, and was steady on others. Second only to Jessop at cover point, he could work his passage in any side.

The ageing of the key players of Surrey's ruling days was reflected in their fall to eleventh in the table.

England in Australia, 1903–04

MCC picked their first overseas touring team in face of England's defeat by Australia in four successive series. Their first choice as captain, F. S. Jackson, was not available: neither were Fry and Ranji. Somewhat surprisingly, Barnes, Jessop and John Gunn were not invited. Criticism was stilled by the event. Warner captained the side and it won the rubber by three Tests to two. The names on the score-sheets are enough to show that the batting on both sides was long and potentially brilliant, and the bowling steady. Technical progress was reflected in the choice of three swing bowlers – Hirst, Relf, and Fielder – in the England party, and the success of Noble, who captained Australia as an all-rounder. If Australia enjoyed the advantage of the weather in 1902, England gained that benefit in this series. In the last analysis, the credit for England's close win should go to Rhodes and Bosanquet.

Before the tour it could be said that Rhodes had gained all his successes in a sequence of wet English seasons. In Australia, while he took advantage of some difficult wickets, he established his ability beyond all question. On pitches where the ball would not turn an inch, he matched as great a batting power as had ever been brought together in one Australian team and, by length, flight and exploiting every tactical resource, proved its master. Bosanquet on a single, but crucial, occasion, proved a match-winner. Arnold's figures appear less impressive, but he may be said to have introduced the cult of the new ball when, employing it in late outswing, he twice broke through the opening batting. Ten of his 18 Test wickets were those of batsmen in the first four.

In the first Test, Australia lost three wickets for 12 to the opening swing attack of Hirst and Arnold before Noble's century took them to 285. England were 117 for four until R. E. Foster and Len Braund (102) put on 192 in the decisive stand. Foster's 287 was the highest score made in any England-Australia

K. S. Ranjitsinhji – 'Ranji' – (Sussex) His batting was an amazing blend of relaxation and speed, delicacy and power. Held in something near awe by even the best bowlers of his time

58

R. E. – 'Tip' – Foster (Worcestershire) of the famous Malvern brotherhood: an England batsman and centre forward

match until then: it remains the highest by any player in his first Test. When Australia batted a second time, 292 behind, Trumper carried his bat for 185 not-out, made in less than four hours, an innings said by some of the more experienced players in the match to be the most brilliant they had ever seen. After another uncertain England start, Hirst, dropped by Laver at short-leg before he had scored, went on to make 60 not-out, and with Hayward (91), ensured an England win by five wickets.

R. E. Foster

'Tip' Foster was one of seven brothers who played for Worcestershire. All were Malvernians, with the steely wrists of rackets players, and several of them were accomplished at more than one game. R. E., who won a full England cap for soccer and represented Oxford University at cricket, soccer, rackets and golf, was the best of the family. As a cricketer he watched the ball well and had a correct defence, but he caught the eye as an upstanding and commanding stroke player, reflecting the off-side bias of his day, but secure against leg stump attack and an effortless long hitter. He played all too little first-class cricket; otherwise, as a natural batsman and slip field, he might long have been an England player.

At Melbourne, England, with the best of the wicket, made a slow, steady start to a total of 315. After rain, Australia were never in the game with a chance. On a typical Melbourne 'sticky' where the ball stood up straight off a length, Trumper – 74 and 35 – and Tyldesley – 62 when England went in a second time – played three of the classic bad wicket innings. But Rhodes – fifteen wickets for 144 runs despite *eight* dropped catches – won the match for England.

The third Test, at Adelaide, was a parade of the best of Australian cricket of the period. Trumper, Duff, Hill, Noble and Gregory, each batted in his own effective and characteristic manner. Trumble, Hopkins, Noble, McLeod and Howell took the wickets. Warner, Hayward, Hirst as batsmen and Bosanquet as a bowler – a portent – could do no more than limit the margin of defeat to 216 runs.

Rain frequently interrupted the fourth game of the series, at Sydney. A. E. Knight of Leicestershire, a patient and orthodox batsman, made the highest score of the match – 70 not-out – which was the effective foundation of England's first innings 249. Australia batted hesitantly against Rhodes, Braund and Arnold for 131 and then, when they were set 329 to win,

B. J. T. Bosanquet (Middlesex) The first bowler to make the googly practicable in Test cricket so that, in Australia, it is still known as the 'Bosey'

Bosanquet came on, as the fifth England bowler, and took six for 51 to settle the game and the rubber.

B. J. T. Bosanquet

Bernard Bosanquet was one of cricket's major innovators. If he did not invent the 'googly' – an off-break bowled with (apparently) a leg-break action – he certainly first developed it to top standard, and by winning two Tests, virtually decided two England-Australia series with it. Bosanquet played his early cricket for Eton, Oxford and Middlesex, as a fast-medium bowler and a rough-edged batsman who used his powerful forearms to force the ball strongly on both sides of the wicket.

A. L. Ford insisted that he had seen Bosanquet's father bowl the googly, but 'Bose' himself asserted that he discovered – or re-discovered – it in 1897 while playing a table game called 'twisti-twosti' with a tennis ball. He has also said he first bowled the ball

that Australians still call 'the Bosey' in the Middlesex-Leicester match at Lord's in 1900 – to Sam Coe, who was 98 not-out at the time. It bounced four times – but it 'beat' poor Coe, and he was stumped!

Bosanquet never 'dropped' his invention consistently on a length. But he was a tall man, whose high delivery set some problems of flight, and the novelty of the off-breaking leg-break reduced such established batsmen of the old school as Shrewsbury, Gunn and Hayward to bafflement, and even indignation.

After 1905, Bosanquet lost his length completely, but he had made his piece of history, and had enjoyed it so much that he could laugh about it, leaving its ultimate development to his successors (who were already at work) and turning to the enjoyment of big hitting in club cricket.

In the last Test, at Melbourne, Australia had the luck to bat before the rains came, but even on a true pitch, only Trumper's masterly 88 arrested Braund, who took eight for 81. After the weather broke, Noble, Cotter and Trumble were all but unplayable: England made only 61 and 101, and Australia won by 218.

Albert – 'Tibby' – Cotter was the New South Wales bowler whom Jack Hobbs considered the fastest he ever faced in a Test. Indeed, Cotter's pace was such as to make good the almost comic mixture of long hops and full tosses of his early years. Later he shortened his run, improved his control without appreciable loss of speed and, for a couple of seasons to 1909, was quite deadly on his day.

The Season of 1904

At last the long sequence of wet summers was broken. Lancashire won the County Championship from Yorkshire and Kent, without losing a match, while the South African touring side, which was allotted no Test Matches, grew significantly in stature and experience.

MacLaren, who had watched Lord Hawke's methods in Yorkshire with much interest, had now built a fresh Lancashire side round his own and J. T. Tyldesley's batting, and Cuttell's stock bowling. He had been unable to keep Barnes who, after some unimaginative handling, had stumped off, back to League cricket. But to the surprise of MacLaren himself, James Hallows, left-handed, came on so far as a competent professional batsman and medium-pace bowler that he performed the double. The side was completed by Walter Brearley, R. H. Spooner,

Jack Sharp, Alec Kermode, Dr Poidevin, A. H. Hornby and either Worsley or Billy Findlay to keep wicket.

Walter Brearley

One of the richest characters in the cricket of the time was Walter Brearley, immensely fit, self-confident, and a bowler of infinite enthusiasm. He took a short run but his pace – only a little short of the very fastest – came from the full swing of his thickly muscular body. His stamina was inexhaustible and, in the new manner, he bowled the outswinger – to an unusually full length for one of his speed.

R. H. Spooner

Reggie Spooner was one of the key figures of Edwardian cricket. He was a natural timer of the ball, who brought to his batting an alert mind and made himself fundamentally sound. He added to that foundation his own almost casual manner, a wristy perfection of hitting and unhurried speed of footwork. He could drive the ball through the covers or mid-off, glance to leg or play to mid-on with any of his contemporaries. But after his off driving, his glory was the cut. He was one of the few – J. T. Tyldesley was another – so quick footed and so certain that they could back away from the stumps and cut Warwick Armstrong's slow leg-theory through the gap between slip and gully. Spooner was a stylist by nature, and those who watched him batting at his best never forgot the sight.

Jack Sharp – double international at soccer and cricket – had renounced his fast-medium bowling and was on his way to becoming an England batsman: the Australian, Kermode, proved an effective stock bowler until he put on too much weight, and Poidevin, also from Australia, and A. H. Hornby were serviceable middle-order batsmen. MacLaren's side was strong all round, and sufficiently well made to remain in the upper reaches of the table for another eight years.

J. N. Crawford

Surrey, again eleventh in the table, brought in Jack Crawford, the finest of all schoolboy cricketers. But for the rank stupidity by which the Surrey club estranged him, he might now rank as one of the two or three pre-eminent match-winning all-rounders.

He first played for Surrey in 1904 as a seventeen-year-old schoolboy on holiday from Repton. His first

Reggie Spooner (Lancashire) An outstanding stylist in an age of style: the beauty of his stroke-play compelled admiration even from opposing bowlers

match began on 4th August – against Kent at Canterbury – when he scored 54 against the run of play, and by the end of the season he was top of Surrey's bowling averages with 44 wickets at 16·25.

Crawford was already a mature cricketer in his teens. His performances for Repton read like those of a man playing with boys, and he was never outclassed on any level of cricket. On tour with MCC after he had left Surrey, he was said to turn his medium-paced off-breaks on Australian wickets so perfect that no one else could make the ball deviate from straight. In 1921 he drove Gregory, then at his fastest, with sustained power. The fact that he played in glasses never seemed to affect his cricket, and his batting was so natural and free that, when Surrey were set runs against the clock, he could measure stroke for stroke with Jack Hobbs.

In his four full seasons with Surrey – 1906 to 1909 – Crawford performed the double twice and once

F. S. Jackson – 'Jacker' – (Yorkshire) The typical Edwardian amateur: in 1905 he captained England against Australia, won the toss in all five Tests, England won the rubber without losing a match and Jackson was first in both the batting and bowling averages

missed it by two wickets. In that period he played twelve times for England and headed the Test bowling averages in Australia, 1907–08. He was only 22 when maladroit handling caused him to leave England for Australia, only returning to Surrey for a few matches in 1919 and 1921. No one who played with him had any doubt that he should have been an England all-rounder for twenty years instead of four.

The Season of 1905

This was 'Jackson's Year'. F. S. Jackson captained the England side that retained The Ashes against Australia, won the toss in all five Tests, and had the best batting and bowling averages of either side.

England won two Tests and three were drawn. The Australian bowling had lost its penetration: neither Trumble nor Saunders made the trip, and Noble's six wickets cost 68 runs each. In consequence, six England batsmen – but only one Australian – averaged more than 40. Eight England bowlers – but only two Australians – took their wickets at less than thirty apiece.

From a later viewpoint it is possible to distinguish in this series the framing of fresh tactical thinking, planned and deliberate moves to shackle the batsmen whose entertainment value was appreciated less by opposing bowlers than by the general public. Warwick Armstrong personified the new approach.

W. W. Armstrong

Warwick Armstrong was a huge man, built on the scale of W. G. Grace, who carried the competitive spirit in Test Matches to a point of arrogant rudeness. The fact remains that he was a highly talented all-round player and, subsequently, a captain of sharp observation and acumen.

In the 1905 series, he angered many critics by his bowling which, in Tests, was designed simply to restrict run-scoring. There is no doubt that Darling recognized the deficiencies of his side and the strength of Jackson's, and that he employed Armstrong's bowling to reduce that difference. In the early matches of the tour Armstrong had shown that, though he did not turn the ball widely, he was quite remarkably accurate for a leg-spinner and capable of taking good wickets as a primarily attacking bowler. Indeed, he took 130 wickets on the tour. In the Tests, however, Darling employed him almost entirely to bowl wide of the leg stump to a seven-man leg-side field and, such was the big man's control of length and line, that he shut up a game for longer than anyone had done since the uniform production of true wickets.

Armstrong's bulk – he weighed twenty stone at the end of his playing career – was such that he could appear clumsy and at times, against well-flighted slow bowling, he positively floundered: but he was a practical batsman who could look after himself against any bowling and, given the opportunity, hit hard, though it was contrary to his nature to take chances in a Test. At slip he would catch almost anything within reach. As a captain he was never out-generalled and, if he constantly fell out with authority, he came through it all unscarred. Others might be disciplined for rebellion, but never Armstrong. He compelled respect, but little affection.

At Nottingham, Frank Laver, who bowled medium pace from a high right arm and set problems of flight and variation, bowled out England. Only Tyldesley – 56 – played him comfortably. Hill and Noble made 106 for the third Australian wicket before Jackson, putting himself on late, took five for 52: Australia led by 25. The second English innings of 426 for five wickets was scored in face of Armstrong's 52 overs for 67 runs. Then, with Trumper away, injured, Australia for the second time lost a Test Match to Bosanquet, who took eight for 107.

A level draw at Lord's, and one when England were prospering at Leeds, and then the rubber was decided at Old Trafford. England, with the advantage of first innings before the wicket was affected by rain, made 446: Jackson scored 113 – his second century of the series – Hayward, as sheet anchor, 82, and Spooner a polished 52: the batting was sound all through. After night rain, Brearley, Arnold, Rhodes and Jackson bowled out Australia twice: England won by an innings and 80, and retained The Ashes.

At The Oval, Darling again used Armstrong to restrict run-scoring and England, with the rubber won, retaliated by piling up runs at their leisure and making a safe draw.

There were still great batting glories ahead, but the bowlers' rebellion was strongly afoot: from year to year in the future runs were to become harder to get.

Yorkshire displayed their strength in depth by winning the Championship from Lancashire, although at various times they were weakened by providing five players – Jackson, Hirst, Rhodes, Denton and Haigh – to the England team. At the end of the season their power was emphasized when they beat the Rest of England by 65 runs.

Northants entered the County Championship this year, having proved themselves largely through the efforts of George Thompson – an immensely loyal professional all-rounder, an untiring and thoughtful medium-pace bowler and a steady bat: his best support came from C. J. T. Pool in batting and W. East as a bowler: they finished thirteenth of the sixteen counties.

Surrey climbed back up to fourth position, an improvement that might be attributed to the bowling of Neville Knox – Kortright's successor as the fastest bowler in the country – and Walter Lees, suddenly improved as a medium-pacer with a difficult flight and occasional off-break. The chief historic importance of their season, however, was that it ushered Jack Hobbs into first-class cricket.

Jack Hobbs

The greatest batsman of modern times, John Berry – later Sir John – Hobbs, did not play first-class cricket until he was twenty-two. In 1905, having come from Cambridge and qualified for Surrey, he opened the innings with Tom Hayward in the county's first match of the season – against the Gentlemen of England, captained by W. G. Grace. Hobbs made 18 in the first innings, 88 in two hours in the second. In the next match, with Essex, he made 28 and 155. Twenty-nine years later, at fifty-one, he scored 121 against Lancashire, the County Champions – the only century made against them at Old Trafford in the entire season. In the years between, he established himself as the master batsman.

Despite the loss of four years to the first World War and most of another to illness, Jack Hobbs scored more runs – 61,237 – and more centuries – 197 – than anyone else. Yet he was never interested in records.

Jack Hobbs was a conscientious professional, concerned with his team's needs and his own duties. He loved to bat, relished the challenge of the game, the fellowship of other cricketers, and the atmosphere of cricket. He took pride in his own fitness and his appearance, cared deeply for his profession; but, above all, given a bat in his hands, he expressed himself and his feeling for cricket on a level of performance quite staggering in its excellence, length, and consistency.

He himself cherished most his batting in the years before 1914, before his infallible professional judgement

Jack – later Sir John – Hobbs (Surrey) The man who raised the craft of batting to an art which he practised with an ease, certainty and grace unequalled by any other player

aggrandizement, he might have made another ten thousand – twenty thousand? – runs. But, behind every innings, there was the man, caring for his craft but never for runs for the sake of runs; always the sparkle of fun lurked in his eye.

Greatness, and his eventual knighthood, sat easily on the shoulders of the spare, quizzical, kindly and gentle man who had lifted batting to new heights. Watching him bat in the days of his established greatness, it was too easy to forget that this was the man who had stepped into the age of Edwardian cricket and met the new challenge of the bowlers, creating fresh techniques to deal with the googly, outswing, inswing and leg-theory, and had made it all look as natural as walking.

England in South Africa, 1905–06

P. F. Warner's MCC side to South Africa would have seemed, a few years earlier, almost unfairly strong for the job in hand. In the event, it was beaten by four Tests to one.

Bosanquet's googly was now turned back on England: it was bowled by four of these South Africans who, between them, took 43 of the 95 English wickets. South Africa summoned fourteen players to the first Test, selected eleven of them and, for the only time since 1884, the same team played through a complete five-match rubber.

In the first Test at Johannesburg, South Africa, set 283 to win, were 105 for six and, for all Dave Nourse's resistance, still 45 short when Percy Sherwell – captain for the first time – came to the wicket, last man in. In one of the historic last wicket stands, he and Nourse batted almost an hour without a mistake and, when Relf cracked under the tension – or was it as a strategem? – and bowled a full-toss, Sherwell hit it for four to win the match, the Johannesburg crowd rushed on to the field almost hysterical with excitement. South African cricket had become a world force.

South Africa went on to take the second, third and fifth Tests by comfortable margins: only at Cape Town, where Blythe took eleven wickets, did England win – and then anxiously, by a bare four wickets.

South Africa's win was that of a team. Eight batsmen averaged over twenty: eight bowlers shared the wickets.

A. D. Nourse senior – Dave Nourse – English born, went to South Africa as an army drummer and stayed

told him that he had reached the age when he must eschew such strokes as the lofted drive over the bowler, mid-off or extra-cover, the forward leg glance or the extremely fine cut off fast bowling. But, in the twenties, when he made runs with such regularity and fluency that it seemed he could score a hundred whenever he wished, he approached technical perfection. The remarkable feature of his batting was that it was so unremarkable. His footwork was so perfect, his range of strokes so wide, his judgement in employing them so sure, that his strokes had the air of unhurried inevitability.

Often when the strong Surrey batting side had been given a firm foundation on one of its perfect wickets of the nineteen-twenties, Hobbs would pick on a deserving bowler of the opposite side and throw his wicket away to him. Had he cared for record-breaking, had he regarded cricket as a vehicle for his own there. Immensely strong, with huge hands, he was a fine slip catcher, occasionally bowled left-arm medium with some inswing, and was a left-hand bat of infinite resolution and power: a fine man in a crisis.

Of the 'orthodox' bowlers, Snooke, like Sinclair, bowled at fast-medium pace with steep rise from the matting wickets which prevailed in South Africa until the second – Cape Town – Test of 1930–31.

The four googly bowlers were R. O. Schwarz, G. A. Faulkner, A. E. E. Vogler and G. C. White. Schwarz played for Middlesex – mainly as a batsman – in the years when Bosanquet was developing his googly. Schwarz watched him, learnt the trick, went to South Africa, and taught this remarkable school of googly bowlers. Schwarz himself, oddly enough, bowled entirely googlies, having discarded the leg-break because it affected his length. Yet, though he bowled only off-breaks, his accuracy and pace off the pitch made him, in the eyes of most opponents, the most dangerous of the four. Vogler was originally right-arm fast-medium, and still often used the new ball, which he could make swing away or break back. He bowled his leg-breaks and googlies at something more than slow pace but was accurate over long spells, and was regarded as the hardest of the four to 'spot'. Aubrey Faulkner – who became a skilful batsman, renowned for his hooking and, later, a fine teacher of cricket – turned the ball extremely sharply. Gordon White – at this time primarily a batsman and only beginning to bowl googlies – took many wickets with what was in fact a top-spinner. All four made the ball leap from the matting and, when they came to England, they impressed their opponents by the pace of their bounce even from the slowest turf.

The Season of 1906

In a summer of brilliant sunshine, Kent won the Championship for the first time in the modern era after a close race, down to the end, with Yorkshire and Surrey. George Hirst performed the unique feat of taking 208 wickets and scoring 2,385 runs in the season, and George Dennett of Gloucestershire – probably the best slow left-arm bowler who never played in a Test – took all ten Essex wickets at Bristol.

Tom Hayward, who scored four centuries in two matches in Whit week set a new record with an aggregate of 3,518 runs for the season.

The chief factors in Kent's success were the batting

Tom Hayward (Surrey) Calm, correct, reliable and, until the 1920s, second to W. G. Grace as the heaviest run-scorer the game had known

65

of K. L. Hutchings and C. J. Burnup, the bowling of Fielder – who took all ten for the Players against the Gentlemen at Lord's – and Blythe, and the all-round play of J. R. Mason and the young Woolley.

Kenneth Hutchings was the surprise of the 1906 season: he had played occasionally for Kent before and caught many eyes by his grace and speed in the outfield. Now, from back-foot defence, he went forward to attack with a whole range of strokes, especially on and off-drives, powered by immense forearms. Hutchings took risks, but his fine eye and good condition carried him through, and he played with such brilliance as to advance from obscurity to Test class in a couple of months.

C. J. Burnup, in strong contrast to Hutchings, was a deliberately limited player: he knew his own powers and played soundly and shrewdly within them, scoring steadily, unperturbed when a game was going badly.

F. E. Woolley

In its comments on the 1906 season, *Wisden* said 'The colt Woolley deserves more than passing notice. . . . It is quite possible that within two or three years he will be the best left-handed bat in England'. At this time, and when he first went into the England team, Frank Woolley was regarded as an all-rounder: indeed, he performed the double eight times. His bowling, slow left, round the wicket, was influenced by Blythe, but Woolley was a shade faster, and from his considerable height – he was nicknamed 'Stork' – his point of pitch was not easy to judge. His long arms helped him in becoming an outstanding slip.

Woolley belongs among the great, however, as a left-hand bat of unforgettable style. He had the reach to play a long way forward, the height to get over the lifting ball when he went back, and he seemed incapable of an ugly stroke. His movements appeared lazy, but the perfectly-timed, long pendulum of his bat invested his driving with fierce power. Against fast bowling he could cut vividly and, until he retired in 1938, when he was fifty-one, his batting was a true echo of the expansive Edwardian days – tinged with risk but gracious, poised, and quite gloriously free. With 58,969 runs (second only to Hobbs), 2,068 wickets and the record number of 913 catches, he stands with Rhodes and Hirst ahead of all other all-rounders in results – and his manner rose above his figures.

In New Zealand, the first Plunket Shield competition took place and was won by Canterbury.

The Season of 1907

The rains came back, and Notts harnessed them to win the Championship from Yorkshire and Worcester, who were jointly second. The South African touring side, granted Test status in England for the first time, overcame the conditions and increased their standing.

Notts' achievement was something of a freak, albeit a striking one. No batsman in the side averaged more than 33, and the Championship was won by Hallam and Wass who took 298 of the 340 wickets that fell to the county. Twelve times this summer they bowled unchanged through an entire innings.

A. Hallam

Albert Hallam, though born in Notts, had played for Leicester and was for six years on the Lancashire staff before he came to Trent Bridge in 1901. In 1907, at the age of 34, he had the best season of his life, and was chosen for England against South Africa at The Oval, but a hand injury kept him out of the game. Right-arm medium, and capable of cutting the ball either way, Hallam was, above all, accurate. His length and direction never wavered, however long the spell. This was the peak of his career: he never again took a hundred wickets in a season and, three years later, faded out of the Notts side.

T. Wass

Tom – 'Topsy' – Wass was a hard nut from one of the richest of Notts nurseries, Sutton-in-Ashfield. He was the straightest of straight speakers and no respecter of persons: some of the most lordly characters in the game felt the rough edge of his tongue. He bowled at genuinely fast pace, though C. B. Fry, for one, said he found him easy enough to play on hard wickets. His outstanding talent was the ability, on damp turf, to turn the ball from leg: Tom Wass was, in fact, the only fast leg-break bowler in the history of cricket. There is no doubt that he spun the ball off the outside tip of his second finger: in his old age, the third and fourth fingers of that hand were inextricably wedged in the palm of his hand from the years of being crammed there to leave free passage for the ball. In 1907, the long sequence of rainy days gave him the perfect setting for his rare gift and he made the most of it. No batsman and a terrible field, Wass remained a useful bowler until 1914: but 1907 was his great year and he still recalled it with gusto in 1950.

England, captained by R. E. Foster, won the only game finished in the three-match Test rubber with South Africa. The issue was closely fought and the effect of the googly on English batsmen – even on their own pitches – is shown by the fact that Schwarz, Faulkner, Vogler and White took all but nine of the 49 English wickets to fall in Tests. R. E. Foster – at first – and Tom Hayward, both off-side players, were particularly bothered by the new 'weapon'. Tyldesley, Braund and Jessop batted England to a safe position in the draw at Lord's, where Sherwell scored South Africa's only century of the series. At Headingley, on a drying wicket, Fry – 54 – was the only English bats-man to score over fifty against Faulkner (six for 17 and three for 58) and White (four for 47), and England were fortunate that, when South Africa set out to make 129 to win, Colin Blythe (who had taken eight for 59 in their first innings) decided the match with seven for 40 in the second. Fry, to whom 'reading' googly bowling was a compelling mental exercise, made 129 at The Oval where Vogler, Schwarz and Faulkner between them took fourteen wickets. The issue was still in the balance – South Africa wanted another 97 to win, with five wickets including those of Sherwell and Nourse still standing – when bad light ended the match.

Worcestershire had the best season they were to know for 35 years. Three of the Foster brothers – G.N., R.E., and H.K. – were at the top of their batting with averages of more than forty. The Austra-lian Cuffe – medium left-arm – was the main bowler, with the briskish Burrows, Arnold, and the faithful Fred Pearson in support.

England in Australia, 1907–08

The MCC side was captained by A. O. Jones of Notts, a hard-hitting but impetuous batsman who was one of the first outstanding specialist fieldsmen. He could be brilliant in the deep, at slip, or short-leg, but he was unmatched in the gully, a position he virtually invented.

His team was by no means the strongest that could have been picked from English cricket of the day – MacLaren, Fry, Tyldesley, Ranji, Jessop, Hirst, Lilley, Spooner and Hayward were all missing. Yet it was not without talent. Rhodes, Blythe and Braund – only thirteen Test wickets between them – simply did not come off as bowlers, yet there was compensa-

tion in the bowling of Crawford – only twenty when the tour started, and top of the Test bowling figures – and of Fielder and Barnes. It might be said that nerve was the deciding factor. In four of the matches there were periods of intense crisis; Australia came through three times, England only once.

A. O. Jones early went down with the illness which proved fatal to him a few years later. So F. L. Fane took over the captaincy for the first three Tests and George Gunn, who had gone to Australia for his health, was brought into the side. He scored 119 and 74 in the first Test.

G. Gunn

George Gunn was a batting genius with an impish streak. When the mood took him he would saunter down the pitch to the fastest bowlers and, though not a strongly built man, drive them with wristy ease. On another day he would inexplicably push and prod at third-rate bowling. Neat footwork was the foundation of his perfect, straight-batted style, and there has been no better batsman against fast bowling in modern times. For years he was worth an England place, but perhaps his irreverent streak did not appeal to officialdom. A drily humorous character, he is generally believed to have missed the South Africa tour of 1909–10 because he put the letter of invitation in his pocket and forgot to open it until after the team had sailed.

Gunn's batting, and the bowling of Fielder, put England in so strong a position that Australia, with 274 to get, stood at 124 for six. At this first 'dominant' of the series, Armstrong rallied the tail and numbers eight, nine and ten – Carter, Hazlitt and Cotter – made 61, 34 not out and 33 not out – to win the match by two wickets.

At Melbourne, Australia twice batted all down the order but without ever breaking away against Barnes and Crawford. Hobbs made 83 in his first Test innings, Hutchings his first Test century. This time England, wanting 282, stood perilously at 209 for eight. Then Barnes ('I could have been a batsman if I hadn't had so much bowling to do') made 38 not-out, putting on 34 for the ninth wicket with Humphries, 39 for the tenth with Fielder, and England came grimly in by one wicket.

At Adelaide, Australia were only 102 on when their seventh second innings wicket fell. At this, the third, testing point, a stand of 243 by Hill and Hartigan put them in a commanding position and, after rain,

Clem Hill (South Australia) Long considered the finest left-hand bat produced by Australia: a strong player, never content to leave the initiative with a bowler

O'Connor – right-arm medium with a puzzling flight – and Saunders shared the wickets and won the match by 245.

There was rain again at Melbourne after Australia had made 214. Saunders and Noble were in their element and Jack Hobbs alone – with 53 in a total of 105 – withstood them. Armstrong hammered home the advantage with a century, and England lost by 308.

In the last match, at Sydney, Barnes (seven for 60), Crawford (three for 52) and Gunn (122 not-out) gave England a first innings lead of 144. Trumper, at his best – 166 in four hours – set England 279 to win. Then, once more, there was rain, and the spin of Saunders, Noble and Macartney cut through to 123 for seven. At this final trial of nerve, the last four England batsmen, Rhodes (69), Crawford (24 not-out), Jones (34) and Barnes (11) almost doubled the score, but the bowling of Saunders – five for 82 in 35

overs – won the match and gave Australia the series by 4–1.

This rubber stands as an example of change even within a single period. Tests in England were still limited to three days, but in Australia it was the practice to play out games without any time limit. Largely in consequence of rain, four ran to a sixth day. The effect may be seen if we take for comparison the last Test between the two sides in England – at The Oval in 1905 – when 1,178 runs were scored at a rate of sixty-five an hour. In 1907–08 in Australia, the overall rate was 43.

The Season of 1908

Once more there was enough rain to please bowlers, especially those of Yorkshire who, undefeated in Lord Hawke's twenty-fifth year as captain, won the Championship from Kent and Surrey. No other county could match the Yorkshire outcricket and, in Championship matches alone, Hirst, Rhodes, Haigh and Newstead took 488 wickets. Newstead's career as a first-team regular lasted only two seasons and this was by far his best summer. He bowled medium pace with an easy action which enabled him to undertake long spells: he relied largely on his length, some nip from the pitch, the off-break, and occasional outswing.

Yorkshire strength is strikingly illustrated by the note 'B. B. Wilson, though he scored 109 against Derbyshire at Leeds in July, was not thought good enough for a second trial'.

Kent were now uniformly strong. Surrey's batting, with Hayward, Hobbs, Crawford, the young Australian stroke-maker, Alan Marshal, and Hayes, was as good as any. They no longer had a Richardson or a Lockwood, but the bowling was well varied between Hitch – young and fast – Marshal, Crawford, Lees, Hayes and Smith.

The first place in the batting averages was occupied by Bosanquet, who had virtually forsaken bowling his googlies. Top of the bowling was J. B. King of the Philadelphian touring side: King, originally a baseball pitcher, could swing the ball abruptly and deliberately either way: his methods were watched with much interest – and considerable subsequent effect.

The Repton team of 1908 was probably the strongest ever put into the field by any school. Four of its members went straight into their county teams in August, and two more had to refuse invitations from counties. One of them, W. T. Greswell, played for Somerset. In his first game, against Middlesex, he was put on to bowl, set his usual school field and bowled his normal slow-medium, right-arm inswingers, starting them well outside the off stump, to hit the wicket. Len Braund and John Daniell, standing together in the slips, watched the over through, put their heads together and, to Greswell's amazement, for his next over, three short-legs were posted close to the bat. Right-arm inswing to a leg trap had begun. Greswell himself was more delighted at another historically significant event in the same match, when C. M. Wells swung his bat back high and threw his left foot across the wicket for the characteristic Edwardian cover drive, and the ball, dipping in far and late, went between his legs and hit the leg stump.

The Season of 1909

Australia, under M. A. Noble, again made their tour in a persistently wet summer, but they retained The Ashes by two Tests to one, and had the best of the two drawn games. Despite the weather, there were some batting triumphs. Three Australians – Warren Bardsley, Vernon Ransford and Warwick Armstrong – took three of the four leading places in the batting averages, and, at The Oval, Bardsley became the first batsman to score a century in each innings of a Test. For Kent v Worcester, Woolley and Fielder made 235 for the last wicket – still the English record. The Imperial Cricket Conference was constituted, with MCC, Australia and South Africa the founder members.

Kent, an entertaining batting side with well assorted bowling – in which Blythe was outstanding – came through strongly in July and August to win the Championship, ahead of Lancashire and Yorkshire.

While the Australian batting was obviously strong, the bowling, on the record, looked less impressive: if there was a deficiency in attack, Noble made it good. His captaincy was the outstanding feature of the Test series. He raised field-setting to a new level; his men no longer moved automatically to the 'orthodox' positions, nor even to set places for particular bowlers, but to places related to the situation. More than one England batsman, for the first time, found the line of his favourite stroke precisely and constantly blocked, or his weakness for the first time subjected to intense pressure. Noble thus gave Australia a psychological

advantage. England suffered, too, from vacillating selection – twenty-five different players were used in the series, and only MacLaren, the captain, and Lilley played in all five Tests.

On a difficult wicket at Edgbaston, the contrasting pair of Blythe and Hirst – unchanged through the first innings – were checked only by Ransford and Gregory in Australian totals of 74 and 151. England scored a mere 121 in their first innings, and it seemed they might be hard put to get the 105 to win; but Fry and Hobbs scored them in an hour-and-a-half: a ten-wicket win for England.

Ham-handed selection produced a distressingly badly balanced England side at Lord's and once Ransford's 143 had given Australia a lead of 89, Armstrong, bowling his leg-breaks with remarkable precision and 'doing' just enough to beat the bat, took six for 35. Australia, 41 for one, won easily by nine wickets.

The Victorian, Vernon Ransford, was a dapper, lithe cricketer, a left-handed batsman whose quick footwork lifted him above most Australians on bad wickets. He had a pleasing cover drive and, in tune with the times, a neat range of leg-side strokes. At cover point he stood out even in so good a fielding side as the 1909 Australians.

For Leeds, England brought back Barnes, who should never have been out of any England side at this time, as he demonstrated with seven for 100. Jessop retired with an injured back and did not bat in either innings. The spin bowling of Macartney – eleven for 85 in the match – was decisive: Australia won by 126.

C. G. Macartney

Charlie Macartney – 'The Governor-General' – came to England in 1909 as a slow left-arm bowler, a quick-moving, clean-handed mid-off, and a number eight batsman. Like all Australian spin bowlers, he gave the ball a sharp twist and had all the wiles of a man who did much of his bowling on the flawless pitch at Sydney.

His batting ability was at first obscured by his unorthodoxy, for he was entirely a self-taught player whose sharp eye enabled him to take some alarming risks. His genius for batting – and it was nothing short of genius – became clear in 1912, and for more than a dozen years he remained an exhilarating batsman to watch, nimble, inventive, an audacious cutter, fearless hooker, masterly legside player, with a quite impudent gift for flick-pulling or cutting a ball pitched on his stumps. 'Mac' was stockily built, with such well developed wrists and forearms that he could leave a stroke late yet still strike powerfully from a short swing.

On another wet wicket at Manchester, Barnes and Blythe shared the wickets in an Australian first innings of only 147: nevertheless, after Laver's eight for 31, that was enough to set them 28 ahead. Had the state of the rubber been different, Noble might have taken risks in attempting to win. As it was, and in face of some shrewd bowling by Rhodes, Australia batted to the safety of a draw.

At The Oval, the English selectors – probably under pressure from MacLaren – brought in the Kent leg-break and googly bowler, D. W. – 'Daddy' – Carr, thirty-nine years old but in his first season, so that this Test match was only his eighth first class game! The wicket was hard and true throughout, but England, having called the Essex fast bowler, Buckenham, to the match, did not play him. MacLaren, typically, opened the bowling with Carr, who took the wickets of Gregory, Noble and Armstrong, to leave Australia 55 for three. MacLaren's point was made, but he now kept Carr on for an hour-and-a-half – a testing stint even for an experienced leg-spinner. Carr lost his bite and length, Bardsley and Trumper collared him, Australia took control and all hope of England levelling the series was gone. Jack Sharp of Lancashire, incomprehensibly included as a fast bowler, scored 105 but Bardsley went firmly on to make his two centuries, and Australia settled for the draw.

W. Bardsley

Australians considered themselves fortunate that they found, in Ransford and Warren Bardsley, immediate successors as left-hand bats to Hill and Darling. Bardsley was cast in the old mould, with an upright stance and a long bat-swing. He employed the cut less often than most batsmen of his day, but his straight drive was a thunderous stroke and he was sound on the on-side. With the years he became increasingly solid and defensive, and still only two Australians – Bradman and Hassett – have bettered his record of 53 centuries.

England in South Africa, 1909–10

H. D. G. Leveson-Gower's MCC team lost the rubber, as the 1905–06 side had done, to googly bowling.

Vogler and Faulkner were responsible for 65 wickets – at less than 22 each – while no other South African bowler took more than four. For all the fact that they won the series, this was the first and only time the googly bowlers were ever mastered on their own matting wickets – by Jack Hobbs who, notwithstanding a double failure (1 and 0) at Cape Town, had an average of 67·37: over twice that of the next English player. Faulkner, now emerging as a dominating batsman, stood similarly positioned above the rest of the South African side. The chief differences between the two teams were that England usually carried two or three men demonstrably below Test standard, and that the South African tail was less pronounced.

G. H. Simpson-Hayward, of Worcestershire, often known as 'the last of the lob bowlers' took 23 wickets in the series. With a low trajectory, he applied buzzing off-spin – his leg-break was slow and inaccurate and employed only for rare variety – and the mat gave him waspish lift and turn against batsmen who did not always take his bowling as seriously as it deserved. Blythe, Thompson and Buckenham were steady but, on matting, not penetrative.

For South Africa it may have seemed ominous that, for seven years, they had discovered no new bowler to take more than two wickets in a series.

The Season of 1910

The monotonous succession of rainy summers continued, but Kent, Champions for the third time in five seasons, were so strong that they would probably have won in any conditions. The Championship for this year was decided on the simple – and perhaps best – basis of percentage of wins to matches played, with no distinction between a draw and a defeat. This year it was decided to count six for a hit over the boundary and not, as formerly, only for a hit out of the ground.

Kent had an embarrassment of resources. Eight of their batsmen – Hutchings, Humphreys, Seymour, Woolley, Dillon, A. P. Day, Knott and Mason – made centuries in Championship matches. Five bowlers – led by Carr in average, Blythe in number of wickets – put out more than thirty opponents each. Kent could, in truth, have fielded two good elevens.

For Derbyshire against Warwickshire at Blackwell, J. Chapman and A. R. Warren set the record – 283 – for a ninth wicket partnership.

W. C. Smith

Surrey's second place was due almost entirely to the bowling of W. C. Smith. Known as 'Razor' because of his extreme thinness, Smith was a slow to slow-medium bowler who, on good wickets, bowled off-breaks steadily but with no great distinction, while his frail physique rarely allowed him to sustain long spells or a full season. 1910 was, for him, the glorious exception. Constant rain created, day after day, the pitches on which he was a bewildering bowler and, thus spurred, he bowled on to finish exhausted in September, but second in the first-class averages with 247 wickets – 72 more than any other bowler in the country. On wet wickets Smith's normal off-break action frequently produced – to his, his wicket-keeper's, slips' and everyone else's amazement – a ball which moved an inch or two from leg. It was the utterly unique opposite of the googly. Smith, with rare wisdom, never sought to discover why this happened. Once it started to happen, he merely shifted his direction to the line of leg or middle-and-leg and let it go on happening. So, for one summer, he became the most destroying agent in English cricket and, had there been a Test series, he must have played for England. As it was, he had to be content – and *was* – with selection for Players *v* Gentlemen at Lord's when, on a wicket ideal for him, he took five for 18.

Two players from overseas – the Australian, Frank Tarrant, left-arm slow-medium and a careful bat for Middlesex, and Charles Llewellyn, South African, who bowled slow left and was a powerful left-hand bat for Hampshire – performed the 'double'. P. R. le Couteur won the University match for Oxford, scoring 160 and taking eleven for 66 – the finest all round performance in the history of the fixture. He bowled leg-breaks and an occasional googly and *Wisden* described his batting as 'very modern in style, a vast proportion of his runs being obtained by on-side hitting'.

South Africa in Australia, 1910–11

The first South African side to tour Australia, captained by Percy Sherwell, lost the series by 4–1. Victor Trumper, in the last great flourish of his Test career, averaged 94·42. Four more Australians – Bardsley, Hill, Armstrong and Kelleway – had figures better than 40. For South Africa, only Faulkner (73·2) who

batted most impressively, approached such a standard against the slow-medium left-arm inswing and natural spin of Whitty – whose 37 wickets were more than half his entire Test tally – Hordern and Cotter. It is revealing, too, that, after Schwarz (25 wickets at 26·04), the next South African bowler was Llewellyn, with 14 at 39·92. Vogler lost his length completely and they had no real fast bowler. Sheer nerves when the game was within their reach probably cost South Africa the second Test, when they collapsed for 80 on a true pitch: but, apart from Faulkner and Schwarz, they were outgunned throughout.

The Season of 1911

At last there came a summer of sunshine and fast pitches on which, for the first time, one of the 'new' counties – Warwickshire – won the Championship.

The first Indian team visited England. Over-praised before they arrived, they disappointed themselves and their hosts by winning only two of their fourteen matches.

A sensational note was struck at the start of the season when, for Notts against Sussex at Brighton, E. B. Alletson scored 189 (out of 227) in 90 minutes – the last 139 in half an hour – the most phenomenal feat of sustained hitting ever performed. He struck eight sixes and 23 fours. In their stand of 152 for the last wicket, Alletson's partner, Riley, scored 10! When Alletson went in, a Sussex win appeared certain: in forty minutes after lunch he brought them to the edge of defeat. This was the only century of his career, though he mounted several similar but shorter assaults. Tall, long-armed and deep-chested, Alletson was originally a brisk right-arm change bowler: later he had brief success with fairly fast leg-breaks until there were objections to his action.

Warwickshire's Championship was due in great measure to the play of their captain, F. R. Foster who, immediately he had been appointed captain for the season, announced his retirement! Pressure was brought to bear upon him, he changed his mind and, after a poor start, Warwickshire won nine of their last twelve matches and, needing to beat Northants in the last match of the season to finish ahead of Kent, they took the title with an innings win. The heavily built and cautious left-hander, 'Sep' Kinneir, was the anchor-man of the batting, and Charlesworth, W. G. Quaife and 'Tiger' Smith – who took over as wicket-keeper when Lilley retired during the season, but who was worth his place for his batting alone – all made useful runs. The fast bowler, Frank Field, for once relatively free from injury, the mature all-rounder Santall, and Quaife with his leg-breaks, all took worthy shares of the bowling. But the man who lifted Warwickshire to the Championship was Foster.

F. R. Foster

Frank Foster had a short cricket career. It began with five matches in 1908: he established himself as a county-standard bowler in 1910, rose to splendid heights as an all-rounder in the twelvemonth from the start of the 1911 English season, and played with distinction until 1914. During the Great War, a motor-cycle accident ended his playing days.

Foster's right-hand batting was never sound, for he played with a cross bat and took many risks, but in 1911, twenty-two years old and in the high summer of confidence, he hit with such spectacular certainty as to take two centuries off Yorkshire and one off Surrey, and, with an aggregate of 1,383 runs in Championship matches, led his county's batting averages.

His left-arm bowling was an altogether different matter. From a full, flowing action, round the wicket, he was fast-medium through the air with explosive lift from the pitch. His inswing was so sharp that, in one of the first leg-theory settings, he often used six leg-side fielders: but he was saved from any hint of monotony by his natural left-armer's break, which he could pitch on middle-and-leg and straighten. For a year he was one of the most menacing bowlers cricket has known and, in that period, he decided a County Championship and a Test series.

The two Northants bowlers, George Thompson and Bill East, took the first two places in the bowling averages and the highest aggregate of the season – 2,562 – was made by Mead of Hampshire.

C. P. Mead

Philip Mead left the Surrey staff to join Hampshire. (It is intriguing to ponder Surrey's power from 1910 to 1930 if they had kept Crawford, Braund and Mead.) Between 1905 and 1936, Mead scored for Hampshire 48,892 runs; more than anyone else has ever scored for one team.

Unprepossessing in style – especially by comparison with Woolley, his chief rival for the place as England's left-hand bat – Mead was little concerned with batting

as such, but he had an insatiable hunger for runs. For many years he never took a net: 'You lead in May, I shall catch you in June' he used to say to the younger players going out to pre-season practice. From his first full season, in 1906, to his last, in 1936, he never failed to score a thousand runs and only Hobbs, Hendren and Hammond made more than his 153 centuries. Utterly phlegmatic, unmoved by pace, at his best on turning wickets, Mead was monolithic in defence, shuffling ungracefully but quickly into position, a master of deflection, precise in his placing. As he once put it 'There's no need to belt the cover off the ball, hard enough for four is hard enough' but, with his long arms, he could hit very hard. Although he had a reputation for slow play, he more than once scored a century before lunch and many of his longest innings were played at a rate of forty or more an hour. In one period during 1923, he scored 1,147 runs in seven completed innings: in 1927, between the end of May and the latter half of June, he played fourteen innings, four of them not-out, for 1,257. He played for England only seventeen times; first in 1911, last in 1928, but few have bettered his Test batting average of 49·37. Woolley's figure was 36·07: but, undeniably, he *looked* better than Mead.

England in Australia, 1911–12

There is little doubt that Warner's 1911–12 side to Australia was the strongest England ever sent overseas. Consider the eleven in the third Test of that series – J. B. Hobbs, W. Rhodes, G. Gunn, J. W. Hearne, C. P. Mead, F. R. Foster, J. W. H. T. Douglas, F. E. Woolley, E. J. Smith, S. F. Barnes and J. W. Hitch. The batting is of top class down to number eight, and the tail capable: Smith, Barnes and – as a hitter – Hitch, all won matches by their batting. With five major all-rounders, the bowling is inexhaustible – Hitch fast right, Foster fast-medium left, Barnes and Douglas fast-medium right, Hearne leg-breaks and googlies, Woolley *and* Rhodes slow left. The close catching is strong, there are two superb outfields and every man is a reliable catcher.

They beat a strong Australian side as conclusively as 4–1 suggests. In the joint figures of the two teams, six English batsmen – Hobbs (82·75), Rhodes, Woolley, Vine, Gunn and Hearne – had better averages than the first Australian (Armstrong), and Foster's was only 0·12 worse. In bowling, Foster,

P. F. Warner (Middlesex) 'Plum' – later Sir Pelham – was the arch-enthusiast of all cricket: batsman, captain, critic and administrator, he lived the game for seventy years

S. F. Barnes (Warwickshire, Lancashire and Staffordshire) The greatest of all bowlers? Accurate, perpetually hostile and with savage lift from the pitch, he harried the finest batsmen in the world for more than thirty years

Barnes – 66 wickets between them – and Douglas all finished above the first Australian – Hordern.

Warner became ill shortly before the first Test and, with many hospital bedside conferences, handed over the captaincy to Douglas.

J. W. H. T. Douglas

Douglas, who captained Essex from 1911 to 1928, was a highly combative cricketer. A fast-medium bowler with a sharp, late outswing that made him extremely dangerous with the new ball, he could maintain pace for long spells. His batting, characterized by determination, was largely, sometimes grimly, defensive. He lacked tact, but never courage, and he died in a heroic attempt to save his father in a shipwreck.

On a good wicket at Sydney, the first Test was won for Australia by batting right down the order – notably Trumper's 113, their only century of the series – and the leg-breaks and googlies of Dr Hordern, who took twelve for 175 in the match.

Douglas opened the bowling with Foster at Sydney, but for the remaining four Tests he gave Barnes and Foster the new ball, and all were won. Barnes began the second Test at Melbourne by taking the first four Australian wickets – of Kelleway, Bardsley, Hill and Armstrong – for one run; he and Foster took fifteen wickets: Hobbs and Hearne made centuries and England won by eight wickets.

J. W. Hearne – 'young Jack' to distinguish him from J. T. – was only twenty at the start of the tour. Never physically strong, he was a neat, copybook batsman,

Wilfred Rhodes (Yorkshire) The ultimate 'senior pro': a surprisingly mature bowler at twenty and the elder statesman of the game at fifty-two: he took more wickets than anyone else who ever played, and made more runs than all but ten others

much concerned with defence. In contrast to the classical rectitude of his batting, Hearne bowled leg-breaks and googlies with a high degree of spin, from a quick rotary arm-swing, at more than slow pace, and he hid his googly well. On a dusty wicket he was practically unplayable.

At Adelaide, Australia batted solidly in their second innings but still fourteen wickets went to Barnes and Foster: Hobbs scored 187, and England won by seven wickets.

In the fourth Test – Melbourne again – fourteen wickets to Foster and Barnes, five to Douglas, and a new Test record of 323 for the first wicket by Hobbs and Rhodes. England, winning by an innings and 225, took the rubber.

Back to Sydney: Foster and Barnes, twelve wickets: Woolley 133 not-out – England won by 70 runs.

Dr H. V. Hordern

Dr Hordern, the first appreciable Australian leg-break and googly bowler, played in only two Test series: he took 32 wickets in this one and 14 against South Africa in 1910–11. After an unusually long run-up, his pace was quite slow but he had a deceptive dip in flight and was so accurate that he sometimes posted a square short-leg, silly mid-on, gully and silly point. He spun googly and leg-break viciously and, a whimsically humorous character, took punishment well. In 1911–12 he was the one consistent bowler in a soundly beaten side. The demands of his dental practice prevented him from coming to England in 1912, restricted his cricket in Australia, and ended it early.

A. F. Somerset took the first MCC team to the West Indies, but the selectors had under-estimated the opposition and the touring side was beaten twice in Barbados and Trinidad, and held, in Jamaica, to the only tie in first-class cricket in the West Indies.

The Season of 1912

This was the year of the Triangular Tournament which has been dismissed, ever since, as 'a failure' – 'never to be repeated' – as if the idea was wrong. Simply enough, it brought Australian and South African teams to England for each of the countries to play three Tests against the other two in the first World Championship of cricket. The suggestion was originally made by Sir Abe Bailey, whose encourage-

C. B. Fry (Sussex and Hampshire) The greatest all-round sportsman England – probably the world – has ever known: athlete and thinker

ment and financial backing materially helped and hastened the rise of South African cricket to Test status. When first mooted, with Australia and South Africa both strong, it was an ambitious and worthwhile idea.

The outcome was dismal because it was attended by grotesque ill-luck. In the first place, 1912 was the wettest summer of the century. Counties untroubled by previous 'rainy' summers felt the pinch. Even Yorkshire, who won the County Championship, showed a loss of £1,000. Then a dispute between a group of Australian players and their Board of Control over the appointment of a team manager resulted in Trumper, Armstrong, Hill, Ransford and Cotter – the 'names' who would have drawn crowds – refusing to make the trip. Finally, South African cricket had slipped from the peak to which the googly bowlers had lifted it, and there was no one to replace them.

England won the unsatisfactory tournament, beating Australia in the only one of their three matches which escaped the weather sufficiently to reach a second innings, and beating South Africa three times. Australia won two and drew the other of their games with South Africa. Fry was unbeaten as captain of England.

The crucial match – England v Australia at The Oval – was the first Test in England scheduled to be played to a finish. It was decided, in four days, on a rain-damaged wicket, by the bowling of Woolley (ten for 49) and the innings of Hobbs, Woolley and Fry. Hobbs, Rhodes and Spooner were the most successful English batsmen, though their final figures were not so good as those of the Australians, Bardsley and Kelleway, who scored heavily against South Africa. Barnes (39 wickets) was by far the most effective bowler in the competition, though Woolley (17 at 8·94) had a better average. Whitty and Hazlitt (fast-medium with an odd 'wobble' in flight, and a highly questionable action) were the main Australian bowlers, but in the first of the nine matches, T. J. Matthews a slow, leg 'roller' performed the hat trick in each innings of South Africa, which remains a feat unique in Test cricket.

Their batting was the ultimate South African failure. After his century in the first Test, Faulkner faded, and no one averaged more than 21. S. J. Pegler – slow leg-breaks – took 29 wickets: Dave Nourse and Faulkner, in support, were expensive.

So ended an unlucky experiment.

Almost half the County Championship matches

75

George Hirst (Yorkshire) Sturdy, strong, reliable and, as batsman, bowler or fielder, a great man at a crisis

were left drawn, and Yorkshire won, in the last analysis, through their ability to finish matches quickly. Everyone except Dolphin, the wicket-keeper, made runs at some time or another, but Denton scored far more than anyone else. Alonzo Drake (medium pace, left-arm stock bowler) and Major Booth (fast right-arm outswinger) had now joined Haigh – rejuvenated by the wet pitches of 1912 – and Hirst in the county's main bowling force; Rhodes had less than 300 overs.

Northants, as runners-up, close on the heels of Yorkshire, afforded the main surprise of the season. They had no truly outstanding player and no batsman who averaged as much as thirty, but calling on only twelve players all season, they became a unity, keen in the field and well served by four bowlers – the West Indian all-rounder S. G. Smith (slow left) the untiring Thompson, Bill East (medium right) and 'Bumper'

Wells (fairly fast right) who each took over forty wickets at less than twenty. They did not again finish so high in the table until 1957.

The Season of 1913

In a warm summer of hard wickets, Kent won the Championship – for the fourth time in eight seasons. In fact, from 1900 to 1914, their average position was a little better than Yorkshire's. K. L. Hutchings had played his last first-class match, but Hardinge was full of runs and Woolley, Seymour, Humphreys, Dillon and Hubble all scored steadily. The attack had nothing to spare, but Fielder's return to form gave Blythe just enough assistance to balance their economy.

Before the season started, there was some unease among the counties. Northants advocated the reduction of playing-time in first-class matches from three days to two. Less openly, Lancashire proposed, at a private meeting with representatives of several other senior counties, the exclusion of four or five of the weaker sides in a reversion to something like the pre-1895 Championship pattern. Eventually both proposals were withdrawn, on condition that there should be no changes – except in methods of scoring – in the County competition until 1917.

Mead and Hobbs both scored over 500 runs more than any other batsman, and Major Booth – Major was his Christian name – starting his outswingers on the middle stump, took most wickets.

England in South Africa, 1913–14

The strongest England side so far sent to South Africa encountered less competition than its immediate predecessors. Of the googly bowlers who had worked such destruction eight and four years earlier, not one so much as appeared in a Test. Had they done so it is doubtful if they could have counterbalanced the bowling of Barnes. In only four Tests – he refused to take part in the fifth after a disagreement – he took 49 wickets which, notwithstanding Laker's performance in 1956, remains the record for any Test series. Coming off the mat terrifyingly steeply and fast, turning the ball the width of the bat both ways from his invariably immaculate length, Barnes reached his ultimate peak. It is doubtful if anyone, before or since, ever bowled better over a sustained period. Only one batsman could stand against him: that was H. W. Taylor. Barnes took his wicket five times in the series, but not without cost: Taylor averaged 50·8, and the clash between the two was memorable.

H. W. Taylor

'Herbie' Taylor was the best of all South African batsmen and a player of world class. More than anyone else, he resembled Jack Hobbs. He had the same effortless movement into the right position, the same shrewd, wide and unbiased selection of strokes, the same understanding of the bowled ball, harnessing it rather than contradicting it, and something of the same relaxed air. He had no noticeable weakness and went forward or back with equal facility. Had Taylor played his cricket in England – for he was no purely hard wicket, or matting wicket, player; his gifts applied in all circumstances – he might have broken most of the batting records, for he had all the skill, and the temperament. He was not a good captain, and it may be that the office detracted from his performance. When cricketing greatness is discussed, Herbie Taylor is too often forgotten. He might be described as the least appreciated of all the great players.

For the rest of the series, in a weak attack, Blanckenberg – tall, medium-pace cutter – pegged away in face of much discouragement and, as a batsman, Zulch plodded gamely. Hobbs played with fluent mastery, Mead with characteristic solidity, while Relf and Douglas mopped up behind Barnes. England won four of the Tests – two by an innings and one by ten wickets – and one was drawn.

The Season of 1914

In a fine summer before cricket gave way to war, Surrey won the Championship for the first time since 1899. They cancelled their last two matches in face of the war-situation, while still needing a first innings lead to be certain of beating Middlesex, who were runners up. MCC exerted their right to decide the winners of the Championship and, with the concurrence of P. F. Warner, the Middlesex captain, awarded it to Surrey. They were, in any case, the best side in England. The ageing Hayward, the mature Hobbs and the younger Ducat and Knight in batting; Hitch, Rushby, 'Razor' Smith and the new leg-spinner, Fender, from Sussex, as bowlers, gave them wide strength, and when they beat Yorkshire by an innings in August, they established their quality.

For Warwickshire against Worcester at Dudley, F. R. Foster scored 305 in 260 minutes; J. W. Hearne made 2,000 runs and took 100 wickets; and Rhodes, taking up his bowling where he seemed to have put it down three years before, performed the double.

A tall, powerful, young man, Arthur Jaques, in his second season for Hampshire, bowled fast-medium inswingers, aimed at the leg stump, to a crowded leg field. It was said, with indignation in some quarters, that he cramped batting: but he took over a hundred wickets and appeared for the Gentlemen at Lord's. Though none of them set fields of this kind, eleven of the first twenty bowlers in the averages employed swing to some degree. The new weapon had been forged. Now, however, it was put down, unimportant in the face of great events. Its exploitation lay more than five years into the future.

Cricket, like many other aspects of life, was never to be the same after the first World War. The rainy seasons of the Edwardian era, and the beginning of the Georgian, had been its blazing summer. It had never stood so high in public esteem before: it was never to do so again. But it had carved out its own shape, and established its high skills on a peak from which they could never be lost.

The Professional Game: 1919–1939

Cricket has always reflected its social setting and, after the first World War, it changed, as the community did, in character. Take up any pre-1914 newspaper and you will find long rolling columns about county matches, written out of certainty that the wide British public was absorbed in all that went on within the game. The cricket of the early part of this book was followed with close interest in Britain, Australia and South Africa. People in Loughborough and Bakewell were absorbed in the progress of the match between Leicestershire and Derbyshire, though neither side was within sight of a prominent place in the Championship. Men in Hanley, Llanelly and Salisbury followed it, though in less partisan fashion, through their morning papers.

After 1918 cricket was briefly a symbol of the return to normality. Once that phase passed, not only in Britain but also in Australia – where the public attitude had always been less romantic – it was to be a matter of star-attraction, Test Matches and winning teams. Except to the caricatured enthusiasts, no other aspect of the game mattered. The allocation of summer days to cricket was now challenged by tennis, seaside excursions, cycling clubs, swimming, athletics, hiking and cinema matinées. For the first time in living memory cricket faced competition.

Competition was growing inside the game as well. In England this was the age of the professional – in two different ways and for several socially sound reasons. The economic revolution caused by war auto-matically reduced the number of men who could spend the entire summer playing cricket. The days when Somerset or Worcester maintained a professional nucleus of two stock bowlers, a sheet-anchor batsman and, perhaps, a wicket-keeper, and completed the eleven with varyingly talented amateurs, were drawing to a close: and not solely because the supply of amateurs had diminished.

Of old, it had been the pride of the northern county professional to don his heavy suit, take his bowler hat and saunter down to the local pub on a winter's morning, to demonstrate that his cricketing success was such that he had no need to return to the pit or the mill out of season. The professional of the inter-war years was also, though differently, romantic and proud to be paid for his cricket. But he was a greater realist, more conscious of wage-levels and the concept of financial stability. He had not left the pit or the farm merely to find himself in another kind of insecurity. He expected to fight for his place in the county team, but he grew increasingly resentful of being dropped in August to make way for an undergraduate or a schoolmaster on holiday – and his resentment was the greater when his replacement was a poor player. Moreover, press criticism of such reductions in team-efficiency was less charitable than it had once been.

So, while some counties managed to continue along feudal lines, they all moved towards a basis of professionalism. There were still amateurs, but fewer of

78

them owed their places to privilege. More of them won their places in competition with professionals. Many of them, indeed, became more professional than the pros.

No paid cricketer ever probed technique or tactics more deeply, or played the game harder, than such inter-war amateurs as D. R. Jardine, R. W. V. Robins, R. E. S. Wyatt, A. W. Carr, V. W. C. Jupp, M. J. Turnbull or P. G. H. Fender. Every year, as acute brains picked out players' weaknesses and brought the sharp drill of technical skill to bear on them, success became harder to achieve. The young batsman or bowler would have a good first season: then he would pass into eclipse as his play was dissected and its flaws exposed.

From 1890 onwards, for good or ill, cricket became less a game for gifted athletes and increasingly one for experts. The inswing bowlers of the twenties looked at the photos of early batsmen with their open stances and high back-lifts and grinned condescendingly. The day of the professional had dawned.

It was, too, the period of the northern professional: between 1922 and 1939 the championship was never taken south of the Trent.

The most determined reactionaries could no longer close their eyes to the fact that the West Indies, New Zealand and India were growing up, so that, if they could not yet beat England, Australia or South Africa, they were at least as entitled to Test status as South Africa had been in 1888.

Finally, the War had widened horizons: the average man no longer believed that cricket was simply a matter of the daily progress of the English season, or a Test series between two of the founder members of the Imperial Cricket Conference – or that the English County Championship was more important than a Test series.

There was no longer one level of 'big' cricket, but two – international cricket and, below it in public estimation and quality of play, the remainder of the first-class game.

1919–1939

Test Matches

1920–21 in Australia, Australia beat England 5–0

1921 in England, Australia beat England 3–0: two matches drawn

1921–22 in South Africa, Australia beat South Africa 1–0: two matches drawn

1922–23 in South Africa, England beat South Africa 2–1: two matches drawn

1924 in England, England beat South Africa 3–0: two matches drawn

1924–25 in Australia, Australia beat England 4–1

1926 in England, England beat Australia 1–0: four matches drawn

1927–28 in South Africa, South Africa v England, series drawn 2–2: one match drawn

1928 in England, England beat West Indies 3–0

1928–29 in Australia, England beat Australia 4–1

1929 in England, England beat South Africa 2–0: three matches drawn

1929–30 in New Zealand, England beat New Zealand 1–0: three matches drawn

in West Indies, West Indies v England, series drawn, 1–1: two matches drawn

1930 in England, Australia beat England 2–1: two matches drawn

1930–31 in South Africa, South Africa beat England, 1–0: four matches drawn

in Australia, Australia beat West Indies, 4–1

1931 in England, England beat New Zealand 1–0: two matches drawn

1931–32 in Australia, Australia beat South Africa, in New Zealand, South Africa beat New Zealand, 2–0

1932 in England, England beat India 1–0

1932–33 in Australia, England beat Australia 4–1

in New Zealand, New Zealand v England, series drawn, 0–0: two matches drawn

1933 in England, England beat West Indies, 2–0: one match drawn

1933–34 in India, England beat India, 2–0: one match drawn

1934 in England, Australia beat England, 2–1: two matches drawn

1934–35 in West Indies, West Indies beat England 2–1: one match drawn

1935 in England, South Africa beat England, 1–0: four matches drawn

1935–36 in South Africa, Australia beat South Africa, 4–0: one match drawn

1936 in England, England beat India 2–0: one match drawn

1936–37 in Australia, Australia beat England 3–2

1937 in England, England beat New Zealand 1–0: two matches drawn

79

1938 in England, England *v* Australia, series drawn, 1–1: two matches drawn: one match abandoned

1938–39 in South Africa, England beat South Africa, 1–0: four matches drawn

1939 in England, England beat West Indies, 1–0: two matches drawn

1932–33 New South Wales
1933–34 Victoria
1934–35 Victoria
1935–36 South Australia
1936–37 Victoria
1937–38 New South Wales
1938–39 South Australia
1939–40 New South Wales

County Champions

1919 Yorkshire
1920 Middlesex
1921 Middlesex
1922 Yorkshire
1923 Yorkshire
1924 Yorkshire
1925 Yorkshire
1926 Lancashire
1927 Lancashire
1928 Lancashire
1929 Nottinghamshire
1930 Lancashire
1931 Yorkshire
1932 Yorkshire
1933 Yorkshire
1934 Lancashire
1935 Yorkshire
1936 Derbyshire
1937 Yorkshire
1938 Yorkshire
1939 Yorkshire

Sheffield Shield Winners

1919–20 New South Wales
1920–21 New South Wales
1921–22 Victoria
1922–23 New South Wales
1923–24 Victoria
1924–25 Victoria
1925–26 New South Wales
1926–27 South Australia
1927–28 Victoria
1928–29 New South Wales
1929–30 Victoria
1930–31 Victoria
1931–32 New South Wales

Currie Cup Winners

1920–21 Western Province
1921–22 Transvaal, Natal and Western Province (equal)
1923–24 Transvaal
1925–26 Transvaal
1926–27 Transvaal
1929–30 Transvaal
1931–32 Western Province
1933–34 Natal
1934–35 Transvaal
1936–37 Natal
1937–38 Transvaal and Natal (equal)

West Indies, Inter-Colonial or Triangular Tournament

1921–22 No result
1922–23 Barbados beat Trinidad
1923–24 Barbados beat Trinidad
1924–25 Trinidad beat Barbados
1925–26 Trinidad beat British Guiana
1926–27 Barbados beat Trinidad
1928–29 Trinidad beat Barbados
1929–30 British Guiana beat Trinidad
1931–32 Trinidad beat British Guiana
1933–34 Trinidad beat Barbados
1934–35 British Guiana beat Trinidad
1935–36 British Guiana beat Trinidad
1936–37 Trinidad beat British Guiana
1937–38 British Guiana beat Trinidad
1938–39 Trinidad beat British Guiana

Plunket Shield Winners

1918–19 Wellington
1919–20 Canterbury
1920–21 Auckland
1921 Wellington

In 1921 the Plunket Shield became an annual competition – winners:

1921–22 Auckland
1922–23 Canterbury
1923–24 Wellington
1924–25 Otago
1925–26 Wellington
1926–27 Auckland
1927–28 Wellington
1928–29 Auckland
1929–30 Wellington
1930–31 Canterbury
1931–32 Wellington
1932–33 Otago
1933–34 Auckland
1934–35 Canterbury
1935–36 Wellington
1936–37 Auckland
1937–38 Auckland
1938–39 Auckland
1939–40 Auckland

'Ranji' Trophy Winners

1934–35 Bombay beat Northern India
1935–36 Bombay beat Madras
1936–37 Nawanagar beat Bengal
1937–38 Hyderabad beat Nawanagar
1938–39 Bengal beat Southern Punjab
1939–40 Maharashtra beat United Provinces

AUSTRALIA DOMINANT

England, weary and out of touch after the war, returned tentatively to cricket. Two of the Olympian figures, W. G. Grace and Victor Trumper, had died in 1915: Major Booth and Colin Blythe had been killed in action: so had other county players of less eminence and a whole sad line of young men, cricketers whose names never appeared in the newspaper reports because they were dead before their gifts could ripen. Even the survivors were not attuned to a life of daily and daylong cricket.

Perhaps 1919 was too early for a full scale County Championship. Worcester, certainly, were in such financial difficulties that they did not take part, and the experiment of two-day matches pleased no one.

In a summer of fine weather, hard pitches and fast scoring, not even longer hours could prevent a large proportion of drawn games.

Some idea of the muddle produced by hurried arrangements was reflected in the final table in which Yorkshire, who played 26 matches and won 12, were taken to the last match of the season before they finished ahead of Kent, who played 14 matches and won six.

Alonzo Drake and Major Booth were gone and Schofield Haigh too old to play, but Yorkshire's winning side soundly blended old hands like Denton, Hirst, Rhodes and E. R. Wilson with a group of young players who were the portent of the reign to come.

In 1920, three-day matches were resumed, and Middlesex won the Championship in a fashion that could not have been better staged. Their last match was against Surrey at Lord's, and they needed to win it to overtake Lancashire. Warner declared and set Surrey 244 to win: Surrey went for the runs and, with ten minutes of playing time left, Stevens bowled their last man to give Middlesex a win by 55 runs – and the Championship. It was Plum Warner's last match as captain of Middlesex and he was carried off the field shoulder-high as the cheering crowd closed in.

It was a happy, moving occasion; and elsewhere in England there was pleasure at the sight of young cricketers of promise, or older men whose powers seemed to have survived the war undimmed. Cecil Parkin, who had been on the Yorkshire staff before the war and had gone by way of Durham to Lancashire, was surprising many batsmen by his bowling methods. Playing for Surrey against Northants P. G. H. Fender struck the fastest century ever recorded – in 35 minutes.

P. G. H. Fender

For a dozen years between the two Wars, Percy George Fender of Surrey was the most astute captain and one of the most effective all-rounders in English cricket. Tall, long-armed, and a relaxed mover, he was constantly alert, probing restlessly at any match in which he took part. After Jessop he was probably the most consistent attacking batsman in the game, gifted with most of the strokes and phenomenally powerful in his cover and extra-cover driving. He bowled leg-breaks and googlies steadily rather than with extravagant spin, had a tendency to spin-swerve and a knack of taking wickets by artful variations. At slip he picked up exceptional catches with a casual air.

E. – 'Patsy' – Hendren (Middlesex) A gay, game batsman; nimble and accomplished, he enjoyed his cricket

As a captain his brain was never still. For years he made a thin Surrey attack far more effective than the total of its apparent powers on the perfect Oval wickets. He observed more, remembered more, and reached his conclusions quicker than almost any other captain of his time, and he never failed to take the maximum advantage of that fact. He was the best English captain who never led an England side.

Hendren, of Middlesex, had become one of the leading batsmen in the country, and was one of five who scored over 2,000 runs in 1920. While two younger – completely contrasted – slow left-arm bowlers, J. C. White and C. W. L. Parker, had advanced, Wilfred Rhodes, at 42, was first in the bowling averages. Vallance Jupp had suddenly become a good enough all-rounder to perform the double and, at the Universities, G. T. S. Stevens, R. H. Bettington, the brothers Hubert and Gilbert

Ashton, A. P. F. Chapman, C. S. Marriott and C. H. Gibson were impressing everyone by the maturity of their play. Moreover, E. R. Wilson, a Cambridge Blue as long ago as 1899, who had played little first-class cricket since 1902, had found time to turn out for Yorkshire – and was second in their bowling averages only to Rhodes – while, behind him, came another young bowler of that unusual and always interesting type – the fast left-arm bowler; Abe Waddington. English cricket was happy at these signs and deeds: but there was no accurate yardstick by which to measure them. English cricket was, in truth, at the bottom of its lowest trough, and the fact was soon to be made plain.

A hastily gathered Australian Imperial Forces team had shown its paces in England in 1919. Yet no-one seemed to appreciate that its results (played 28: won 12: lost 4), for what was no more than a stopgap services side, bespoke immense Australian power at home.

Australia had asked for a visit from MCC in 1919–20: but English opinion deemed that too early. So was 1920–21; but it would have been impolitic not to resume the pattern of tours. Reggie Spooner, who at first accepted the captaincy, was forced to resign it to Douglas, but otherwise, whilst it is possible to make a case for including Holmes or Mead, the side chosen was just about the best available on form. *Wisden* could only describe its performance as 'disaster'. For the first and only time a Test series was won 5–0; with all Tests played to a finish, England could not even hope for the mercy of a draw.

Some cricket had been maintained in Australia through the war years, and their side was more than competent: it had not a real weakness and it was captained with characteristic ruthlessness by Warwick Armstrong. Except for the switch between Oldfield and Carter – two wicket-keepers so good that there was little to choose between them – and replacement for injury or illness, only one change was made in the team for the five matches.

So quickly had the new generation found its feet that Australia included only four men who had played against England before the war. Bardsley was still there, and Kelleway had become an even more valuable all-rounder with his lively bowling and obdurate batting. Macartney was ill and missed the three middle games of the series, but his 170 in the last Test confirmed him in his high place. Armstrong batted ponderously, bowled artfully and, most relentless of all captains, never let England climb back to their feet after the first knock-down.

H. L. – Herbie – Collins was Bardsley's new opening partner. Lean and tough, he was a cool batsman, economic of effort, with a defence like rock and a precise judgement in the use of his pads. He averaged 61 and 'Nip' Pellew – one of the fastest and finest of all outfields and a quick-footed stroke-maker – 53.

The issue was clinched by two 'new' bowlers, of whom Mailey had toured New Zealand with Noble's side of 1913–14; Gregory was a post-war product, who emerged from club to international class during the AIF tour of England.

A. A. Mailey

Arthur Mailey's 36 English wickets in 1920–21 is still the record for an Australian bowler in a Test series. He was an expansive leg-break and googly bowler who threw the ball well up. No one ever spun the ball more, and he extracted life from the hardest baked Australian wickets. The extent of his spin often affected his length but rarely his line, and his googly often hit the stumps. Alert, observant, with a questing mind, he was quick to notice batsmen's weaknesses, and nothing delighted him more than out-thinking an eminent opponent: and so he was dangerous even on a perfect pitch.

Throughout Mailey's Test career, Australia had runs to spare, so that he could experiment and, if necessary, 'buy' his wickets: and he was always philosophic in face of punishment. When Victoria made their score of 1,107 – still the record single innings total – Mailey's figures were 64 (eight-ball) overs: 0 maidens: 362 runs: 4 wickets. In extenuation, Mailey once remarked that his figures would have been better but that he had four catches dropped by a man wearing a brown coat in the members' stand.

Mailey was an amusing and sometimes revealing caricaturist, a perceptive cricket reporter, a drily humorous essayist and diverting conversationalist, with a wise man's sense of proportion about cricket and life.

J. M. Gregory

To a whole generation of young and impressionable cricket followers in England and Australia during the early twenties, Jack Gregory is still the personification of fast bowling. Six-feet-three tall, with a long, bounding run-up and an intimidating leap at delivery, he was unquestionably high in pace and on hard grounds he made the ball rear alarmingly. He lacked subtlety and at first his direction was not always good, but his speed and bounce provided constant material for his wicket-keeper and slips, and, to drive home an advantage, he would keep up full effort for long periods.

Gregory was the unusual combination of right-arm bowler and left-hand bat. His batting, for all its rough-hewn air, was sound enough in defence and productive enough in scoring to place him among the relatively few Test class all-rounders, for his concentration, length of reach and sureness of hand made him the best Australian slip field of his period.

Gregory, Mailey, Kelleway and Armstrong were so adequate for Australia's attacking needs that Macartney bowled only three overs in his two Tests.

Hobbs – 505 runs in ten innings – was by far England's best, and the dogged Douglas her only consistent batsman, though both Russell and Make-peace made courageous defensive centuries: Hearne was ill and did not play after the start of the second Test: for the rest, the tour was a humbling experience.

It was in bowling, however, that the poverty of English cricket was most mercilessly reflected. Only Fender (12 at 34·16) and Parkin (16 at 41·87) took more than nine wickets or – apart from E. R. Wilson, who played only in the last Test when he had three for 36 – had an average below fifty!

Australia in England, 1921

The Australians sailed with the MCC party back to England where, until the rubber was won, they proved even stronger than in their own country. The last two Tests were drawn after rain. At Old Trafford England had gained a strong position, but at The Oval their situation was not so good as the score might indicate, since Armstrong treated the closing stages of the game so casually that, in his last gesture of contempt for English cricket, he read an evening newspaper in the outfield and allowed men who did not normally bowl to put themselves on and off as they wished. Taxed with this discourtesy, Armstrong declared he was reading the paper to find out the score.

The Australian strength lay in the improvement of McDonald, who, with Armstrong, Gregory and Mailey (Kelleway was inexplicably not included in the party) made up so complete an attack that no one else bowled as many as sixty overs in Tests.

Gregory and McDonald quite dominated the cricket of 1921 when, in a blazing summer of hard wickets, they swept through English batting like a gale through bean-sticks, seizing the public imagination and winning a Test series.

E. A. McDonald

In 1921 it was said that Ted McDonald was not so fast as Gregory. Nevertheless, the difference in speed between them cannot have been great and Gregory's terrifying approach must have made him look faster. Certainly, McDonald often beat batsmen by sheer pace, and his bouncer – which was a planned in-gredient of his strategy – flew like a tennis ball.

His action was perfect. His run to the wicket, absolutely straight, was as smoothly tip-toe as a sprinter's, and his delivery, from a fully cocked wrist,

Ted McDonald (Victoria and Lancashire) A saturnine fast bowler with a glorious action: on his day, an utter destroyer

was a perfect high arc. On slow, wet grounds, he could reduce his pace and bowl medium off-breaks to a close field with his well-hidden yorker in reserve.

McDonald was already twenty-eight when he began his Test career, which lasted little more than a year. He then returned to England where he played in League cricket, qualified for Lancashire and, as late as 1930, rated as one of the best fast bowlers in English cricket.

If the English defeat of 1920–21 could not fairly be attributed to errors by the selectors, that of 1921, at home, should be. It was important that, through illness, Hobbs, the best batsman on either side, never lifted his bat in the series, and Hearne played only once. It is nevertheless true that, like their successors of some twenty-odd years later, the committee of 1921, knowing full well that the danger was the Australian fast bowling, did not take the obvious step

84

of concentrating on batsmen who were sound against pace. By trial and error they reached some such basis of choice by the fifth Test – when it was too late – and included Mead, Russell, Tennyson, Brown, Woolley (whose 95 and 93 at Lord's were England's only fighting gestures in the early matches), Ernest Tyldesley and Douglas, who finished in that order in the first seven places of the final batting averages. But why was George Gunn, the best English batsman against pace, left out? In all, thirty different players were chosen for England in the series which, even in face of overpowering opposition, must still bespeak bad selection. Parkin – alone as a bowler with sixteen wickets – was never given the sympathetic direction or the steady supporting bowler he needed. Taking the captaincy from Douglas and all but hawking it around before giving it to Tennyson was pathetically clumsy. While all this fantastic chopping and changing was going on, Australia won the first three Tests for the rubber: they could afford to jockey England into drawing at Manchester and The Oval.

C. H. Parkin

No bowler has ever been more difficult to label than Cecil Parkin. It can be said definitely that he always bowled with his right arm: after that he defies precise definition – except that he always used the same run-up – of about ten to twelve yards. Slim, gay, lively and inventive, with the fingers of a conjuror – conjuring was his hobby – he could bowl anything and everything. As a young and successful bowler in League cricket his pace was on the fast side of medium. In county cricket his basic method – so far as he had one – was medium to slow-medium off-breaks. As a Test cricketer he frequently opened the bowling with fast-medium outswingers. In some circumstances he employed a leg trap for his off-breaks. On less receptive pitches he might give his off spin more air and pitch along the line of the off stump. His 'slower' ball was regarded at first with intense respectful suspicion, later with some derision, but at both stages it brought him wickets. He would toss it right up – as leg-break, or wide-turning googly – sometimes deliberately as a full-toss; and, if it was often hit for four, it also persuaded good batsmen to 'get themselves out'.

Parkin was an impatient man. He modelled himself on Barnes, but he lacked Barnes's persistence and accuracy. He saw no virtue in mechanical, or even sustainedly accurate, bowling. He always wanted to take wickets quickly – and usually did – but was never averse to 'buying' them. Often a match-winner, a vibrant personality whose quick wit and tongue often led him into trouble – and kept him out of Test Matches – he left county cricket after a disagreement with Lancashire, and became the first of the highly paid League professionals.

G. Brown

Whenever the subject is raised of 'the greatest all-rounder', George Brown's name must always be considered. He kept wicket for England, opened the innings for England; took over six hundred wickets as a fairly fast right-arm outswinger; he was considered the best mid-off in England and was outstanding at silly point, while a pre-1914 reference book described him as 'the furthest thrower in the game'.

A man of immense courage – did he not show his contempt for an opposing fast bowler by withdrawing his bat from a bouncer and deliberately breasting it down? – he was lifted to his best by such challenge as that of the 1921 Australians. George Brown was one of the few players who could be said genuinely to relish fast bowling, and, brought into the England side for the third Test of 1921, he was the one batsman to play in as many as half the Tests without failing once. His scores were 57, 46, 31, 32 and 84: and only once did one of the fast bowlers take his wicket. Although he was not Hampshire's regular wicket-keeper, he was a 'natural' who could pull on any old pair of gloves and, without practice, take any type of bowling with ease.

His left-handed batting was sound; against fast bowling he was especially powerful on the leg side; and against every type of bowler he drove with the full, uninhibited flow of his terrific strength. A colourful, generous cricketer, George Brown might worthily have played in three times as many as his seven Tests. There has never been a braver player nor one who more often succeeded in a crisis.

Outside Tests, the Australians had four totals of more than 600 and, against Notts at Trent Bridge, where they won by the immense margin of an innings and 517 runs, Macartney, dropped when he had made nine, scored 345 in less than four hours. Five bowlers of 1921 took all ten wickets in an innings: the remarkable Cecil Tyson, in his first first-class match, scored 100 not out and 80 not out for Yorkshire against Hampshire, only to end his career with the county ten days later.

Middlesex were once more Champions: the title did not come south again until they next won it, in 1947.

On the way home, Australia played three Tests in South Africa, won one and left two drawn. Armstrong, who was ill, handed over the captaincy to Collins and his place in the four-man bowling unit to Macartney. For South Africa, Nourse, Taylor and Frank batted usefully and Carter and Blanckenberg took 27 wickets, but against weak change bowling, Ryder, Macartney, Collins and Gregory made more than enough runs for Australian security.

Domestic Patterns and Problems

Australia were so strong that England and South Africa were now inescapably faced with the need to find a fresh generation of players to reinforce their batting and completely re-stock their bowling.

Fortunately there was a brief pause in which all three countries could turn to their domestic cricket. In England, Yorkshire completed their second great team-building operation and won the Championship of 1922 with a highly efficient cadre of thirteen players. Once it had been decided to replace Norman Kilner with Leyland and when, in August, E. R. Wilson took over the captaincy from Geoffrey Wilson, the eleven – sound in batting and highly penetrative in attack – was P. Holmes, H. Sutcliffe, E. Oldroyd, R. Kilner, W. Rhodes, E. Robinson, M. Leyland, G. G. Macaulay, A. Dolphin, A. Waddington, E. R. Wilson.

This was the foundation on which Yorkshire built their towering position in English inter-war cricket – eleven times Champions, twice runners-up and only once as low as fifth, in eighteen seasons. Apart from changes in captaincy, every Yorkshire cap awarded in that period was sternly – sometimes bitterly – contested. Two of the 1922 eleven – Sutcliffe and Leyland – were still regulars in the team that won the Championship in 1939. Round them, over the years, the side developed like a healthy organic growth in which, as any member aged past peak efficiency, he was replaced with an infallibility and adequacy that filled the rest of cricketing England with dismay and envy.

Meanwhile, a full dozen men whom Yorkshire did not seek to retain as reserves left to become first-rate county players in other teams. Lancashire, Notts and, in 1936, Derby, on the same basic design of a pro-

fessional eleven with an amateur captain, kept the Championship in the north to the end of the era, though Sussex, Kent, Surrey and Middlesex had made gallant challenges at different times.

Apart from Derbyshire, who grew steadily in strength and came through from the lower to the upper reaches, the standing of the counties changed little during the seventeen years from 1922. The power group at the top was followed relatively closely by Sussex, Kent, Middlesex and Surrey. Gloucester – apart from a few isolated spurts – and Essex existed on the upper fringe of the middle belt; Warwick on the lower; then, through Somerset, Hampshire and Leicester to the three poor relations. Glamorgan – who in 1921 became the last county admitted to the Championship – and their closest predecessors, Worcestershire and Northants, lived on the fringe of bankruptcy as chopping blocks for the other counties. Between the two wars Glamorgan finished only twice in a single-figure position, Worcester once, and Northants never. Each produced a few outstanding players but never a complete eleven of true county-class.

The Warwickshire-Hampshire match at Edgbaston in 1922 produced the most remarkable recovery in cricket history. Warwickshire, batting first, scored 223 and then, on a true wicket of no great pace, Harry Howell and Gough-Calthorpe bowled out Hampshire for 15. Following on, Hampshire, on the second day, lost their sixth second innings wicket with all their measurable batsmen except Brown gone, and still needed 22 to avoid an innings defeat. This was the great challenge of George Brown's career: he was one of the few cricketers capable of believing he could meet it. He and Shirley put on 85, but McIntyre was out cheaply and, at 274 for eight, Hampshire were a mere 66 on. Yet some strange fire of resistance had been kindled. This one innings apart, Walter Livsey – even with the aid of 15 not-outs – averaged only a fraction over nine for the season. Now he stayed with Brown while they put on 177 for the ninth wicket. Then Brown was out for a chanceless 172: but the miracle continued. Stuart Boyes (batting average for the season 6·04) made his top score of the year – 29 – and kept an end secure in a last wicket partnership of 70, while Livsey went on to make the first century of his career. Hampshire, all out 521, had seized the initiative and Warwick, psychologically routed, were put out by Kennedy and Newman for 158. Hampshire won by 155 runs.

In Australia, Queensland were admitted to the Sheffield Shield competition in 1926–27 but, apart from three successes by South Australia, New South Wales and Victoria – who rarely fielded less than half a dozen Test players apiece – tended to decide it between themselves.

In Australia the eight-ball over was established in 1922 and, except for reversion to six-balls for the English visits of 1928–29 and 1932–33, has remained in force ever since.

The long-standing Australian attitude in favour of playing matches to a finish had stemmed, reasonably enough, from the desire to achieve definite results in the relatively few matches of their season. It is strange that the absence of the time factor – always regarded as a fundamental ingredient of cricket – should have had a less adverse effect on their batsmen than on those of visiting teams. Australians in England have rarely played with less urgency than English cricketers in the setting of the three-day match. But English and South African batsmen in Australia have often tended to reduce their normal tempo in 'play to a finish' matches, frequently with poor results.

Australian opinion during the twenties hardened in favour of stricter time limitation and, in 1930–31, the fifth day extension in Sheffield Shield matches was abandoned in favour of four-day fixtures.

In South Africa, Transvaal and Natal stood far above the other Currie Cup sides; they could often have fielded a second eleven too strong for most of their competitors.

South Africa were faced with a special problem. They could not afford to be the only Test-playing country using matting wickets. Many of their best bowlers, who made the ball move and lift dangerously off the mat, found themselves lacking in resource and unable to make the constantly necessary length adjustments when they played on turf. Matting wickets went because they were the exception and not the rule. Those with the widest experience of pitches throughout the world had no doubt that the mat was the supreme test of the cricketer, that it emphasized the gap between the good and the great. They instance Barnes and Lohmann as bowlers, Hobbs and Taylor as batsmen, who stood high above all their contemporaries in the pre-turf Tests in South Africa. The fact remained that South Africa was at a disadvantage in world cricket so long as she was alone in playing on mat. Turf had to come and, in 1931, it did: but problems of climate made its maintenance

difficult and expensive and the standard of pitches there has never been so steady as in England and Australia.

In New Zealand the Plunket Shield went the rounds; and in the West Indies, where the distances involved unhappily kept Jamaica out of competition with the other three major sides, British Guiana, Trinidad and Barbados all had their winning turns.

England and South Africa, 1922–23 and 1924

Frank Mann's MCC team was a careful rather than a forward-looking selection; and at the end of the series neither side could feel better fitted to face Australia than before. Taylor stood high above all other batsmen on the two sides. Without Hobbs, England lacked distinction, though Russell solidly made his way to a century in each innings of the Durban Test, Mead was reliable, as usual, and Woolley struck one handsome century.

A. E. Hall, a fastish bowler who divided his cricket between South Africa and his native Lancashire, was chaired off the field at Cape Town after he had pursued England to a nervous, one-wicket win with seven for 63 in the second Test. The English batsmen had more respect for Blanckenberg, and though Nupen did not hold his place throughout the series, he decided the first Test with a foretaste of the form that was to make him one of the finest of all bowlers on matting. Kennedy's bowling – he was top of the English averages with almost twice as many wickets as the next man – tilted the series in the last match at Durban. Kennedy is remembered as a county rather than a Test bowler; only five men have taken more than his 2,874 wickets. Steady as a rock at medium pace, right-arm, he was a fine craftsman, swinging the new ball and cutting the old, tireless and unendingly resourceful. He performed the double five times and he and his harness-mate, Jack Newman (2,032 wickets, 15,333 runs), were nine-tenths of the Hampshire bowling and solid props of their batting for well over twenty years.

F. T. Mann, an unusually popular captain, finished third in the batting averages but the two 'experimental' choices, Arthur Gilligan and Greville Stevens, did little in Tests.

In England in 1923, Yorkshire, in winning the Championship, played 32 matches and won 25 – 13 of them by an innings: three of their bowlers – Rhodes,

Roy Kilner and Macaulay – stood in the first three places of the national averages.

E. Hendren

Baptismally Elias, but traditionally 'Patsy', Hendren was the leading batsman of the 1923 season, and he stands second only to Hobbs in number of centuries – 170. The most human of cricketers, he scampered the first run of an innings with the anxious eagerness of a schoolboy and his humour and mimicry cheered any game. Below average height and chunkily built, he was busily fast on his feet, quick to move down the pitch to drive slow bowling, a hard, brave – and often battered – hooker, and an impudent cutter. He liked to get on with a game, and on true pitches it was not easy to keep him quiet, for he had strokes for all kinds and directions of bowling. When the ball turned, his nimbleness served him well, and for thirty years he was a relishable and reliable batsman.

A capable professional footballer as a young man, Hendren was a fine runner and catcher in the deep; later he settled in the slips where he was watchful and sure-handed. On all levels of the game he was one of the best loved of all cricketers.

The 1923 West Indian side in England played no Tests but, overcoming the handicap of a cold summer, they made a favourable impression through the batting of the captain, George Challenor, the pace attack of Francis and John – two essentially straight fast bowlers – and the spectacular fielding of Constantine.

1924 was one of the most exciting formative years of English cricket, when a whole group of players stepped up to a new level of performance and stamped themselves as true Test cricketers.

Herbert Sutcliffe

In 1921 and 1922–23 Russell made a strong claim to open the England innings with Hobbs. In 1923 and 1924, however, his batting in county matches was undistinguished and, already in his middle thirties, only current form could have justified his selection. So the place went to Sutcliffe, who established himself from his first match. Firmly built and spruce, he was first and foremost a dogged batsman and secondly an invariably cool one. Beaten by three consecutive balls, he would play the fourth completely unrattled. Sound in back foot defence, like every Yorkshireman, he was also strong in driving, especially straight. He had not the speed of movement of Hendren but he was an immensely brave player, who faced fast bowling unflinchingly and was an assured and prolific hooker.

Herbert Sutcliffe was a self-reliant cricketer who asked no favours from the game. He accepted bad wickets with good, never found any situation too desperate, nor any too easy. In 1931, a wet season, he scored 3,006 runs at an average of 96·96. He was the only man to play regularly in every inter-war season; and he scored over a thousand runs in each. He took pride in everything about his cricket and, if he was not such a rough diamond as some Yorkshire cricketers, he was as hard, at core, as any of them, a batsman who set out with complete concentration to score runs and was not to be deterred. Probably to a greater extent than anyone else, he could make runs when he was out of touch; that quality made him a great, instead of a good, Test batsman.

Roy Kilner

Yorkshire first played Roy Kilner, before the 1914 War, as a left-hand batsman. Subsequently, at the side's need, he bowled well enough to become an England all-rounder. His batting was straightforward; reliable in a corner; upon opportunity, he hit with the full power of his stocky frame, driving, pulling and hooking forcefully.

As a slow left-arm bowler, he had such precision of length and direction that he could close up a game for long periods, bowling unwaveringly to his field. In the same side as Rhodes, however, he sought to provide a different type of attack and frequently bowled over, instead of round, the wicket. With considerable variety of flight and spin, sometimes near to medium pace, he constantly strove to produce surprise within a pattern of accuracy. A friendly and modest man, Kilner died at 37, when he was still a candidate for any England side.

George Macaulay

George Macaulay was a determinedly aggressive cricketer. A lean, wiry man, he was originally a fast, right-arm bowler but, on the Yorkshire staff, he reduced his pace and concentrated on off-spin. He could still take the new ball and bowl outswingers on the lively side of medium, but it was as a brisk off-spinner, who turned the ball abruptly from a grudging length, that he made his reputation. On a sticky wicket his pace and degree of spin made him quite brutish, and he was always attacking. He could bat usefully, but he expressed himself in his bowling.

Maurice Tate (Sussex) He had the perfect action, the gaiety of a boy, the heart of a lion, the stamina of a mule and a pace from the pitch which made him unique among all bowlers – fast-medium through the air, truly fast off the pitch

Maurice Tate

There have been few happier accidents in cricket than the bowling of Maurice Tate. From 1912 when, at the age of seventeen, he first played for Sussex, until 1922, he was regarded as a homespun but capable batsman and a fair right-arm change bowler of slow-medium off-breaks. In July 1922, he had bowled long and unprofitably to Philip Mead when, suddenly, he swung his body fully into a faster ball which bit back off the pitch and hit the stumps. Within a year Tate was the finest fast-medium bowler in England.

He retained his original slow-medium bowler's run – seven full paces and a four-feet jump – and derived his pace from the mighty lever of his body-swing. His perfect action made him a fast bowler off the pitch. He had the arms, shoulders, hips and feet of a pace bowler, immense stamina and a zest for bowling. Some of his spells of sustainedly hostile bowling, especially

in the heat of Australia or India, would have left most men in a state of collapse: and he smashed his left foot with the thunderous stamp of his delivery stride. For a decade he was the finest of his kind in the world. A natural bowler, he made the new ball swing away late. The worn ball he swung in; and often it would move 'the other way' off the seam. His length and direction were unfailing: he never bowled a 'no ball' in his life and only one wide – when he threw up a slow ball which was carried wide by the wind. He opened the Sussex innings for some years and in Tests scored 1,198 runs as well as taking 155 wickets.

A humorous character with a relish for life and a great enthusiasm for the game, Maurice Tate felt that his bowling made some amends for his father's error in the Old Trafford Test of 1902.

Arthur Gilligan

Maurice Tate's Sussex and England bowling partner was not a great player, but an extremely useful one. His right-arm bowling was fast enough to disconcert the hesitant. He batted straightforwardly, strong in driving, always looking for runs, and a fighter when his side was in trouble. A keen and fearless mid-off and a constantly enthusiastic captain, he was exactly the man English cricket needed in 1924. By quite mischievous ill-luck, he was hit over the heart by a lifting ball in the Gentlemen v Players match at The Oval. He went on to make a century against the run of the game, but he never bowled really fast again and, in the single moment of his injury, England lost the almost priceless asset of a pace bowling *pair*.

Fred Root

As twenty years earlier, some batsmen had felt that the googly was 'not quite fair', so their successors were ill at ease about leg theory. Yet the inswing of Fred Root was, for bowlers, a logical consequence of the batsmen's off-side revels in the Edwardian era.

Root, the first man to perfect leg theory, was no slavish pusher of inslant. Out of his high-stepping run and wheeling arm-swing, his pace could be little short of truly fast and his inswing, even with a worn ball, was late and sharp. He could, too, bowl the ball that went with his arm or, on a 'green' wicket, make his inswinger hold and, in contrast to many of his successors, he bowled to a full – even generous – length, backing his swing and change of line to take wickets. Fred Root was a consciously professional cricketer and, undoubtedly, contemporary feeling against leg

89

theory prevented him playing for England as often as he would have done in the post-1945 period. Certainly, none of his followers have excelled him.

A. P. F. Chapman

Through the twenties, for Berkshire, Cambridge University, Kent and England, Percy Chapman batted with a physically magnificent and mentally boyish quality of athleticism. He was a left-hand bat of fine strength and a wonderful eye, who sent the ball through the off side like a spear. He was technically fallible but, for several years, his physical attributes over-rode professional detection of his flaws: and for so long his batting was one of the glories of English cricket.

The same prodigal gifts and his contempt of danger made him a staggering close catcher, one who would push his hand in front of a full-blooded drive, confident that his fingers would close on it. In his heyday he was a truly spectacular cricketer.

In the first match of the 1924 series, at Edgbaston, Sutcliffe, Kilner, Chapman, Tate and G. E. C. Wood – the Cambridge University and Kent wicket-keeper – played their first Tests. Taylor won the toss after rain and sent England in to bat. Hobbs and Sutcliffe made 136 for the first wicket: England totalled 438 and then Tate – who took a wicket with his first ball in Test cricket – and Gilligan bowled out South Africa for 30. Following on, South Africa were a different side: Bob Catterall, a handsome and militant right-hand bat, scored 120 in a total of 390. Nevertheless, they lost by an innings and 18. Parkin took 0 for 18 and wrote himself out of Test cricket in a Sunday newspaper.

At Lord's, Catterall made another century. But Hobbs with 211 – the highest Test score thus far in England – Sutcliffe (122), Woolley (134*) and Hendren (50*) took England on to a dismaying 531 for two. Dick Tyldesley of Lancashire, a portly man whose mildly turning but accurate leg-breaks had a peculiarly hanging quality, helped Tate and Gilligan to bowl South Africa out twice. Again England won by an innings – and 18.

At Headingley, Tate took nine wickets: Hendren scored a century: England by nine wickets. Rain wiped out the last two matches: England won the series 3–0. South Africa had found a striking batsman in Catterall, but, apart from the patient leg-spinner, Pegler, and Parker, the pace-bowler called in from Lancashire league cricket, their bowling was threadbare.

England, on the other hand, could believe, with good reason, that they had struck a rich vein of talent.

Australia v England, 1924–25

A 4–1 result to a Test rubber sounds positive enough. Yet this defeat marked the turning of the tide towards England. On the one occasion – in the fourth Test at Melbourne – when England won the toss and batted, they won by an innings and 29.

It is probable that the rubber had been settled the previous July, when Gilligan was injured. There was no other adequate bowling partner for Tate who, nevertheless, in one of the greatest of all one-man bowling performances, set a new record with 38 wickets (at 23·18) in a Test series. Only two other bowlers of more than slow pace bowled for England. They were Gilligan, reduced now to medium (10 wickets at 51·9), and Douglas (one at 104). Apart from Tate, only Kilner (17 at 23·47) of the English bowlers took more than eleven wickets or had an average below 46.

Australia based their batting strategy on keeping out Tate at one end and taking runs at the other. With the support that any one of half a dozen English bowlers could have given twelve years before or six afterwards, Tate might have won the series for England. Perhaps, indeed, the written-out Parkin (200 wickets in England in 1924) or Root could have done it. As it was, Tate was a solitary menace and Collins, the new Australian captain, devoted himself to blunting his edge.

The other opening bat, Bardsley, was routed and Collins alone – putting defence first, using his pads with cold realism, shielding the other batsmen – prevented Tate from cutting through even more devastatingly than he did. So, Jack Ryder – an angular, devoted, right-hand bat – Johnnie Taylor – quick-footed batsman and outfield – and the rising power of Australian batting, Bill Ponsford, took the decisive runs from the slow bowlers. Sutcliffe, Hobbs, Hendren and Woolley batted so well that the regular Australian bowlers, Kelleway, Gregory and Mailey, were expensive and, at the end, Grimmett had better figures.

W. H. Ponsford

The heavily built and pugnacious-looking Victorian, Bill Ponsford, was the first of the modern school of record-breaking batsmen. In 1922–23 he broke the

Bill Ponsford (Victoria) The broad-based, phlegmatic batsman who first set the modern pattern of record-breaking scores: Brooks (Surrey) is the wicket-keeper

record for an individual innings with 429 against Tasmania: in the next Sheffield Shield season he averaged 88·16. He made a century in his first Test – against Gilligan's side – and in 1926–27 in Australia scored 214, 151, 352, 108 and 116 in consecutive matches. A year later he broke his own record with 437 for Victoria v Queensland. He was ill on the 1926 tour of England and a fractured hand kept him out of two Tests of 1932–33. Yet, but for Bradman, we should think of him as the Australian batting wonder.

Ponsford was an apparently clumsy mover, with an ugly habit of taking short fast bowling directed at the leg stump – which he enjoyed no more than most

batsmen – on his heavy stern. It seemed, too, that he often moved so far across the stumps that he was apt to be bowled behind his legs. Yet all this can detract little from his figures: in fourteen years of first class play he scored 13,819 runs at an average of 65·18. He was a relentless punisher of anything over-pitched, for his front-of-the-wicket strokes were not only strong but placed with considerable precision. Against fast and short bowling, his cutting and glancing, if not elegant, were well controlled and rarely lifted. A man of unfailing concentration, a durable player, always hard to get out, Ponsford was matched for consistency by few batsmen of our time.

Clarrie Grimmett (Victoria and South Australia) Wily and ageless, he snapped his leg-breaks and googlies nagglingly at batsmen, gave away nothing and, by his sharp spin, took much

C. V. Grimmett

With a bustling, almost round-arm action, Clarrie Grimmett bowled leg-break, googly and a 'flipper' which nipped straight through. His trajectory was low and ungenerous, his length remarkably tight for one who spun so much. Short and bony, with the air of a veteran from the start, observant and astute, Grimmett was, in the apt description of Neville Cardus, the 'Artful Dodger' of cricket. He was to remain a Test bowler – apparently no older and un-diminished in skill – for a dozen years to come.

England, though beaten, could return home con-fident that the corner had been turned. All they needed was that *one* extra bowler. On the Australian side, Gregory had declined from his high peak of pace and had no McDonald at the other end. It was Australia's turn to think.

HOBBS, THE MASTER

When Jack Hobbs came back from the Australian tour of 1924–25, he was forty-two years old. He was about to embark on an Indian summer more than seven years long, in which he reached such a standing in English cricket as only W. G. Grace had enjoyed before, and which no one since has ever approached. Four times in those years he was top of the first-class averages. In 1925 he led off with a dozen centuries by 20th July but then, unnerved for the first time – by the posse of press and film men who followed him, waiting for him to draw level with Grace's record of 126 centuries – he faltered for more than three weeks before, at Taunton, he equalled the record in the first innings and passed it in the second.

He could no longer play all the strokes of his youth, but the mellow certainty of his play revealed batting as a craft lifted near the level of art. Here, for once, was a public idol without feet of clay. The man could bat: and he had true humility and a flawless courtesy which came from the heart. Young men became better players for watching him; in that respect his influence was incalculable: any English batsman who grew up in those days could tell how much he learnt from 'The Master'.

It was one of the happinesses of Jack Hobbs's life to have been part of the return of English cricket to the high plateau and, when Collins brought his Australians to the series of 1926, Hobbs and Rhodes were co-opted as the first professionals to be members of an English selection committee.

In 1925 Yorkshire won the Championship without losing a match: Tate scored a thousand runs and took two hundred wickets for the third consecutive season, and 71,000 people attended the three days of Roy Kilner's benefit match at Leeds. In 1926, Lancashire – largely through Ernest Tyldesley, Harry Makepeace, Cecil Parkin and Ted McDonald – won the County Championship. Rhodes – rising forty-nine – was top of the first-class bowling averages and completed the double for the sixteenth time: Hobbs and Sandham put on 428 for Surrey's first wicket against Oxford University: and Essex and Somerset played a tie at Chelmsford.

For two years, however, cricketing England and Australia had been looking forward with unusual interest to the 1926 Test series.

Australia had two significant men who had not yet

Hobbs and Sutcliffe – the finest of all opening pairs; masters of the changing situation, they set a standard of mature, cool command which has never been equalled in Test cricket

played in a Test – Woodfull and Richardson.

W. M. Woodfull

As Ponsford's opening partner in the Victorian side, Bill Woodfull earned the nickname of 'The Unbowl-able'. He was well-built, as solid in appearance as in character. He batted right-handed with a short back-lift, an utterly – sometimes painfully – straight bat, and a text-book rectitude of stroke. He forced the ball away in front of the wicket through strength of fore-arm, but he was an inveterate gatherer of runs, scoring faster than he seemed to do because he had strokes to bring him one or two runs every time the bowler strayed from length or line. As a Test captain, in later years, Woodfull was eminently sound; he was modest and polite, never sought publicity, and made few mistakes. Between his first appearance in the

Sheffield Shield and his complete retirement to school-teaching, he scored 13,392 runs at an average, which may surprise some, of 65 runs an innings.

A. J. Richardson

Australia has produced few outstanding off-spinners by comparison with England, and Arthur Richardson might not have made the tour of 1926 if he had not been a worthwhile all-rounder. He was a right-handed batsman who used a bat of immense weight, which gave spectacular additional force to his driving, but restricted his other strokes. Strongly built, he played in spectacles – which did not seem to affect him – and for some years was a mainstay of the South Australian side. In Australian opinion, he tended to overdo 'leg theory' on turning wickets: he, for his part, felt that, on English pitches, he was wise to follow local prac-tice. He spun the ball hard but his Australian length left batsmen room to play back on English wickets. In 1926 he was entrusted with Australia's solitary and slim chance to win but, in the last analysis, he lacked the experience of English techniques to exploit it.

The English selectors had in mind seven players who had made the 1924–25 Australian tour. Their first priority was an opening bowler to pair with Tate: the candidates were Larwood, Geary and Root. They had been sufficiently impressed by Stevens to send him to South Africa in 1922–23: they were bound to consider Ernest Tyldesley of Lancashire as a batsman and, in English conditions, Parker of Gloucestershire suggested himself.

Harold Larwood

Every generation in every country where cricket is played has its symbolic fast bowler. For seven years, from 1926 to 1933 that figure, in England – and, if truth be told, in Australia as well – was 'Lol' Larwood. He was only of average height but he had strong hips and legs, the muscular back of a coal miner, and long arms. At the end of a menacing, rocking run, his right arm came over high and straight as a hop pole. He was a safe catch and good enough bat to score 98 against Australia, but as a fast bowler he is legendary.

His pace was that rare, vicious, shattering yard faster than that of other men legitimately called fast. He kept himself fit, worshipped bowling; linked his speed, eventually, to control of length and direction nearly as precise as a slow bowler's. He bowled a late outswinger, a break-back as sharp as that of the classical fast bowlers, and sometimes made the ball

93

Harold Larwood (Notts) Batsmen whose experience stretched back long before his day, and others who played into much later years, thought 'Lol' beyond all question, the fastest bowler they ever saw

run he was as fast as any bowler in England for several more years.

George Geary

During the twenties a group of English bowlers combined the merits of the old and the modern schools; they could swing, cut and spin, had length, stamina, tactical sense and fidelity. One of the best of them was George Geary, who, for Leicester, had to be an all-rounder and who at Headingley in 1926 served England well by his batting.

Over six feet tall, deep-chested, long-armed and with huge hands that made him a safe slip and a commanding manipulator of the ball, he bowled right-arm medium, a shade faster when conditions indicated increase. On a helpful wicket he could make the ball leap and turn; when the shine was on he could swing both ways, not extravagantly, but enough – and late. His length was impeccable and his judgement of a wicket unerring.

G. T. S. Stevens

Greville Stevens was an outstanding cricketer as a boy. He scored 466* in a house match at University College School and is the only player to have taken part in Gentlemen v Players while still at school. His talents were such that, though he never played a full first-class season after he came down from Oxford in 1923 (he played only seven matches for Middlesex in 1926), he was never out of the selectors' minds so long as he was available for even a limited number of matches.

He was, as by instinct, straight and correct in defence and he had, in the Woodfull manner, a shallow back-lift, but by his immense power of forearm he drove prodigious distances. He bowled leg-breaks and googlies with emphasis on spin, which produced some bad balls, but others good enough to beat the best batsman; he concealed his googly extremely well and never lost his leg-break. A capable catcher in the gully, alertly intelligent, with extensive capacity for enjoyment, he had much to offer to cricket and he left the game before it could spare him.

Ernest Tyldesley

The younger brother of the outstanding Edwardian batsman, 'J.T.', Ernest Tyldesley concealed similar resolution under a modest appearance. He and his cricket were well-mannered and, if his bat was a little crooked in backlift, his style was generally unexceptional.

run away off the seam. But his supreme asset was the highest peak of speed anyone now alive has ever seen produced by a legitimate action.

Experienced batsmen with thousands of runs under their belts were frightened to bat against Larwood. The observant student of *Wisden* will note frequent injuries or ailments that prevented men from playing against Notts in his heyday.

In 1926, only twenty-one, he was raw, lacking in the meticulous control and the experience of batsmen he learnt in the next few years. But he had the rare and unteachable gift of bowling a ball of such pace as whistled through the defence of experienced batsmen before their eyes were in – and sometimes after. He injured his left foot in Australia in 1933 and rarely, subsequently, bowled full out. But even off a shortened

He had the knack of the masters – making difficult bowling look simple. He was an accomplished bad-wicket player, poised and unhurriedly quick, a militant hooker and neat cutter of pace: and he passed the acid test of the matting wicket. Perhaps he was too quiet: almost unobtrusively he came to 102 centuries and throughout a career of twenty-seven years he averaged 45 runs an innings – five more than his more celebrated brother, and far more than a number of inferior players picked for England ahead of him. He received much less than his due from the selectors.

C. W. L. Parker

If there was an unluckier player in their period than Ernest Tyldesley it was, surely, Charlie Parker of Gloucester. It is quite incomprehensible that he played for England only once – against Australia at Manchester in 1921, when he took two for 32, which remains his entire Test tally.

Parker was a left-arm spin bowler, often nearer medium than slow in pace. On batsmen's wickets he lacked the flight or subtlety to match such slow left-arm masters as Rhodes, and he did not relish being hit. But, given a scrap of turn in a wicket, he would exploit it, and on a 'sticky' he was the most destructive spinner of his time. His low flight gave the batsman no opportunity to get to him, and his spin was so savage that it gave him lift as well as turn. Parker might have made a career as a golfer, and he did not emerge as a first-class bowler until 1920, when he was thirty-five: then, for another fifteen years, he was an utter destroyer. In his benefit match, against Yorkshire at Bristol in 1922, he hit the stumps with five consecutive balls, the second of which was a no ball. He could rub by as a batsman and, from 1921 to 1930, he should never have been left out of an English team in England if there was any possibility of rain, for on a wet wicket he could bowl out any side in the world.

Australia in England, 1926

The Tests of 1926 engrossed England – including several million people who never saw a ball bowled – as only two other series have done in this century – 1902, when England lost, and 1953 when, as in 1926, they beat Australia after a sadly long period of defeat.

Arthur Carr of Notts, a hard cricketer, forceful, straight batsman, keen close field and firm handler of men, was chosen as captain. At Trent Bridge, Root

Charlie Macartney (New South Wales) 'The Governor-General' – a militant batsman, brilliant, strong and aggressive

was picked as opening bowler with Tate, but after Hobbs and Sutcliffe had made 32, the game was washed out. At Lord's England played three pace bowlers – Tate, Root and Larwood. They went on in that order and took two wickets each: Bardsley, who carried his bat for 193, was the core of an Australian total of 383.

Now, after the years of waiting, England held a whip hand in batting: Hobbs (119) and Sutcliffe (82) made 182 for the first wicket and Woolley (87), Hendren (127*) and Chapman (50*) carried on to 475 for three declared. Macartney (133*) and Collins – 24 in two-and-a-half hours – were content to see Australia safely to a draw.

The third Test, at Leeds, was probably the most eventful draw ever played between the two countries. The wicket was soft after rain yet Parker, one of twelve English players summoned to the match, was left out and then Carr, winning the toss, sent Australia in to bat. From the first ball of the match – bowled by Tate – Bardsley was caught at slip, and Macartney edged the fifth to Carr, at third slip, and was dropped. Thus reprieved, Macartney, cutting and driving exultantly, went on to score a century before lunch, murdering Macaulay's bowling in the process. Woodfull went at his own pace to 117 and the second wicket did not fall until 235: Richardson made exactly 100 and the Australian total was 494. Geary and Macaulay's 108 for the ninth wicket could not save England from following on. But rain and an opening partnership of 156 by Hobbs and Sutcliffe left England to draw the game without anxiety.

At Old Trafford, Parker was again called to the match and even more inexplicably left out: his anger was justifiable. He thought there was a personal bias against him: if there was none before his outburst, there certainly was afterwards. Rain cut the first day's play to a few minutes. Carr was taken ill at the weekend and on Monday Jack Hobbs took over as the first professional to captain an official England team. Woodfull and Macartney (his third in consecutive Tests) again made centuries: Australia scored 335. England made 305 for five – Ernest Tyldesley top-scorer with 81 – in the draw which was inevitable in little more than two days left after rain.

So, after four draws, the decision went to the fifth Test at the Oval – to be played to a finish. England chose Brown as wicket-keeper, but he was injured and Strudwick kept the place: Rhodes, at forty-eight years old, came in: amazingly, Ernest Tyldesley was

dropped: and in a storm of controversy, Carr was replaced, in the team and the captaincy, by Percy Chapman.

It is now almost forty years ago since that match was played, but none since has so gripped England, and it was estimated that 103,000 people watched it.

Chapman won the toss and England batted on a two-paced, but not really difficult, wicket. Hobbs and Sutcliffe started fluently enough and had made 53 in the hour when Mailey – as he recalled ever after with mirth – bowled Hobbs with a dipping full toss. Mailey, spinning the ball hard and tossing it well up, went on to a characteristic set of figures – six for 138 – and only Sutcliffe and Rhodes solidly, Chapman and Tate brightly, brought England to as many as 280. Larwood took the early wicket expected of him and Australia were 59 for four and 90 for five: but in their traditional fashion they recovered, trebled the score for the last five wickets and, with 302, took a first innings lead of 22. No doubt Chapman, who had no experience of captaincy, received sound advice from Hobbs and Rhodes – and Rhodes, brought on at appropriate moments, took two for 35.

Hobbs and Sutcliffe made 49 together by the end of the second day. There was a thunderstorm in the night and sun the next morning. Was the wicket difficult? It usually is at The Oval after rain. It seems certain that Richardson and Macartney lacked the experience of such purely English conditions to exploit them properly. It was said – and denied – that Hobbs and Sutcliffe bluffed Collins by treating Richardson with exaggerated respect. There is, though, no doubt that Richardson made the ball turn considerably and occasionally quickly. The conclusive factor was that Hobbs (100) and Sutcliffe (161) batted with high competence. They made 172 for the first wicket and, though no one else except Tate scored more than thirty, an England total of 436 set Australia 415 to win on a pitch stirred by more rain.

In such conditions, Larwood made the ball rise steeply and Rhodes – who had played for England before Larwood was born – made it turn: they chopped Australia down to 35 for four. No effective recovery was possible: England won by 289 runs and took a Test rubber from Australia for the first time since 1912.

For Arthur Mailey (nine wickets for 266 in the match), Charlie Macartney (an average of 94·6 for the series), Bardsley (twice captain in the absence of Collins, and who averaged 57·75), Andrews, Collins and Richardson, this was their last Test match. Of Australian bowlers, only Mailey and Grimmett took more than four wickets: Gregory's three cost almost a hundred runs each. For Australia it was the end of an era and a generation.

England, at last, could contemplate resources adequate for several years to come, and in 1927, Walter Hammond stepped up to his place as one of the four greatest batsmen of this century.

Walter Hammond

Walter Hammond's potential as a cricketer was obvious when he was no more than a boy. Only a protest against his Gloucestershire qualification and an illness in 1926 delayed his advance.

In 1927, a few weeks before his twenty-fourth birthday, he scored a thousand runs in twenty-two days of May – the same time as W.G. had taken thirty-two years earlier: no one else has ever done it so quickly.

Walter Hammond had only to walk three or four strides to identify himself as an athlete, and he could turn to any ball game, without practice, sometimes without previous experience at all, and play it with an ability which reduced ordinary men to admiring envy. He was one of the three batsmen – Hobbs and Bradman were the others – who, at their best and given reasonable circumstances, could have backed themselves to score a century.

His fine proportions partly concealed his great physical strength while, even when he put on considerable weight in his later years, he still moved gracefully – and quickly. He regarded the hook as uneconomic: otherwise he had a scoring stroke for any ball which did not compel defence. Memory recalls him hitting through the covers, from front foot or back, like a roll of thunder, so that the fastest fieldsmen could not hope to stop it unless it came straight to them. The suggestion that he could not play on the leg side is nonsense to anyone who ever saw him go down on his right knee and sweep so accurate a left-arm spinner as Verity, off a length and the stumps, against the break to square-leg. There were frequent occasions when Hammond scored almost twice as fast as anyone else in a match: yet he always gave the impression of playing within himself. He struck some of the strongest and longest blows of modern times, yet he did so without the impression of effort.

No single incident reveals Hammond's high skill

Wally Hammond (Gloucestershire) One of the half-dozen greatest players in cricket history, he had the strength of a giant, the lissom poise of a dancer and he hit a cricket ball with magnificent clean power. The blue handkerchief showing from his trousers pocket was his only mannerism

A. P. – 'Titch' – Freeman (Kent) whose slow spin and flight tempted all but the best of inter-war batsmen into self-destruction

The England side of 1927–28 to South Africa, without Hobbs, Tate and Larwood (a tour to Australia lay only a year ahead) drew the Test rubber without discovering anything fresh. For South Africa, Catterall and Taylor were still by far the best batsmen, but they were relieved to find two fresh bowlers in Cyril Vincent – intelligent slow left-arm – and Bissett who, with a gale at his back, was fast enough to win the fifth Test.

In the batsman's summer of 1928 Hobbs had a batting average of 82, and nine others more than 60. Larwood was first in the bowling table and next to him was Freeman, with the record number of 304 wickets in a season.

'Tich' Freeman

In each of the six seasons from 1928 to 1933, A. P. – 'Tich' – Freeman took more than 250 wickets. He was an extremely small and unathletic-looking man whose hand would barely go halfway round a cricket ball. Yet, for year after year, he bowled his leg-breaks and googlies to an unwavering length. He also took wickets – usually lbw – with a ball which gathered speed after pitching and went straight through. Batsmen of his day argued bitterly as to whether this was a deliberate top-spinner or a 'leg-break that didn't': Freeman never enlightened them.

At the highest level he was not an effective bowler. The quick-footed batsman who went down the pitch to him could punish him heavily: and he never worried the better Australians. But he was a destroyer of the rank and file of county batting. His spin was not great – enough to beat the bat was enough for him – but his flight was not easy to judge and he was never afraid to put his fieldsmen deep and pitch the ball up near – but just short of – half-volley length. He stands second to Rhodes for the number of wickets taken in a career – 3,776 – and since the day in 1936 when he played his last match for Kent, there has been no one like him.

An injury kept Jack Hobbs out of cricket from early June until mid-July and in the Surrey side much responsibility rested on the shoulders of his opening partner, Andrew Sandham. Sandham – like Percy Holmes who went in first with Sutcliffe – might well have played many more than his fourteen Tests in any other period. He was a neat batsman, imperturbable and correct, an excellent cutter, and he scored 107 centuries, modestly content to play in the shadow of Jack Hobbs whom he liked and admired so much.

more clearly than the occasion when, joking with a famous spin bowler who had just tumbled out a county side on a turning wicket, he said 'I don't know how they get out to you – I could play you with the edge of the bat'. The bowler bridled: they went out to the still difficult pitch and Hammond, with the bat sideways on, played an entire over of jumping off-breaks back to the incredulous bowler.

In 1927–28, he opened England's bowling against South Africa and, as a fast-medium outswinger (when roused, genuinely fast) he could have been a Test cricketer if he had never made a run. At slip his catching has not been excelled in our time, though it may be equalled by the Australian, Bobby Simpson.

Walter Hammond gave the public his performance at cricket, but nothing more. He allowed himself a single mannerism – the corner of a blue and white handkerchief showing from his right trouser pocket. For the rest, his life was his own.

98

Douglas Jardine (Surrey) Of cool mind and unflinching courage, he studied cricket and played it hard: if the Harlequin cap he wore angered his opponents, he was amused

Jack White (Somerset) whose slow left-arm bowling was so accurate and so subtle in flight as virtually to decide a Test series against Australia

When Hobbs did come back, it was to extend his dominion by scoring a century for England against the West Indies. If that was not a testing series, it gave England the chance to complete their team-building for the Australian tour ahead by bringing in four players who were to leave their marks on Test cricket; Jardine, Leyland, White and Duckworth.

D. R. Jardine

Many experienced English cricketers still contend that they never played under a better captain than Douglas Jardine. An Oxford blue, he matured as a batsman in the strong Surrey batting side of the nineteen-twenties. His strength was as a defensive player, for in resistance he best expressed himself. He was essentially a modern player, somewhat limited in his off-side play but completely equipped on the leg, playing his strokes late and powering them from the wrists and forearms. His craggy height, upstanding position at the wicket and patrician features gave him an imperious air and, against fast bowling, he was at his stern, uncompromising best. He had a keen, cool, analytical brain and, as a captain, was cast in the modern mould; strict, decisive, careful never to lose a scrap of advantage, and, when he could not win, a master of the rearguard action.

J. C. White

Almost all the famous line of slow left-arm bowlers were genuine spinners; but Jack White, of Somerset, was a flight bowler. On a good wicket he hardly ever turned the ball and, even on a responsive one, spin was not his strongest asset. With a rather plodding approach but a mechanically sound action, he made the ball dip into the bat through the air and took more than a few wickets when batsmen who did not know him played for the turn which was not there. Sinewy and strong, he was as nearly tireless as any cricketer who ever played and, at the end of a four or five hour spell, he was as accurate as when he started. His variations were minute and were aimed largely at deceiving the batsman as to pace and pitch, making him play fractionally too soon or too late. A workmanlike batsman and a faithful, if not nimble, fieldsman, he was a capable all-rounder and a sound captain.

Maurice Leyland

Unless it be George Hirst, no cricketer ever more truly reflected the best qualities of Yorkshire cricket than Maurice Leyland. His burly build and lack of height militated against the usually accepted canons of style, but his left-handed batting had an unforgettable, sturdy character. His heavy forearms created the impression, in some of his strokes, of a man wielding a hammer, and he could hit with flailing power. For all his thick physique, he was quick on his feet and, while he had all the skill on the leg side that the cricket of his period demanded, he was strong through the covers and less reluctant than many of his contemporaries to lift the off or straight drive over the field. Pre-eminently, however, Maurice Leyland was the man for a difficult situation: then, defending to rescue an innings or hitting to win a match, he was at his best. For all his good nature, he relished a fight; he was one of those rare men whom challenge and crisis really did make a better player. He was an eager outfield, a cool, safe catcher and a quick, low thrower: and he bowled the 'Chinaman' with amusement and occasional success.

George Duckworth

The England selectors made several experiments before they settled on George Duckworth as Herbert Strudwick's successor. He was to lose his place to Ames's superior batting, but for at least eight years there was no better wicket-keeper in the world. The first of the modern, acrobatic school of wicket-keepers, he covered much ground standing back to fast bowling and he took McDonald's deliberately wide range of bounce and line with great certainty. He was, though, a complete wicket-keeper who stood up

to the stumps to Tate at his fastest, and took spin bowling safely. His ear-splitting appeals were a reflection of his keenness and he was always *in* a game, a great asset to any captain in lifting the spirits of a flagging team.

It was long since English cricket had been so rich in talent. Indeed, the batting was so massive that Charles Hallows, the Lancashire left-hand bat who scored a thousand runs in May, could not find a place in the team to Australia in September.

THE FIELD WIDENS

The West Indies became the fourth Test-playing country in 1928 when their side under R. K. Nunes met England in three matches. It was a dismal start – they were beaten by an innings in each game.

Francis, Constantine and Griffith made an awkward fast-bowling combination on fast pitches. But in the Tests they were tameable; and the batting proved so naïve that their highest individual score was Roach's 53 at the Oval, and Freeman, in his only run of success in Tests, took 22 of their wickets at 13·72.

Learie Constantine

The number of cricketers who have positively drawn large crowds is small – W. G. Grace, Ranji, Gilbert Jessop, Jack Hobbs, Victor Trumper, Don Bradman, Keith Miller, Walter Hammond, Denis Compton, Ted Dexter, Harold Larwood, Garfield Sobers, Trueman, Bland, Graeme Pollock and Learie Constantine. 'Cons' was the finest fieldsman cricket has ever known. He was also a right-arm bowler, first of pace and later of a mixture which included almost everything the hand can do with a cricket ball, and a volcanic batsman. A gloriously exuberant cricketer with a superbly lissom body, his outfielding – running, swooping pick-up, long, low, fast returns and safe catching would alone have been enough to establish his reputation. For more than good measure he was a fine close field, brave and intensely quick. His batting was probably nearer to that of Jessop than anyone else's: cutting, driving, hooking, indulging every kind of extravagance and rebelling against being pinned down; if he batted for an hour, a crowd would be entranced – and he would probably have made a century.

In Test cricket his batting did not come off: his

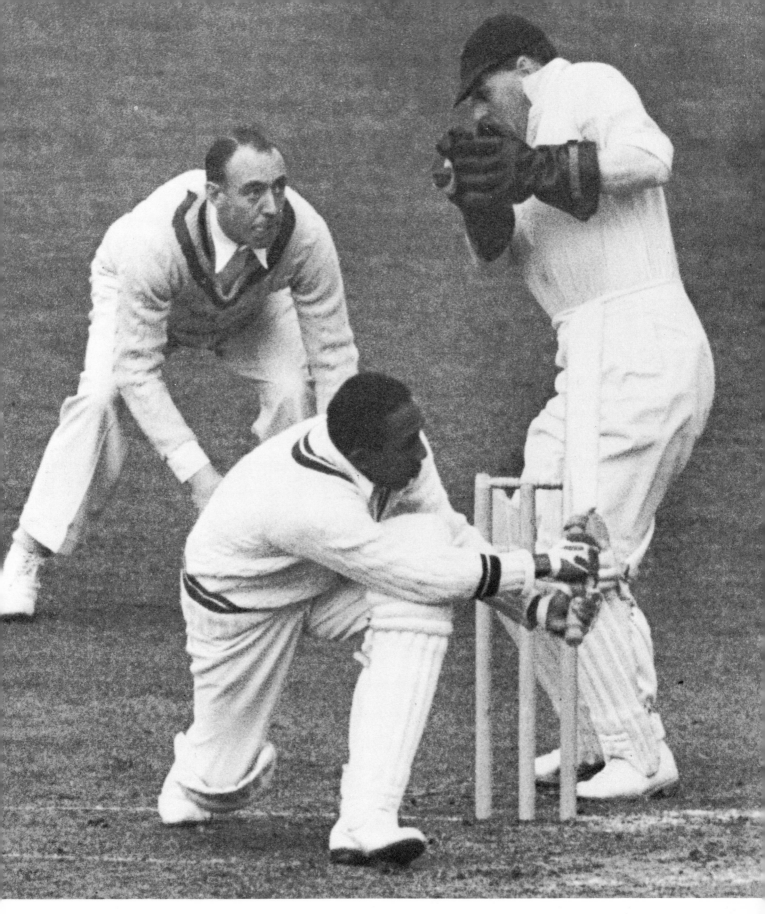

Learie – now Sir Learie – Constantine (Trinidad) The most dynamic cricketer of his time: explosively unorthodox batsman, exuberantly fast bowler and the greatest of all fieldsmen: slip is Garland-Wells, wicket-keeper, Brookes, both of Surrey

average was only 19, and he had a disastrous tour of Australia in 1930–31: but his fast bowling and his fielding would have taken him into any side, and he will be remembered, vividly and pleasurably, long after many who made more runs have been forgotten.

The West Indies had never won a Test in England until 1950 but they drew one series and won another, by their batting power on their own wickets, before the 1939 war.

George Headley

The first West Indian batsman of world stature was George Headley. Born in Panama of Barbadian parents, he played for Jamaica and remains that island's finest batsman. Headley was below average height, quick on his feet and perhaps more completely a back foot player than any other batsman who is entitled to the label 'great'. Completely self-taught, he was difficult to contain on fast pitches for he had strokes all round the wicket and, moving back on to his stumps, he drove through mid-on with remarkable facility. He was, too, the first West Indian batsman to look sound on bad wickets and for six years he must have been worth a place in a World eleven.

Apart from the dogged Ivan Barrow, Headley had little batting support in England and, though the West Indian sides of the early years produced fast bowlers – such as Constantine, Hylton, Francis, Griffith and Martindale – with impressive regularity, their spin bowling was never strong until 1950.

Before 1914, two of the best West Indians had come to England to play – S. G. Smith for Northants and C. A. Olivierre for Derbyshire – and subsequently their domestic play suffered from the loss of players like Constantine, Headley, Martindale, St Hill and Achong to English league cricket.

New Zealand entered Test cricket in 1929–30, when A. H. H. – Harold – Gilligan took a fair England second team there and played four Tests, of which England won one and three were drawn.

New Zealand have never been a power in cricket: indeed, Australia have only once accorded them a Test Match – beating them by an innings and 103 runs in March 1946. Their home cricket, however, has always been happy, and Test tours have kept it refreshed. Their early Test sides, captained by T. C. Lowry, a wicket-keeper-batsman who previously played for Cambridge University and Somerset, could point to a leg-spinner of ability in W. E. Merritt, a capable wicket-keeper in K. C. James, and a first-class

batsman in C. S. Dempster: it was unfortunate for New Zealand cricket that all three were attracted to England by the prospect of professionalism or regular cricket which did not exist for them at home.

J. W. E. Mills, a slim, correct, opening bat; C. F. W. Allcott, a hard-working slow left-arm bowler; I. B. Cromb, a new ball bowler who made some hurry off the pitch; and the all-rounders, R. C. Blunt, M. L. Page and H. G. Vivian; all played their parts in the establishment of New Zealand cricket. J. A. Cowie, the best of their pace bowlers, was unlucky that the 1939 war took what should have been his richest years.

Their gravest loss was Martin Donnelly, a promising nineteen-year-old when he toured England in 1937 who was, by the nineteen-forties, arguably the finest left-hand batsman in the world. He spent some post-war years in England and then settled in Australia.

India, somewhat formally inducted to Test cricket with a single match at Lord's, in 1932, were the most impressive of the three 'new' countries on entry. Indeed, if they could have included Duleepsinhji and the Nawab of Pataudi – as it must be felt they should have been able to do – they might have given England a close game. To recall that side – captained by C. K. Nayudu – is to realize the vast change in the character of Indian cricket in less than thirty years. Naoomal Jeoomal and, at need, Wazir Ali were competent defensive batsmen, but the rest batted in a style obviously founded on the cricket of English servicemen in India. Nayudu himself was the perfect example of this early Indian school of batting. Tall and lithe, he was a militant player who used his feet well and drove very hard, cut brightly and revealed his fast-wicket upbringing with a horizontal-bat stroke to the on side. The fact that the team had a genuine fast bowler, that the bowling was an attacking and not a restrictive force, and that the fielding was eager and often of the highest-class, completed a picture far removed from Indian sides of recent years.

The massive Mahomed Nissar was a genuinely fast bowler who, from his height, made the ball rise awkwardly, and who bowled a violent break-back. Amar Singh – also right-arm – had an ugly run-up, but was one of the best fast-medium bowlers of his time; he cut the ball, swung it both ways, had a disconcerting dip in flight and, in English conditions, made the ball do some remarkable things; he came off the pitch almost as surprisingly fast as Tate. Jehangir Khan, a busy medium pacer, also had useful speed off the wicket and was a thoroughly serviceable all-round cricketer, a player of character, determined and zestful.

When D. R. Jardine took an England second team to India in 1933–34 – winning two Tests and leaving one drawn – the change in that country's cricket was already becoming apparent and, on matting wickets, only Amar Singh matched the resource of the England bowlers.

Their 1936 team to England had a fine opening pair in Merchant and Mushtaq Ali, and substantially the same bowlers as in 1932, but there were deep rifts between the players – Amarnath was sent back home part way through the tour – and in direction, tactics and temperament they fell far below Test standard.

In 1930–31, the West Indies went to Australia, where their bowling was savagely mauled by Ponsford and Bradman, and they lost three Tests by an innings and another by ten wickets. But in the last game of the series, Martin – a solid left-hander – and Headley both made centuries, and, after rain, the fast bowling of Francis, Griffith and Constantine, with Martin – slow left-arm – won the match. They had to wait twenty years for the opportunity to meet Australia again.

After their Australian tour of 1931–32, Cameron's South Africans went on to New Zealand, where they won the two Tests quite easily. In recent years the two sides have played two happy series in South Africa.

The extension of Tests created two levels of international play. While the West Indies soon moved into the higher class, South Africa have had an erratic career, alternating between strong sides and weak, but, in general, having a small nucleus of top-class players. New Zealand, India and Pakistan – who played their first Test in 1952–53 – however, have remained on a lower level of performance and while, in India and Pakistan, the difference has often been reduced by the effect of the climate on visiting sides, none of them have ever been anything like a match for a full strength England or Australian team in its own country.

There has been a steady replacement of matting wickets with turf through India and Pakistan, but pitches there have become so easy that they might be prepared specifically for the breaking of batting records. As a result, Indian batsmen in particular have developed a 'stay there and the runs will come' attitude; bowlers have been discouraged from such

pace as Nissar commanded, and outcricket has become a chore. The batsmen, artificially built up at home, have proved sadly vulnerable in other countries, especially to fast bowling.

THE BRADMAN ERA

England won the 1928–29 series in Australia by four Tests to one and were clearly, though not widely, the stronger side. They had so much batting that Mead made the top score – 73 – in the second innings of the first Test and was never picked again. Leyland did not get into the eleven until the last Test, whereupon he made a hundred. Hammond, with four centuries – one in each innings at Adelaide – had the prodigious average of 113·12 for the series and Hendren, Sutcliffe and Hobbs all had figures of more than fifty. But Jackson, Bradman, Ryder and Woodfull all averaged over fifty for Australia.

The conclusive factor was the English outcricket. The catching was almost faultless. Their decisive bowlers were not, as had been expected, Larwood and Tate – though they took 18 and 17 wickets respectively – but Geary and White. Geary was first in the averages with 19 wickets at 25·10 but White had 25 at 30·4, and he bowled 406 overs. Day after day his bowling was as steady as if grooved and, in the tense closing phase of the fourth Test, when England won by only twelve runs, he carried on with perfect precision and took the last two wickets in his sixty-fifth over to finish with eight for 126 in the innings.

Grimmett, easily the chief wicket taker for Australia, with 23, had an average of 44·52: Don Blackie, an old fashioned type of off-spinner who spin-swerved away and broke back, played for the first time in a Test at the age of 46 – the oldest man to appear for Australia – and had 14 wickets at 31·71.

The series was full of incident. At Brisbane, where Gregory broke down – never to play Test cricket again – England won, after rain, by the record margin of 675 runs. On a bad wicket, Australia were all out for 66: Woodfull carried his bat for a highly expert 30*. At Sydney, England – Hammond 251 – had a record Test innings total of 636 – and won by eight wickets. At Melbourne, when England needed 332 to win, Sutcliffe, Hobbs and Jardine played three masterly bad wicket innings, the quality of which was emphasized when four wickets were lost in scoring the last 14 runs to win.

Adelaide saw a dramatic Test Match. Hobbs and Sutcliffe began it with a stand of 143 and then, apart from Hammond – 119* – the rest of the innings slipped away to 334 all out. Australia reversed the process: they were 19 for three before Jackson, in his first Test, stabilized their batting with his memorable 164: Ryder, Bradman, a'Beckett and Oldfield backed him capably and Australia had a first innings lead of 35. Again the English batting was patchy: except Hammond with 177 – his second century of the match – Jardine (98) and Tate (47), no one made more than 17 and Australia needed 348 to win. Ryder again batted toughly, if luckily, and they had reached 320 with seven wickets down when, with the game in the balance, Hobbs ran out Bradman from cover point. White – 124 overs and thirteen wickets for 256 in the match – coolly bowled England to a twelve run win.

The gap was narrowing. Back to Melbourne where Jack Hobbs, in his last Test in Australia, made a calm, certain 142 in three-and-a-quarter hours, and Leyland, playing against Australia for the first time, 137 at number seven; Hendren's 95 was the other high score in a total of 519. For Australia, Woodfull and Bradman made centuries; Geary bowled 81 eight-ball overs to take five for 105 and England had a narrow lead of 28. Then England collapsed like a side of tired men: Hobbs with 65, Leyland 53* and Tate 54 found little difficulty, but Wall took five for 66 and Australia were left needing only 286 to win. No batsman failed and, after two escapes in the field, they won by five wickets.

In the first Test Australia played a new batsman, D. G. Bradman, who went in at number seven, seemed somewhat out of his depth against Tate, scored 18 and 1, and was dropped. He was brought back for the third Test and his scores for the rest of the series were 79, 112, 40, 58, 123 and 37*. He was to play for Australia for another nineteen years and, in that entire period, they lost only one Test rubber.

Don Bradman

Only W. G. Grace towered so high over the cricket of a period as Don Bradman. Jack Hobbs was the equal of either in skill, but to him cricket was always a game: he lacked the single-minded determination to succeed of the other two.

There are many points to be made about Don – now Sir Donald – Bradman: but the first must be that he approached more nearly to infallibility than any other batsman. One in every three of the innings he played was a century: over a career of twenty-one years, he had an average in all matches of 95·14: in Tests of 99·94: these are figures so far above anyone else's as to set Bradman completely alone as a run-scorer.

His style was complete utility. He lacked the advantage of height but he was compactly built, with wide shoulders, steely wrists, leanly muscular forearms and neat feet. He was as fast as a cat in movement and never off balance. He had every 'business' stroke in the book and a number – often improvised – which have never been defined but which he, in his speed of judgement and sense of striking, could make work. In many hands the hook was a risky stroke: but when Bradman played it he rolled his wrists – in a masterpiece of timing – and kept the ball down.

He could bat on bad wickets, but it seemed that he did not care to do so. He was interested in runs and, unlike most record-breakers, he was never content to let them come: he *made* them, and made them quickly. High among his merits comes the certainty of his punishment of the bad ball. More consistently than any other player, he hit the bad ball for four: and he would take a single or two runs from a ball only marginally off line, which most other players would have been content to stop.

He played, altogether, 338 innings and made only 16 'ducks': he was only seven times out in the nineties – he was too much of a realist to believe that batting was different on the brink of a century: and only fifteen times between 100 and 109 – he did not relax when he had scored a hundred.

Bradman had, so far as could be ascertained, no real weakness. Like any other batsman, he was more vulnerable to the perfect length, fast turning leg-break or googly, or the extremely fast ball on the leg stump, than to others inherently less good. But he was a greater batsman, and his figures are relatively more impressive, because for twenty years he was the primary target in world cricket. Such was his standing that, if a young bowler hit his stumps in the nets, it would be prominent news in the sports pages of the press. Timing, patience; an acute tactical judgement which told him when to attack a bowler, when to defend; touch and placing; unwinking concentration and unfailing run-hunger: he had all the attributes of the great batsman. He set out to break all the batting records, and he succeeded.

A fit, fast, certain outfield, he moved later to mid-off

Don – now Sir Donald – Bradman (N.S.W. and South Australia) the most relentless and least fallible of all run-makers

or cover point where he never nodded, and could observe the game more closely. As a captain he was firm, astute, with an almost uncanny gift for reading a game and foreseeing its developments. He was as hard as Armstrong or Jardine but never paraded his toughness. In 1948, full of years and honours and certain of winning the rubber, he could at last relax. In that year, for the first time, he appeared fallible, especially at the start of an innings when he took longer than of old to accustom himself to the pace of the pitch – but he averaged 72·57 for the series. He captained that overwhelmingly strong side with the air of an elder statesman, and received a knighthood at the end of the tour. He continues, powerful and clear-thinking in the councils of the game. His is modern cricket's most complete success-story.

A. A. Jackson

In this – 1928–29 – series, Bradman made no deeper impression than another fresh Australian player, Archie Jackson. A slim, poised, right-hand bat, Jackson was cast in the mould of Trumper, different in method, because he was opposed by a different type of outcricket, but with the same vitality and joy in his play. At seventeen he 'walked' a place in the New South Wales team and averaged 58 in Sheffield Shield matches: at eighteen he scored two centuries in a match against South Australia: and he was only nineteen when he scored a century in his first Test (the youngest man to perform the feat). If his square driving of fast bowling made a deep impression because of its unusual strength and certainty, he had every stroke and the ability, through his speed and

H. G. – 'Nummy' – Deane (Transvaal) One of the wisest and most understanding of Test captains, he made his team stronger than the apparent total of its component parts

adjustment, to attack bowling which pinned down other batsmen. Percy Fender described him as 'the finest player at his age I have ever seen'. This was Jackson's short life of glory. He came once to England – in 1930 – but showed only glimpses of his quality, for he was already a sick man and, on 16th February 1932, the day when England beat Australia at Brisbane and won The Ashes, he died, only 23 years old.

In the same Australian season Alan Kippax (260*) and Hal Hooker (62) set one of the most remarkable records in cricket. Coming together when New South Wales, with one wicket standing, were 263 behind Victoria on the first innings, they batted for over five hours in a last wicket stand of 307. It remains the record last wicket stand for all cricket. Nor was it a merely mathematical feat – it won the match *and* the Sheffield Shield.

The rising power of Australian batting conditioned the English players' and selectors' thinking in the

home series with South Africa in 1929. England took the rubber by 2–0 but, despite experiments, added no probables to their list for the Australian visit in 1930.

South Africa, cutting their losses, dropped a number of their older players and sent a young side under Deane.

H. G. Deane

Few captains in cricket history have achieved so much of far-reaching importance in a single tour as H. G. – 'Nummy' – Deane did for South Africa in 1929. He brought over a team in which only three men – himself, Taylor and Catterall – had been to England before. At one point on the tour, injuries so far reduced the strength of the side that they sent for J. P. Duminy, who was on holiday in Switzerland, to complete the eleven for the third Test. Yet, given the solitary advantage of a dry summer, Deane moulded his raw players, brought up on matting wickets, into a happy side which achieved far more than could have been reasonably expected and which formed the basis of South African cricket for years to come.

Deane was a friendly guide, perceptive, quick to appreciate and harness players' gifts. He was a brave catcher, and a batsman whose intelligence lifted his performance. At the Oval, after South Africa had been in trouble at 20 for three, Deane and Taylor saved them with a fourth wicket stand of 214. Using their feet well to 'Tich' Freeman, who had upset their batting in earlier games, they hit him out of Test cricket with an analysis of 0 for 169.

H. G. Owen-Smith

A natural athlete, 'Tuppy' Owen-Smith was a triple Oxford Blue – at cricket, rugby and boxing – and captained England at rugby. He was only twenty when he made his first impression on Test cricket. In the Leeds Test of 1929, England seemed to be winning easily when he made his century – completing it in the course of a South African record last wicket stand, with Bell, of 103, to alter the whole shape of the game and reduce England's winning margin to five wickets – which was, in fact, more precarious than it sounds.

Owen-Smith was a gay and nimble cricketer, eager and quick, yet cool in assessment. He was not only sufficiently fast to move down the wicket to spin bowlers, but accurate in his judgement of their pitch. He was a fine driver and puller of slow bowling, a dextrous cutter and hooker of pace. In the covers his speed, balance and ball-sense made him thrilling to

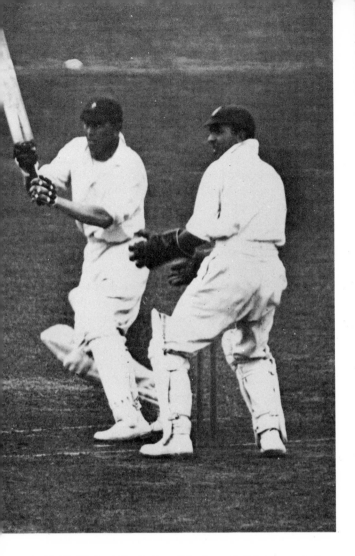

H. W. Taylor (Natal) One of the finest of all batsmen, who has received less than his due; the only player ever to master the bowling of S. F. Barnes on a matting wicket. The wicket-keeper is L. E. G. Ames

H. G. – 'Tuppy' – Owen-Smith (Western Province) Boxer, rugby player, cricketer: he relished battle but never lost his sense of humour: Frank Chester is the umpire

watch. In the days of the thirties, when Hendren stood at slip and any of Owen-Smith, Robins, Human, Hulme, Carris and Hart spanned the arc between third man and mid-off to a leg-spinner or slow left-arm bowler, the Middlesex off side fielding was an exhilarating spectacle.

Owen-Smith was one of the most popular of cricketers because his play reflected the sparkle of the man himself. He could be a responsible player – he enjoyed contest – but he faced responsibility gaily as well as staunchly.

Bruce Mitchell

For twenty years the start of the South African innings saw Bruce Mitchell, tall, slim, fair and quiet, walking out to open the innings. Yet he came to England in 1929 as an all-rounder who started the

tour as a number seven batsman and a change bowler of leg-breaks. By the time of the first Test, Deane had moved him up the batting order to number one, where he proceeded to make 88 in seven hours. He and Bob Catterall put on over a hundred for the first wicket in each innings and Mitchell's place was established. He continued, throughout his career, to be primarily a defensive batsman, pleasantly upright in style, able to play a graceful and often powerful off drive but, most of all, a man of impeccably correct defence, dedicated, concentrated. A superb slip catcher, he was one of the most useful South African cricketers of modern times.

H. B. Cameron

The 1929 South Africans pleased crowds by their play and their personalities. One of their most attractive figures was 'Jock' Cameron, a wicket-keeper-batsman of high quality. When the situation demanded it, he could play in strokeless and reliable defence, but it was his nature to hit the ball: he was an immense, straight-batted driver and an impulsive but effective hooker, good enough to make fast hundreds without mistakes.

As a wicket-keeper, he occasionally irritated purists by casual, one-handed and sometimes untidy taking of returns from the field, but so long as there was the chance of taking a wicket he was alert and adroit, working close to the stumps and as fast a stumper of the batsman who did no more than lift his heel as anyone in his time. He died suddenly and tragically on his return from the England tour of 1935.

In their match with Wales at Colwyn Bay, the South Africans once again faced Sydney Barnes, so often the destroyer of their batting in the years before the first World War: he was now 56, but he took ten of their wickets in the match for 90 runs and they thought him as fine a bowler as any they faced on the tour.

Notts, with their battery of pace bowlers in support of the batting of Gunn and Whysall, won the County Championship. It is probable that fast bowlers were favoured by the two new experimental rules, which applied in Championship matches only. The first provided for a larger wicket – an inch higher and an inch wider: the second made it possible for a batsman to be lbw even though the ball had snicked his bat or his hand. The larger wicket stayed: the 'snick' rule, however, was discontinued after 1934.

Bowlers in the 1929–30 series between England and the West Indies were swamped by the batting of Headley (two centuries in the Test at Georgetown), Roach (209 in the same match), Hendren (an average of 115·5) and Sandham – 325 at Kingston, where England, in their first innings, set a new record total of 849. Each side won one of the two Tests that were finished.

England v Australia, 1930

Even before the season of 1930 began, the talk among cricketers was all of the Australians. It was thought that their bowling was thin. In the event Grimmett, with his infinite capacity for work, took more than twice as many Test wickets as anyone else on the side – 29 in 394 overs. His assistance, loyal but uninspired, came from Wall – straight and steady but not quite fast; Fairfax, big, fast-medium, right-arm, who bowled well within himself; and Hornibrook, slow left-arm, a plodder on good wickets, something more when the ball would turn. There was talk of Ponsford the record breaker, of Woodfull, the amazing young Jackson and Bradman: the four of them were linked in the public mind as forming a mighty core of batting.

The tour had barely begun, however, when Bradman stepped up to the isolated eminence he was to enjoy for a generation. Had he never played, we should talk of Ponsford, Woodfull and McCabe as the three great Australian batsmen of those days. But they, and a number of their capable successors, were overshadowed by this springy little man with the vast capacity for scoring runs.

In the first match of the tour, at Worcester, he scored 236, quite overshadowing Woodfull's faultless innings of 133: in the next game, 185* against Leicester. A score in the seventies, one in the eighties, two in the forties, then 252* against Surrey. Ponsford's 220* against Oxford University passed almost unnoticed. Bradman was headline news. On 31st May he came to the Hampshire match needing 46 runs to complete a thousand by the end of May (not a thousand in May: the first part of his Worcester innings was played on 30th April). Hampshire won the toss; Grimmett (seven for 39) bowled them out and Bradman opened the Australian innings. As he moved through the thirties rain began to fall, increasing in intensity until, when his score was 43, Newman bowled one down the leg side, Bradman – infallibly Bradman-like – hit it firmly wide of long-leg for four, reached 1,001, and the players ran for the pavilion: there was no more play that day.

On Monday, Bradman went on to 191 and he now commanded expert attention throughout the country. All at once he – not Woodfull, Ponsford or Jackson, but Bradman – was the problem for England.

Was he vulnerable at any particular point? If so, it was not obvious. To Tate – who had harried him in his first Test? Perhaps. To high pace? Possibly: most batsmen are. It was noted, too, that since he had been in England his wicket has gone four times to leg-break and googly bowlers; and acute observers suspected that he could not 'pick' the googly.

On this not unreasonable hypothesis, the selectors set out to probe him with the best concealed googly bowling at their disposal – that of R. W. V. Robins and I. A. R. Peebles.

R. W. V. Robins

The prototype of the modern, expert, serious amateur, Walter Robins had the natural gifts of an all-round cricketer, a questing mind and a restless, competitive attitude to the game.

He was an outstanding schoolboy all-rounder and played for Middlesex while still at Highgate. He owed his first two Cambridge blues to his batting and fielding: his spin bowling in 1928 came as something of a surprise.

The key to his cricket was urgency; he could not bear a static cricket match. Physically trim, and nimble, he was a fast, keen fieldsman, brilliant in the covers. His batting was restricted by lack of height, which left him at a disadvantage with the lifting ball and may have influenced his tactics in constantly trying to 'get at' the bowling and dictate its length. He would go far down the wicket to drive spin bowling and he cut the faster bowlers or lashed them square. He made few long scores, but his batting – by averting collapse or making runs against the clock – often won matches.

He was most important, in 1930, as a bowler. With healthy impatience, he set out to bowl the unplayable, with violence of spin as his first objective, even at cost of flight and, sometimes, length. No one else at this time turned the googly so sharply and so fast, and the intensity of his spin sometimes made the ball dip sharply.

Business restricted the amount of Robins's first-class cricket but in 1947, as captain of Middlesex, he cut through to essentials – the winning of matches as quickly as possible – and Middlesex finished as Champions. He was an artful tactician, with a sharp eye for the weaknesses of opponents but unswerving urgency was the keynote of his captaincy. As one of the thinkers of the game, he was a realistic and valuable Chairman of Selectors.

I. A. R. Peebles

The South African Test player, Aubrey Faulkner – probably the finest-ever teacher of cricket – was chiefly responsible for Ian Peebles – at the age of nineteen – appearing in Gentlemen v Players at the Oval in 1927. It was, though, not until 1929 that Peebles became an effective leg-break and googly bowler: in 1930 he won an Oxford Blue as a Freshman and played for England against Australia.

Tall, long-armed and with a model, high, sideways-on action, he set some problems of flight from the height of his delivery, particularly after he reduced his early pace. 1929 probably was his best season, for then, from a fairly steady length, he turned sharply both ways and hid his googly remarkably well. He had, too, a much faster ball which he delivered without apparent change of action and could direct up on yorker length.

In 1930 he bowled fewer and fewer leg-breaks and, within a year, had 'lost' it altogether, though he was effective purely as a googly bowler because of his turn, bounce, length and flight. It was not until many years afterwards that an operation discovered and repaired the damage done by the strain of bowling back-of-the-hand spinners on immature tendons in his shoulders. Bradman himself confessed that he could not pick Peebles's googly and it was tragic for Peebles that he should have beaten Bradman conclusively with the leg-break at Old Trafford in 1930 – at precisely the time when he was losing the ability to bowl it.

One of the best of cricket story-tellers, Peebles has become an understanding and felicitous cricket reporter.

The first series of four day Tests to be played in England began at Trent Bridge on a difficult wicket and England, through an old master of an innings by Hobbs and quick fifties by Chapman and Robins, reached 270. With some help from the pitch, Tate and Robins bowled out Australia for 144 (Tate bowled Bradman for 8). Hobbs again, Sutcliffe and Hendren all batted well and Australia needed 429 to win. So long as Bradman was there, they threatened to make them. In, for him, subdued mood against the turning ball, he had batted more than four hours for 131 when he made no attempt to play the googly from Robins which bowled him. England won by 93.

Sutcliffe and Larwood were injured and could not play at Lord's and England brought in Duleepsinhji and Allen in their places.

K. S. Duleepsinhji

Kumar Shri Duleepsinhji, nephew of Ranjitsinhji, was one of the most gracious of batsmen. Slim almost to the point of frailty, he usually batted with the sleeves of his silk shirt buttoned to the wrists and seemed to sway into his strokes, which were surprising in their power. To watch him hook the short, fast inswing of Voce or Clark through their leg-trap, sweep down the pitch to drive Freeman's spin anywhere through the arc from extra-cover to mid-wicket, or go back

K. S. Duleepsinhji (Sussex) 'Duleep' was Ranji's nephew, a suave batsman with steely wrists and superb timing: illness stopped his cricket career as he was reaching the highest level

and cut a slow leg-break from Dick Tyldesley delicately yet with such timing as to add pace to it and send it for four – these were among the loveliest sights to be seen on English cricket fields between the two wars.

Like his uncle, Duleep played for Cambridge University and Sussex, but illness cut his playing career to only eight full seasons. In that period he scored 15,537 runs with an average of 50 – 58 in Tests. A superb, unhurried slip fieldsman, he was as graceful and elegant a cricketer as even the Edwardian age ever boasted.

G. O. B. Allen

From his first appearance for Eton against Harrow at Lord's in 1919 (when he was run out, backing up, before he had taken guard) 'Gubby' Allen has been near the hub of the game which has been the abiding interest of his life. In his schooldays and as a Cambridge blue he was something of a tearaway, striving for extra pace often at the expense of length and line. As he thickened physically, however, he developed a good circling action and control at substantial speed. He bowled outswing with the new ball, an occasionally awkward break-back and, as his accuracy increased, a disconcerting yorker.

His batting was studied in defence and he was always a strong driver and a competent, if reluctant, deflector off the back foot. Near to the wicket he was brave, intent and a reliable catcher. When he was fifty he scored a century for the Free Foresters against Cambridge University and remained, by dint of enthusiastic net practice, a bowler of some pace far through his forties.

There was no flaw in Allen's play that could have been eradicated by study or practice and he thought unendingly about the game, concerned for its traditions and becoming a Chairman of Selectors for whom no point was too small to be treated with care.

The wicket and the weather were good at Lord's, Duleepsinhji made a century in his first Test against Australia, and England's 425 seemed a healthy total – until Australia passed it with only two wickets down. Woodfull made 155 – and Bradman capped it with 254. When Woodfull declared, at 729 for six – a new record for the series – the English bowlers could contemplate such analyses as Allen, 0–115; Tate, 1–148; Robins, 1–175; White, the most successful of them, 3–172. Chapman's characteristic 121 saved England from an innings defeat and when Australia set about making 72 to win, Robins and Tate caused a flutter of distant hope by taking the first three wickets for 22: then Australia coasted in by seven wickets.

Bradman now was in the saddle. At Leeds he went in when Jackson was out for 1, scored a hundred before lunch and 309 by the close of play: next morning he went on to 334 – out of an Australian total of 566. Hammond made 113, and, while Grimmett bowled steadily on (five for 135), England worked their way to 391. That was not enough to avoid the follow-on, but time and bad light gave them a draw.

At Manchester the wicket was wet at the start: Woodfull and Ponsford put on 106 and then Bradman, showing little relish for the turning ball, faced Peebles; was almost bowled first ball, dropped at slip off a leg-break at 10, and out in the same fashion at

110

14. Rain made another draw and all was on the Oval Test – which would, therefore, be played to a finish.

The selectors dropped Chapman from the captaincy. Admittedly he was no great strategist but he had batted gallantly at Lord's and was still a fine close-catcher. He gave way to a very different kind of player in R. E. S. Wyatt of Warwickshire.

R. E. S. Wyatt

Another of the early 'professional amateurs', Bob Wyatt was a quiet, studious enthusiast. Unathletic in appearance, he was a solid, correct batsman, leaning on defence, precise in placing the loose ball for runs and, at a crisis, cool and reliable. He bowled medium pace right-arm through little curves and with occasional cut, and his knowledge of his opponents brought him some good wickets. He was a tidy fielder.

Wyatt's captaincy was undemonstrative but efficient: he rarely missed a trick, was helpful to his bowlers, considerate to his batsmen, meticulous in placing his fieldsmen. If ever there was a sound cricketer it was Bob Wyatt.

Larwood, fit again, came back into the side; so did W. W. – 'Dodger' – Whysall, also from Notts, a dour raw-boned bat with a strong defence, considerable power in the drive and remarkable facility in the pull-stroke: he was surprisingly preferred to Hendren.

England won the toss and batted: Sutcliffe ballasted the innings with 161, Hobbs, Duleep and Wyatt batted usefully, and the total was 405. Australia passed it with three wickets down, before Bradman had completed his innings of 232.

Rain removed the last shreds of England's hope: Hornibrook had learnt the lesson of England and now, at the last, took seven for 92. When Hobbs came out for his second innings, the Australians cheered him to the crease. This was the end of Test cricket for him. This was a fitting finish, on his home ground, against the old enemy. Bradman's average for the series (without benefit of not outs) was 139·14: the next Australian, Woodfull, 57: but – Sutcliffe 87, Duleep 59. If Australia had not had Bradman, England who, after all, had one of their stronger teams, might have won. They were the first country to go down to Bradman, but not the last.

The Tests overshadowed the rest of the country's cricket except in Lancashire – Champion county – and Gloucestershire. Gloucester, after many lean years, were runners-up and, in a dramatic match still remembered in the West Country, they tied with the

Australians. Their advance was attributable to the reinforcement of Hammond and Parker by Goddard and Sinfield and the captaincy of Lyon who had demanded, and been given, complete control of the team.

B. H. Lyon

Modern captaincy reached one of its high points in 'Bev' Lyon. His was not only a good cricket mind: he carved out a separate and equally successful business career. More than one change was made in the Championship rules to plug gaps he had found and exploited. He was a good man with other men and a practical cricketer. As a batsman he won matches by outwitting bowlers and, though he played in glasses, he was a fearless and secure close catcher. He will be remembered, however, as the captain who, never afraid to risk losing in the attempt to win, lifted Gloucestershire cricket back to its old reputation. He found it all extremely diverting, and his humour never failed.

T. W. Goddard

There have been more subtle off-spinners than Tom Goddard, but none more relentless. Tall, lean and tough, he first played for Gloucester as a fast-bowler, with little success, but, set on a cricket career, he joined the staff at Lord's where he was turned into an off-spinner.

Returning to Gloucestershire he found there, in B. H. Lyon, the ideal captain for him. Working out his field, encouraging him by relying on him, Lyon gave Goddard the impetus he needed to become a first-rate attacking spinner. He was not a subtle flighter, but his length was steady and that long index finger of his, wrapped round a ball, gave it a terrific twist. Tom Goddard needed only a scrap of turn in a pitch to bowl all day, and punishment merely made him more determined. With Charles Parker he formed a deadly pair when the wicket helped and, even at the age of fifty-one, given the sun on his back, he was still one of the most hostile of his kind.

West Indies made their first tour to Australia in 1930–31. Ponsford averaged 77, Bradman 74: Iron-monger, a medium-paced left-arm spinner, highly effective in Sheffield Shield cricket for many years but with an action that did not please everyone, took 22 wickets at 14·68 and Australia won the rubber by 4–1.

A good, but not full-strength, England side was beaten in South Africa by the only Test finished – and

the only one played on matting. The second of this
series – at Cape Town – was the first in South Africa
to be played on turf, and matting was never used in
any subsequent Test. Fittingly, Nupen, a master
bowler on the mat, was the South African captain:
he took his final chance – 11 wickets on that last
matting – but never proved so effective again.

In the Championship of 1931, Gloucester were
again runners-up, this time to Yorkshire, whom they
beat after one of Beverley Lyon's 'freak' declarations
which disturbed the traditionalists but produced
results. In Yorkshire there was pride that, immediately
upon Wilfred Rhodes's retirement, they had produced
another of the great slow-left-arm bowlers to take his
place.

Hedley Verity

The earlier Yorkshire slow-left-arm bowlers had been
genuinely slow, men who set their fields deep and
flighted the ball up to a full length. Their successor,
Hedley Verity, was a man of his time. Tall, with a
smooth, high action and almost without mannerisms,
he bowled tight, sometimes little below medium pace
so that, on a slow wicket, he hurried, and often
pierced, the batsman's stroke. His length was rigidly
accurate, his line meticulous: he spun his natural
break relentlessly and his faster ball was an effective
and sparingly used surprise.

Until the 1939 War, in which he lost his life, he
was England's unquestionable first choice and, whenever there was rain, he was master of any batting side
in the world.

A quiet, studious cricketer, with a sensitive face
and already a mature air when he first came into the
Yorkshire team as a twenty-five-year-old, Verity's
form never wavered. On the verdict of statistics he
is the most successful bowler of the twentieth century.
His career was short – 1930 to 1939 – but he took 1,956
wickets (an average of nearly 200 a year) at the
remarkable figure of 14·87.

At times he batted well; and off his own bowling
and in the gully, he caught some stingers.

South Africans in Australia, 1931–32

It was now the turn of the South Africans to come
under the lash of Bradman. He was injured and did
not bat in the fifth Test, but his average for the rest
of the series was a staggering 201·5. The South

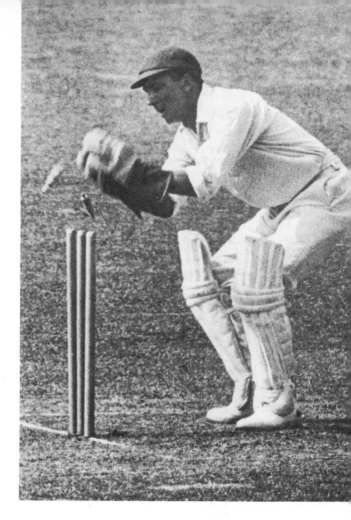

*Leslie Ames (Kent) Stands beyond all challenge as the finest
wicket-keeper-batsman the game has ever known*

Africans observed that in the fourth Test (when,
nevertheless, he made 299*!) he was uneasy with the
short, fast, lifting ball on his leg stump: and there is
no doubt that the news was passed to England.
Australia won all five Tests, three by an innings, in
sustained steam-roller fashion.

The English season of 1932 was one of preparation
for Australia. Yorkshire won the Championship, and
Holmes and Sutcliffe, with 555 against Essex, beat the
first-wicket record by one run – a hastily discovered
leg-bye, to balance the scoreboard: in a match at
Leeds, Hedley Verity took all ten wickets of Notts for
ten runs. Sussex, captained by Duleepsinhji, burst up
to second place – Tate bowled magnificently. For
Kent, who were third, Ames scored 2,432 runs and,
as a wicket-keeper, made exactly 100 dismissals.

L. E. G. Ames

Worth his place in any side as a batsman alone, Leslie
Ames is proved by figures the best wicket-keeper-

batsman – in the sense that demands high standards in each capacity – any country has ever had. His wicket-keeping may not have been quite so good as Duckworth's but he was neat and economical, and is credited with going through the 1932–33 Test series in Australia without missing a single chance. Since he was then keeping to bowling of a pace he never encountered in his normal play with Kent, that places him above reasonable criticism. His whole style was easy and relaxed: to slow bowling he squatted low and he took Freeman without error for weeks on end.

His batting was fluent, based on quick footwork, and his driving was strong, long and safe. He never overplayed his hand but he was a uniformly fast scorer and a reliable punisher of the bad ball. To have scored over a hundred centuries and more than 30,000 runs places him high amongst all batsmen, while no other wicket-keeper approaches such a record.

Preparation for Australia was apparent in Notts' cricket in August of 1932. Larwood, after a couple of overs to his normal off-side setting, frequently switched to a leg field similar to Voce's. So, for appreciable periods the pair of them maintained fast leg theory from both ends. The tactic was not particularly successful and, on slow wickets at Leyton and Cardiff, it proved expensive.

W. Voce

The Australians were sufficiently apprehensive of Bill Voce in 1930 to depute McCabe and Victor Richardson in their match against Notts to hit him out of the running for a Test place. He took only one wicket for 112 and they had succeeded. Then he bowled usefully in South Africa in 1930–31 and was clearly earmarked for a place in the side to Australia.

Voce joined Notts as a medium pace left-arm bowler, became for a brief period a slow orthodox spinner and then switched to fast-medium. Indeed, but for Larwood at the other end, he might have been called fast. He bowled inswing varied with the breakaway. Tall and deep chested, Voce was surprisingly lissom for so massively-built a man and his body swing, high action and pronounced wrist-whip gave his bowling awkward life from the pitch. He often undertook long spells without losing pace and, though some critics thought he should have bowled round the wicket rather than over it, his line unsettled many batsmen, and made his ball that left the bat off the pitch more likely to produce a catch to slip or

wicket-keeper. He was at first a foil for Larwood but he played for England in his own right for many years after Larwood went. Voce has the strange record of playing against Australia in eleven Tests, all of them in Australia.

W. E. Bowes

The third bowler in England's planned strategy for Australia, 1932–33, was Bill Bowes of Yorkshire. Six-feet-four tall, he maintained fine bodily control for one of such gangling build, and for his pace, which could be quite fast, he was commendably accurate. His chief merit was his steep lift from the pitch so that, in hard conditions, the ball frequently rose, off a length, to the batsman's knuckles. With his strong hands and long fingers he swung the new ball sharply and often made it 'move' off the seam.

After the 1939 war, although he was in his late thirties and weakened by a spell in a prisoner of war camp, he came back to cricket to meet Yorkshire's need and, reducing his pace and 'doing' more with the ball, he was one of the best bowlers in the country for a couple of seasons and opened the bowling for England against India.

England in Australia, 1932–33

In the most bitterly controversial of all Test series, England were captained by Douglas Jardine, who, through a storm of protest, coolly persisted in his pre-determined tactics and beat Australia by 4–1.

Argument has raged ever since about the English bowling of fast leg theory which was dubbed 'Body-line' and, in some quarters, bitterness about it persists even now, more than thirty years afterwards.

A number of facts are clear beyond all question. Larwood, Voce – and, in his one Test, Bowes – bowled mainly on or outside the line of the leg stump to a concentrated leg side field and constantly employed the 'bumper'. It is true that they took wickets by hitting the stumps and by slip catches but they would have been less capable bowlers than they were if they had not sometimes changed their line as 'variety'. Since Larwood rarely bowled inswing, and there is no doubt of his accuracy, his line must have been aimed *directly* at the leg stump or beyond.

Five England batsmen, but only two Australians, had averages of more than forty. Bradman – the effective difference between the two sides – was the target, and the success of the plan is shown in his figures. His Test average in England in 1930 was 139, in this series it was 56·57 (by far his lowest in any Tests): Woodfull's figures for the same two series showed a drop from 57·5 to 33·88 and Ponsford's from 55 to 23: 139 runs an innings is the margin between winning or losing a Test rubber.

Bradman, who missed the first Test through illness, was out seven times – to Larwood four times and Bowes once. Ninety-three Australian wickets fell in the series – 33 to Larwood, 15 to Voce and one to Bowes: 49 altogether to leg theory. Allen, the fourth pace-bowler, who firmly employed his normal field setting, completed the pattern of pace and took 21 wickets. Verity, the stock slow bowler, had only 11.

That this method of attack was Jardine's fixed purpose is clear from his handling of Maurice Tate. Tate was given only one match before the first Test. Although he was England's greatest new ball bowler of the post war period, he was not put on until both Larwood and Voce had bowled the shine away without taking a wicket. Nevertheless, as soon as he came on, Tate took the wickets of Wendell Bill – opening batsman – Bradman and Kippax and, in his second spell, McCabe: four of the best batsmen in Australia for 53 runs in a total of 273. He was given six overs in the second innings and only played in one more major match (in which he had a mere fourteen overs) until the Tests were over. Tate had finished fourth in the first-class averages in England in 1932 and such a performance as this – with the old ball, too – immediately before the first Test, must have been sufficient to play anyone into a Test eleven in normal circumstances. The inescapable conclusion is that Tate had to be kept out because he would have embarrassed Jardine's plans.

It is significant that, as in England immediately after the two World Wars, there was no genuine fast bowler in Australia – certainly no one remotely approaching Larwood in pace – and their batsmen were completely out of tune against such speed. They were routed by pace – and by its line.

The repercussions of so-called 'Body Line' were numerous and regrettable. Bad feeling was engendered on a disproportionate, national scale and representations were certainly made to the Colonial Secretary. The Australian Board of Control sent a cable of protest against the English tactic to Lord's, and MCC offered to withdraw the team without finishing the series. There were crowd scenes, luridly publicized

dissension between the dressing rooms, and relations between the two sides, originally impaired by Armstrong, deteriorated even further, and did not become truly cordial again until 1964.

Fast bowlers have always regarded the occasional short ball as legitimate intimidation, or a 'surprise' weapon: certainly Gregory and McDonald employed it in England in 1921 when at least one England batsman was seriously injured. Now, for the first time, it was employed as a consistent system of attack. The feeling among the Australians was that 'Body-line' was not unplayable and that a good batsman could make one or two good scores against it – as several of them did – but that he would take such physical hammering in the process that he was still feeling the effects when he next faced it.

Attention was focused so intently on the three main figures in the affair – Jardine, Larwood and Bradman – that two important new players – Eddie Paynter and O'Reilly – received less attention than they deserved.

E. Paynter

At Adelaide and at Brisbane – where he batted weak and ill from a throat infection and returned to a hospital bed each evening – Eddie Paynter shored up the English batting at crucial stages of the match. A compactly built left-hander, he took some years to play his way into the strong Lancashire batting side of his day and he was almost thirty before he scored his first century (1931). Once established, he stood out as an attractive and highly individual batsman. Short and alert, his training gave him a foundation of defensive orthodoxy and he built on it a masterful scoring style. Mobile and strong in the wrists, he drove harder than his size promised, cut full-bloodedly and pulled with unusual certainty. In ability, character and temperament, Eddie Paynter was a cricketer of Test stature, unfortunate to play in only twenty Tests in which he had one of the highest averages of his period – 59·23.

W. J. O'Reilly

Until the nineteen-thirties, leg spinners, even at Test level, tossed the ball high, relying on flight as well as turn to beat batsmen, and no one was surprised if, in striving for high spin, they sometimes sacrificed length. Clarrie Grimmett and then Bill O'Reilly were the first to set tight standards of control in the bowling of wrist-spin. They were a strongly contrasted pair, Grimmett small, wrinkled and unobtrusively busy,

O'Reilly tall and so openly hostile as to earn himself the nickname of 'Tiger'. From a fairly long and shambling run, and with a stoop at delivery which lost him the advantage of his height, O'Reilly bowled leg-breaks and googlies at almost medium pace. His leg-break was more rolled than truly spun, but he pushed it through briskly and it turned the essential distance, which is half the width of a bat. His googly, which was a shade slower but still allowed the batsman little time to use his feet to it, turned more sharply and bounced high enough to justify one – sometimes two – men at short-leg.

It may be argued that, from 1932–33 (when he was easily Australia's most successful bowler, with 27 wickets at 26·81) until 1938, when his bowling at Leeds gave Australia the win that drew the series, O'Reilly was as important a match-winner as Bradman.

He was a bowler of forbidding aspect, yet a sensitive craftsman with a wide range of methods of altering his length, pace and arc. It was as nearly as makes no matter impossible to collar him, and his spirit was unquenchable; he would bowl on, tight yet attacking, on perfect batsmen's wickets without complaint. A friendly man off the field, when he was bowling Bill O'Reilly hated batsmen with an intensity that was by no means assumed and, at his fiercest, he seemed to make the pitch shorter than it was.

English cricket in 1933 seethed with argument and counter-argument about the series in Australia. Larwood, suffering from a foot injury, bowled only ten overs for Notts, and Voce fell away to almost half his number of wickets of the previous year at twice the cost. Verity took seventeen wickets – for 91 runs – in a day for Yorkshire against Essex.

West Indies in England

The West Indies, in their three-Test series, were at a loss about how to deal with the leg-break and googlies of Robins at Lord's and, at the Oval, of C. S. Marriott, Kent, a Dulwich schoolmaster playing the only Test of his career. But at Old Trafford, where Barrow and Headley made centuries, they had by no means the worst of a drawn game.

There, Constantine – in the only Test for which his league club released him – and Martindale turned fast leg theory against England. Hammond was hit on the chin and had to go off, but Jardine, with an almost disdainful courage characteristic of the man, refused to rub his bruises and batted composedly and surely for five hours to make 127: that innings, his only Test century, was in some ways his finest triumph.

Yorkshire were again Champions, and by a large margin, although they were twice well beaten by Sussex who finished second. James Langridge, a conscientious craftsman and the best type of professional, played a considerable part in both those Sussex wins. A slow left-arm bowler and left-hand bat, he took 158 wickets and scored 1,578 runs in the season.

In the series with the West Indies, and even more convincingly in India in 1933–34, Walters emphasized his right to the place of England's opening bat, never adequately filled since Hobbs left it in 1930.

C. F. Walters

As a Glamorgan player as early as 1923, Cyril Walters had obvious gifts, but it was not until after he moved to Worcester in 1930, and, after careful thought changed his method of play, that he became a class batsman. Right handed, of average height, he was a wristy striker whose batting had an air of easy self-confidence. He had always been a pleasant off-side player but he matured into one who with sharp eye and good balance became a precise, stylish maker of runs to leg, glancing and on-driving. He had put an unquestionable seal on his ability in the series against Australia in 1934, then, after an injury in the following summer, he retired from first-class cricket when, still short of thirty, he had just reached his best.

K. Farnes

No cricketer has ever had a finer physique than Kenneth Farnes; six-feet-five tall, he weighed sixteen stone and was perfectly proportioned. Extremely strong and with a good action from a short – ten stride – run, he bowled with a snap of the wrist, and on his day – such as Gentlemen v Players at Lord's in 1936 – he bowled as fast as anyone in modern times. Lift from a length came naturally from his height and action, and he occasionally moved the ball into the bat through the air or off the seam. Speed and angle of bounce, however, were enough to make him a menacing bowler in any conditions or against any opposition.

With Maurice Nichols he made the Essex opening attack of the time a dangerous proposition on any wicket with pace in it. Nichols, a powerful man who bowled right and batted left, was a major county player and fell only a little short of the heights as an all-rounder.

Australia in England, 1934

The Test series of 1934 was bitter with the after-taste of 1932–33. Jardine himself withdrew from the series and decided to report it for the press. Larwood made statements in the press which were certainly sincere, but which ruled him out of selection; and Voce simply was not picked. Thus England's attacking strength of 1932–33 was abandoned. Local indignation was paraded in some harsh scenes at the Notts-Australians match and eventually Arthur Carr was deposed from the county captaincy.

There was a feeling abroad that England would lose, and they did – by two-one – though Bradman was not so consistent, neither did he score so heavily, as in 1930. Again he began with a double century at Worcester but then he dropped into a trough, only to rise out of it an even more brilliant player than before. Treating bowling almost with scorn, he played some innings of quite heady brilliance, masterful, expansive, lofting the ball with safety, playing strokes of sheer invention and scoring faster than ever.

Wyatt captained England with his usual care but little luck. Farnes, after taking ten wickets at Trent Bridge, was never fit through the series. Now that Hobbs – retired from Test cricket – and Duleepsinhji – too ill ever to play again – were gone, only Leyland, Sutcliffe, Walters and Hendren batted reliably for England. Hammond and Wyatt were said to have failed: it would be a more accurate reflection of the cricket to say that they went down before the effective match-winners of the series, O'Reilly and Grimmett, who together had 53 wickets at less than 27 each. The remaining Australian bowlers took 18 between them.

Ponsford had a batting average of 94·83 and Bradman, after a run of low scores in the first three Tests, made 304 at Leeds and 244 and 77 at the Oval.

The Trent Bridge Test of 1934 was the only one in which Australia beat England without a century from Bradman between the beginning of the 1930 series and Lord's in 1948. No other Australian batsman scored a century there, but most of them made runs – including Chipperfield's long remembered 99 – and O'Reilly (eleven wickets) and Grimmett (eight) were simply too much for the England batting, though the last wicket fell only ten minutes before time to give

Hedley Verity (Yorkshire) A master of the craft of slow left-arm bowling: imperturbable and intelligent, he enforced respect on good wickets by his unfailing accuracy; where the ball turned, his spin was deadly

Australia the match by 238. At Lord's, England made 440 and Australia 192 for two before the rain came. Then, on a turning wicket, only Woodfull (43) could cope with Verity (15 for 104 in the match). The remaining eighteen Australian wickets were taken for only another 210 runs and they lost by an innings. At Old Trafford the match was a draw from the first ball bowled on the plumb pitch: 1,307 runs were scored and only twenty wickets fell. In the fourth Test – Headingley – England went down before O'Reilly and Grimmett for 200. Bowes made Australia 39 for three overnight but then came a stand of 388 between Ponsford and Bradman. Both were missed in the seventies and between them they made 485 of Australia's 584 all out. Rain ended the match with

England struggling to avoid an innings defeat.

So the rubber depended on the Oval. Hendren was injured and the English selectors brought back Woolley, who had been in fine form for Kent, but was now forty-seven years old. Bowes bowled well, and took nine wickets for 219 in the match, but Ames was injured (Woolley took over as wicket-keeper) and again the English catching and ground fielding were poor. This time Ponsford (266) and Bradman (244) put on 451 for the second wicket in little more than five hours. It was the steam roller at its heaviest. Only Leyland and Walters offered real resistance to Grimmett and O'Reilly and, set 708 to win in the last innings, England crumpled. Woolley made 4 and 0, a sad end to his Test career. For the second time Australia won a rubber on Woodfull's birthday.

Lancashire were County Champions and George Duckworth chose their match against Surrey for his benefit. Jack Hobbs had played only a few early games for Surrey and Duckworth wrote asking him particularly to play in his benefit match. Hobbs – now fifty-one – came, scored 116 – the only century made against Lancashire in a Championship match at Old Trafford that season – in the first innings and 51* in the second. That was his 197th and last century in first class cricket. At the end of the season he retired, having made more runs – 61,237 – than anyone else in the history of the game.

England now was full of good county cricketers but none were clearly to be seen who looked likely to topple the Australians.

THE MOUNTING CHALLENGE

In the West Indies in 1934–35, England, with six men who had played against Australia, lost the four-Test rubber by two-one. Their win was in the first Test, at Barbados on a rain-damaged wicket, when only 309 runs were scored and only one innings was completed. Wyatt declared England's first innings closed, Grant declared West Indies' second, and England scraped home by four wickets. It is doubtful if the three Yorkshiremen, Bowes, Verity and Sutcliffe, who did not make the tour, could have adjusted the overall balance. On West Indian wickets, Headley stood head and shoulders above any other batsman on either side and Martindale, Hilton and Constantine were a strong hand of fast bowlers.

South Africa in England, 1935

Two new pieces of legislation took effect in 1935, one firm, the other experimental.

In November 1934, a statement was issued from Lord's of agreement by the Imperial Cricket Conference of the principle 'That any form of bowling which is obviously an attack by the bowler upon the batsman would be an offence against the spirit of the game'. Direct attack was defined as 'persistent and systematic bowling of fast short-pitched balls at the batsman standing clear of his wicket'.

On the same day it was announced by MCC that, in 1935, a trial would be given to an amended lbw rule, by which a batsman could not be out lbw if he stopped with his body not only a *straight* ball, but also one which pitched on the *off side* of the line of the stumps so long as he was in the line between wicket and wicket when he did so.

Here, indeed, was a strange irony, for these two pieces of law-making dealt separately with cause and effect within cricket. Fast body-line bowling may have been worked out by Arthur Carr and Douglas Jardine: but, historically, it sprung from the bowlers' rebellion against pad-play. In the 1924–25 and 1926 Australia-England series Collins had calmly pushed his pad into the line of the ball from Maurice Tate which came back from outside the off stump. He was not alone. The most successful batsmen in the world – even as far back as Ranjitsinhji, if in his case only rarely – had met the pace-bowler's classic weapon of the break-back, when it was pitched on its true line, outside the off stump, with a studied bend of the leg to take it on pads often specially reinforced for the purpose. If the 'new' lbw law had been introduced in 1921, the term 'Body-line' might never have been invented – nor the tactic needed.

The new ruling had not, yet, as some had feared, over-emphasized off-break and inswing bowling. The time was to come when bowlers would exploit it – but no more balefully than batsmen had exploited the lack of it.

The main event of the season was South Africa's winning of their first Test and first rubber in England. Their fresh strength lay in three batsmen and two bowlers: Dalton, a strongly built forcing bat; K. G. Viljoen, a correct and determined player of pace, and E. A. B. Rowan, a jauntily confident batsman, also strong against fast bowling: X. C. – Xenophon –

Balaskas, who had first made his mark as a batsman, was now a leg-break and googly bowler, with a low flight and considerable spin: he was the effective match-winner at Lord's, after which a shoulder injury kept him out of the remaining Tests. A. B. C. – 'Chud' – Langton, at twenty-three, was the youngest member of the side. Six-feet-three tall with a high action, Langton used the new ball well, swinging it late: with a worn ball he cut it with variety of pace and accuracy of length, working in the manner of the English county stock bowlers, with the additional advantage, from his height, of a steep angle from the pitch.

Herbert Wade captained the side skilfully and sensitively; he was a brave close fieldsman and, several times in this series, a valuable batsman when things were difficult.

England used twenty-five players in the series without making any advance towards a better side than that of 1934. N. S. Mitchell-Innes, a handsome bat, still up at Oxford, later to become a Somerset player; W. F. Farrimond, a fine wicket-keeper who had the misfortune to spend most of his career with Lancashire as understudy to Duckworth; Dennis Smith, a stylish Derbyshire left-hander who, on his day, was the nearest approach we have seen to Woolley; Jack Iddon, a steady Lancashire all-rounder, slow left-arm bowler and dogged bat; E. R. T. Holmes, a gay cricketer, a strong driver and fair medium pace bowler; T. B. Mitchell of Derbyshire, who took to leg-break bowling late in life and maintained length and spin for some years; J. Sims, drily humorous and wise Middlesex leg-spinner; W. Barber, solid Yorkshire right-hander; A. Mitchell, another Yorkshire batsman and brilliant close field; A. H. Bakewell, sometimes brilliant bat of Northants, who never fully realized his immense promise, a fine catcher; J. C. Clay, the Glamorgan off-spinner of artful flight and appreciable spin; H. D. Read, Essex, probably, after Farnes, the fastest bowler in the country, but erratic and lacking in resource: these were the best county cricketers in England now tried out among the known and established players. Not one of them seemed of the standard that would be demanded in the series of 1936–37 in Australia. England had slightly the better of four drawn games but, at Lord's, South Africa won well. The decisive performances were Mitchell's 164* in the second South African innings and Cameron's 90 in the first; the bowling of Balaskas – nine for 103 – and Langton, six for 89.

Sutcliffe, at Lord's, and Tate, at Old Trafford, played their last Tests; and their true successors were not to be seen.

Yorkshire, their weighty batting given point by the bowling of Bowes and Verity, won the County Championship. Derbyshire, the mounting power, were second: Smith, Worthington and Alderman as batsmen; Mitchell as a bowler, with a county record of 160 wickets, had four men behind him – Copson, the brothers George and Alf Pope, and the all-rounder Townsend, who all took more than sixty wickets. Middlesex, with Robins, Smith, Peebles and Sims a sharp attack to back the batting of Hendren, were third.

H. Gimblett

In early May of 1935, Somerset gave a trial to Harold Gimblett, the twenty-year-old son of a Bicknoller farmer. It was decided not to engage him: he was given his expenses and was leaving the ground when a telephone call told the secretary that Hawkins was unfit and could not play in the match with Essex starting the next day at Frome. Such was Somerset cricket, even in 1935, that there were only six professionals on the staff and, while it might have been possible to make up the side in the morning if the match were being played at Taunton, that was not practicable for Frome. So – incredible as it may seem, especially to North Country cricketers – the young man was told to play 'to make up the number'. He had never played far from home, nor for a more pretentious club than Watchet, and he had to hitch-hike to Frome for the match. He went in when the pace bowling of Nichols had reduced Somerset to 107 for six and, in sixty-three minutes, scored the fastest century of the season and went on through the new ball to 123. His innings decided the match: Somerset won by an innings and Harold Gimblett remained a regular member of the side until illness put him out of the game in 1954.

For almost twenty years Harold Gimblett was the most audacious opening bat in cricket. A right-hander, he was strongly built with thick arms and he cut, drove, hooked and pulled with great power and determination. He would attack any bowling from the first ball sent down, and it was not unusual for him to take three, or even four, fours off the first over of an innings. He often paid for his temerity, but he scored 23,007 runs at an average of 36. On his day he would murder the best attack and, in 1950, he mounted an assault on the spin bowling of Ramadhin so impressive that he was picked for the Test at Trent Bridge. On arrival, he had a carbuncle which put him out of the game; and, oddly enough, although England were beaten, he was not picked again. So his Test appearances were limited to two against India in 1936 and one against West Indies in 1939 – 129 runs at 32.25. Yet there were times when a player of his approach and powers might have won a match which slower players could not save.

Also in 1935, Cyril Smart of Glamorgan took 32 runs – 664664 – from a six-ball over bowled by Gerald Hill of Hampshire.

It was all pleasant domestic cricket, but those concerned with selection knew it was no more. England had now lost three consecutive Test rubbers – to Australia, West Indies and South Africa – in less than two years.

Australia in South Africa, 1935–36

Victor Richardson – a forcing batsman and outstanding close field – took the third Australian side to South Africa and won the rubber by 4–0 with one game drawn. Even without Bradman – who was 'not available' for the tour – Australia won three games by an innings and a fourth by nine wickets. They were only once put out for less than 400: McCabe, Fingleton and Brown scored consistently for Australia but the series was won by the bowling of Grimmett (44 wickets at 14.59) and O'Reilly (27 at 17.03) backed by superb catching close to the wicket, particularly by Fingleton and Richardson.

Only one South African – Nourse – had an average of more than 34 and only one of their bowlers – Mitchell with his leg-breaks – had a better bowling figure than 43.

A. D. Nourse junior

His innings of 231 against the 1935–36 Australians established Dudley Nourse in the South African team for fifteen years. Son of Dave Nourse, he was a short and powerfully made man with immense strength in the shoulders and arms. A right-hand bat, unflinching against pace, he was a superb player of leg-break and googly bowling. Surprisingly quick on his feet for one of his bulk, he had a wily dead bat in defence when he needed it, but his usual method against spin was of measured attack. He had an uncanny eye for the spinning ball and could leave his stroke late yet still hit strongly in any direction.

The 1936 season in England was not a happy one: several counties were hanging on the brink of bankruptcy and public interest in the Tests with India was slight. There was, though, general pleasure at the 'new' lbw law – especially among umpires. England won two of the Tests and had the best of the one left drawn. Then, at Manchester, their progress was arrested by the second innings opening partnership of 203 by Merchant and Mushtaq Ali.

V. M. Merchant

Vijay Merchant was a studious bat who could produce all the strokes but whose game was based on defence. Patient, sound, tireless, devoted to cricket, a cold killer of the bad ball, he was of the school of record breakers and if the war had not interrupted his career, he might have produced even more impressive figures than 12,876 runs at 72.74.

Mushtaq Ali, a tall left-hander, was essentially a stroke-maker who cut and drove spectacularly but was always in danger, with his full flow of the bat, early in his innings.

Derbyshire were County Champions and two of their players – Worthington and Copson – were chosen for the tour to Australia. Stan Worthington was a big, strong, right-hand bat, mainly a front-of-the-wicket player, strong in the drive with an on-side bias, but useful against the swinging ball and a good hooker and square cutter. Wilfred Copson was physically not unlike Larwood, not much above average height but deep chested and long-armed. He had an easy, almost lounging, approach to the wicket and his power came from his huge shoulder-heave in delivery. Much faster than he looked, he came surprisingly quickly even off slow pitches and he had a distinct and late swerve.

J. Hardstaff

There have been few more handsome batsmen in recent years than 'Young Joe' Hardstaff whose father played for Notts and England before him. He was a slim, poised, fair-haired man; a right-hand bat, full of attractive strokes. His average in Tests against Australia – 40 – shows that he passed the hardest trial. He was at his best on fast pitches when his driving, especially through the covers, was as handsome as even the Edwardians could have wished. He was, too, a fine outfield.

C. J. Barnett

Another member of a cricketing family, Charles Barnett, like his father, C. S., played for Gloucester. One of the most aggressive opening batsman of his day, he was well made, strong in arms and wrists, and he hit commandingly. Most of his runs came from drives, which he was not afraid to lift and at times struck long distances. He cut, especially square, with fine eye and judgement, for he was always reluctant to allow a fast bowler to bowl wide of his off stump unpunished. He sometimes lost his wicket through what seemed an impetuous stroke but he also, and frequently, took opposing attacks by the scruff of the neck and hammered them off length. A good outfield and a useful medium pace swing bowler, he was a good county all-rounder. He was an England batsman because he would carry the fight to the bowlers in any cricket, even a Test against Australia.

Fishlock and Fagg were also taken on the tour to Australia. Laurie Fishlock, Surrey left-hand opening batsman, amateur soccer international, and outfield of Australian class, was a cricketer of good temperament, fine straight and off driver, and with all the left-hander's usual ability on the leg side. For some years on either side of the second World War, Arthur Fagg, when in good health, played fast-bowling as well as anyone in England. Right-handed, grim in approach, with powerful arms and outstanding as a hooker, he lost what should have been his best years to illness and the war.

England in Australia, 1936–37

G. O. Allen's MCC side achieved its most important and long-term aim by re-establishing English cricket in the estimation of an Australian public still smouldering with the anger roused by the Jardine-Larwood attack of four years earlier.

In other respects the series was unsatisfactory. Unusually for Australia, four of the five Tests were affected by bad weather and on both sides illness, injury and zig-zag form tilted the balance of matches oddly. In the English party, Wyatt was kept out of the first three Tests by illness: Robins was never fully effective after he broke a finger at fielding practice – which he needed less than most – between the first and second Tests: Fishlock fractured a finger and Fagg became so ill with rheumatic fever that he returned home before the end of the tour. McCormick and

Bill Voce (Notts) Hostile left-arm pace: remembered as Larwood's partner but a major bowler in his own right

Badcock of Australia, too, fell ill during Test Matches. Apart from such unavoidable misfortunes, the series suffered from the Australian tactical decision – which caused O'Reilly to be used as a defensive instead of an attacking bowler – to attack Hammond's leg stump. This certainly slowed Hammond's scoring, but did not stop him, and he ended with an average three runs an innings higher than in 1932–33.

An unusually large number of players on both sides, too, were out of form. For the first time in Test cricket a side two down with three to play – Australia – won a rubber. Each Test went with the toss but, once more, Bradman decided the issue. The unfancied English team was not so strong as it might have been: Sutcliffe was missed for his experience and stability, and the bowling of Bowes could have made an appreciable difference to the side.

In the first Test, at Brisbane, McCormick – in whom Australia had at last found a bowler of genuine pace, if not of accuracy – struck at the England opening and three wickets were down for twenty before Barnett and Leyland rebuilt the innings so that it reached 358. The Australian batting went entirely the other way: at the start Fingleton scored his fourth century in consecutive innings (following three against South Africa in 1935–36) but, once their third wicket had fallen at 166, Voce, bowling as well as he ever did, bundled out the rest of their batting for 234. Allen's 68 was the main factor in England setting Australia 381 to win. Bad light and then rain put the task far beyond them. On a vicious Brisbane 'sticky' Allen and Voce bowled unchanged and Australia, out for 58, lost by 322.

J. E. Fingleton

Disconcerted by Larwood in 1932–33, Jack Fingleton had the courage and the ability to play his way back as a reliable Test opening bat. Although he could punish anything short by square cutting, hooking and glancing, his power lay in his sound defence and steady concentration. He had an intelligent approach, studied opposing bowlers with much perception and was content to wait for the bad ball and punish it as much by precise placing as by his appreciable power of stroke. Even among Australian outfieldsmen – over the years the best in the world – Fingleton stood out for his speed and safety.

S. J. McCabe

Of Bradman's physical stamp, though a little bigger, Stan McCabe was the only batsman of his time to match 'The Don' in combined brilliance and certainty of stroke-making. Fast to adjust himself to the length of a ball, blessed with good arms and wrists, he hit hard off front or back foot and, in any circumstances, was a difficult man to contain. At one moment he appeared a superb cutter; within a few minutes he would drive as if that were his main gift and then he would parade a hook of force and control to compare with any. Here again was an Australian batsman who never feared his fate too much but who, at a crisis, still believed in the bat as an aggressive weapon and who coolly but fearlessly set out to attack bowlers who only shortly before had seemed in command. He was yet another who would have shone more brightly if he had not spent his career in the shadow of Bradman.

In a number of Tests when Australia's bowling lay largely in the hands of O'Reilly and Grimmett or Fleetwood-Smith, McCabe used the new ball – medium pace right-arm – bowling largely inswing

with occasional nip from the pitch and general accuracy. He was another whose fielding left him nothing in debt when he went to bat.

At Sydney, Hammond, restricted but secure, made 231* in England's 426 for six before heavy weekend rain. Allen declared and, on another ugly wicket, Australia, with Badcock absent, went down before Voce and Allen for 80. Allen took the risk of enforcing the follow-on on an improving pitch where Fingleton and Bradman took Australia to 162 before the second wicket fell. McCabe, with 93, continued well enough but Voce cut through the middle of the batting. England, winners by an innings and 22, were surprised to find themselves two up.

At Melbourne, only McCabe (63) offered any real resistance to the well-handled English bowling, even before the rain which persuaded Bradman to declare at 200 on the second day. Hammond and Leyland made a brave show on yet another unpleasant wicket but, once they were gone, and while Allen, in his turn, pondered a declaration, five more batsmen were out for nine runs between them. When eventually Allen did declare – at 76 for nine – Bradman reversed the Australian batting order and lost only O'Reilly before the end of the day. The pitch rolled out well but still five Australian wickets were down for 97 before – with the rubber almost lost – Fingleton (136) and Bradman (coming off best, as usual, with 270) in a record sixth wicket stand of 346, played Australia to an impregnable position. Leyland, Hammond and Robins made brave gestures towards an almost impossible 689 which allowed Fleetwood-Smith to buy his wickets: he did – five for 124 – to give Australia a win by 365.

L. O'B. Fleetwood-Smith

In 1932–33, Hammond was charged with the task of hitting Fleetwood-Smith out of Test selection and he discharged it with ruthless efficiency. Now, four years later, 'Chuck' (a nickname which cast no aspersions on his perfectly fair action), with nineteen wickets in the last three Tests, played a leading part in Australia's winning run. He was then unique in top-level cricket as a slow left-arm wrist spinner who bowled the 'Chinaman' – or left-armer's off-break – and its complementary googly. He was not always accurate but his immense spin and pertinacity enabled him to get rid of good batsmen on plumb wickets. On his day, which was by no means every day, Chuck Fleetwood-Smith was a match-winner of the Mailey type.

The fourth Test, at Adelaide – the only one of the series unaffected by weather – was England's real chance to win the rubber. Only W. A. Brown, who made 42, McCabe (88) and Chipperfield (57*) settled in against Allen, Farnes and Hammond. In this match Verity was used in a despairing attempt to find an opening partner for Barnett: they made England's two best opening stands of the series – 53 and 45 – but Allen must have longed for Sutcliffe. Barnett's 129 took England to a first innings lead of 42 and two Australian second innings wickets had gone for 88 when Bradman once more changed the course of a match – with 212 of a total of 433. Nevertheless, on a still true wicket, 392 should not have been beyond the powers of an England side in which Hardstaff, Allen and Robins batted at numbers seven, eight and nine. It was the kind of position from which Australia might have won; England simply did not bat well. Fleetwood-Smith happily paid 110 runs for six wickets. Though six English batsmen played themselves in, none stayed to make the major innings the situation demanded, and they lost by 148.

Australia batted first in the decisive fifth Test at Melbourne and took the chance offered when England dropped four catches. Bradman made 169, McCabe 112 and Badcock – a strong thick-set right-hander whose career petered out in an unhappy series in 1938 and War – 118. In their total of 604, Farnes's six wickets for 96 was a magnificent effort to stem the tide. Although Hardstaff made a calm and stylish 83, England were already struggling before the rain again made batsmen's lives difficult and Nash – a thickset, fastish bowler from Victoria – O'Reilly and Fleetwood-Smith bowled Australia to a win by an innings and 200.

1937 – England's New Generation

In 1937 two obvious pieces of history were made when, after two years of trial, the 'new' lbw law was confirmed, and J. H. Parks, of Sussex, became the first player to take 100 wickets and score 3,000 runs in a season.

Less obviously, there emerged in England a new generation of cricketers entitled to be reckoned among the great.

England, captained by R. W. V. Robins, won one and drew two Tests of an unremarkable series against New Zealand in which the essential difference between the two sides was reflected in the fact that, while half a dozen New Zealand batsmen stayed long enough to make fifty, none of them, against expert bowling and field-setting in Tests, approached more nearly to a century than Hadlee's 93.

Yorkshire, with what now amounted almost to monotony, won the County Championship, but were closely pressed by Middlesex who, if they had won their last two matches, would have taken the title. During August, when competition between the two was close, Walter Robins issued a challenge to Brian Sellers, the Yorkshire captain, to a match on a neutral ground. It was duly played at the Oval in September: Yorkshire won by an innings and 115.

On the 28th July, Paynter for Lancashire v Sussex, and Moore for Hampshire v Warwickshire both scored a hundred before lunch: Paynter went on to 322 and Moore to 316* in the day.

Of greater eventual significance, Hutton, Compton and Washbrook played for England for the first time; Wright took 107 wickets for Kent and Edrich was top of the Middlesex batting averages.

Leonard Hutton

Sir Donald Bradman's successor as the best batsman in the world, Len (now Sir Leonard) Hutton, scored 0 in his first innings for Yorkshire second eleven, Yorkshire first team and England.

He came to success the hard way. Bradman's successor in eminence, he also followed him as the chief target in cricket and became one of its most battered players. During the war his left arm was broken, set, re-broken and re-set so that, by the time he resumed cricket, it was thinner and almost two inches shorter than the other. Pale, broken-nosed, often withdrawn, Hutton was an imaginative man who trained himself to dourness in batting and in public behaviour.

In the quality of his strokes he had no peer in his time. But he never used them injudiciously. When he cared to improvise, he could bat as thrillingly as Bradman, McCabe or Weekes. That, however, was not the manner of his play. For many years he was the ballast of the England innings and he cared too deeply for his craft and his position to take chances. To the best bowling he proffered impeccable defence, forward or back, against pace or spin. He took his runs when the bowler erred, and he had a sharp eye for such error. It was said that his shortened left arm left him open to the off-break and there were times when those watching – perhaps *too* closely – thought

Denis Compton (Middlesex) A gay and spontaneous batsman who mastered the problems of his age by courage, intuitive skill and timing

he had a weakness there. If so, he overcame it as he solved all the other problems of an injury which might have undermined the technique of a lesser player. At his greatest he cut and drove through the covers with an elegance unsurpassed in any era. Yet memory sees him as an embattled player or a lonely captain, pressing ahead with his job – to make sure that his side won or, if that were impossible, resisting to the end. His batting was never violent. Like Hobbs, he seemed to harness the break, swerve or pace of the ball to his strokes, and he killed the lifting ball on a sticky wicket with deep understanding of spin.

Batting, for him, was no joke; it was his job, and he used it to win matches; sometimes he broke records along the way. Hour after hour he presented that sternly straight bat to the bowler and lay in wait for the bad ball which he hit surgically to the most profitable place.

As with J. W. Hearne, one was surprised that a batsman of such care should bowl leg-breaks as

Hutton did – at times, in his early years, quite successfully. He had, too, a safe pair of hands anywhere.

As a Test captain, Hutton was undemonstrative but implacable; never losing a scrap of advantage, never taking any situation for granted. He came through the bad days to captain an England side that beat Australia. Then, with his 129 hundreds, his batting average of 55·51 – slightly but meaningfully higher, at 56·67, in Tests – and his knighthood to come, he left the physical and nervous strain of cricket for business and reporting.

Denis Compton

Their 'supporters' did Len Hutton and Denis Compton a disservice by comparing them. They were too dissimilar for comparison; they had in common only that they were gifted batsmen, and that for a dozen years they were far and away England's best.

Compton, like Hendren, whose successor he was in many ways – including playing at outside left for England in a 'Victory' international – was a personal batsman, who showed his humanity at every twist and turn of his play. He had the same eagerness to snatch his first run, the same inclination to joke, the same ability to switch from laughter to single-minded concentration on the next ball bowled.

Compton was a natural cricketer who, with maturity, never lost the air of a boy at play. His batting had an air of spontaneity, for all its soundness. Responsibility found a streak of iron in him. In his first match for Middlesex, when he was eighteen, he went in last and stayed with his captain to gain his side a first innings lead. In later years he stood firm when the rest of the England batting was going down around him.

There were times, such as the summer of 1947, when he reeled off runs like a record-breaker and, against North-eastern Transvaal in 1947, and in the Trent Bridge Test of 1954 with Pakistan, he went on for over after over, producing every stroke in the book – and some invented on the spur of the moment – in such a headlong tumble of run-scoring that it seemed he must be out at any moment. Then, hair rumpled, rosy with warmth, he embodied all the gaiety of cricket.

Compton was a cricketer of his age in his power on the leg side, and no one else has ever been stronger against the off-spinners who exerted such a hold over the batting of the nineteen-fifties. His sweep, an apparently loose-limbed stroke, placed the off-break anywhere between square-leg and fine-leg with an accuracy which beat the most careful field-setting. Then, when that side was packed, he would dash down the pitch and drive or, when the bowler sought to trap him by dropping short, cut against the spin or play a short-armed, back foot drive which travelled at great speed. His cover-driving forced the best leg-spin or slow left-arm bowlers to set a defensive field to him, but still his power sent the ball through.

Defence irked him: while he put his head down to save a match, he still struck the loose ball hard and happily. He had out-of-form spells, notably in Australia in 1950–51, without losing his progressive approach and, as on the occasion of benefit matches at Lord's, he had a quite uncanny knack of making a century when it was most appropriate.

He was, it must be said, an atrocious runner between wickets and some of his escapades, humorous in retrospect, seemed tragic at the time.

Compton bowled the 'Chinaman' with a well hidden googly, not always accurately but at least well

enough to take over six hundred wickets and, in the Cape Town Test of 1949, as England's emergency orthodox slow left-arm bowler, he took five for 70.

In his young days a good outfield, he became a good close catcher, if liable to lapses. His 18 centuries and aggregate of 3,816 runs in 1947 are still unexceeded and only Hammond, Bradman and Hutton have scored more than his 5,807 runs in Tests. He remains the picture of the happy cricketer.

Cyril Washbrook

The post-war partnership of Hutton and Washbrook endured as no other had done for England after Hobbs and Sutcliffe, and as none has done since. Washbrook, short, high-shouldered and stocky, was an assertive batsman. He had all the Lancashireman's ability to present the dead bat in defence, but he was rarely content to lean upon it. His strength and his weakness lay in cutting and hooking; in the end he always attacked the pace bowlers and did so well enough to score 76 centuries; and if long experience of dealing with the faster bowlers tended to emphasize his back foot play, he was a commanding on-driver. With an assured air and quick reflexes, he always sought to dominate the opposing bowling and he was never content to accept a game as lost.

One of the finest cover-points in the latter day game, Washbrook was a positive cricketer and an individualist.

D. V. P. Wright

No bowler in cricket can have reaped so little reward for so many balls verging on the unplayable as Doug Wright. He inherited 'Tich' Freeman's position as Kent's leg-break bowler, but the two were completely unlike in method. Freeman, after the fashion of his day, tossed the ball up and invited attack. Wright, from a unique, and precariously balanced, sprung-rhythm run-up, bowled at something near medium pace with a faster ball which beat some of the best batsmen with their bats half way down. He spun both leg-break and googly acutely and, though his length sometimes wavered, he might, at any time and on the easiest of wickets, beat the defensive stroke of the best batsmen in the world, even though they were well set. At times he turned his googly so sharply as to justify two men at short-leg: at others he would bowl leg-breaks of such fire that the batsman could only grope: then, again and again, the ball would beat the edge of the bat and stumps as well.

THE PROFESSIONAL GAME: 1919-1939

He performed the hat trick seven times – more often than anyone else – and he always maintained a remarkably low overs-per-wicket return.

An ordinary batsman and field, he was worth his place in the England side for a dozen years as the man more likely than anyone else to bowl the unplayable ball.

W. J. Edrich

For several years after the second World War, Edrich and Compton, coming behind Robertson and Brown, made the Middlesex batting so weighty that, but for sure handling, it might have swamped and drawn matches.

Bill Edrich was a short, vibrant man of wiry strength and a highly developed combative streak. His straight driving of fast bowlers and his pulled drive over mid-on reflected his attitude to bowling and he hooked short, fast bowling in a way that brought him many runs, but which experienced Test bowlers often exploited to take his wicket. In defence he bristled with resistance and took some severe beatings from fast bowlers without a hint of flinching. In his early days he tended to correct his over-anxiety by taking risks. As he matured, he became a colder player, still difficult to pin down, but more shrewd and controlled in his attacking strokes.

He served often as an all-rounder in Test cricket, for, in a period when England were short of fast bowlers, his bounding, slinging fast right-arm was as quick as anything England had available. First an outfield, he became a good slip. His spring and vitality kept him constantly *in* a match and he would fight the most hopeless game fiercely down to the last ball.

Australians in England, 1938

Bradman's Australian party of 1938 reflected the state of Australian cricket – wealth in batting and, apart from O'Reilly, poverty in bowling. In attack, all rested on O'Reilly and the fitfully successful Fleetwood-Smith. McCormick, spoken of as the fastest bowler Australia had ever sent to England, was no-balled for over-stepping the crease nineteen times in his first three overs of the tour. That may have un-settled him for, except in the Lord's Test, he did nothing to justify his home reputation.

Waite, a leg spinner who sometimes bowled medium paced swingers; White, slow left-arm and Ward, slow

leg-breaks, would hardly have been chosen for any other Australian team between the two wars.

Barnett was a neat wicket-keeper and, if Badcock batted disappointingly in Tests, two other young batsmen, Hassett and Barnes, showed the powers that were to expand after the war.

S. G. Barnes

Built on the square, strong-armed lines of so many Australian batsmen, Sydney Barnes was a right-hander with a belligerent approach. When he first came to England, his strength lay on the off side where he drove well. With the years he became more and more a back foot player, scoring almost all his runs square of the wicket or behind it. He was of the mental cast to make long scores and, eminently safe against pace and all but the best spin, he scored heavily so long as he cared to play first-class cricket. He was an intrepid close field.

A. L. Hassett

There have been few more poised batsmen than Lindsay Hassett and none in our time whose footwork was so perfect. Only five-feet-six tall, small-boned and neat, he moved into position with unhurrying speed so early that it seemed that he might have done any-thing with the ball when it arrived; then, like George Gunn, he would often, almost mockingly, allow it to strike a dead, defensive bat.

Especially after he took over the captaincy of Australia, Hassett cast himself in the role Collins assumed during the early twenties, allowing the full force of the early bowling to waste itself against his immaculately straight defence. He watched the ball carefully and, when he was of a mind to attack, he hit with remarkable strength for one so small; he cut stylishly, could hook the highest pace, and pulled impudently. He enjoyed teasing bowlers, either by his unfailingly patient defence or by beating their field-placings, and he maintained a puckish humour in some difficult corners. His good nature was an im-portant factor in the steady improvement of relations between Australian and English teams after the War. He fielded brilliantly in the deep and was an alert captain, with a gift for keeping his players in good heart.

W. A. Brown

This was the second of Bill Brown's three tours of England and his most successful. He was a quiet man,

Stan McCabe (N.S.W.) The compact, combative stroke-maker who played two of the finest innings of Test cricket between the two wars

thoughtful and dedicated to the game and always in the best of physical condition. He could at times reveal a whole battery of strokes and in another period might have used them more often. Coming into Test cricket at a time when Australia were rich in young batsmen, he preferred the more certain path of planned run-scoring and at times his play was slow though, because of his smooth, erect style, it was never ugly. Most important from his point of view, he rarely failed to make runs when they were needed.

Only once during the 1938 series – when the Leeds pitch helped spin – did either side look capable of bowling the other out twice to win a match within the allotted four days. The Old Trafford Test was completely washed out by rain and the last, at The Oval, was to be played to a finish.

The series produced so many batting records as to make their repetition wearisome, and often the cricket reflected the players' realization that, unless a batsman made a mistake, he need hardly be out.

Hammond, who had become an amateur, was hustled forthwith into the captaincy, and the new generation of English batsmen announced themselves in a lively start to the series. Barnett – 99 not out at lunch – went on to 126: Paynter made 216* and Hutton and Compton, in their first innings against Australia, 100 and 102 towards a total of 658 for eight declared. Farnes and Wright, supported by Verity and the off-breaks of Sinfield, the useful Gloucester all-rounder, gave England a first innings lead of 247, which must have been much larger but for McCabe. He scored 232 out of the Australian 411, batting so gloriously that Bradman, watching from the balcony, called out the other Australians from the dressing room with the words 'Come and watch this, you may never see an innings like it again'.

When Australia followed on, their only possible objective was to avoid defeat. Brown – 133 – and Bradman – also suiting his method to the demands of the occasion with 144* in six hours – steered them safely to a draw.

At Lord's, England replaced Sinfield with Arthur Wellard of Somerset, who bowled fast medium out-swing as penetrating as any in England and who, as a firm-footed hitter, struck more sixes in his career than anyone else.

England again batted first, and though McCormick made early inroads into their batting, Hammond (240) and Paynter (99) built the total to 494. But for Brown who carried his bat for 206* – Hassett's 56 was

Bill O'Reilly (N.S.W.) The tightest and briskest of all leg-spinners, the 'Tiger' who never relaxed his attack, and never gave any batsman best

the next highest score – Australia would have been far more than 72 behind. Hammond again declared and set Australia 315 to win in under three hours: they were not tempted and Bradman made a draw certain with 102*.

Australia's strategy for the series was to hold on until they came to a wicket suitable for O'Reilly, and they found one – granting some turn and a little pace without being treacherous – at Headingley. O'Reilly duly won the match by taking ten wickets, backed by Fleetwood-Smith with seven. Only Hammond – 76 – scored more than 30 in either English innings. Also in accordance with Australia's plan, Bradman gave O'Reilly elbow room by scoring 103, with a capable and responsible 76 by Ben Barnett – sent in as night watchman – his main support. Australia needed 105 to win and, as the pitch and light deteriorated, England harried them.

Hassett batted with cool resource, and his 33 was the conclusive Australian effort. Wright, put on, perhaps, too late, took the wickets of Bradman, McCabe and Hassett for 26 runs but Hassett had by then brought Australia to the edge of their five wickets win.

The Oval Test of 1938 was one of many records, and is more stirring in summary than it sometimes seemed to those who watched it. England had, at last, a batting strength to compare with Australia's in length and depth, and they set out to wipe off many old and bitter scores. They left out Charles Barnett (who had an average of 43 for the series) and Wright also. Hutton, who had missed Headingley through injury, Leyland and Arthur Wood, the cheerful and reliable Yorkshire wicket-keeper, came into the side.

Hammond won the toss, England batted and the Australian bowling was opened, somewhat sadly, by McCabe and Waite. Edrich was out to O'Reilly at 29 and then the runs began to grow to mountainous heights. Hutton batted into the third day for 364 – a new record individual score for a Test: Leyland (187) put on 382 with him for the second wicket. Hammond made 59, Hardstaff 169* and Wood 53 in the record Test total of 903 for seven wickets made by tea time on the third day, when Hammond declared. Bradman and Fingleton had both been injured in the field and did not bat in either innings of Australia. Bowes with seven wickets and Farnes, five, mopped up and England won by – another record – an innings and 579 runs. It was magnificent, but one wondered at times if it was cricket. England had drawn the series but Australia retained The Ashes.

For all that Hutton took his Test record from him, Bradman was again the dominant figure of the summer. Once more he began with a double century at Worcester and made a thousand runs by the end of May. He scored a century in each Test in which he batted, and, although he did not play after the last Test, he made 2,429 runs in the season and averaged 115·66.

Yorkshire and Middlesex were again Champions and runners-up, well clear of the remainder of the counties. Edrich, like Bradman, scored a thousand by the end of May – all of them at Lord's. Maurice Nichols, for Essex against Gloucester at Bristol, scored 159 runs and took 15 wickets for 115. C. I. J. Smith of Middlesex scored 50 in eleven minutes, also against Gloucester. 'Big Jim' Smith, a huge Wiltshireman, was at lowest estimate a first-class county bowler, genuinely fast, straight, lively and strong: and a firm-footed hitter of mighty strength and carry.

Hugh Bartlett

Two of the most spectacular innings of 1938 – or any other year – were played by Hugh Bartlett – 175* in under three hours for Gentlemen v Players at Lord's and 157 – the first hundred in 57 minutes – for Sussex against the Australians. A tall, finely built left-hander, Bartlett had been a strong hitter from his schooldays at Dulwich. Of late he had worked to improve his defence and, from that platform, he proceeded, in 1938, to launch an offensive against all types of bowling. Most of his runs came from drives – between square cover and straight – old-fashioned pulls towards mid-wicket, and a savage slash through point. Linking strength to his natural timing, he drove with almost frightening power and, when on the kill, he was magnificent to watch. He served during the war with considerable gallantry and distinction but, when he returned to cricket, the finely balanced mechanism of his batting had been disturbed beyond the power of so essentially instinctive a cricketer to adjust it.

England in South Africa, 1938–39

The challenging and lively matting wickets of South Africa had now given way to over-good turf pitches. Batsmen flourished throughout. England, with the strongest team they had ever sent to the Union, won the only Test finished. At Johannesburg, Paynter scored a century in each innings; Gibb, the Cambridge University and Yorkshire wicket-keeper-batsman, stolid and of infinite patience, who played in spectacles, made 106 and 93, and Valentine, the free hitting Kent right-hander, 97, for England. Goddard did the hat trick, but Dalton's 102 was the basis for a South Africa recovery to 390. Hammond's declaration gave the strong South African batting no chance to win.

In the second Test, England put themselves out of danger with 559 for nine, including centuries by Hammond, Valentine and Ames. Despite a brave 120 by Nourse, South Africa followed on, when Van der Byl and Rowan resolutely saved the game.

In the third Test, at Durban, the wicket was again good, except for one period of mild disturbance on the last day. Hammond won the toss for the third time; he scored 120 and Paynter 243, South Africa dropped catches, and the England innings was closed at 469 for four. Farnes, Wright and Wilkinson bowled out South Africa for 103 and again, in their second innings, in face of determined resistance from Mitchell – 109 – Rowan and Viljoen, for 353, to give England an innings win.

At Johannesburg rain blotted out the third day and, after even and capable batting by South Africa had given them a first innings lead of 134, England had no trouble in making a draw.

The last Test at Durban was to be 'timeless': in the outcome it was left drawn after ten days – with an intervening Sunday. There was no play on the eighth day (i.e. the second Saturday of the match) but otherwise some cricket was always possible, until rain or poor light ended each day: and always the wicket rolled out true next morning.

Hammond lost the toss to Melville for the only time in the series and South Africa batted solidly: Van der Byl and Nourse made centuries: Melville, Dalton and Grieveson over fifty, in an innings of 530. Perks of Worcester took five for 100 – impressive figures in such a total – in his first Test. Reg Perks had just reached the height of his career when war came. He was a tall, strong fast-medium bowler who contradicted his square-on action with a perfectly fair delivery and hostile pace from the pitch. Although he lost six years to war, he took a hundred wickets in each of sixteen seasons and posed problems of pace and swing on good wickets.

No England batsman played a long innings, and they were 204 behind on the first innings. 'Timeless Test' tactics dictated that South Africa build up an impregnable total and Van der Byl – a solid bat who won an Oxford Blue in 1932 – followed his first innings century with 97, narrowly missing being the first South African to score a hundred in each innings of a Test against England. Melville made a century, the batting ran long to 481 and South Africa had set England 696 to win.

Hutton and Gibb began with 78 for the first wicket and then Hammond, in an imaginative piece of captaincy, sent Edrich in at number three, his usual place for Middlesex. Edrich's previous scores in the series had been 4, 10, 0 and 6 and since, in the series against Australia, he had played six innings for 67 runs, there was considerable weight of opinion in favour of ignoring his obvious natural talent and dropping him. Nothing could have been more characteristic of the man than that, at this crucial juncture of the match

Len – now Sir Leonard – Hutton (Yorkshire) The modern master: sometimes his determination concealed the grace and beauty of his movement, but he was essentially a stylist

and his career, he proceeded to score 219. Hammond, in one of the finest innings of his life, scored 140, Gibb plodded grittily to 120 and Paynter made 75. Gradually the ports at which the English team could catch the Union Castle boat home decreased: and, timeless Test or not, the tenth day had to be the last. South Africa pinned down the batting until the tea interval, when England, at 654 for five, wanted 42 to win. The rain came down again, and the game was left drawn.

The longest match and the highest fourth innings total in Test cricket, and only a draw to show for it, made a joke of the idea of timeless Tests.

Many of the South African batsmen had fallen far below the scoring standard of which they were capable. It was clear, however, that their strength was growing. In 'Marble' Gordon who, even against such a strong batting side, took 20 wickets – albeit at 40 each – they had found a medium pace spin bowler of rare ability. Unhappily neither he, Van der Byl, the talented wicket-keeper, Grieveson, nor the two men killed in the War – Langton and Briscoe – were able to take their places in what had been reasonably foreseen as the best of all South African sides, when it remustered in the years of peace.

West Indies in the English season of 1939

An air of apprehension and unreality hung over the summer of 1939. So far as its facts are concerned, England won one Test against R. S. Grant's West Indians and the other two were drawn; Yorkshire and Middlesex were again first and second in the Championship, with Gloucestershire third. It was decided to try out the eight-ball over in first-class cricket, an experiment shelved after the War.

England won the first Test at Lord's when, though Headley for the second time scored a century in each innings of a Test, hundreds by Hutton and Compton – an earnest of days to come – and an admirably balanced attack of Bowes, Copson, Wright and Verity, proved conclusive. Two declarations by Hammond – at 164 and 128 – at Old Trafford threw the West Indies unhappily into the problems of a bad wicket and, against Bowes, Copson, Goddard and Wright, they barely scrambled to a draw. At The Oval, where

the English catching was deplorable – eleven catches were dropped off Perks, who nevertheless took five for 156 – the West Indies took a first innings lead. Constantine had five for 75 in the first English innings and hit a violent 79. Hutton and Hammond with hundreds saw England and the rubber secure.

There was no happier event of the season than Northants beating Leicestershire by an innings at Northampton – to win their first Championship match since the start of the 1935 season. Down at Bournemouth, as August ran out towards War, a young South African-born leg-spinner, Tom Dean, took four Worcestershire wickets in five balls – including the hat trick: by 1946 his bowling gift was gone.

On 1st September, the German army moved into Poland. Only one first-class cricket match was in progress on that day: it was the benefit match for Jim Parks senior – Sussex v Yorkshire, at Hove. Hedley Verity took seven wickets for nine runs and put out Sussex for 33. It was the last first-class game of Verity's life, and England's last for six years.

The Post-War Scene, Concentration and Expansion: 1946–1965

The post-War era has been a separate and quite distinct stage in the evolution of modern cricket. In the 1890s, England, the country where most first-class cricket was played, and whose Test teams had proved, on results, stronger than any other, dominated the scene. There the county Championship was, insularly, thought the most important part of the game, so that there was resistance to increasing the number of Tests from three to five on the grounds that it would interfere unduly with the Championship. Between 1900 and the first World War, Test cricket grew in importance and extent, but still English county cricket was a major facet, and the Sheffield Shield and Currie Cup competitions absorbed much attention in Australia and South Africa. Between the two wars, Test cricket moved clear of all other play. Attendances at any fixture of less than international standing fell away, though touring teams' matches against counties, states or provinces drew fair crowds.

Since 1946, cricket has taken different courses in different countries so that it is not possible to generalize about it.

In England and Australia, summer interests have become more diverse and there is less *social concentration* on cricket. With increased prosperity, the *family* car has ended the day when the working man played or watched cricket while his wife stayed at home or went shopping. The car may be used to go to a Sunday afternoon match in the country but rarely to weekday cricket.

In England, the novelty of an annual visit from an overseas team had already worn off by 1939. The West Indies – regarded as 'colourful' – attracted spectators; South Africa did so at their best. But the only team to fill cricket grounds was Australia. India and New Zealand tours were hard pressed to make a profit. The renewal of cricket after war drew some nostalgic crowds: and the winning West Indies side of 1950 put themselves almost level with Australia in public estimation. But soon a sequence of one-sided and slow-moving Test series with other countries had such a disenchanting effect that the whole schedule of tours was altered to make Australian and West Indian visits more frequent and to shorten those by South Africa, New Zealand, India and Pakistan.

In Australia, where cricket had been a sterner kind of religion, the beaches proved a greater attraction than the playing of club cricket and the great stadia that had been full to watch Bradman were humiliatingly empty for Sheffield Shield matches; they did not fill again until Worrell's West Indians kindled public imagination in 1960–61.

In South Africa, interest spread in the nineteen-forties. Until then cricket had been regarded as the game of the section of the population with British origins. When, after 1947, the Afrikaans sector began to accept it, it became, for the first time, a truly national game in the Union.

The mounting success of West Indies teams maintained the always high enthusiasm for the game there and gave it added sophistication. Air travel, too, allowed Jamaica – hitherto kept out by the great distances involved – to join in inter-territorial competition. That isolation accounts, to some extent, for the smaller general cricket interest in that island than in Barbados, Trinidad and British Guiana.

While interest and attendances waned in England and Australia, they grew in India and Pakistan. There cricket is faced with less competition for its audiences than in other countries. It has become – not altogether happily – involved with national prestige, particularly in Tests between the two countries. To the disappointment of the Indian and Pakistani public, a number of leading players of other countries have been disinclined to make tours there. The main reason for their reluctance is certainly the effect of the climate and food on the health and performance of visitors from more temperate countries. On the other hand, the consuming interest of the public in international matches, even with non-representative touring sides, is so great as to make any tour there a financial success.

New Zealand, of all the Test playing countries the one least concerned with its own importance, continues to foster cricket healthily and happily, content to keep its ideas fresh through tours abroad and making friends through the unfailing charm of its teams.

Ceylon has already played representative matches with Indian and MCC teams and undoubtedly aspires to official Test Matches. Such recent players from Ceylon as Jayasinghe, Inman, Goonesena, Piachaud and Bartels have shown ability in England.

The Fijians have a native talent for both rugby and cricket and have surprised Australian, New Zealand and West Indian teams by their talents for fielding, fast bowling and long hitting.

Of the African countries, Kenya – who have played representative games with selected teams of 'Non-European' (their own term) cricketers from South Africa – and Uganda have play of good standard.

Technically, cricket since 1946 has, like many other games – Rugby and soccer, for instance – become highly intellectualized, and based on restriction of scoring. This restrictive method reached its first high level in the Lancashire side of 1951 where Tattersall – off-breaks – Berry and Hilton – slow left-arm – bowled with remarkable precision to carefully set defensive fields. It continued along the line of bowling directed at, or wide of, the leg stump: inswing, inslant – the

ball which the right-arm bowler, from the edge of the return crease, aims to or outside the leg stump – left-arm over the wicket as bowled by the South African, Goddard, and off-spin as practised by the successors of the Gloucestershire Goddard. All relied on a strong leg side field and, in 1957, legislation aimed primarily at the inslant bowlers restricted the number of fieldsmen on the leg side to five, of whom only two could be behind the batsman's wicket. This move did stop some negative bowling but it also penalized the off-spinner, especially on a turning wicket.

For some years, however, the off-break bowlers exerted great power and every side in the world except Australia employed them (Ian Johnson, though he went through the motions of off-spin, was in effect a slow, flighty outswinger).

Field-placing and the general standard of fielding – particularly in close catching and throwing – rose to new heights. Runs became harder to make than ever before. The traditional slow bowling – the ball tossed up in the hope of luring the batsman into giving a catch in the deep field – disappeared. The high hitting batsman became uneconomic and those who remained developed such proficiency on the leg side that they would often hit the slow left-arm bowler or the leg-spinner from outside the off stump to midwicket.

Test cricket has become grimmer than ever before. Fast bowlers are directed mercilessly and, despite the legislation against 'direct attack', the bouncer is employed too frequently to be called a 'surprise weapon'. Cricket, especially on representative level, is now not only a searching technical examination, but a harrowing nervous experience. The players of the post-1950 period look at photographs and films of cricket between the two wars and laugh – insisting that, in those days, runs must have been utterly easy to make. More convincingly, such heavy scorers of earlier days as Jack Hobbs and Philip Mead said frankly that, against accurate bowling to modern field-placings, their scoring would have been severely curbed. Walter Hammond, asked by the English side of 1956–57 in South Africa how he would have scored against Trevor Goddard's medium left-arm leg-stump attack, confessed that he could see no escape from the stranglehold it imposed.

In 1957 it was decided to award bonus points in the County Championship to a side which took a first innings lead at a faster scoring-rate than their opponents'. Immediately, it was converted, in tactical minds and in practice, into a matter not of the positive attempt to score faster than the opponents, but setting out to compel *them* to score *slower*.

When knock-out cricket, with an overs-limit for each innings, which had proved so entertaining on lower levels, was introduced, in the shape of the Gillette Cup competition, for the counties, alert brains applied themselves to its particular problems. The essential conclusion was that, in the number of overs allowed, a fielding side would do better to limit its opponents to, say, 150 for no wickets, than bowl them out for 151. Forthwith elaborately restrictive – in fact constrictive – field settings were employed. But the Cup, with its one-day result, did bring back the crowds.

In standard of performance, bowling has become far more accurate and control of the swinging ball has reached new heights of precision. Throughout the game it is increasingly difficult for players to continue to such ages as they formerly did. The forty-year-old now frequently is struggling to keep pace with his colleagues as effectively as fifty-year-olds did before 1940. Particularly this is true in the field; of old it was possible to hide two – or even three – ageing fieldsmen; now every man has to be of high standard or mobility or team efficiency suffers.

Undoubtedly there is less fun – for both players and spectators – in the game now than there was thirty years ago. On the other hand, it is certainly played on a higher all-round level of skill. First-class teams nowadays simply do not carry passengers and players who might have 'got by' between the wars, despite a flaw in technique, now find that their weakness is discovered and unfailingly exploited.

In England, slow and grassy wickets have extended the province of the seam bowler and reduced the amount of spinners. Leg-break bowling has almost gone out of existence so that Australia have been able to employ it with considerable effect against English batsmen unaccustomed to it. In India, the slow pitches have killed off the fast bowler while the leg-spinner has flourished. Year after year, MCC have exhorted the countries to produce fast, true wickets on which matches will move quickly. The response, however, has been slight: either because ground committees do not want fast wickets, or groundsmen cannot prepare them.

Cricket economics have altered vastly since 1946, with the Australian states suffering the most acute financial hardship they have ever known.

In England, the distribution of wealth has been turned upside down. Soon after the War ended, several of the poorer counties formed supporters' clubs which, in turn, organized football pools with, in some cases, quite phenomenal financial success. Those first in the field – Glamorgan, Warwickshire, Northants, Derby, Worcestershire and Leicestershire – are now more than solvent, and their new wealth has been reflected in most cases in playing results. There has, too, been a marked growth in county membership which has, to an extent, offset reduced gate-receipts. The counties' shares of profits from home Tests and overseas tours, and of radio and television fees, have also helped to meet the steeply rising costs of running a county team. Almost all counties now either house a Test Match, have a large membership, or a substantial income from their supporters' clubs. Only Hampshire, Gloucester and Somerset may not be financially secure.

The single wealthy patron of cricket, such as kept some counties solvent, practically disappeared with the War of 1939 and has been replaced by the thousands of shilling-a-week contributors to the football pools. A new influence is the commercial patron, spending money on cricket instead of on advertising space or more restricted forms of public relations. Thus we have the Gillette Cup, the Carling single-wicket competition and sponsorship of a domestic tournament in the Caribbean by petrol and tobacco firms.

Ambitious projects of this nature have been undertaken by Rothmans of Pall Mall, the cigarette-makers. They began by under-writing the International Cavaliers club, which has made several overseas tours of the type which has become popular in Rhodesia, India, Pakistan and Ceylon. They sent a touring side of recent Test players to Jamaica in 1964; that venture was sufficiently successful to be repeated in 1965. In 1964 they subsidized an eleven of West Indian Test players under Sir Frank Worrell to play three matches against representative England teams.

In this season, they have marked their jubilee by backing the public selection of a World XI to play two matches against England teams.

The healthiest aspect of post-war English cricket has been the levelling up within the Championship. For many years the top places were shared between the same few sides while others never emerged from the lower reaches. Since 1946, however, every county has been at least once in both the first five and the last six places.

Surrey, with a side which must rank with the best the competition has ever known, were Champions for seven consecutive seasons from 1952 to 1958, while Yorkshire, only once truly out of the hunt since the 1946 re-start, have been six times first and five times runners-up. Most stimulating of all, however, three of the former tail-enders – Glamorgan, Hampshire and Worcester – have won the Championship for the first time, and Warwickshire for the second.

Surrey, 1952–58

During Surrey's second great period in the Championship the captaincy was held first by Stuart Surridge and then by Peter May. The batting – spread, over the years, between May, Barrington, Fletcher, Clark, Constable, Fishlock and Stewart – was adequate but never so weighty as to make their cricket top-heavy with runs. The task of the batsmen was to make room for a keen, tight and balanced attack in which the three constants were Alec Bedser, Laker and Lock; the extra pace opening bowler was first Surridge and then Loader, while Eric Bedser reinforced both the spin bowling – when it needed reinforcement – and the batting. Surridge was a demanding and stimulating captain who set the high standard of fielding and catching which made the side's outcricket so menacing.

Yorkshire, 1946–65

Yorkshire's six Championships since the war have been won under five different captains – Sellers, Yardley, Burnet, Wilson (the first professional to hold the office there in modern times) and Close. As after the first World War, they won in 1946 with a skilfully composed blend of elders and learners. Through the middle period the batting of Hutton and the bowling of Trueman, Wardle and Appleyard were strong points. Latterly there has been long, and sometimes brilliant batting, with Close as its keynote; it broke Surrey's run in 1959 when, in the final and decisive match, against Sussex, Yorkshire set to score 215 to win in an hour-and-three-quarters, made them with seven minutes to spare.

Glamorgan, 1948

The last county to enter the Championship, Glamorgan, startled even their friends when they won the title in 1948. To many this was a memorial to Maurice Turnbull, their captain of the thirties, whose efforts during the thirties averted the threat of bankruptcy and set a fresh standard of outcricket. J. C. Clay, one of the main bowlers in the county's first Championship season, 1921, was, happily and valuably, a member of the Championship team. His off-breaks, coupled with the spin of Muncer and Trick – especially on turning wickets at home – the all-round cricket of Watkins and the batting of W. E. Jones, all contributed to the win. There were, however, stronger batting and bowling sides in the country: Glamorgan beat them because they were the best fielding team England had known until then, and were captained with unremitting drive by Wilfred Wooller.

Hampshire in 1961

This team, moulded by Desmond Eagar and taken over in 1958 by Colin Ingleby-Mackenzie, won after some nicely judged declarations, through a shared effort: six batsmen scored over a thousand runs – Marshall and Horton over two thousand – and six bowlers of varying paces and styles – led by Shackleton – took 45 wickets or more.

Worcestershire in 1964

When Tom Graveney joined Worcester from Gloucester, he completed a batting order long, solid, and capable of fast runs. The pace bowling of Flavell, Coldwell and the medium paced Standen, with Carter in reserve, and the contrasting slow left-arm of Slade and Gifford gave Kenyon, a mature captain, an attack for any conditions and always economical. The team grew in power and confidence over the season and carried through unwaveringly to win from Warwickshire.

Middlesex in 1947 and 1949, Warwickshire in 1951, Lancashire – who shared with Surrey in 1950 – reflected the broadening of the competition: eight different counties won the Championship in a span of twenty years.

Tom Graveney (Gloucestershire and Worcestershire) the gracious, prolific and mature batsman who, puzzlingly – and perhaps by no more than bad luck – failed to hold his place at the highest level of the game for twenty years. The wicket-keeper is Dick and short leg is Pollard

In 1951, H. E. – Tom – Dollery became the first professional to captain a Championship-winning county side. The first of the modern professional captains was Ewart Astill, of Leicester, in 1935 – that county's most successful season between the two wars: and Leslie Berry was appointed by Leicestershire for 1946 to 1948. After that every county except Essex, Glamorgan and Hampshire had at least one professional captain before the distinction between amateur and professional was abolished in 1962. It was a true reflection of the thinking of the times, as well as an expedient move, to make Len Hutton the first professional captain of an official England team in 1952.

The results that follow show the immense growth of Test cricket in the past twenty years and why, in the critical and historic mind, it must be divided into first-class and second-class play. Australia, England, and the West Indies are the three contestants for the title, which exists in the modern cricketing mind without ever taking concrete form, of a World Cricket Championship. South Africa may achieve successes against England or Australia: they do not, of course, play the West Indies – but they would not be a match for the strongest sides of the other two.

1946–1965

Test Matches

1945–46 in New Zealand, Australia beat New Zealand, 1–0

1946 in England, England beat India 1–0: two matches drawn

1946–47 in Australia, Australia beat England, 3–0: two matches drawn

in New Zealand, New Zealand *v* England: one match drawn

1947 in England, England beat South Africa, 3–0: two matches drawn

1947–48 in West Indies, West Indies beat England, 2–0: two matches drawn

in Australia, Australia beat India, 4–0: one match drawn

1948 in England, Australia beat England 4–0: one match drawn

1948–49 in South Africa, England beat South Africa, 2–0: three matches drawn

in India, West Indies beat India, 1–0: four matches drawn

1949 in England, England *v* New Zealand, series drawn, 0–0: four matches drawn

1949–50 in South Africa, Australia beat South Africa, 4–0: one match drawn

1950 in England, West Indies beat England, 3–1

1950–51 in Australia, Australia beat England, 4–1

in New Zealand, England beat New Zealand, 1–0: one match drawn

1951 in England, England beat South Africa, 3–1: one match drawn

1951–52 in India, India *v* England, series drawn, 1–1: three matches drawn

in Australia, Australia beat West Indies, 4–1

in New Zealand, West Indies beat New Zealand, 1–0: one match drawn

1952 in England, England beat India, 3–0: one match drawn

1952–53 in India, India beat Pakistan, 2–1: two matches drawn

in Australia, Australia *v* South Africa, series drawn, 2–2: one match drawn

in New Zealand, South Africa beat New Zealand, 1–0: one match drawn

in West Indies, West Indies beat India, 1–0: four matches drawn

1953 in England, England beat Australia, 1–0: four matches drawn

1953–54 in South Africa, South Africa beat New Zealand, 4–0: one match drawn

in West Indies, West Indies *v* England, series drawn, 2–2: one match drawn

1954 in England, England *v* Pakistan, series drawn, 1–1: two matches drawn

1954–55 in Australia, England beat Australia, 3–1:

one match drawn

in New Zealand, England beat New Zealand, 2–0

in Pakistan, Pakistan *v* India, series drawn, 0–0: five matches drawn

in West Indies, Australia beat West Indies, 3–0: two matches drawn

1955 in England, England beat South Africa, 3–2

1955–56 in Pakistan, Pakistan beat New Zealand, 2–0: one match drawn

in India, India beat New Zealand 2–0: three matches drawn

in New Zealand, West Indies beat New Zealand, 3–1

1956 in England, England beat Australia, 2–1: two matches drawn

1956–57 in Pakistan, Pakistan beat Australia, 1–0

in India, Australia beat India, 2–0: one match drawn

in South Africa, South Africa *v* England, series drawn, 2–2: one match drawn

1957 in England, England beat West Indies, 3–0: two matches drawn

1957–58 in South Africa, Australia beat South Africa, 3–0: two matches drawn

in West Indies, West Indies beat Pakistan, 3–1: one match drawn

1958 in England, England beat New Zealand, 4–0: one match drawn

1958–59 in India, West Indies beat India, 3–0: two matches drawn

in Pakistan, Pakistan beat West Indies, 2–1

in Australia, Australia beat England, 4–0: one match drawn

in New Zealand, England beat New Zealand, 1–0: one match drawn

1959 in England, England beat India, 5–0

1959–60 in Pakistan, Australia beat Pakistan, 2–0: one match drawn

in India, Australia beat India, 2–1: two matches drawn

in West Indies, England beat West Indies, 1–0: four matches drawn

1960 in England, England beat South Africa, 3–0: two matches drawn

1960–61 in India, India *v* Pakistan, series drawn 0–0: five matches drawn

in Australia, Australia beat West Indies, 2–1: one match drawn, one match tied.

1961 in England, Australia beat England, 2–1: two matches drawn

1961–62 in Pakistan, England beat Pakistan, 1–0: two matches drawn

in India, India beat England, 2–0: three matches drawn

in South Africa, South Africa *v* New Zealand, series drawn, 2–2: one match drawn

in West Indies, West Indies beat India, 5–0

1962 in England, England beat Pakistan, 4–0: one match drawn

1962–63 in Australia, Australia *v* England, series drawn, 1–1: three matches drawn

in New Zealand, England beat New Zealand, 3–0

1963 in England, West Indies beat England, 3–1: one match drawn

1963–64 in Australia, Australia *v* South Africa, series drawn, 1–1: three matches drawn

in New Zealand, New Zealand *v* South Africa, series drawn, 0–0: three matches drawn

in India, India *v* England, series drawn, 0–0: five matches drawn

1964 in England, Australia beat England, 1–0: four matches drawn

1964–65 in South Africa, England beat South Africa, 1–0: four matches drawn

in India, India *v* Australia, series drawn, 1–1: one match drawn

in Pakistan, Pakistan *v* Australia, one match drawn

in Australia, Australia *v* Pakistan, one match drawn

in New Zealand, New Zealand *v* Pakistan, series drawn, 0–0: three matches drawn

in Pakistan, Pakistan beat New Zealand, 2–0: one match drawn

in India, India beat New Zealand, 1–0: three matches drawn

in West Indies, West Indies beat Australia, 2–1: two matches drawn

1946–1965

County Champions

1946 Yorkshire
1947 Middlesex
1948 Glamorgan
1949 Middlesex and Yorkshire
1950 Lancashire and Surrey
1951 Warwickshire

1952 Surrey
1953 Surrey
1954 Surrey
1955 Surrey
1956 Surrey
1957 Surrey
1958 Surrey
1959 Yorkshire
1960 Yorkshire
1961 Hampshire
1962 Yorkshire
1963 Yorkshire
1964 Worcestershire

Sheffield Shield Winners

1946–47 Victoria
1947–48 Western Australia
1948–49 New South Wales
1949–50 New South Wales
1950–51 Victoria
1951–52 New South Wales
1952–53 South Australia
1953–54 New South Wales
1954–55 New South Wales
1955–56 New South Wales
1956–57 New South Wales
1957–58 New South Wales
1958–59 New South Wales
1959–60 New South Wales
1960–61 New South Wales
1961–62 New South Wales
1962–63 Victoria
1963–64 South Australia
1964–65 New South Wales

Currie Cup Winners

1946–47 Natal
1947–48 Natal
1950–51 Transvaal
1951–52 Natal
1952–53 Western Province
1954–55 Natal
1955–56 Western Province
1958–59 Transvaal
1959–60 Natal
1960–61 Natal

1962–63 Natal
1963–64 Natal

West Indies Inter-Territorial Tournament

1956–57 British Guiana drew with Barbados
1957–58 Jamaica beat Barbados
1958–59 Barbados beat British Guiana
1959–60 British Guiana drew with Jamaica
1960–61 Barbados beat Trinidad
1961–62 British Guiana beat Barbados
1963–64 British Guiana

Plunkett Shield Winners

1945–46 Canterbury
1946–47 Auckland
1947–48 Otago
1948–49 Canterbury
1949–50 Wellington
1950–51 Otago
1951–52 Canterbury
1952–53 Otago
1953–54 Central Districts
1954–55 Wellington
1955–56 Canterbury
1956–57 Wellington
1957–58 Otago
1958–59 Auckland
1959–60 Canterbury
1960–61 Wellington
1961–62 Wellington
1962–63 Northern Districts
1963–64 Auckland
1964–65 Canterbury

'Ranji' Trophy Winners

1940–41 Maharashtra
1941–42 Bombay
1942–43 Baroda
1943–44 Western India
1944–45 Bombay
1945–46 Holkar
1946–47 Baroda
1947–48 Holkar
1948–49 Bombay

1949–50 Baroda
1950–51 Holkar
1951–52 Bombay
1952–53 Holkar
1953–54 Bombay
1954–55 Madras
1955–56 Bombay
1956–57 Bombay
1957–58 Baroda
1958–59 Bombay
1959–60 Bombay
1960–61 Bombay
1961–62 Bombay
1962–63 Bombay
1963–64 Bombay
1964–65 Bombay

Qaid-I-Azam Trophy Winners

1953–54 Bahawalpur
1954–55 Karachi
1956–57 Punjab
1957–58 Bahawalpur
1958–59 Karachi
1959–60 Karachi
1961–62 Karachi Blues
1962–63 Karachi
1963–64 Karachi Blues
1964–65 Karachi

AUSTRALIAN CHAMPIONS

Australia were ready and eager for Test cricket after the second World War, as after the first, and pressed for the visit of an MCC side. Their request was publicized and it became a matter of national pride for England to meet it.

English cricket of 1946, so long as it stood in relative isolation, seemed healthy enough. Those with clear recollection and judgement of the pre-war years knew otherwise. They were right – as can be seen now by reference to the number of men who first played county cricket in 1946 and 1947 and, found wanting, were never seen there again. There were good bowlers and batsmen but too few of them for the game to be truly strong. Too many runs could be scored from

*Vinoo Mankad (Gujerat) in 1946 one of the most accomplished
all-rounders in the world: keen but steady and shrewd*

Vinoo Mankad

More than any other India player, Vinoo Mankad
was cast in the mould of the English professional. In
1946 he performed the feat, rare for a touring player,
of the all-round double. His bowling was slow left-
arm, varied in flight and well spun, he took punishment philosophically and was never easy to master on
the best of batsmen's wickets. His batting – right-hand
– was based on Merchant's and at this time it was
careful and correct, straight and patient and, if he
lacked the strokes of Merchant, he was completely
reliable. Subsequent Lancashire League experience
led him to a freer style, less sound but more attractive.
He was a safe-handed field and a steady, balanced
character.

From the English point of view, this rubber was
valuable for the introduction of two of the players who
were to stand with Hutton, Compton, Washbrook
and Edrich as pillars of English cricket through the
bad times to the good. They were Alec Bedser – who
took 24 of the 49 Indian wickets that fell in Tests – and
Godfrey Evans, brought in as wicket-keeper at The
Oval.

A. V. Bedser

The history of Maurice Tate was repeated in Alec
Bedser. Unless we quibble about an odd appearance
for Surrey in 1939, he did not begin his first-class
career until 1946, when he was almost twenty-eight;
then he laboured mightily and almost alone to sustain
the English pace attack and burnt away much of his
fire before adequate support was found for him.

Massively built – six-feet-four tall and weighing
fifteen stone, like his twin brother, Eric – he bowled
fast-medium. In his early days he was almost entirely
an inswinger but he developed a full technique, sometimes made the ball go a little the other way in the
air, moved it in both directions off the pitch and
developed a leg cutter which, on a helpful wicket, was
utterly devastating. His stamina and fortitude matched
his build and, off an easy eight-pace run, with an ideal
body-action, he flogged life out of many a reluctant
pitch in spells, and over a period of home seasons and
overseas tours, such as would have broken the strength
of any ordinary man. Only two English bowlers –
Trueman and Statham – have taken more than his
236 wickets in Tests: both of them played in more
Tests and with better support. Bedser could bat well,
though wise captains saved his strength for bowling;
and the ball dropped easily into his huge hands. Often

indifferent change bowling; raw batting provided too
many easy wickets.

It was significant that Alf Gover, of Surrey, at
thirty-eight, was the fastest bowler in the country – a
standing he would never have claimed in his best
years, up to 1939. Indeed he opened the bowling for
England in one Test of 1946. Gover, a bowler of
courage, stamina and thought, became the best-
known coach in England.

India were beaten comfortably enough in the only
one of the three Tests finished. They were captained
by the Nawab of Pataudi, who had played for England
against Australia in 1932–33 and 1934 – a capable
bat, strong on the leg side, patient and determined in
method. Their best players were Merchant, now a
steady-scoring batsman of infinite patience and control, Amarnath, a genuine all-rounder – subtle and
accurate medium pace bowler and a punishing batsman on hard wickets – and Mankad.

139

Godfrey Evans (Kent) Played in more Tests – 91 – than any other cricketer and, by his vitality and exuberance, was a stimulus to everyone who played in or watched any one of them

it seemed that he stood quite alone as England's one attacking hope: his labours squeezed much sweat and some wry humour from him: and for eight years he never flagged.

T. G. Evans

No cricketer ever had more vitality than Godfrey Evans, who kept wicket for England in 91 Tests – the greatest number played by any cricketer – and was responsible for 219 dismissals, another Test record.

Supremely adroit, he read spin bowling well; stood up to the stumps to Alec Bedser although he had no comparable experience in his county side and, standing back to fast-bowling, covered vast distances to make catches of astounding acrobatic brilliance.

His batting was usually gay and daring (he could rarely resist the temptation to cut) though in 1946–47, in Australia, he batted for over an hour-and-a-half

before he scored in his stand with Compton that saved the Adelaide Test. More characteristically, in 1959, at Trent Bridge, he scored the fastest fifty ever recorded for England in a Test; against the West Indies in 1950 he made a hundred on an 'impossible' wicket at Old Trafford.

Godfrey Evans had an extra value in his unfailing high spirits: he would make bad returns from the field look good, find a joke when his side was out of luck, and generally provide a psychological fillip which was of immense service to his captains and fellow-players.

England in Australia, 1946–47

Luck seems invariably to be against the weaker side in a Test series, and so it proved for Hammond's team in Australia. They lost the rubber by 3–0 and were twice defeated by an innings. Although there were good and brave individual performances – by Edrich, Compton, Hutton, Bedser, Evans, Wright, Ikin, and Yardley – they never all came off at once and the out-cricket and general quality of play fell far below Australia's.

This was the first series of official Tests in Australia played to a time-limit – six five-hour days. The first – Brisbane – Test established the pattern of the series. Bradman, who was thirty-eight – elderly by Australian Test standards – and had been invalided out of the forces, was considering retirement so seriously that he did not trouble to make the 1945–46 tour to New Zealand. He appeared at Brisbane, as yet uncommitted as to his future in the game, and had made 28 when he sent a ball from Voce to Ikin at slip: Ikin took it, Bradman – believing he had 'pinched' the ball between bat and ground – stood his ground: Ikin appealed, and the umpire gave Bradman not out. He stayed to make 187, to average 97·14 for the series and, as batsman and captain, put England twice more to rout.

Hassett, too, scored a century and Australia made 645 before the inevitable Brisbane rain created a viciously sticky wicket and though Edrich, above all, Hammond, Compton, Yardley and Ikin batted with courage and skill in such circumstances, they could only delay an innings defeat.

At Sydney both Bradman and Barnes scored 234 and Wright, who constantly beat both bat, bat's edge and stumps, finished with the tragically unjust figure of one for 169. Edrich made 71 and 119, Ikin 60 and Compton 54 but the English batting, on an easy pitch, went down before Ian Johnson's outcurving off-spinners and McCool's leg-breaks and googlies, in the most naïve fashion.

At Melbourne, the time-limitation saw the first drawn Test in Australia since 1881–82. England were in the game until Lindwall – who scored one of the three Australian centuries – and Tallon put on 154 for the eighth wicket of their second innings. The leg-spin of McCool and Dooland again found the English batting crease-bound and Yardley and Bedser hung on for the draw.

At Adelaide, both Morris for Australia and Compton for England scored a century in each innings. At last the Australian leg-spinners were resisted. Compton and Evans held out on the last day to leave little batting time for Australia, who, with nine wickets standing, needed only 99 to win when they made a quiet draw which ensured that they won the rubber.

At last England made an impression on the Australians when, in the last match, Wright with seven for 105 and Hutton – 122 before he retired ill – gave them such a chance that, if Bradman had not been dropped at 2, Australia might never have achieved their five wickets win.

His seven for 63 in this match established Lindwall with Miller, Tallon and Morris in the new generation of Australians who were to exert such power in Test cricket during the next few years.

R. R. Lindwall

The technique, control and resource of a medium-pace bowler, coupled with speed which could be genuinely fast, made Ray Lindwall the finest of post-war bowlers. He had a glorious, smooth, sweeping run-in, an unusually low arm for one who must be placed among the great, a whole range of pace and precise control of length and line. How he bowled so sharp an inswinger from such a low arm must remain a mystery: he had an equally abrupt outswing and his bouncer – well hidden and sparingly used – and yorker were often deadly.

His artifice was such that he would often persuade a batsman to start to duck at an expected bouncer only to bowl him a good length ball: his effect on some English players in 1948 was all but hypnotic.

A batsman with all the essentials of soundness, a forthright approach, some power in driving and square cutting, he made most of his innings quickly, and in

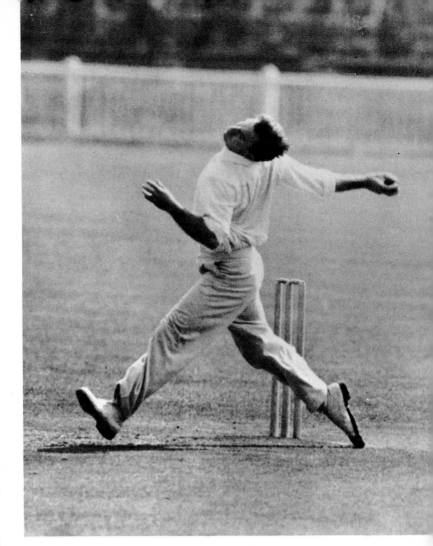

Ray Lindwall (NSW and Queensland) truly fast with the technical repertoire and control of a medium-pace bowler: with Miller, he made as fine a pair of opening bowlers as cricket has ever known

Tests he scored 1,502 runs to go with his 228 wickets. Only a little over average height, well built, but not large, he was always fit and supple and continued to the age of 38 as a Test bowler of high skill and variety.

K. R. Miller

With the physique of an athlete, and aptitude for every part of cricket, Keith Miller was a towering player, who won matches by his batting, bowling and fielding. A bat, to him, was an attacking weapon. Inherently a forward player, he struck the ball on fast wickets with force and majesty. He could be reduced to ordinary level by spin bowling on a real 'turner' but he could, too, rise to the challenge of a difficult situation and tilt a match – and do it gloriously.

If one of his powers has to be set above the others, it must be his bowling, for with his high, flowing action he could bowl up to full fast speed and yet make the ball move late in flight, or off the seam, so penetratingly as to beat the best batsmen in the world on plumb wickets. His bouncer was sudden and venomous. He took any run-up that occurred to him: off fifteen yards he would check at the last moment and deliver a blind length googly, or he would toss back his huge flop of hair and, from three paces, blast through a batsman's defence with a yorker. He rarely employed his medium pace off-breaks, but in suitable conditions he bowled them well enough to win matches.

At slip or in the covers he hurled his body prodigious distances to scoop the ball out of the air, catching men from strokes which seemed to be going safely wide of him for four: and his throwing was straight and sharp as an arrow.

Sometimes cricket bored him: when it challenged him he was at his princely – though apparently negligent – best. Gay, spontaneously generous, and convivial, Keith Miller was one of the most colourful and brilliant of all cricketers.

D. Tallon

Lean, quiet and tough, Don Tallon was a wicket-keeper with superb hands, who moved with economy yet made distant catches with uncanny certainty exactly in the middle of the palm. He could have kept wicket in skin-tight gloves. He was never hurried or baffled by spin bowling and he took pace with cool ease. As a batsman he was always likely to be useful at a pinch, and no crisis ever disturbed his cold efficiency.

A. R. Morris

With a century in each innings of his first inter-state match in 1940, when he was only nineteen, Arthur Morris made an impact on Australian cricket from the start of his career. A calm left-handed batsman, he watched the ball closely and often left his stroke to the last possible moment. His weakness – exploited by Alec Bedser with some success – was a tendency to shuffle across his stumps, leaving himself open to be bowled behind his legs. A Test record of 3,533 runs at 46·48 shows that it was no ruinous flaw.

A strong bottom-hand player – he suffered from bruising between thumb and first finger of his left hand – he was assured in the placing of his strokes, especially round the arc between square-point, in front of the wicket, to mid-wicket and, out of his

Arthur Morris (NSW) One of Australia's four great left-handers, only Alec Bedser disturbed his composure or restricted his power

certain balance, he invariably kept the ball along the ground. Although his defence was strong, he was quick to move out from it, and his punishment of the loose ball was always harsh.

Ian Johnson, Ernie Toshack – slow medium left-arm stock bowler; George Tribe, who bowled the 'Chinaman'; Colin McCool – thickset leg-spinner and hard-driving bat; Bruce Dooland – another leg-spinner-all-rounder; all did something useful in the series: the last three eventually came to English county cricket. So completely had the new generation taken over that only Hassett, Barnes and, of course, Bradman, retained their places from the team that had toured England in 1938.

England had seven of their players from that series, and could count only Yardley and Ikin as discoveries from the tour.

N. W. D. Yardley

An unspectacular but consistently useful cricketer, Norman Yardley took over the captaincy when Hammond was kept out of the Sydney Test by fibrositis, and retained the post for three subsequent series. He was a steady bat, strong on the on-side and sound under pressure. His medium-pace bowling, with a little cut and some swing, took some extremely useful Test wickets and his catching was always good. A steady, equable man, well trained by his Yorkshire mentors, he was a captain whose firmness was sometimes obscured by his pleasant manner but who was never frightened to take a reasonable chance to snatch a win.

J. T. Ikin

Without ever attaining the heights, Jack Ikin was a batsman who stood up staunchly in a losing side. Unflinching against pace or when his side was being hammered, he had the left-hander's power through the covers, concentration and a patient defence. His right-arm leg-spin bowling was better than he ever had much chance to show at Test level and he was one of the first of the specialist short-leg fieldsmen. Some of his catches from full blooded hits underlined his quickness of eye as well as his courage.

South Africa in England, 1947

The England players went home to the relative quiet of a series – which they won by 3–0 – against a South African team which could not harry them with pace or wrist-spin, as the Australians had done. There was something of a surprise at Trent Bridge where Alan Melville, the South African captain, scored two centuries and, thus, three in consecutive innings: he had scored one in the second innings of the 'timeless' Durban Test of 1938–39. He made a fourth at Lord's. Melville, who captained Oxford University and Sussex during the thirties, was a stylish batsman whose health was never good, and the strain of the tour reduced his playing power. In this game England followed on, and only Compton's innings of 163, Yardley's 99 and a last wicket stand between Martin and – to his enduring amusement – Hollies, denied South Africa the chance to win.

This was the Edrich-Compton summer, when those two made such a profusion of runs in the sun. Both of them passed the former record aggregate for a season – Hayward's 3,518 of 1906: Compton's 18 centuries in a season was also a record and between them they scored 2,056 runs against the South Africans. So Tuckett (fast-medium), Athol Rowan (off-breaks) and 'Tufty' Mann (slow left-arm) suffered more heavily than their merits promised. Nourse and Mitchell both batted well at times but, though Bedser had temporarily lost his nip after being over-bowled in Australia, a mixed bag of English bowlers were good enough to take the decisive wickets within the margin the runs of Compton and Edrich allowed them.

England in West Indies and India in Australia, 1947–48

There could have been no sharper foreshadows of the coming 1948 England-Australia Test series than the results of the tours in the preceding overseas season. In the West Indies, a half-strength MCC side under G. O. Allen lost the Test rubber by 2–0 and did not win a single first-class match on the tour. The party was unlucky in the matter of injuries and Hutton was flown over in an attempt to make good the damage. It was personally happy that S. C. (Billy) Griffith – an unlucky wicket-keeper to play so few Tests – should have been sent in first in the Trinidad Test and scored his first century. Little else was cheering for the English side. Another player of promise – Maurice Tremlett of Somerset – hustled too early into representative cricket, and subsequently badly mishandled, made the tour as a gifted young man out of his depth. The lesson of the tour, soon to be even more heavily underlined, was that English county form meant nothing at the highest international level, where the West Indies now stood.

Meanwhile, India had gone to Australia full of a hope which was to be ruthlessly crushed. Bradman had an average of 178 in Tests against them and Hassett 110, while five Australian bowlers took their wickets at less than 17 each. The Indians finished completely demoralized, after the most savage mauling any side has ever suffered in Test cricket.

Australia, meanwhile, added two more major figures to their already powerful forces in Harvey and Johnston.

R. N. Harvey

The batsmen of modern times who even approached Neil Harvey's Test total of 6,149 runs – second only to Bradman's among Australians – based their game on defence. Harvey has shown on occasions that he has the ability to defend soundly; but the essential quality of his batting was always attack. A small, neatly-made, left-hander, he rarely hesitated to throw his bat at the ball – especially in the square slash by which he made so many runs. In his early days, the off-spinners – and always the faster bowlers, who swung the ball away – might make him play and miss. His achievement was that, by audacious pulling, wristily strong driving and exhilarating cutting, he made many runs quickly. Light and fast on his feet, he could dictate length to all but the cleverest bowlers and, when he was set and 'on the kill', his quickness of eye and power of wrist made him most difficult to contain. For all his modest manner, his cricket had a streak of aggression and, early mature in temperament, he frequently took control of a match.

His speed, the certainty of hand he developed as a baseball player, his long throwing and eager anticipation, made him one of the finest outfields of his time.

W. A. Johnston

A left-arm bowler who began as a slow spinner, adopted fast-medium swingers, and eventually covered the range of pace between the two – who could swing, cut and finger-spin – Bill Johnston was one of the most versatile of bowlers. Six-feet-two tall, with, despite a peculiar duck of the head before delivery, a high sweeping action, he made the ball swing sharply in to the right-hand bat. Valuably, he could also loop it away to a length which tempted, and often betrayed, off-drivers. He varied his inswing with a sharply cut

breakaway and could bowl the left-armer's natural spinner as sharply as the specialists.

So in the same match he was often used as both shock-bowler and stock-bowler, positively beating batsmen on the defensive stroke, or tempting them to destroy themselves. He stands sixth among Australian bowlers for number of Test wickets – 160 in eight years – and, for one of such variety, he bowled surprisingly few bad balls and a number of surprisingly good ones.

As a man 'Big Bill' was of infinite good nature, resilient, an earnest cricketer who was never without humour. His batting was something of a joke, though in 1953, when an injury in a practice match at the beginning of the tour inhibited his bowling, he achieved an average of 102 – by dint of being out only once on the tour (a feat performed, to the bowler's great delight, by Vic Cannings of Hampshire). Not always a good field, Johnston had a phenomenal throw; a valuable bowler for any captain to have at his command.

Australians in England, 1948

History repeated itself. As Gregory and MacDonald ripped through the England batting in 1921 after the first World War, so did Miller and Lindwall in 1948, after the second. The batting under Bradman was even weightier than Armstrong's; Bill Brown played in only two Tests. If there was ill luck, Australia suffered it. Bradman won the toss only once: Lindwall could not bowl in the second innings at Trent Bridge nor Miller at all at Lord's: Barnes, injured at Old Trafford, was still unable to play at Leeds: they had the worst of the wicket at Manchester and at Leeds. They were probably the strongest side Australia ever sent to England: rarely needing more than four bowlers, they always had five – six at Headingley. Seven of their batsmen – including, grotesquely enough, Toshack who was only once out – averaged more than 40 in Tests.

The English side was not a poor one. Of the 21 players used, too many were either unsettled by pace, or never had an adequate chance to justify themselves, and Hutton, now the chief target of the fast-bowlers, was once dropped. There were brave enough performances for England: bowling by Bedser; batting by Compton – at his courageous best in making a century at Old Trafford after snicking a no-ball from

Lindwall into his head – Hutton, Washbrook and Edrich. It was the measure of the series that England twice appeared to have taken the initiative at Headingley, yet still lost. On the first occasion, Dick Pollard, the Lancashire fast-medium bowler, took the wickets of Hassett and Bradman in one over, but Miller and Harvey (a century in his first Test in England) retrieved the situation for Australia with powerfully assertive play. Then, after competent batting in both England innings, Yardley declared and set Australia 404 to win in five-and-three-quarter hours, on a broken wicket: England missed six chances. Morris and Bradman made centuries and Australia steamed home, easily: seven wickets. There was not even any consolation for England at the end: at The Oval, Lindwall (six for 20), Miller and Johnston bundled them out – despite Hutton, who fought down to the end – for 52: and Australia won Bradman's last Test by an innings. Bradman, cheered all the way from the pavilion, reached the wicket through an applauding corridor of England players, promptly failed to read a googly from Hollies and was bowled for 0. It was an unusual, but warmingly human, display of fallibility to close his Test career.

England in South Africa, 1948–49

George Mann's team won – 2–0 – a rubber they might easily have lost. They took the first Test by two wickets with a leg bye off Gladwin's thigh from the last possible ball, and the fifth by three wickets after a surprisingly generous declaration by Nourse.

Nourse, Eric Rowan, the perennial Mitchell, and Wade all batted proficiently for South Africa, while Cuan McCarthy – genuinely fast but with a doubtful action – and the two spinners, Athol Rowan and Mann, bowled as well as anyone on the English side. Jenkins, though, might have had an outstanding tour but for the remarkable mastery Nourse exerted over him: no other South African played him confidently.

E. A. B. Rowan

A wiry, perky man, Eric, the elder of the two Rowan brothers, was an extremely positive character. As an opening batsman, he was basically a back foot player who gave the impression of having time to spare against fast bowling. His batting was, in general, soundly orthodox: he cut neatly, hooked with relish and drove well. He would at times, however, set out to prove a point, when he could be impregnably defensive or extremely venturesome.

He caught well close to the wicket but his consuming interest was in captaincy. Quick-witted and assertive, he directed a side with much acumen, especially in attack, thinking well for his bowlers and handling them skilfully.

A. M. B. Rowan

The taller, younger Rowan brother – Athol – was a wide-shouldered, humorous and relaxed person. A knee injury sustained from the recoil of a gun in the North African campaign was so serious that, before the tour to England in 1947, he played both hockey and cricket with his left leg in irons. The injury interrupted his cricket career, and ended it prematurely. With an individual grip, Athol Rowan bowled sharp off-breaks with a marked outward spin-swerve. He was a useful middle-order batsman in defence or attack, and at cover-point he was fast and safe.

Rowan was the first off-spinner to rout a modern Australian team when, playing for Transvaal against Hassett's side of 1949–50 on a turning wicket at Johannesburg, he took nine for 19 in their first innings and six for 49 in the second – as well as making second highest score in the first Transvaal innings and the highest in their second. He had little luck in Test cricket and he played only briefly, but he must be reckoned among the best of modern off-spinners.

N. B. F. Mann

The slow left-arm bowler of Melville's 1947 team in England, 'Tufty' Mann was a courteous person but, at that time, a raw cricketer. On that tour, however, he bore an immense burden of work, he became match-hardened and his technique improved from day to day. Mann was, originally, of the old school of slow left-arm bowlers who gave the ball plenty of air outside the line of the off-stump. With experience he became altogether tighter and more varied in method and bowled accurately to a restrictive field for long spells. He played in spectacles and his batting and fielding were not important, but he was an intelligent bowler, of whom South Africa could have expected long and valuable service, but for the illness which ended his life when he was only thirty.

R. O. Jenkins

Short, and moving as if muscle-bound, 'Roly' Jenkins,

of Worcester, was an 'old-fashioned' leg-spinner, who tossed the ball high and backed his flight and spin against the bat. His spin was certainly considerable, he hid his googly well, usually dropped on length and line, and stood up well to punishment. A safe close catcher, good enough batsman to perform the 'double' and be classified as an all-rounder, Roly was an earthy, Midland character, an immense trier and obsessed, above all, with the theory and practice of leg-spin.

Hutton and Washbrook set a new Test record for the first wicket with 359 – made at more than a run a minute – at Johannesburg, and they and Compton formed the hard core of the English batting. Cliff Gladwin – one of the tightest of all bowlers of inswing – and George Mann of Middlesex, an enterprising front foot batsman and alert field, both played well without promising that they would be effective against Australia. In the match with North-Eastern Transvaal, Compton produced an innings of joyous savagery – 300 in three hours, the last 180 at two runs a minute: it was batting of utter, but happy mastery, such as few other batsmen of any age could have played.

At the same time, the West Indies, visiting India for the first Tests between the two countries, won the only one of the five Tests to be finished. West Indies were already building their massive batting power while India were adopting the policy of slow, waiting cricket which was soon to permeate their entire thinking.

New Zealand in England, 1949

In a season of old-fashioned amiability, English cricket took breathing space. For tension, there was the County Championship in which Middlesex won five matches in succession to end their season: Yorkshire had to beat Glamorgan in their last match to finish level with them – and they did: it was the first Championship tie for sixty years.

This year Devon, who had shown much initiative, including the floating of a Festival at Torquay, applied for admission to the Championship, but were not admitted.

New Zealand, at first allotted three four-day Tests, asked for four of three days each. Firstly, that would save them the loss of three times two blank days – which might balance their budget – and, secondly, they believed that they could avoid defeat by England in three-day Tests. So it proved. New Zealand came under as good dual-control – by Walter Hadlee as

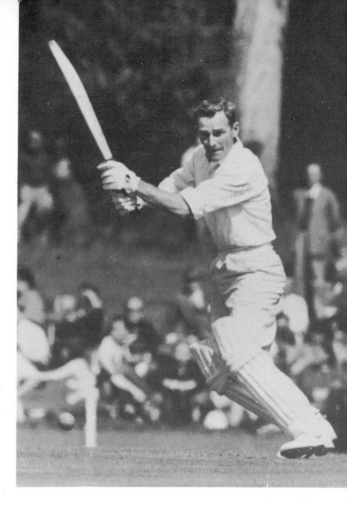

Bert Sutcliffe (Northern Districts) in 1965 the senior playing Test cricketer and generally regarded as the best batsman produced by New Zealand

captain, and Jack Phillips, a manager of wisdom and good nature – as any modern touring team has had. Their bowling relied largely on Jack Cowie, a now ageing fast-medium bowler who moved the ball dangerously off the pitch and maintained accuracy and life through some long spells; and Tom Burtt, a phlegmatic, accurate slow left-armer who spun when he could, and bowled a good length and line at other times. Their batting had the stern Verdun Scott as opener, Mervyn Wallace who – quick on his feet and playing very close to the pad – made a good start and then faded, and Hadlee (who played a memorable innings against Surrey when Alec Bedser was making his leg-cutter rocket like a startled partridge), Sutcliffe and Donnelly.

B. Sutcliffe

Bert Sutcliffe, once he had cured a tendency to untidy hooking, became a menacing attacking left-handed batsman whom few bowlers could confine. Fit, fast on his feet and possessed of a keen eye, he was

146

hard to bowl at, always looking for runs and capable of hitting his way out of trouble by measured attack.

Martin Donnelly

When there is discussion of left-handed batsmen in the post-war period, it must always be argued that Martin Donnelly was as good as any. Short, lively of mind as well as movement, he was a punitive batsman, utterly sound because his method was firmly grounded, but of temperament and ability to attack any bowling. He pulled with amazing certainty and, from good wrists, he could leave his strokes late yet play them strongly. Quite unassuming, he would take control of a match with the assurance of a great player and, had his first-class career been longer and on higher planes, we might now talk of him as being among the great batsmen of all cricket.

Several interesting England cricketers appeared in the series.

L. Jackson

Les Jackson, of Derby, a fast-medium bowler with a slingy action, amazing accuracy and ugly pace from the pitch, played the first of his two Tests. Undoubtedly the most under-estimated bowler English cricket has ever known in terms of representative selection, he was respected by every batsman who ever faced him. In his type and period it may be that he was inferior to Alec Bedser, but not to any other bowler of any country. He would drop for over after over within a square foot and, on a soft pitch, he would knock a dinner-plate-sized hole and make the ball rise devilishly out of it. He moved either way off the pitch by sheer nature, and simply could not be collared. In the ultimate, he was deadly accurate and unpleasantly faster than he looked.

R. T. Simpson

The modern, easy-labelling tendency has been to regard all Notts batsmen as solely good wicket players and, certainly, Reggie Simpson – lithe, upstanding and polished – was, like any other player, at his best when the pitch was on his side. In the manner of Joe Hardstaff, he hit the ball regally through the covers and, in his later years, he was recognized as a player of fast bowling with few equals in poise and certainty. His century at Melbourne in 1950–51 took England far towards winning their first post-war Test against Australia and, given a little more luck, or a little less devotion to stroke-play when the going was hard, he might have been a major Test batsman.

T. E. Bailey

With the elevation of Trevor Bailey to Test status in 1949, the England strength that was to defeat Australia was almost complete. Here, without doubt, was the cricketer who 'by taking thought added a cubit to his stature'. He had – and has – one of the best cricket brains, and he applied it early in life to attaining success on the highest level – in Tests against Australia. In his young days he was an attractive stroke-maker of no great resistant power. He became as determined and impregnable a defensive player as England has ever thrown in against Australia. His bowling was lively but tight. He worked on it until, though his pace was not great, he could do what he wanted to do. His control was such that he could produce the ball he chose to probe any particular batsman, and could deliver it to the exact point he desired. So his bowling became, as it were, an extension of his alert cricket mind.

In the field, too, he concentrated unremittingly and made some fine catches, especially at slip. Over the years, Bailey was a fine match-saver and, as is frequently forgotten, often a match-winner. His forward defensive stroke reduced some of the best Australian bowlers to something near despair, but it was the instrument of a defence which turned Test Matches. Bailey has ability, brains and character and he applied them effectively to Test cricket.

Australia in South Africa, 1949–50

Without Bradman, Australia beat South Africa by 4–0. Harvey had a batting average of 132 and five others of more than 40, while five of their bowlers took over ten wickets at less than 25 each. South Africa could not match such figures. Mitchell had gone and Nourse and Rowan were the sinews of their batting. Their chief bowlers, Mann and Tayfield, took wickets at more than 38 each. South Africa was faced with the inescapable need to build a new team and, in Tayfield, they had its kernel.

H. J. Tayfield

Taking over as South Africa's off-spinner on the retirement, through injury, of Athol Rowan, Hugh Tayfield became one of the best of all post-war slow-

Hugh Tayfield (Rhodesia, Natal and Transvaal) the most successful slow bowler in South African Test history, precise and subtle in flight: useful bat and brilliant field

bowlers. He did not turn the ball so much as Rowan, but he was an unrelenting and unendingly resourceful bowler, never better than on plumb wickets. His nickname – 'Toey' – came from his habit of stubbing his toe on the ground before he began his short run, in a mannerism he barely noticed in his intense concentration on the ball he was about to bowl. Phenomenally accurate, a master of flight in all its variations, and only thirdly a spinner, he set the closest possible field and successfully dared the best batsmen in the world to hit him. He backed his field with amazing stops to his own bowling and created an atmosphere of the tightest restriction. No truly slow bowler since J. C. White was so difficult to hit. Tayfield's batting was by no means negligible but he

devoted himself passionately to that rare tactic, aggressively restrictive slow bowling.

WEST INDIAN INTERLUDE

1950 demonstrated that, as the members of more recent English touring teams to the West Indies knew, cricket there was on its way to the top. Their side under Goddard, accorded four five-day Tests, won three to England's one. That was less of a surprise than the method of their winning. That they should bring four great stroke-makers was to be expected from cricketers who could produce a Headley. It was expected, too, that their attack would be based upon pace. It was not. For the first time the West Indies produced match-winning spin-bowling. Moreover they, whose batting had often been unstable – so that Headley had to make his brilliance subservient to security – were now equipped with a sheet-anchor batsman of sound technique and steady temperament.

The four stroke-makers were Weekes, Worrell, Walcott and Stollmeyer; the two spin-bowlers Valentine and Ramadhin; and the ballast-batsman, Rae. For their two main pace-bowlers, a first visit to England came too late: Hines Johnson reached his fortieth birthday and Prior Jones his thirty-third during the tour. In a less strong side, others might have stood out: Robert Christiani, a fluent batsman who could keep wicket; John Goddard, the captain, courageous close field, dangerous medium pace off-spinner and a batsman with a world record stand (502 for the fifth wicket, with Worrell) behind him; Gerry Gomez, a tough all-rounder, economic medium-pace bowler, good field and dogged bat when things went badly: in this eleven they were the journeymen.

Attempts to rank the 'Three Ws' lead to fruitless argument: we may treat of them in alphabetical order, noting that all three were born within the space of eighteen months in the 166-square-mile island of Barbados and that all were natural, uncoached players.

C. L. Walcott

Clyde Walcott's greatest period came a little later than that of the other two when, between 1952 and 1956, in twelve Tests he scored twelve hundreds. Against Australia in 1955–56 he twice made a century in each innings of a Test and his 827 was the highest

148

Clyde Walcott (Barbados and British Guiana) powerful, watchful and a mighty striker of the ball from the back foot

aggregate of any West Indian batsman in a single series. He was a vast man with huge limbs and a broad smile. A capable close fieldsman, he kept wicket in Tests and was a useful medium pace bowler, as well as one of the finest batsmen of his time.

Walcott had strokes all round the wicket from either foot; he hooked with easy certainty, cut with surprising delicacy and, when he moved on to the front foot to drive, he matched anyone in the world for strength. But he was at his regal best when he played off the back foot. When bowlers dropped even a little short to him, his command was absolute: wrists, forearms and shoulders blended their strength in strokes which left deep fieldsmen powerless, tearing past them along the ground or flying low and long for six. Even when he had little room to play back, a single convulsive twist of the wrists dispatched his on or off drives with tearing speed. He bore the stamp of the man with time to spare about his strokes: it was as if he played a defensive stroke only to gain breathing space, and then his bat seemed impenetrable.

E. de C. Weekes

No batsman since Bradman had mounted such a withering attack on bowlers as Everton Weeks when, on the West Indies' 1950 tour of England, he had scored five double centuries by mid-July. Short, with stocky power, he was quick of eye and footwork. He would move far down the wicket to a half-volley and send if for four with no more than a twist of the wrists. Some slow left-arm bowlers found it almost impossible to bowl to him. He would pull with absolute impudence and, if his leg-side strokes were usually confined to the arc between mid-wicket and the bowler, he struck the ball through every degree of the off-side. Like Walcott, he needed a ball only fractionally short of a length to use an attacking stroke. His cover-driving, totally unlike Hammond's in style, matched it in consistent power and control. More than once in 1950 he drove an opposing cover-point almost to the boundary, yet still forced the ball past him. His most spectacular stroke was the square cut, which he could play to a ball extremely close to the off stump or even on it, when he squatted down on air to make himself room for a wristy, savage, horizontal blow like the swing of a machete. Lively and springy, Weekes played cricket intensely and, if he was happiest to field in the slips, where he pounced like a cat, his speed made him a fine cover-point.

F. M. Worrell

The first knighthood ever bestowed on a West Indian cricketer – Frank Worrell – recognized services to cricket: in his own country, to which he gave a quality of captaincy few teams have known in modern times; in Australia, where his team of 1960–61 re-established the game in public esteem; and in England, where his batting in 1950 and his captaincy in 1963 were outstanding.

Slim and relaxed in an almost feline fashion, Worrell was first and foremost a stylist: his unhurried bat fell effortlessly into the classical lines. It was never possible to isolate any single stroke as his best because he had them all and he played them in their context. He gave the impression of disinterest remarkable in one with the concentration to make such long scores – he took part in two stands of over five hundred runs; he averaged 147 in Tests against England in 1947–48 and 89·93 in 1950. At times he seemed uncertain at the start of an innings, but once 'in' he made fewer errors of judgement – of length or line – than many other batsmen of high standing.

Though his main achievements were as a right-hand bat, he first played for Barbados as a slow left-arm bowler and he could always bowl spinners usefully. In 1950, however, used as an opening bowler in the Tests at Trent Bridge and Lord's, he bowled fast-medium round the wicket and made the ball move sharply and come off the pitch at rattling pace.

His captaincy was shrewd and quite ruthless: he gave his players consideration and, in return, expected that he could ask all they had to give – and get it. He could take an unyielding stand with a smile and, whatever the strain or the emergency, he was never flustered and never raised his voice. He played Lancashire League cricket to subsidize his studies at Manchester University, where he took a degree in Social Anthropology and Sociology: and he became a Warden at the University of the West Indies. He still laughs easily and remains convivial.

J. B. Stollmeyer

His innings at Old Trafford in 1950 alone was sufficient to stamp Jeffrey Stollmeyer as a superb batsman. The wicket was so explosive that, though the tall Clyde Walcott, as wicket-keeper, stood up straight, Valentine's slow spin jumped from a length so steeply as to pass over his shoulder. In such grotesque conditions, Stollmeyer batted with something unbelievably near repose. His slim build argued that his hitting-power stemmed from perfect timing. His footwork was certain, he was never out of position and, late as his decision had to be, his strokes were as elegant as if he were playing on a perfect pitch. The shape of modern cricket made him a good on-side player, but on the off he played with the polish of the Edwardians.

A. F. Rae

The specific task of Alan Rae in the 1950 West Indian side was to guarantee against such collapses as, through deficiencies of temperament or technique, had befallen their predecessors. The fact that he finished second to Worrell in the Test batting averages shows how thoroughly he discharged that duty.

A left-hand bat, with wide experience of English conditions as a club player while he was studying law in London, Rae watched the ball, and all a game, with a close eye and brought an alert brain to bear on its problems. He accepted his allotted role and, at Lord's, his long and patient innings was the basis of the West Indies' first Test win in England. He attracted less attention than the more brilliant players in the side, but the extent of his value may be measured by study of the defeat of the 1957 team which lacked such steadiness at the start of the innings.

A. L. Valentine

Two matches represented Alfred Valentine's entire first-class cricket career when he sailed to England in 1950: by August of that year he had taken 33 wickets in four Test Matches. Amiable and, though tall and fairly strong, completely unathletic in appearance, he was a poor field – who needed glasses long before he took to them – and no batsman. His approach to the wicket was a leaden-footed plod, but his slow left-arm bowling, wheeled away for hour after hour, was unwavering, never off length, never off line and spun so hard that it would turn off any surface. His spinning finger bled, calloused, bled again, and still he went on with plodding accuracy. He had few variations –

Alf Valentine (Jamaica) maintained vicious left-arm spin, utter accuracy and unfailing good humour through some immensely long spells

even the ball that went on with his arm was a late development; his wickets came from length and spin maintained over immense spells and ultimately he and Ramadhin settled the rubber. His comment was a wide, friendly and gold-filled grin.

K. T. Ramadhin

Like his colleague, Valentine, Sonny Ramadhin had played only two first-class matches before he came to England in 1950 and took more wickets – 135 – than any West Indian bowler had ever done on an English tour.

Of partly Indian extraction, a little man – only five-feet-four tall and small-boned – he bowled slow off-breaks and leg-breaks from a brief skipping run. He was not a leg-break and googly bowler, for he never turned his wrist fully: he took the seam in the stretch between his first and second fingers and bowled somewhat in the manner of Sydney Barnes, applying the spin with the inside of those two fingers. Had he bowled either off-break or leg-break alone he would

have been difficult to play, because his length was good, his spin sharp enough to beat the bat, his flight was not easy to pick up and he came nippily off the pitch.

His extra power lay in the concealment of his break, which no English batsman in 1950, except possibly Washbrook, could penetrate. In 1957 he again plagued the English batsmen until it was decided to treat him as an off-spinner which, in the main, he always was (he often posted as many as three short-legs). His leg-break afforded the surprise and variety which made batsmen so tentative about playing his off-breaks. Of all the English batsmen of 1950, Hutton, who used his feet well to him, probably played Ramadhin best, but the quick arm-swing and unidentifiable spinning action reduced many others to near-desperation.

The first Test was played at Old Trafford on a travesty of a Test wicket, about which the West Indies were moved to complain, though eventually they contented themselves with a recommendation at the Imperial Cricket Conference that instructions should be issued to Test groundsmen which would ensure reasonable conditions.

In such a booby trap, a dogged innings by Bailey, one of poise by Hutton, and of determination by Edrich were capped by Evans's century of incredible eye, bravado and quickness. In reply, West Indies could offer only Stollmeyer's memorable 43 and 78, and game gestures by Weekes, Walcott and Gomez, as they were bowled out by Berry and Hollies. This was the first Test and best performance by Bob Berry, a Lancashire – subsequently Worcester and Derbyshire – slow left-arm bowler who usually relied on length and flight, rather than spin. Eric Hollies, Warwickshire's main bowler for many post-war years, rolled leg-breaks and googlies to a steady length and with an acute sense of tactics and of batsmen.

Some English apologists attribute England's defeat to the absence of key players: Compton, for instance, was not fit for the first three Tests after an operation on his knee. But the margins by which West Indies won the last three games – 326, ten wickets, and an innings and 56 – are conclusive proof of their superiority. Their batting was both secure and capable of fast runs, and the effect of Valentine and Ramadhin was such that they took 59 Test wickets – the other bowlers 18 between them.

Lord's saw the high-water mark of the Valentine-Ramadhin dominance. They rendered some of the

K. T. – 'Sonny' – Ramadhin (Trinidad) the most baffling spin-bowler of recent years, he formed, with Valentine, the most effective spin-bowling partnership in Test cricket since Grimmett and O'Reilly

THE ENGLISH REVIVAL

England in Australia, 1950–51

The defeat by West Indies profoundly disturbed England's team-building ideas and the side for Australia in the following winter contained some hopeful makeshifts and some experiments. The question of captaincy was not settled until late in the summer: it eventually devolved on F. R. Brown, the only one of the experiments to prove successful.

F. R. Brown

In the early thirties, Freddie Brown made a mark as a brisk – sometimes almost unplayable – leg-spin and googly bowler, one of the hardest of all front-of-the-wicket hitters and fine outfield, for Cambridge University and Surrey. He was picked for the 1932–33 tour of Australia but did not appear in a Test, though he played six times for England between 1931 and 1937. In 1949, after only intermittent first-class cricket for some years, he became captain of Northants, and, in the fourth Test of 1950, took over the England side from Norman Yardley. As a post-war player – he was thirty-nine when he first captained Northants – he was constantly useful. If his leg-breaks were not so dangerous as formerly, he could use the new ball intelligently and accurately at medium pace. His hitting was still unusually powerful, his hands safe, and his experience wide. No one played a larger part in the revival of Northants cricket than he did between 1949 and 1953.

Australia, now without Bradman, Barnes and Brown, were not the monolithic batting power they had been. They still had the established bowling cadre of Lindwall, Miller, Johnston and Johnson with, in this series, the assistance of Jack Iverson. Already thirty-five when he appeared in his first Test, Iverson had learnt with a table-tennis ball to impart spin by gripping the ball with the thumb against the bent-back middle finger which he used to flick off-break or leg-break spin, or merely to propel a straight ball, at the moment of release. His bowling may have been a freak but it took him to the top of the Australian Test bowling in this series with 21 wickets at 15·23.

Before the tour, English anxiety centred on the

England batting abject. Gilbert Parkhouse, the Glamorgan batsman, usually regarded as at his best against pace, played the spin sensibly, but despite his 48 and a determined century by Washbrook, England were a beaten side all through.

At Trent Bridge, 261 by Worrell and 129 by Weekes left England so far behind that another century by Washbrook and firm batting by Simpson, Parkhouse, Dewes (the Middlesex left-hander) and Evans served only to make West Indies bat again.

At The Oval, West Indies scored well all down the order and Goddard added his spin to that of Valentine and Ramadhin so that Hutton had the rare experience of carrying his bat for 203, yet seeing his side beaten by an innings.

Alec Bedser (Surrey) a mighty labourer in the sun, he carried England's bowling through the lean years with the strength, stamina and endeavour of a giant

bowling; there was no outstanding opening partner for Bedser (who took 30 wickets). In the event Bailey, though handicapped by injury, took 13; Brown – alternating between leg-breaks and 'seam-up' – 18; and Wright 11. It was the batting that failed: Hutton had an average of 88 – twice that of any Australian, and fifty more than the next Englishman.

Brisbane produced its usual thunder-storm freak. While the wicket was still good, Bailey, Bedser, Brown (leg-breaks) and Wright did better than they could have hoped and bowled out Australia for 228. On the sticky wicket after rain, Brown declared the England innings at 68 for seven: Hassett retaliated by closing at 32 for seven. England wanted 193 to win: the wicket was still difficult, if not so bad as it had been. Hutton, in one of the finest Test innings anyone has ever played – off-driving majestically – scored 62*: of

the remainder, only Brown – 17 – reached double figures and England, out for 122, lost by 70.

The second – Melbourne – Test was tensely close. For the first time in a Test between England and Australia in this century, no one of the four completed innings reached 200. Bedser rose to his peak in a mighty spell: Bailey backed him well and only Harvey, Hassett and the hearty all-rounder, Loxton, brought Australia to 194. England, after a collapse, were steadied by Hutton (moved to the middle of the order) and Evans to take a first innings lead of three. Brown (medium pace), Bailey and Bedser took the Australian wickets in the second innings and England were left with three days to make 179 to win. Not for the first time, they became over-careful. The ball kept low from a slow pitch: Hutton made 40 while the rest of the side played so inhibitedly that Iverson and Johnston, costing less than two runs an (eight-ball) over, bowled Australia to a narrow win by 28 runs. It was, however, a triumph of character rather than of superior technical ability. Only Hutton, Bedser, Evans – who kept superbly – and Brown matched Australia in fibre.

At Sydney, England were certainly unlucky. They batted first, whereupon, in their first innings, Bailey's thumb was broken and Wright strained a leg muscle so that neither could bowl. Bedser, Brown (leg-breaks and medium pace) and Warr, maintained the bowling with only six overs of relief, for two days and, as they tired, Australia, largely through an unusually calculated century by Miller, built up a total of 426. On a turning wicket, the English batting again went down, with Brown resisting, to Iverson – and an innings defeat. So the rubber was decided.

The Lancashire bowlers, Statham and Tattersall, were flown out as replacements for injured players before the fourth Test, which was given its decisive tilt when Morris, after a series of failures against Bedser, scored 206. Though Hutton carried his bat for 156, Compton was in the worst 'run' of his career and the rest of the batsmen were deficient in skill or temperament.

At last, in the final Test at Sydney, England emerged from their long eclipse. Morris and Hassett took Australia to 111 before the second wicket fell: then Bedser (five for 46) and Brown (five for 49: at medium pace) cut through the rest of the innings to 217. Again the under-valued English bowling had given the batsmen opportunity. Even now only two of them – Hutton, 79, and Simpson 156*, with 235

Jim Laker (Surrey) the greatest of all off-spin bowlers, takes his tenth wicket in the second Australian innings at Old Trafford, 1956. Players, from left to right – M. C. Cowdrey, I. W. Johnson (other batsman), L. Maddocks (out lbw), T. G. Evans, J. C. Laker, G. A. R. Lock, D. S. Sheppard, A. S. M. Oakman

out of a total of 320 – made the most of the situation. Bedser broke open the Australian second innings which stood at six for two wickets: resistance hardened through Hassett, Harvey and Hole, but Wright cut into the middle batting and Bedser – five for 59 – ended it peremptorily. 95 to win and Hutton, who had waited so long for this opportunity, made sure, with 60*, that it was not lost: by eight wickets England had beaten Australia for the first time since August 1938. As in 1924–25, hope shone clear ahead.

South Africa in England, 1951

England returned to the setback of defeat in the first Test by South Africa. Nourse, the visiting captain,

batting in constant pain from a recently fractured and pinned thumb, scored 208 in their 483 for nine. Hundreds by Compton and Simpson took England to 419 before, as the wicket became difficult after rain, Brown declared with nine wickets down. Bedser, with six for 37, and Tattersall, the steady slow-medium off-spinner of Lancashire, bowled out South Africa for 121 and England had over five hours to make 186. Since Nourse was unable to field, Eric Rowan took over the captaincy and handled the bowling of his brother, Athol, 'Tufty' Mann and the fast, erratic McCarthy so imaginatively to precisely set attacking fields that, once Ikin was out for 33, only Wardle, with a hard hit 30, checked South Africa, who won by 71 runs.

England took the second, third and – with a few

alarms – the fifth Tests to win the series 3–1. After Trent Bridge, Nourse never played another Test innings of more than 29 and, especially against Bedser who took 30 wickets in the series, the middle batting of South Africa was never secure. Tayfield did not show his home bowling form and Athol Rowan, despite a damaged knee, kept him out of the Test side. Geoff Chubb bowled gamely and sometimes better than that at medium fast pace; Eric Rowan was always hard to get out; and McLean hit the ball in the best South African tradition: but the odd three or four men did not measure up to Test cricket, and it was there that South Africa fell short.

England could find pleasure that a winning team, at the highest level, was being built. Laker, with ten wickets at The Oval, established himself; May scored a century in his first Test; Graveney batted well in unfriendly circumstances at Old Trafford and Wardle gave signs of his subsequent powers.

J. C. Laker

English cricket for twenty years had promised, as historic certainty, to produce the ultimate off-spinner, at the end of a line which ran through Parkin, Goddard, Jupp, Astill and Clay. He appeared in Jim Laker. Yorkshire-born, he first made a mark in North African wartime cricket and joined Surrey after the War. Cool, laconic, a man who seemed to bowl with his tongue in his cheek, he had every item of equipment to be hoped for in an off-spinner. If he had not turned the ball at all he would have been a top-class bowler for his length, line, variation of pace and flight. But he spun the ball so much that the batsman at the non-striker's end heard it leave his hand with a buzz. On anything approaching a sticky wicket, he was deadly: vicious break-back was varied with a ball which he appeared to spin like the others but which ran on to slips. There was a faster ball – and he was in general a little faster than he looked – while he could change his direction for left-hand or right-hand bat with absolute and meticulous certainty.

After he had routed Australia in 1956, the attitude of their batsmen was 'Just give us the opportunity to get at him on our own pitches'. In due course – 1958–59 – he went to Australia and, on their perfect wickets and though his spinning finger was so affected by arthritis that he had to miss one Test, he bowled more overs and took more wickets than any other English bowler in the series, was top of the bowling table, and cost only two-and-a-half runs per eight-ball over. This was the retort of the truly great bowler.

Laker was a good catch in the gully and at least once batted capably in a Test. He stands alone for complete mastery of bowling slow off-spin: there can never be a better in that kind.

P. B. H. May

From school at Charterhouse, through his days with Cambridge, Surrey and England, until he gradually eased himself out of first-class play in 1963, Peter May was an outstandingly successful batsman. Six feet tall, with good arms and shoulders and never hampered by any excess weight, he was a fit, hard player of games with undoubted ball-sense. When he first entered county cricket he was susceptible to off-spin and used to be caught at short-leg too often for his own peace of mind. The Australians sensed his potential early and, in 1953, turned the full blast of their pace attack on him when he played against them for Surrey and MCC in May. His single-minded application carried him through both challenges. He was a cricketer of great moral strength, with a pleasantly boyish charm and a courteous manner but, underneath, he was as hard as Hutton, who had a considerable effect on him as batsman and captain.

May's batting sprang from natural aptitude but he gave it much thought. He could play forward soundly in defence from the start; his back play grew safer with experience. Among his strokes, one is tempted to dwell upon the on-drive because it probably is the most difficult of all to play and he executed it to a higher degree of perfection than anyone else in his time. He did not employ the sweep, and quite soon he ruled out hooking of high pace as uneconomic: but he *could* hook – as he could glance and cut – though most of his runs came between midwicket and the left hand of cover-point.

He could hit hard, even spectacularly – and at his best he was complete against all types of bowling. His cardinal quality was his coolness – there was a cold hardness about his cricket: less than almost anyone else was he a mood player or one affected by the setting of his innings, except that he became a little harder in an emergency.

Between 1955 and 1961, he captained England in 41 Tests, a record number for any captain of any country. In that period his thoroughness exposed him to immense strain which was reflected physically so that, at the age of thirty-one, he decided that the stresses and his future career outweighed the

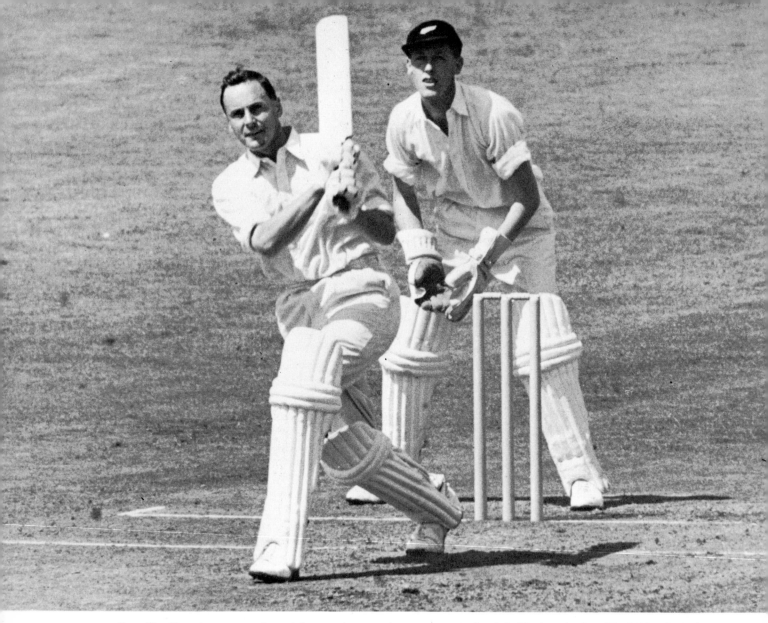

Peter May (Surrey) a correct and essentially strong batsman whose courtesy covered an inflexible determination: Ward (New Zealand) is the wicket-keeper

satisfaction he found in cricket.

His captaincy, like his batting, was cool, and hard; he was a capable close catcher and a man who contrived to live long in the bright light of publicity with an unmarred image.

T. W. Graveney

Modern cricket has known few more handsome batsmen than Tom Graveney, whose play was shaped by the changing bowling methods of his period. At the start of his first-class career – in 1948 – he was predominantly a front-foot, off-side batsman. With the years, the bowling he faced turned him into a back-foot on-side player with a costly tendency to play across the line towards mid-on. Since leaving Glouces-

tershire for Worcestershire, he has matured into an eminently skilful all-round batsman and probably at the moment is more complete in temperament and technique than in the days when he was a regular Test choice.

Tall and slim, Graveney could not bat other than gracefully and he drives, straight and through the covers, with a lazy ease that concealed power. He is the only purely post-war player to score a hundred centuries and certainly the best professional batsman England has produced in that generation. If he has suffered some setbacks he might have escaped in an earlier period, he still draws those who care for the aesthetic delights of cricket and for the making of runs in a memorable way.

J. H. Wardle

From 1947, when he won his county cap, until the dispute which, in 1958, ended his connection with Yorkshire, Johnnie Wardle was one of the best slow left-arm bowlers in the world and certainly the most versatile of his kind the game has ever known. In the orthodox manner, from a rhythmic action, and with a deceptive arc of flight, he could, for long spells, restrict good batsmen on perfect wickets and his finger spin was keen. Rarely, but often enough to underline his ability, he bowled the wrist-spun 'Chinaman' and its googly as accurately and well as anyone has ever done – and effectively enough to win at least two Test Matches. His recent appearances for Cambridgeshire are convincing evidence that he remains as good as any bowler of either type in England.

He caught well and his left-hand batting was sufficiently firmly grounded for him to defend capably and hit with remarkable power. His clowning delighted many crowds. It is regrettable that his achievements, appreciable as. they were, fell short of what they might have been.

W. Watson

Modest, quiet and the model of left-handed batting style, Willie Watson was unlucky to play for England in only 23 Tests. He played coolly under the heaviest pressure, struck the ball regally on fast wickets and retained his poise and certainty of stroke on the most awkward bowlers' pitches. Merely to watch him play a back stroke in defence and drop the ball at his feet was to relish something near perfection in the handling of a bat. He will always be remembered for his century which saved the Lord's Test in 1953 and gave England the chance to win that rubber against Australia: it is sad – and almost incredible – that he was dropped from the England side for the final match that won back The Ashes. Perhaps he was too modest: certainly for ten years England had no better left-hand batsman. His cricket sense was sound, his behaviour impeccable, and he moved well and caught safely in the outfield, though a shoulder injury impaired the early power of his throwing.

West Indies in Australia, 1951–52

Effectively the same side as had beaten England in 1950 went under John Goddard to Australia and lost. In two Tests the margins were so narrow that West Indies might have taken the series by 3–2. The difference between the two sides lay less in runs than in temperament. Australia had the stronger pace-bowling combination and Miller, Lindwall and Johnston never allowed the West Indian batting to build up its accustomed huge totals. Finally, however, the rubber turned on nerve. At Brisbane, West Indies dropped catches and, in the second Australian innings, Valentine and Ramadhin bowled 85 overs – without even changing ends – and Valentine was hit for 117 runs for his one wicket, when either Gomez or Worrell might have bowled tight: Australia scraped in by three wickets. At Melbourne, the last two Australian batsmen – Ring and Johnston – had 38 to make to win; the West Indian outcricket cracked and, amazingly, the runs were made.

The West Indian form was best summarized in the fact that Gerry Gomez was their most successful batsman and bowler, finishing well above players of greater ability by virtue of his harder resistance to the psychological pressures of a series in Australia.

India in England, 1952

Under their first officially-appointed professional captain, Len Hutton, England took the rubber by 3–0 from India, who were never truly in the hunt. Manjrekar, their newest young batsman, made an accomplished century at Headingley; Hazare, the captain, played some courageous, straight-batted innings, and Ghulam Ahmad bowled his off-breaks steadily. The best performance for them was by Mankad, released by his league club for three Tests, who, at Lord's, scored 72 and 184 and, in 97 overs, took five wickets for 251.

Hutton bore his responsibility seriously, and had a batting average of 79. Public excitement in England, however, centred on the discovery – at last – of a fast bowler, Trueman, who three times tore the heart out of the timid Indian batting. At Leeds, in the second innings, their score stood at 0 for four wickets; in the first at Manchester, 17 for five; at The Oval, six for five. In the series Trueman took 29 wickets at 13 each and English cricket followers flocked to see their hope of a counter to Miller and Lindwall.

F. S. Trueman

In 1952 Fred Trueman, a story-book fast-bowler, arrived in story-book fashion to reduce England's opponents to 0 for four wickets in his first Test. In the next dozen years he became the first bowler to take 300 wickets in Tests, behaved in an exaggeratedly extrovert fashion, was in trouble, dropped from the England side, recalled to it, was never out of the news and only for short periods out of some kind of controversy.

A little under six feet tall, strong in shoulders and arms, deep of chest, wide-hipped, with the thick legs and broad feet of the ideal fast-bowler's physique, he had, at his best, a long, curving, menacing run-up and a complete cartwheel, high, sideways-on delivery. With the new ball he made the outswinger move sharply and late; at least once he ran through a Test side by bowling off-cutters; his yorker took some good wickets and his bouncer was sudden and intimidating.

At times on good wickets he could look innocuous and, after he was thirty, he did not always bowl at full pace, often in county cricket contenting himself with steady fast-medium with a fast ball as a stern 'reminder' to presumptuous batsmen. Still, on his day and stimulated by wickets, the crowd, or the opposition of a favourite enemy batsman, he could be a killer. Employed in short spells, as a shock bowler, Trueman was one of the most dangerous bowlers of his time. An unusually good close catcher, he was also capable in the deep field and an ambidextrous thrower; his batting was good enough to bring him three centuries and at times he hit slow bowling unorthodoxly but mightily. Unpredictable but never dull, he has reaped the rewards and suffered the rebuffs of a character-cricketer in the modern game.

The sensation created by Trueman diverted attention from the first Test century of Sheppard and the entry into Test cricket of Lock, who took four for 36 at Old Trafford: both were to play important parts in English Test cricket for some years to come.

The Rev. D. S. Sheppard

From a first appearance for Sussex in 1947, when he was eighteen, until the end of the tour in Australia of 1962–63, David Sheppard engaged attention by his batting. Upstanding, with a high grip on the bat handle and predominantly a front-of-the-wicket player, capable of weighty driving, he, like so many of his generation, was forced increasingly on to the back foot and to on-side play. Like Peter May, he was a serious cricketer who gave much thought to the problems of the game. In 22 Tests he had an average of 37. In his single season – 1953 – as captain of

Sussex, he was regarded by the players under him as remarkably capable for one with so little experience of the office, and the 1954–55 MCC team to Australia was only given to Hutton by a narrow decision over Sheppard. He made himself into a safe close field. He was ordained in 1955 and left first-class cricket in 1963.

G. A. R. Lock

There never was a more fiery enthusiast for cricket than Tony Lock, slow left-arm bowler, one of the finest of all short-leg fieldsmen, and a batsman of greater ability than is generally recognized.

When he first appeared in county cricket in 1946, he was quite a slow bowler, with some flight but little spin. In 1952, after he had performed his National Service and spent a winter of bowling practice in a low-roofed hall, he came back to the Surrey team with a quick, low arc of flight and a high degree of spin but with an action which, especially when he delivered his faster ball, was suspect. From 1952 – when he was three times 'called' for throwing – he waged a struggle with Wardle for the place of England's slow left-arm bowler, which seemed to be his when Wardle went out of the first-class game in 1958. In 1958–59, however, Lock had an unsuccessful tour of Australia and, in New Zealand, was shown a film which convinced him that his action was unfair. Characteristically, he set about remodelling his bowling. He was 'called' twice more and dropped from the England team but, by 1961, with a fresh and unexceptionable action, he was recalled to the Test side against Australia. That was the finest of all his triumphs.

A fierce trier, prepared – despite the handicap of a badly damaged right knee – to bowl for hours in any climate and on any wicket, 'Locky' is still the most aggressive of bowlers. In 1963, he decided to emigrate to Australia where he played for Western Australia in the Sheffield Shield. He returned to England for the summer of 1965, primarily to play as a League professional, but the invitation – and, we may suspect, the challenge – to play for Leicestershire in mid-week matches was too great for him to refuse, and he returned to the county game in such mid-week matches as he could contrive while still maintaining his League engagement.

With his 'illegal' action Lock turned the ball viciously and his faster ball was very quick indeed: nowadays he has more flight and fair turn, good length and the same unfailing persistence. Some of his catches at backward short leg have been amazing and,

Tony Lock (Surrey) fieriest of all cricketers: great short-leg field, the only bowler successfully to switch from an illegal to an acceptable action and, as a batsman as in all else, one who rose to a challenge

as he showed against the West Indies in 1963, he can bat capably and not without style and aggression.

South Africa in Australia, 1952–53

There had been no more surprising result in post-war Test cricket than the 2–2 tie made in Australia by a young South African side, after critics in their own country and in Australia had suggested that, in view of the weakness of South African cricket, the tour should be cancelled. The party was managed by K. G. Viljoen, who had been a member of the South African teams massacred by Australia in 1931–32 and 1935–36 – six innings defeats and only once so much as a draw – and there is little doubt that he thirsted for revenge. The captain, Jack Cheetham – a keen cricketer and gritty batsman – co-operated enthusiastically. The South African success was founded on the bowling of Tayfield – 30 wickets in the series –

and the sometimes amazing catching of a side of young and highly trained players.

Harvey scored almost 400 more runs than any other batsman on either side and had an average of 92: there were six centuries for Australia and only one – by Russell Endean, a dedicated, 'made' batsman and eager fieldsman – for South Africa. But the touring side, though seemingly outweighed, hung on. At the last – Melbourne – Test, Australia batted first and made an apparently impregnable 520. No one for South Africa made a century but, of the seventeen innings played for them in the match, eight were of fifty or more and only one batsman – Fuller, at number eleven, 0* – did not reach double figures. Fuller, Tayfield and Mansell – aided by seven catches – put out Australia for 209, and South Africa won the game by six wickets, to level the series. Significantly, Miller and Lindwall were unable to play in this match – the first time Australia had taken the field without at least one of them since the war. Their importance to the side was increasing rather than diminishing.

At the same time, Pakistan, the newest member of the Imperial Cricket Conference, played her first Tests – against India in India – and lost the rubber by 2–1.

Australia in England, 1953

Hassett's 1953 side showed many changes from Bradman's of 1948: Bradman, Barnes and Brown were missing from the batting; Toshack and Johnson from the bowling. Several of the new players, however, were notable, such as Benaud, Davidson, Gil Langley, a rugged, game and reliable wicket-keeper. Graeme Hole was an attractive stroke-maker who eventually proved vulnerable to high pace; Ron Archer, a finely made pace-bowler, forcing bat and brilliant field, was put out of cricket sadly early by an injury.

R. Benaud

A cricketer with a hungry mind, high ambition and rich all-round ability, Richie Benaud was, for almost a decade, a personality of cricket and one of its most successful captains. His first claim to selection was as a leg-break and googly bowler: not quite slow in pace, using a top-spinner, a 'flipper', and every possible variation of flight and point of delivery, he perpetually harried batsmen. He was always hungry to bowl and, considering the extent of his experiments, he was, of his kind, an accurate bowler. He took more Test wickets – 248 – than anyone else except Trueman.

As a batsman he was a stroke-maker of aggressive bent, whose height and shoulders lent power to his driving, and whose inclination was to meet an emergency with measured attack: and he averaged 24 in Tests. His fielding, especially in the gully, was fearless and brilliant.

A man of high confidence and a quick brain, Benaud enjoyed captaincy, made some bold decisions and, while he rarely refused a reasonable chance to go for a win, he could be tenacious in guarding an advantage, and no one could accuse him of quixotry.

A. K. Davidson

Mighty-shouldered, tall and supple, Alan Davidson was Keith Miller's successor in the Australian team as a match-winning all-rounder. He was primarily a bowler – fast left-arm over the wicket, swinging the ball late into the right-hander, making it lift steeply from all but the deadest surface and, given a little greenness in the wicket, often making it leave the bat off the ground. His Test bowling average – 20·58 – is the lowest among those Australian bowlers of this century who have taken a hundred wickets.

His batting was free and powerful and at least once – in 1961 – it played a decisive part in a Test rubber against England. In any position he was among the finest catchers of all cricket. More worried than most cricketers by injuries, he was not always fit, but often when he appeared most weary he produced his best bowling.

The Test series of 1953 was historic and stirring. The people of England, who had not known what it was for their team to beat Australia anywhere for twenty years, nor at home for twenty-seven, were gripped – and moved – by the series as it ran to its decision in the last match.

Trueman, now in the RAF, played only ten matches for Yorkshire when, understandably, he seemed neither match-fit nor in full form.

Trent Bridge was dramatic and ultimately disappointing. Australia batted first and had reached 237 with only three wickets down before Bedser battered his way through and bowled them out for 249. England went down before Lindwall once more and were 105 behind. Again Bedser retrieved the position – he took fourteen wickets for 99 in the match, one of the best performances by any English bowler against

Alan Davidson (NSW) married unusual strength with easy grace; a bowler of high pace and late movement, a prehensile catcher and powerful batsman

Australia – and, on the third evening, England wanted only 187 to win on a good pitch and with nine wickets standing. Then, cruelly, rain made a draw where there could have been a tight finish.

At Lord's another century by Hassett was matched by Hutton and England led by 26. In the Australian second innings, Morris (89), Miller – unusually subdued in making 109 – and Lindwall with some late blows, set England 343 to win in the last hour of the fourth day and all the fifth. Lindwall, bowling against England – a clash which never lost its dramatic intensity – threw the Lord's crowd first into silence and then dejection as he had Kenyon taken at short mid-on and Hutton at slip: Langley held a wide catch from Graveney off Johnston, and England were 12 for three, with Compton and Watson together. The wicket was taking spin and soon Hassett brought on Ring, pitching his leg-breaks dangerously in the rough outside the left-handed Watson's off stump. In the last over of the day, one such ball whipped quickly in: Watson played it into the hands of Lindwall, close up at short-leg – and it popped out. England were 20 for three at the close of play.

Tuesday, 30th June, 1953 was the most dramatic day's cricket played in England for many years. The only question in the minds of most of those present – and, by contrast with the previous days, the morning crowd was small – was the time at which Australia would win. To save the game regardless of runs, England still needed to bat all but ten minutes as long as they had done in their entire first innings, but now Hutton, Graveney and Kenyon were gone. Lindwall and Miller bowled: then they gave way to Johnston and alternation of the two leg-spinners, Ring and Benaud. At twenty minutes to one Johnston pitched a ball middle-and-leg to Compton: it straightened and kept low and Compton was lbw. When Bailey came in, his average in nine innings against Australia was under eight, his highest score 15.

At lunch Watson and Bailey were still together: 116 for four: four hours left. Down the afternoon the two held on. As news of the resistance spread, the crowd grew from four thousand of the morning to three times as many. At five-to-three a silence fell on the ground as Hassett called up Miller and Lindwall to take the new ball, and set a close attacking field. The mood of the crowd was a half-hysterical mixture of incredulity and hope. Bailey would push forward to Miller and roll the ball a few yards down the pitch or Watson would rock on to his back foot to Lindwall and play a dead bat defensive stroke – and suddenly someone would break the tension with applause. Three times the lifting ball ground Bailey's hand against the bat, but the two were still there at tea. Just on half-past-five, Watson swung Ring high towards the Tavern, Benaud rushed in and attempted a catch, could not touch the ball, and it went on past him for four and Watson's hundred. Watson had been in five-and-three-quarter hours for 109 when he edged Ring, by way of his pad, to Hole, who caught him at slip. The crowd stood to Watson as he walked in. Within a few minutes Bailey mishit Ring to Benaud in the gully and went out, head down in chagrin, through the cheers. Thirty-five minutes left and only Brown – one of the selectors, brought in for this match to make good the lack of an all-rounder – and Evans stood between the Australian bowlers and the tail of Wardle, Bedser and Statham. Both Brown and Evans were known to be vulnerable to Lindwall; but, inexplicably, Hassett did not bring him on. In the last over Brown, who had been chancing his arm,

edged Benaud to slip. For a moment the possibility of Benaud taking the three remaining wickets in the last four balls struck the crowd with cold chill: but Wardle made all safe. The game had been saved in a fashion more epic than many a win. All at once, after so many years, England felt themselves a match for Australia.

At Old Trafford, a century by Harvey and a pleasing 66 by Hole took Australia to 318 but, after rain, play started at 2.10 on the last day with the English first innings still uncompleted. Once England had avoided the follow-on the game seemed to be petering out. Australia were left with an hour to bat in their second innings – but on a turning wicket. By the end of play their score was 35 for eight against the cut of Bedser, the finger spin of Laker and Wardle: few can have dreamt how sharply it foreshadowed 1956: but to Laker, Hutton and May it was no dream.

At Headingley, the batting of Hassett, Harvey, Hole and Archer, and the bowling of Lindwall – eight wickets – and Miller – six – left Australia in a strong position. After tenacious, delaying innings by Edrich, Compton (with an injection in an injured hand), Bailey (38 in four hours twenty minutes) and Laker – who played Miller and Lindwall boldly – Australia needed 177 to win in 115 minutes. Since the wicket took spin, Hutton, recalling that last hour at Old Trafford, attacked through Bedser, Lock and Laker. Hassett went early, but Morris, Harvey and Hole counter-attacked so effectively that Australia needed only 66 in 46 minutes. At this point Hutton could no longer take risks to win. He called up Bailey who closed down the game by bowling wide of the leg stump to a leg-side field. Once more, he saved England from threatened defeat, and took them to the Oval with The Ashes dependent on the result.

The final Test was decided by the respective selection committees. The Oval wicket had favoured spin all the season yet the Australians left out all three leg-spinners – Benaud, Hill and Ring – and relied on a pace attack with only Johnston who could use a turning pitch. England brought in Trueman and, as it proved, crucially, played Lock and Laker on their home ground.

Trueman earned his place with four wickets, Bedser took three, and another responsible innings by Hassett and some firm hitting by Lindwall were the main contributions to the Australian total – 275. Miller and Johnston took seven English wickets and again Hutton and Bailey were the chief English scorers – in

306, for a lead of 31. Then, as the pitch began to respond to spin, Lock, five for 45, and Laker, four for 75 (the other wicket was a run out), were checked only by a brave hitting partnership of fifty by Archer and Davidson for the seventh wicket. England needed 132 to win and Hutton, Edrich, May and Compton made a slow way to their objective – of match, rubber and Ashes – at a rate of barely two runs an over before the crowd swept, cheering, across the ground.

Bedser's 39 wickets at 17·48 was the outstanding single performance of the series, with Hutton's 443 runs at 55 and Lindwall's 26 wickets at 18 next behind him. Over all there was little between the two sides except the Australian deficiency in spin, which cancelled out their superiority in the field. For once, however, England – especially at Lord's – had reacted to crises in a way Australia could not have bettered. Hutton, an unobtrusive but relentless captain, had ensured that England played the game as resolutely as Australia, and had missed no tactical trick.

England in the West Indies, 1953–54

This tour was not a happy one: its atmosphere was imperilled from the start by public insistence that it was for 'The Championship of the World'. Bottle-throwing incidents, some doubtful umpiring decisions – and reprehensible reactions to them – and the no-balling of Lock for throwing, all contributed to a tense and sometimes bitter atmosphere.

In some ways this tour was Hutton's greatest personal performance for, after England had lost the first two Tests, he lifted them by his own efforts to draw the series. At Kingston, Jamaica, long West Indian batting, led by the stylish J. K. Holt junior, and the bowling of Valentine, Ramadhin and Gomez put England so far behind that, although Stollmeyer did not enforce the follow-on, Watson's century in partnership with Hutton could not avert defeat by 140 runs against the fast leg theory of the Oxford Blue, Esmond Kentish.

In Barbados, 220 by Walcott, 166 by Holt, and seven wickets to Ramadhin, were conclusive after an English first innings in which only Hutton stood firm.

England batted first at Georgetown and Hutton, playing with all his concentration and professional skill, made 169 while the rest of the side, in greater or smaller measure, resisted beside him. The total was 435: nine West Indians bowled; Ramadhin took six

for 113. Statham broke into the West Indian first innings and they never recovered from being 16 for three: Weekes and Holt (twice) batted gamely but England won by nine wickets.

There never had been a result in a Test played on the coconut matting of Port-of-Spain and no one expected one now, in the last to be played there before the switch to turf. 1,528 runs were scored for 25 wickets and a draw.

So back to Jamaica where England needed a win to level the series: and, when Hutton lost the toss for the fourth time in the series, it seemed that they might have to labour to save the game. In the event, Bailey, on a straightforward pitch of no great pace and to general amazement, in his best Test bowling performance, took seven for 34. Only Walcott scored more than 22 against him and West Indies were out for 139. Hutton now put the issue beyond doubt with an innings of 205 made with grim purpose in a little less than nine hours. A century by Walcott and 64 by Stollmeyer saved an innings defeat but England, winning by nine wickets, shared the rubber.

Hutton, with an average of 96, was the decisive batsman of the series, though Walcott, Weekes and Holt all had figures above fifty. Ramadhin took 23 wickets, but no other West Indian bowler had more than eight, while four England players – Statham, Bailey, Laker and Lock – had between 14 and 16.

J. B. Statham

No fast-bowler in the history of cricket can have maintained such accuracy and consistency for so long as Brian Statham. Since his first entry into county cricket on his twentieth birthday in 1950, he has bowled at truly fast pace with the precision of a slow bowler. His run-up is smooth and flowing, through to a final delivery which involves a huge whip of body, shoulder and highly flexible wrist. He rarely swings the ball, his movement is generally off the pitch, and in to the right-hander: though occasionally, for reasons he does not understand, the ball suddenly starts to go the other way.

It is not possible to estimate the number of wickets Statham set up for others by making it all but impossible for batsmen to play strokes against him. His own tally of Test wickets – 245 – is below only those of Trueman and Benaud, and on the whole he has been unlucky – especially against left-handed batsmen who have played and missed outside the off stump times beyond number.

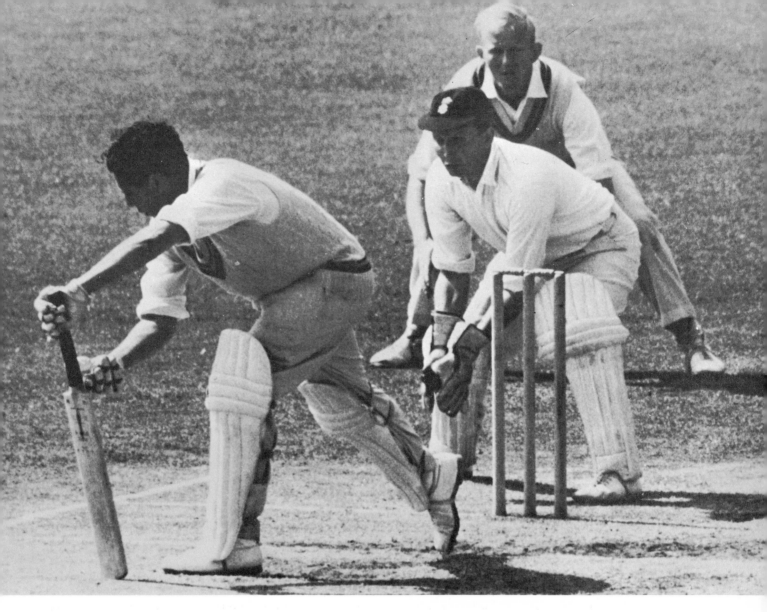

Trevor Bailey (Essex) by courage, concentration, care and an acute intelligence made himself one of the most complete cricketers: a match-winner as well as a match-saver. Long is the wicket-keeper and Storey, slip (both Surrey)

Quiet, steadfast, and devoted to cricket, Brian Statham has been the best of professional cricketers and, in 1965, took over as captain of Lancashire after his county had experienced some unhappy seasons.

His left-hand batting has sometimes been violently useful, his catching in the deep is utterly reliable and his throw long, low and accurate. He is generally known as 'George', and even his opponents like him.

New Zealand in South Africa, 1953–54

South Africa won a happy series by 4–0. The batting of McGlew, van Ryneveld, Cheetham, Endean and McLean, the spin of Tayfield and the pace of Adcock were the decisive factors in the series. Reid, Sutcliffe and the captain Rabone – who missed two Tests through injury – were the main New Zealand batsmen but when Rabone was away, McGibbon carried too great a weight of the bowling.

Pakistan in England, 1954

On the first visit to England, Pakistan drew a four-Test rubber when they won at The Oval to level the score at 1–1.

The first Test, at Lord's, could not be started until 3.45 on the fourth day and a draw was inevitable. At Nottingham, Appleyard – five for 51 in the first innings – Bedser, Statham and Wardle bowled out Pakistan twice. Simpson made 101, and Compton murdered the leg-spin of Khalid Hassan – at sixteen the youngest man to appear in a Test – to score 278 in less than five hours before Khalid at last bowled him. England won by an innings and looked likely to do so again at Old Trafford when rain ended the game.

At The Oval, the England selectors left out Bedser and Bailey in order to give Test experience to Tyson and Loader who had been picked for the imminent tour to Australia. On a wicket responsive to spin not one of the four innings reached 170 and the issue was decided by Fasal Mahmood who took 12 wickets for 99.

On the touring side Kardar, who had formerly played for India (on the tour of 1946), Oxford University and Warwickshire, was a captain with much experience of English conditions; Imtiaz Ahmed was a serviceable wicket-keeper-batsman; Maqsood Ahmed batted attractively in the early stages of the tour; Shuja-id-Din and Zulfiquar Ahmed were useful natural spinners. Their outstanding players, however, were Fazal and Hanif.

Fazal Mahmood

A strongly built fast-medium bowler, Fazal learnt his craft on matting wickets. With a somewhat shoulderish action he swung the ball both ways, but his chief ability lay in cutting the ball, especially from the off, though batsmen found it hard to distinguish his off-cutter from the rarer one which moved from leg. He bowled steadily, a little short of a length, and on this tour was certainly over bowled. Always dangerous on the mat, he would have flourished, too, in regular English cricket.

Hanif Mohammad

Neat, balanced and dextrous, Hanif began the 1954 tour of England preoccupied with defence. Later in that summer he showed a whole range of strokes and, at nineteen, looked a world-class batsman. Although quite short, he hit with wristy strength and his hooking was splendidly certain. Subsequently he relapsed into defence and broke records on easy wickets without revealing his full powers. He has scored far more runs for Pakistan than any other player, but such is the mood of cricket in the sub-continent that he does not always reveal his full stature.

England were at this time producing players of high quality and they took to Australia three men who had not been considered a year before – two of them still regarded somewhat askance even when chosen in late 1954: they were Appleyard, Cowdrey and Tyson.

R. Appleyard

Illness interrupted, and early ended, the first-class cricket of Bob Appleyard who first appeared for Yorkshire in 1950, created a record by taking 200 wickets in his first full season – 1951 – and, after playing only one match in 1952 and 1953, retired in 1958 with a record of 708 wickets at 15·48, and after playing nine times for England.

Tall and well-built, Appleyard bowled between slow-medium and medium, swinging the new ball, cutting and spinning the old. In many ways he was cast in the mould of stock bowlers of old, in that accuracy was his prime asset, for he rarely wavered from length or line. He learnt, rapidly and thoroughly, to disguise his variations, and his change of pace often proved as effective as his swing or turn. He was at his best in English conditions because he was so effective on slow turning wickets where the orthodox slow spinner does not come quickly enough off the pitch to beat the better batsmen. Appleyard was a natural stock-bowler and, if he had remained fit, he could have filled that post for England for many years.

M. C. Cowdrey

England has had no more gifted batsman in recent years than Colin Cowdrey who, when he is in tune, can play every stroke against every type of bowling – and with time to spare. At his best he looks like a man playing with boys: then, his hooking of the fastest bowling is an unhurried, precision stroke and his driving an apparently simple exercise in perfection. Against spin, he will go forward and play in the shadow of his pad with such solidity as makes the bowling seem innocuous. Massively built, yet never ponderous, he moves into position instinctively and his reactions are abnormally quick.

His weakness stems from his strength. He is so near the stage at which he can play everything with certainty that the slightest hint that the bowler might be able to beat him seems to undermine his confidence. In essence, he has quite abnormal ability linked with normal humility. If he recognized that he is an unusually gifted player and based his batting on that fact he might, with little trouble, pass many of the batting records. Quiet and fascinated by cricket, he is

Colin Cowdrey (Kent) a player of such outstanding natural gifts as to make batting appear a simple matter: his achievements have been limited only by self-doubt

not merely a natural games player, he seems to have an extra sensitivity in bat-play. Only self-doubt stands between Cowdrey and the highest eminence. He is an unruffled catcher at slip or gully and he sometimes bowls leg-breaks, one of which was struck by Alan Davidson, in 1954, to the roof of the grandstand at Sydney, a carry few bowlers have ever experienced.

F. H. Tyson

Whenever, during the middle fifties, Frank Tyson delivered his first ball before a crowd that had not seen him before, there would be a spontaneous, mass gasp which was the ultimate comment on his speed.

Indisputably the fastest bowler in post-war cricket, he was, for a period of about four years, one of the few men – say half a dozen – in the entire history of cricket who regularly beat good batsmen by pace alone.

He relished fast bowling, but he recognized it as a brief and precarious calling. Therefore he took a University degree so that, as soon as the day came when he felt his powers were waning, he could leave professional cricket for an assured living as a schoolmaster.

To his enduring disappointment, his native Lancashire were not interested enough to offer him an engagement. (What a combination he and Statham would have made in county cricket!) So he joined Northants in 1952 but his University studies probably spared him the damage young fast bowlers suffer through six-day-a-week cricket by deferring his first full season until 1954. Then, yards faster than anyone else in the country, he was chosen for the last Test against Pakistan.

For four years he was the fastest bowler in the world and, as his pace declined, he exploited swing and cut – still fast, but not so fast as he had been. This did not satisfy him, the slow Northampton wicket had always been a handicap to him and, true to his plans, at the end of the 1960 season he retired from first-class cricket.

Tall, with long arms and fine chest and shoulder development, Tyson was made for bowling. The length of his run varied. At times it was much more than twenty yards: in his youth, and again during his high peak, in Australia in 1954–55, it was thirteen yards, a rhythmic progression, ending with a mighty swing of body and shoulders, with his arm stretched up from his full six feet of height, and a spectacular final leap down the pitch after the ball. His plunging follow-through pummelled his left foot and once caused a hair-line fracture which inhibited him for some time.

A large number of his best wickets were clean bowled when he simply sent the ball through before the bat could be brought down. He rarely bowled the bouncer except for surprise, preferring to employ the yorker which was more direct in effect.

In the second Test of 1954–55, he was knocked unconscious by a bouncer from Lindwall, who later came in to bat against Tyson. Never, surely, can a bowler have been more tempted to let a batsman 'have one': Tyson bowled Lindwall with a half-volley.

Frank Tyson's career contained four great performances when, within the space of six months, he four times ran through a Test innings. Many men have laboured long for less. By coincidence, each of these feats was performed after a dinner on the previous night with burgundy as the accompanying wine.

For the brief and glorious period of his highest speed, Frank Tyson was a match-winner, a unique experience for batsmen and one of the spectacles of cricket. He enjoyed it, earned his salt and went away content, leaving his legend behind.

England in Australia, 1954–55

To Len Hutton, to defeat Australia on their own grounds now represented the pinnacle of ambition. Over the preceding three years he had forged the weapon for the task and accustomed himself to handling it. Wisely, he was never over-confident; rarely even mildly confident: he accepted nothing in cricket as certain until it was accomplished fact.

At Brisbane, England packed their side with pace-bowling and when Hutton won the toss he sent Australia to bat. In the previous match – MCC v Queensland – the pitch had been 'green' on the first morning: at the Test it was not. Hutton's decision to put Australia in has been adduced as the reason for England's defeat. That ignores the fact that twelve catches were dropped in the Australian innings and that Compton was injured. Morris – twice missed – made 153, Harvey 162 and Australia 601 for eight. The familiar, deadly combination of Miller and Lindwall cut England to 11 for three and, thereafter, the batting of Cowdrey, Bailey in the first innings, Edrich, May and Tyson in the second, slowed, but never threatened to prevent, Australia's progress to an innings win with a day to spare.

While the defeat at Brisbane still hung heavily on the English players, Alec Bedser was surprisingly left out of the side for Sydney. The wicket would have suited him: but he had been off colour and Hutton, from long experience at the receiving end, wanted the highest pace available. Arthur Morris, acting as captain in place of the injured Johnson, put England in and Lindwall, Johnston, Archer and Davidson, in steadily switched variety of seam-bowling, broke through to 88 for seven, and only a splutter from Wardle and Statham lifted England to 154. Statham, Bailey and Tyson, finding some pace in the pitch, kept the game still within England's reach by containing the Australian innings to 228. May's century and 54 by Cowdrey took England to 296 and set Australia 223 to win, of which they made 72 for two by the end of the fourth day. On the morning of the fifth, the game was fascinatingly balanced. Harvey

took control of the Australian batting. Hutton held back his main pace attack – Tyson and Statham – until the last moment, and then threw them in to bowl for the rest of the match – and win it or lose it. They took five wickets. Then Harvey farmed the bowling to put on 39 for the tenth wicket with Johnston before Tyson, near the end of his tether after an hour-and-a-half spell since lunch, at length found the edge of Johnston's bat and Evans made the catch.

Tyson, with ten wickets in the match, had won it: but Statham – three for 45 bowling against the wind in the second innings – was his essential partner in the operation.

At Melbourne, England batted and Miller bowled one of the greatest spells in post-war cricket. At full pace, with sharply angled movement from the pitch, in nine overs during the hour-and-a-half to lunch, he took three wickets for five runs. Cowdrey, playing with impressive maturity, made 102, with Bailey as his main partner. Australia batted evenly and only Statham – five for 60 – kept their lead to 40. May – 91 – with Bailey again shoring up the second half, helped England to 279.

The pitch showed ominous cracks early in the game and was crumbling by the end of the second day – Saturday. In a rainless weekend, Sunday was a day of the scorching north wind yet, on Monday, the cracks had disappeared and the pitch was wet and sound. It was officially denied that the pitch had been watered. This time Australia were set 240 to win and made 79 of them for two wickets on the fourth day. Next morning, Hutton threw in Tyson and Statham again. In an hour-and-twenty-minutes the remaining eight wickets went down for 36 runs and England had won by 128. In that morning spell Tyson bowled 6·3 overs and took six for 16; Statham, in six overs, two for 19.

Again at Adelaide there was little difference between the two first innings – Australia 323, England 341. When Australia batted again, Hutton took off Statham after two overs and, on a wearing pitch, put on Appleyard who took three for 39 by the end of the fourth day. Next morning, when everyone expected Appleyard to bowl again, Hutton once more employed full pace. In an hour-and-a-half, Statham took three for 12, Tyson three for 17, and Australia were out for 111. England's passage to the 94 they wanted to win was contested by Miller, who put out Hutton, Edrich and Cowdrey in the course of twenty balls and then caught May at cover. Compton and

Frank Tyson (Northants) briefly but gloriously the fastest bowler in the world: he recognized and enjoyed the shortness of such a career

Bailey balanced the innings, and England took the match by five wickets to keep The Ashes.

With the rubber won, Sydney threatened anti-climax, particularly when torrential rains – which caused loss of life and damage in the valley of the Hunter River – prevented any play until after lunch on the fourth day. Graveney scored his first hundred against Australia; May, Compton and Bailey all made runs. England declared at 371 for seven, and Australia were 82 for two on the fifth evening. The next day, when the match was expected to drift out quietly, Wardle proceeded to bowl his 'Chinaman' so effectively (five for 79) that Australia – all out 221 – followed on against England for the first time since the Oval Test of 1938. Now Wardle took three for 51, but there was not sufficient time for England to force a win.

This series was decided by the two England fast bowlers, Tyson, who took 28 wickets, and Statham, 18: and it is, by modern standards, surprising that they barely employed the bouncer at all. On a number of the Test wickets the ball came through at varying heights and, at Tyson's speed and with Statham's straightness, that was all the assistance they needed. Five English and six Australian bowlers took ten or more wickets: May and Cowdrey established themselves as Test batsmen. Hutton had achieved his ambition, and he could now relax. But, almost thirty-nine and much battered, tired and troubled by a back injury, he played only a few matches in 1955 and then retired.

England in New Zealand, 1954–55

Before returning home, England played as usual in New Zealand, where only Bert Sutcliffe offered any substantial opposition to the English bowling in the first Test. In the second, Sutcliffe, Reid and Rabone built a first innings total of 200 – only 46 less than England's – but, when New Zealand batted again, Tyson, Statham, Wardle and Appleyard dismissed them – and dismissed is the word – for the lowest recorded Test score – 26.

Australia in the West Indies, 1954–55

Immediately after their home series with England, Australia went to the West Indies where they made a complete batting recovery and became the first overseas side to win a rubber in the Caribbean. In fact, they were never beaten on the tour and their batsmen, with no such pace as Tyson's to face, scored twelve centuries between them. Walcott, with five hundreds in the rubber – one in each innings of the second and fifth Tests – was the heaviest scorer in the series while, at Bridgetown, Atkinson and Depeiza made a record seventh wicket stand of 348. The issue was settled by Miller and Lindwall (40 wickets between them at a lower figure than that of any West Indian) with Archer as third pace-bowler, and Benaud and Johnson as the spinners. Australia won the first, third and fifth Tests: the other two were left drawn. In the fifth – at Kingston – seven centuries were scored. By then, Australia had hit Valentine and Ramadhin out of the West Indies team. After Australia had stood at seven for two wickets, McDonald made 127, Harvey 204, Miller 109, Archer 128 and Benaud 121: Walcott's two hundreds – 155 and 110 – did not even serve to make Australia bat a second time.

South Africa in England, 1955

Cheetham's team which had been tempered in Australia in 1952–53 formed the basis for his side in England and again the militant Ken Viljoen was the manager. Although they lost the rubber by 3–2, they were the first South Africans to win two Tests in a series in England, and at least seven of their players had matured into capable Test cricketers.

D. J. McGlew

The discipline of Ken Viljoen struck an answering chord in Jackie McGlew. Short, with the jutting jaw of a fighter, as fit as constant training could make him, he developed a resistant quality in his cricket, reduced the scoring strokes of his youth and made his wicket one of the hardest in the world to take. No stylist, though straight in his forward defensive push, he was quick on his feet, watched the ball unremittingly and, on his back shuffle, adjusted quickly to the moving ball. It was the essence of the man that, in 1955, after a 'pair of spectacles' at Lord's, he went on to score a century in each of the next two Tests. As well as his passionately determined effort to keep one end safe for his side, he was a fast and keen fieldsman in the covers – or anywhere else.

Jackie McGlew (Natal) a belligerent cricketer and a captain capable of infusing some of his own determination into a losing side, he resisted to the last ball of any game

T. L. Goddard

South Africa has produced no all-rounder since Aubrey Faulkner of such value as Trevor Goddard. Six-feet-two and lithely built, he was a cricketer of his time, brought up in the South African school which set out to make itself, first and foremost, hard to beat. Goddard bowled left-arm medium pace over the wicket with a little swing and a little cut but, above all, to an economic length, on or outside the leg stump to a leg-side field, so that the best batsmen in the world found it difficult to make strokes against him. His left-handed batting, which tended much to the back foot, was balanced and scholarly, with an air of style and sound defence; like McGlew, he was hard to get out. His fielding has hardly been bettered since the war and some of his running catches were triumphs of balance and timing.

W. R. Endean

First a wicket-keeper then an outstanding fieldsman, Russell Endean was a strong batsman who, in 1954–55

for Transvaal against Orange Free State scored 197 before lunch – a feat unapproached in first-class cricket. In Tests he usually was a dogged batsman, a pusher and deflector on the leg-side with a rather individual bottom-handed push square on the off. His somewhat plodding approach to batting was belied by his fielding: through unremitting concentration, he made some amazing catches both close to the wicket and in the deep.

J. H. B. Waite

The best wicket-keeper-batsman of his day, John Waite set a Test record when, against New Zealand in 1953–54, he took 23 wickets in the Test series. At six feet, he was tall for a wicket-keeper, but he was slim, bent easily and was neat, relaxed and quick: a thoughtful cricketer and often a valuable steadying influence. His batting was calm, fluent and, unusually for a South African, assured on bad wickets.

R. A. McLean

In a series of South African sides where the batting tended towards grimness, Roy McLean was not always regarded with approval. He was by nature an attacking batsman and, in a day of tight bowling, the risks he chose to take cost him his wicket often enough for him to be several times left out of the South African team while he was at the height of his powers. With a good eye, strong wrists and an inborn sense of timing, he would carry the fight to the best bowlers and, on his day, his cutting, driving, hooking and glancing brought him runs at fine pace and in exciting fashion. He was not consistent, but he was a match-winner – and a gay cricketer.

N. A. T. Adcock

South Africa's most consistent fast bowler, Neil Adcock, was six-feet-three and leanly built. His run up was long and fluent but in delivery he was almost purely an 'arm' bowler, with a high, complete cartwheel of the arm but little body swing. By his height he made the ball rear awkwardly from only a little short of a length and took many wickets through catches to the wicket-keeper or slips, particularly on the 1960 tour to England.

As had been foreseen, May inherited the England captaincy from Hutton and, at Trent Bridge, after he had won the toss, England made a strong start to the series. Most of the batsmen made runs, but slowly against defensive bowling and field placing: 334 in

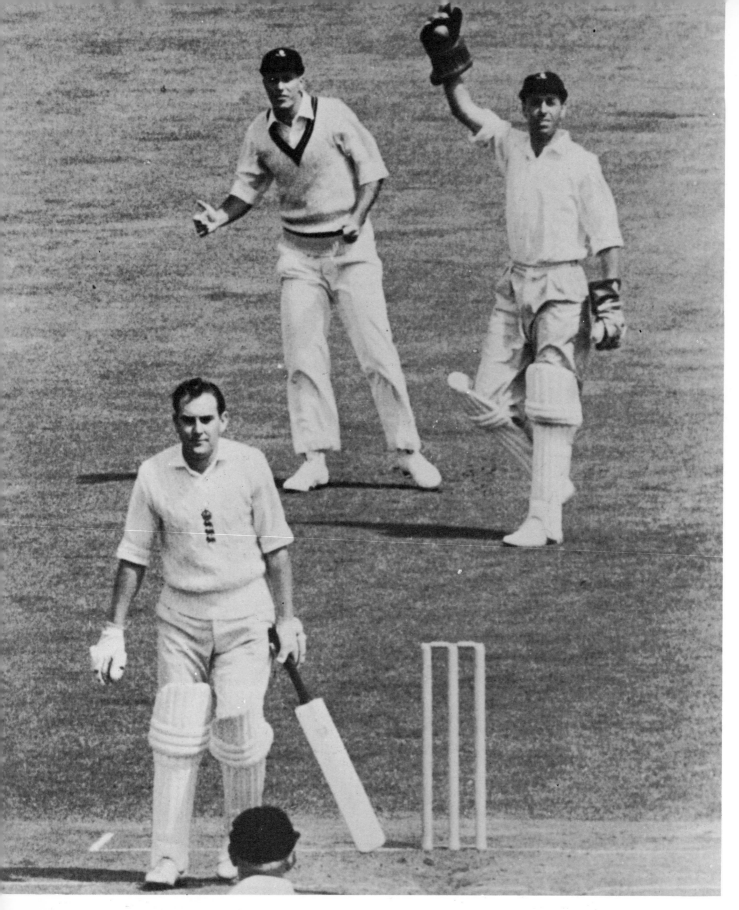

John Waite (Transvaal) the outstanding wicket-keeper-batsman in post-war cricket: here he has caught Ray Illingworth (Yorkshire): Trevor Goddard is at slip

nine hours. Once Tyson and Statham had made initial inroads – to 35 for four – the South African batting became even slower – 144 in five-and-three-quarter hours on Saturday, when Appleyard and Wardle steadily finished off the innings for 181. May enforced the follow-on and McGlew and Goddard made 46 on Saturday evening without losing a wicket. There was weekend rain and play did not start until one on Monday. Tyson, mellowed by Dr Howell's Beaujolais at Sunday dinner, bowled as fast as he had done in Australia. In one spell he took five for five and swept away the South African batting. England won by an innings and five runs.

Tyson could not play at Lord's, where Trueman and Titmus came in. May won the toss; England batted on a grassy wicket, and Peter Heine – six-feet-five, fast right-arm and discovering, to his delight, the possibilities of pace-bowling in English conditions – and Adcock broke through to 45 for four and England never recovered. Goddard took the tail-end wickets and England were out for 133. The first two South African batsmen, McGlew and Goddard, were both out for 0, to Trueman and Statham; then, with Endean and Keith to keep the other end secure, McLean played a fine hitting innings: with the fortune to be dropped, and accelerating on the second morning, he went on to 142. South Africa's 304 gave them a lead of 171. May – 112 – Graveney and Compton in a spell of spirited batting took England to 277 before the fourth wicket fell: Tayfield and Adcock ended the innings at 353, leaving South Africa only 183 to win. In the last half-hour on Saturday, Statham took the wickets of McGlew and Goddard, and Cheetham retired hurt when a short ball from Trueman struck him on the elbow (he did not play again until late July). Play on Monday was stopped by bad light for two hours, punctuating Statham's unbroken spell, from start to finish of the innings – 29 overs, in which he took seven for 39, to win the match for England by 71.

England batted first on another lively wicket at Old Trafford. Kenyon and Graveney were out early – then Compton, after a shaky start, found his touch and, with support from May and Bailey, made 158 of England's 284. McGlew went off hurt after he had made 77 and South Africa were still behind at 245 for five when Paul Winslow – a tall, slim young man and a natural straight hitter – came in to Waite. Waite scored his first Test century, and Winslow, with a towering six over the sight-screen, reached his first

and only hundred in first-class cricket. Their 171 was a record seventh wicket partnership for South Africa. McGlew returned and went on to 104* in a total of 521 for eight declared: 237 on. England lost Kenyon and Graveney for two; then May – 117 – Compton and Cowdrey rebuilt the innings to 381. South Africa wanted 145 in 135 minutes to win. They went for the runs from the start; McGlew and McLean forced the pace effectively but four wickets fell quickly and, from the last three overs, and with three wickets left, they needed 10 runs: Waite coolly saw them in with an over to spare.

Headingley was the occasion of a courageous South African recovery. Batting first, they were 38 for five, 98 for seven, before Endean, Tayfield and Heine struggled up to 171. Then, after four overs, Adcock injured his foot and took no further part in the game. Tayfield, Goddard and Heine shouldered the bowling and only May and Compton – 108 out of 191 – offered them any check. Centuries by McGlew and Endean and seventies by Goddard and Keith made a second South African innings of 500. Once Insole and May were out, Goddard and Tayfield, bowling 109 overs between them, worked their way steadily through the innings to beat England by 224 runs and leave the rubber to be settled at The Oval.

There the re-shaped England batting – Ikin, Close and Watson came in – did little better than before. On a pitch which granted a little turn, but no lift or unevenness, Goddard and Tayfield ran down the innings, without important opposition, for 151. Laker and Lock, in their usual turn on this pitch, bowled England to a lead of 39. May's conscientious 89* was the chief innings that set South Africa 244. Now Lock and Laker shared nine wickets and England took the rubber with a 92 runs win.

West Indies in New Zealand, 1955–56

To the ordinary reader, the fact that West Indies won this series by 3–1 sounds unremarkable. But, for New Zealanders, their first Test win – after twenty-six years – was a great cricketing occasion. In each of the three preceding Tests of the series, Weekes had made a century, and the spin bowling of Valentine, Rama-dhin and, latterly, Atkinson had been enough to bring them two innings wins and one by nine wickets. Now, on a difficult pitch, John Reid's 84 was the highest score of the game and, in the fourth innings, Cave and

Beard bowled out the West Indies for 77, and New Zealand beat them by 190.

Australia in England, 1956

Although Australia lost the rubber by 2–1, it was arguable that they were the better side: certainly they won the only Test to be played out on a hard true wicket – at Lord's.

Ian Johnson, the slow off-spinner and serviceable bat who had been a member of Bradman's side but not Hassett's, was the captain. He probably was not wise to announce early in the tour that his team would regard other matches as practice for the Tests. Apart from the captain, only Miller, Lindwall and Harvey remained from Bradman's 1948 team.

I. D. Craig

In 1952–53, when he was seventeen, Ian Craig became the youngest cricketer to play for Australia (he scored 53 and 47 against South Africa). He came on the English tour of 1953 without playing in a Test. Neatly made, well-balanced and intelligent, he moved well on his feet and his strokes were deft, clean and unhurried. He missed several seasons of cricket in order to concentrate on his studies as a chemist. Nevertheless, his ability as a batsman was obvious and his maturity of mind such that, after some responsible batting in the latter part of the 1956 tour, he was given the captaincy of the Australian side on a short tour to New Zealand and then of their team to South Africa in 1957–58. He thus became the youngest Test captain. Although his side won the rubber 3–0 Craig himself had little success as a batsman and the post passed to Benaud.

K. Mackay

The choice of 'Slasher' Mackay for the English tour of 1956 was a surprise to the Australian public and to Mackay himself who, at the age of thirty, had never before been chosen for any representative match. His strength lay in unattractive but safe left-hand batting: he scored more runs for Queensland than any other player. Using a heavy bat, Mackay pushed and deflected most of his runs though, if provoked, he hooked hard. His judgement in leaving a ball un-played was exact and his patience and concentration made him a hard batsman to dismiss on good wickets. Off-spin puzzled him in England and he was helpless against Laker at Leeds and Manchester in 1956 (four runs in four innings).

Normally, however, he was a valuable all-rounder who, at right arm medium pace, swung the ball appreciably both ways and bowled a steady length, and was a safe catcher. Mackay, as an all-rounder, became an important member of Benaud's side. An incessant chewer of gum, with the walk of a stage villain, and a finicky way of patting, brushing and studying the pitch while batting, Mackay was a tough enthusiast, and a character.

C. C. McDonald

When Australia were being routed by Tyson and Statham in 1954–55, they turned from such recognized stroke-makers as Flavell and Hole to more solid batsmen, one of whom was Colin McDonald. He scored 48, 29, 72 and 37 in his four innings of the series and remained in the Australian side for another six years while, with 3,106 runs, he passed the aggregates of all but five Australian Test batsmen. Stumpy in build, with an alert mind, McDonald was never an attractive player but he had a sharp eye for the ball, was phlegmatic against pace or spin and, unlike some Australian batsmen, could delay his stroke to cover late deviations. His scoring was steady but rarely fast: his asset was solidity – of technique and temperament.

J. W. Burke

Preoccupation with defence weighed against Jim Burke's selection for Australia for some years. Cap-a-cock, tall and lean, inclining more and more towards back play, he was a watchful cricketer with a shallow back lift and a determinedly defensive attitude: a good man when his side was in trouble. His square-on method of back play found him often in trouble against sharp-turning off-spin, but he had the courage to hang on even when he was being beaten. A man of pleasantly dry wit, he sometimes bowled off-breaks himself – with an action more than merely suspicious.

P. Burge

Slow to mature, Peter Burge reached the heights of his cricket in his innings at Headingley which decided the 1964 Test series. Tall and strong with huge arms, he was the Englishman's idea of an Australian. He was always a brave player of pace, solid and straight in defence, quick and powerful in the hook. He learnt slowly to deal with off-spin; in time, however, he evolved a sideways-on or forward defence to it, coupled with an effective sweep and, by 1964, played Allen and Titmus as well as any Australian. Burge always reacted truculently to challenge and, a masterful striker of the ball, fought against any suggestion of domination by a bowler.

P. E. Richardson

Seeking a successor to Hutton as opening batsman, the England selectors in 1956 chose Peter Richardson – then of Worcester, subsequently of Kent – for all five Tests. He finished third in the batting averages with a figure of 45: but in each of his eight Test innings he was caught by the wicket-keeper from one of the faster bowlers. Once the Australians discover such a weakness in an opponent they never cease to exploit it and, in 1958–59, they harried him mercilessly.

Richardson, left-handed like his brothers – Dick of Worcester and Bryan of Warwick – remains one of the most prolific scorers in county cricket. He is not a powerful stroke-player, though he hits well through the covers and cuts cleanly: but he is a perpetually busy batsman, always keeping the scoreboard moving with pushes or deflections into gaps, quick running and a quick-witted appreciation of the bowling, the field and the state of the game. A lively field at cover, he is a sprightly cricketer, amused by the game and amusing about it.

D. J. Insole

No student of the copy-book would accept Douglas Insole as a class batsman because both his bat and his strokes were frequently crooked. He had, however, a good eye and guts, was quick on his feet, hit the ball strongly and never worried himself about correctness so long as he was playing long innings, which he constantly did. A useful emergency wicket-keeper, an enthusiastic field in the covers, a safe catcher at slip and a change bowler with the knack of taking wickets, he was a useful man in any side. As captain of Essex he proved a close observer of the game, one of its warmer wits, and concerned to understand his players, not only as cricketers but as men.

Before the first Test, Laker took all ten wickets in the Australian first innings against Surrey, who became the first county since Hampshire, forty-four years before, to beat an Australian touring side. The deficiencies of the Australian batting against off-spin were obvious, while their own slow bowling resources were thin. Johnson and Wilson were largely flight and length bowlers, who did not turn the ball appreciably.

Rain, which took the equivalent of more than two days from the playing time, made the Trent Bridge Test a draw. England's new opening pair, Cowdrey and Richardson, put on 53 in the first innings and 151 – the first century opening for England against Australia since Hutton and Washbrook's 129 at Headingley in 1948 – in the second. May, too, batted valuably and England twice declared. Of the thirteen Australian wickets that fell, Laker took six and Lock four. Only Burke, Harvey and Burge played the turning ball convincingly.

The Lord's Test was Miller's match. Australia had planned to use him mainly as a batsman but, without Lindwall and Davidson who were injured at Nottingham, they now needed him as an all-rounder. He scored 28 and 30, took five for 72 in the first innings of England and five for 80 in the second. In his support, Johnson won the toss for the only time in the series: McDonald and Burke put on 137 for the first wicket: Archer took six wickets: Benaud, at a crucial stage of Australia's second innings, played a fine forcing innings of 97: and the cheerfully reliable Langley set a new Test record with nine 'wicket-keeper-wickets' – five of them catches off Miller. Only May – 63 and 53 – scored more than 32 in either England innings and, by 185 runs, Australia won their first Test in England since 1948.

To strengthen the batting at Leeds, England called back Washbrook – now a selector – and brought in Insole and Oakman. Miller, suffering from a sore knee, was unable to bowl for Australia and Maddocks took the place of Langley who was injured.

Had Miller been able to bowl, the match might have gone differently. Archer began it by taking the wickets of Richardson, Cowdrey and Oakman for three runs and England were 17 for three when Washbrook came in to May. Their partnership made 187; May reached 101 and Washbrook, unlucky but not dissatisfied, 98: England 325 all out. To the horror of the Australians, the wicket began to break up on the second day: Laker turned the ball widely from the moment he came on and Australia were 81 for six when bad light stopped play on Friday evening. Rain prevented any more cricket until Monday afternoon. The wet wicket was at first easy but, as the sun came out, the ball turned appreciably and Lock and Laker ended the Australian innings at 143 and they followed on. Harvey, quick footed and resourceful,

Keith Miller (Victoria and NSW) a Test player as batsman, bowler and, as nearly as may be, fielder; a match-winner who played like a prince. Evans is the wicket-keeper: Alec Bedser at slip

batted four-and-a-half hours for 69 while Lock and Laker, occasionally switching ends for variety, bowled 81 persistent overs between them, took nine wickets for 95 and gave England the game by an innings and 42.

The Old Trafford wicket was even more unfit for Test cricket than that at Leeds. The English selectors, encouraged by the success of Washbrook in the previous game, recalled David Sheppard, now a curate in London, who had played only four innings for Sussex in the season. May won the toss, England batted, and Richardson and Cowdrey began with a partnership of 174. Before the first wicket fell, puffs of dust were rising when the ball pitched, but neither Johnson nor Benaud seemed to extract any turn for

their spin. Richardson made 104, Cowdrey 80, Sheppard 113 and England, with 439, were at least safe. McDonald (32) and Burke (22) scored 48 for the first wicket: then Laker took the wickets of McDonald and Harvey at 48: at tea Australia were 62 for two. With the first ball on the re-start, Lock had Burke caught at slip and then, in 22 balls, Laker took the remaining seven Australian wickets for eight runs (nine for 37 in the innings). The wicket was, indeed, bad – but not so bad as to put Test cricketers in quite such helpless straits.

When Australia followed on, McDonald went off with a knee injury and Harvey hit his first ball from Laker – a full toss – into Cowdrey's hands at silly mid-on: he had been given a 'pair'. At the end of

Friday's cricket, Australia were 51 for one. There was rain in the night and on Saturday, limiting the day's play to 45 minutes. In that time Australia scored six runs, Burke was caught at short-leg, and McDonald returned to take his place. Sunday's gale continued through Monday, when only two brief spells of cricket – amounting to an hour altogether – were possible: Craig and McDonald made 27 more runs, and no wicket fell. Play began only ten minutes late on Tuesday when McDonald – who had now batted in this innings on four days – and Craig, plodded to 112 for two by lunch. Then, as the wicket dried under the sun, Laker took four more wickets in the course of nine overs before Benaud dug in with McDonald for over an hour until tea. In the last session – of five minutes less than two hours – England had to take four wickets to win. Occasionally May switched Lock and Laker but, in fact, Laker took every one of his wickets in the match from the Stretford end. Immediately after tea, McDonald, who had batted five-and-a-half hours for 89, was caught at short-leg. Laker and Lock moved in for the kill; Lock, bowling at full bore to decide the match, often beat the bat but never found its edge or hit the stumps. Laker bowled Benaud: Lock caught Lindwall off him at short-leg and, at half-past-five Maddocks was out lbw. Jim Laker had taken all ten wickets of the innings for 53 runs – in 51 overs. The feat was, remarkably, spread over four days. He had 19 for 90 in the match. It was a performance beyond all probability of parallel. No one before had ever taken 19 wickets in a first-class match, nor all ten in a Test innings. There can be no doubt that Laker bowled superbly: but Australia, perhaps disgruntled and thrown off balance by the state of the wicket, batted poorly. McDonald and Burke – twice – Craig, and Benaud, played Laker firmly: the remaining Australian batsmen barely offered, and some of their strokes were abject.

For The Oval, where Australia could still square the rubber, Compton, whose kneecap had been removed by operation in the previous year, followed Washbrook and Sheppard in recall to the England side, and Tyson played his first Test of the series. Australia had a full strength eleven. England reached 222 with only three wickets down when Compton was out for a nostalgically happy 94: then the rest of the batting went down around May (83*) to 247 all out. Archer – five for 53 – bowled like Miller's heir. Rain on Thursday night and sun on Friday left Australia another ugly wicket where, however, Harvey, Miller,

Benaud and Lindwall batted so resolutely that, though Lock and Laker took six wickets, Australia were only 45 behind on the first innings. Richardson and Sheppard took risks to attack the bowling on the drying pitch. Then, from lunch time on Saturday until lunch on Tuesday, rain made play impossible. With four hours left, England moved to 182 for three before May declared, leaving Australia two hours to make 228, which was impossible. Instead, they lost five wickets – three of them to Laker – for 27. There was some criticism of May for failing to give his bowlers time to win the match. To do so he must have given Australia, also, time to win it. In the realistic manner of Test captains since these games began, with the rubber his for the holding, he saw no point in giving his opponents the chance to share it.

The quality of the English bowling – and, it must be said, of the Test weather and wickets – was reflected in the fact that, for the first time, no Australian scored a century in a five-Test series. Laker's 46 wickets set a new record for a single rubber against Australia – though still short of Sydney Barnes's 49 – in four Tests – against South Africa in 1913–14, but his average of 9·6 was better than Barnes's. The divergence in spin bowling between the two countries grows more marked. English batsmen become more vulnerable to unaccustomed leg-spin, Australians to off-spin – and here they were opposed by the master of that method in conditions ideal for him. Strikingly enough, of Laker's 132 wickets for the season, 63 were Australian.

For the first time since the introduction of regular five-Test series between the two countries, in 1897–98, England had won three consecutive series. Miller, Langley and Johnson retired from Test cricket at the end of the tour.

Away from the Tests, when Lancashire beat Leicestershire by ten wickets at Old Trafford, no Lancashire batsman was dismissed in the match.

England in South Africa, 1956–57

A strong side under Peter May, with Insole as his vice-captain, was held to a 2–2 tie in the series by the South Africans captained by the Oxford Blue, Clive van Ryneveld. In a rich period of faster bowlers, England took Loader of Surrey in preference to Trueman, who had only 33 wickets for Yorkshire in the county season of 1956.

P. J. Loader

Originally a leg-break bowler, Loader bowled well on the fast side of fast-medium and could slip a disturbing and well hidden slow leg-spinner into a sequence of pace. He varied his length subtly and, though slightly built, came quickly from the pitch. His bouncer, a genuinely menacing ball, was, unfortunately, delivered with an action which was exceptional.

On a slow pitch at Johannesburg, both sides batted slowly and, though Adcock took seven wickets in the match for 69, a century by Richardson and Bailey's five for 20 – to put out South Africa for 72 in their second innings – brought England a comfortable win.

At Cape Town the margin was as great as 312. Richardson (45 and 44) Compton (58 and 64) and Cowdrey (101 and 61) put May in the position to declare safely with six second innings wickets down. Then Wardle, who had taken five for 53 with his 'Chinaman' in the first innings, took seven for 36 with it in the second. The South African batsmen, baffled by his length, turn and concealment of spin, were all out for 72, and England were two up with three to play.

In their fighting mood of recent years, South Africa rallied at Durban. A controlled innings of 100 by McLean gave them a first innings lead of 65. If Tayfield, with eight for 69, had not been held up by Insole – 110 – South Africa would have had ample time to win. In the event, set 190 at 45 an hour, they ran into more trouble with Wardle – now mixing orthodox, slow left-arm with wrist-spin – and held out for a draw.

The fourth Test was South Africa's first win in a home Test against England since they had abandoned matting wickets. On a good batting pitch they tackled Wardle firmly: McLean was again top scorer but the batting was good all down the order. May's 61 – his best innings of, for him, a disappointing series – still left England 89 behind. A slow first-wicket partnership of 62 by Pithey and Goddard was broken by Laker and then South Africa, going for quick runs, collapsed to 142. England had more than a day to make 232 and the innings resolved itself into a contest between Tayfield – who bowled from the start of the last day until the end – and the English batsmen. At first Richardson, Insole and Cowdrey attacked him, but Tayfield persisted. The issue grew closer and the atmosphere more tense and, an hour after tea, Tayfield's brother, Arthur – fielding substitute for

Funston – caught Loader on the boundary. Tayfield had taken nine for 113 in 37 overs and South Africa had won by 17.

The recently relaid pitch for the last Test at Port Elizabeth was so slow as to undermine batsmen's confidence with a phenomenal number of shooters. Wardle, injured, could not play and South Africa had the luck to bat first, before the wicket disintegrated. Endean's careful 70, top score of the match, virtually decided it. Bailey made 41 in England's second innings and Tyson, at high speed off a short run, took six for 40. Against Tayfield – six for 78 – England never seemed likely to make the 189 they needed and South Africa levelled the series when they won by 58 runs.

West Indies in England, 1957

The great players who had beaten England in 1950 had aged significantly by 1957. But Goddard had some fresh talent which had already matured in the sadly long period since the last visit of so strong a cricketing power to England.

O. C. Smith

Gayest of cricketers, and bracketed with Headley as the finest products of Jamaican cricket, Collie Smith had played only two first-class matches before he scored a century in his first Test – against the 1954–55 Australian side – when he was twenty-one. Short, nimble and a natural maker of strokes, he learnt to curb his urge to hit every ball: but, at the least opportunity, he used his attacking power, which covered every line all round the wicket, and he was never afraid to back his length against the field by lofting a drive, pull or hook.

His off-break bowling – well flighted and spun – and spontaneously happy fielding completed the picture of an attractive person and a gifted cricketer. He came to league cricket in England and was killed in a car accident in 1959, shortly before he would have returned to the West Indies for the Test series with England. He was only twenty-six: some of the rare joy in modern Test cricket was lost with him.

G. Sobers

No all-rounder in the history of Test cricket can be rated higher than Garfield Sobers. Yet another uncoached genius from Barbados, at sixteen he appeared

Garfield Sobers (Barbados) the newest West Indian master, who pulls far more than his weight: Barrington is at slip

for that island as an orthodox slow left-arm bowler: at seventeen he played his first Test and, with four for 75, was the best West Indies bowler in an England innings of 414. Turning to batting, four years later he set the fresh record for an individual score in a Test with 365* against Pakistan.

Fairly tall, lithe and loose-limbed, he is a brilliant left-hand bat, with all the recognized strokes and the ability to improvise others as the ball is on its way to him. There is little doubt that, on hard wickets, if he cared to avoid risks, he could make a hundred almost as often as he chose. So far, he has usually preferred to go his own exciting and inventive way, but under the responsibility of captaincy he played some more restrained innings against the 1964-65 Australians.

His fast-medium left-arm bowling moves through the air, and off a wicket with any 'green' in it, and nips off the pitch. In other conditions, he will bowl left-arm wrist-spin, making his 'Chinaman' and its googly break a long way from a good length. The best of current West Indian close fieldsmen, he is the most effective player in present day cricket. He has divided recent years between playing in the Lancashire League, for South Australia – where, in 1962-63, he became the first player to score 1,000 runs and take 50 wickets in an Australian domestic season – and in the West Indies. A purposeful cricketer, he is a relaxed and convivial man.

R. Kanhai

A Guianese of Indian extraction, Rohan Kanhai takes more risks than any other successful batsman in the world today. Slightly built, fast on his feet and utterly audacious, he happily attacks any bowling and hits with power and originality. He can defend, but he is restive when he does and, in tactical terms, his attack is a worthwhile risk, for he is more likely to collar the best bowling than anyone else now playing. He often hooks at fast bowlers so convulsively – and with an unusual rotary swing of the bat – as to throw himself off his feet on to his back. His footwork is such that many bowlers find it impossible to confine him: and when he is set – in so far as one whose play is balanced on such a knife-edge can ever be said to be set – he seems able to play any stroke off any ball. At one period, in an attempt to strengthen the batting, West Indies played him as a wicket-keeper, but he was not of Test class in that capacity, and is worth his place solely as a batsman of exhilarating and match-winning gifts.

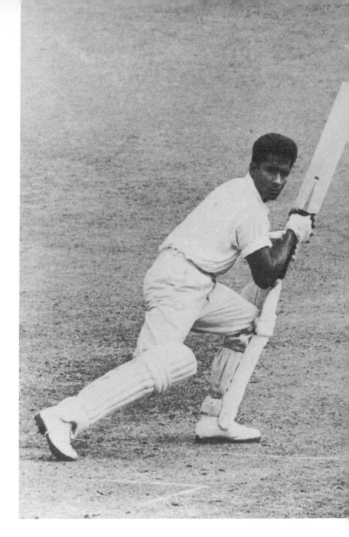

Rohan Kanhai (British Guiana) has the eye, speed and wrists to walk a knife-edge of audacious stroke-play against the best bowling in the world

R. Gilchrist

For a brief period, Roy Gilchrist inherited from Tyson the title of the fastest bowler in the world. Of no great height but with long arms, a strong wiry frame, and an action which was sometimes questioned, he could move the ball violently. His bouncer was savage and he subsequently used a 'beamer' – fast, head-high full-toss – which was dangerous in the extreme. He was sent home partway through the West Indian tour of India and Pakistan in 1958-59.

D. Atkinson

Captain of West Indies in seven Tests between 1954 and 1956, Dennis Atkinson was a useful all-round player who bowled off-cutters at brisk pace and was a sound and hard-driving batsman who, in an innings of 219, shared with Depeiza in the record seventh wicket stand in the Bridgetown Test of 1954-55 against Australia.

178

F. C. M. Alexander

The Cambridge Blue and English amateur international soccer player, 'Gerry' Alexander, captained West Indies from 1957 to 1960. A tough, unflagging wicket-keeper – one of the best West Indies have ever had – he also surprised some people when he was first in their Test batting, with an average of 60, against Australia in 1960–61. He was a less gifted batsman than several members of that team but his courage, determination, knowledge of his own limitations and refusal to be overborne by Australian tactics, made him a successful player under pressure.

D. B. Close

Between 1949 – when, at eighteen he became the youngest player to perform the double and to play for England – and 1963, Brian Close appeared for England twelve times in seven different Test series. Tall and well made, he is a left-hand bat of considerable ability, watchful, brave and correct in defence, or one of the best punishing players in English cricket. His off-break or medium-pace seam bowling can be useful at county level, for it is informed by a good cricket mind: but it is not such as should trouble Test batsmen. Anywhere near the wicket and especially at slip, he catches well. Made county captain of Yorkshire in 1963, he took them to the Championship in his first season and has maintained firm control of the side through some difficult phases.

The West Indies lost the rubber by 3–0 and had the worst of the two drawn matches. By comparison with the side of 1950, the 'three Ws' were less consistent; there was no opening bat of the stability of Rae or the quality of Stollmeyer, and the spin-pairing of Ramadhin and Valentine was no longer the automatic answer to a captain's problems.

The issue was effectively decided in the first Test, at Edgbaston. England batted first on a good, true wicket of fair pace. As in 1950, their batsmen failed signally to read Ramadhin's spin. Even without the assistance of Valentine – who lost his control and had an unhappy tour – he took seven for 49 and England, it seemed, were back in the trough of seven years earlier. Against an England attack of Statham, Trueman, Bailey, Laker and Lock, the West Indies batted with all their old certainty and, more than ever, it seemed like 1950 over again. Collie Smith, with 161, became the first batsman to score a century on his first appearance against both Australia and England. Though Walcott and Worrell went lame

and had to have runners, they scored 90 and 81 respectively. By the middle of Saturday afternoon, West Indies, 474 all out, had a lead of 288 and, as it seemed in realistic terms, two-and-a-half days in which to bowl out England for a second time.

Because of Worrell's injury, Atkinson opened the West Indian bowling with Gilchrist, whose pace caused less anxiety than the threat of Ramadhin. Surely enough, he deceived both Richardson and Insole as to the direction of his break within two overs and England were 65 for two and, apparently, no nearer the solution of their long-standing problem. Close – leaning heavily on his long, forward defensive stroke – and May stayed to 102 for two at the close of Saturday's play.

Over the weekend some good cricketing brains were brought to bear on the problem of Ramadhin. Bill Bowes was firmly of the opinion that he should be played off the front foot as an off-break bowler, which meant that his leg-break – unless pitched outside the leg stump – would miss everything. Whoever else shared the opinion, it was accepted. On Monday morning, Close was out to Gilchrist: 113 for three: and Cowdrey came in to May. Each played forward to 'Ram' in the shadow of the pad, covering against the off-break. That day Ramadhin bowled 48 overs: 20 of them were maidens and only 74 runs were made off him: but he took no wickets and May and Cowdrey were still together, at 378 for three, when Monday's play ended. On Tuesday, both batsmen moved gradually out of defence to attack. When Cowdrey was caught in the deep, driving Smith, they had put on 411, the highest stand for the fourth wicket in any Test and the third for any wicket in all Test cricket. May went on to 285, until then the biggest individual score in post-war Tests. At 583 for four, he declared. Ramadhin had not taken a wicket since his two on Saturday evening and his figures for 98 overs were two for 179. By the end of play on Saturday he had taken nine wickets: in the remainder of the series he took only five more.

May had given West Indies no chance to win: they needed 296 at more than two a minute. Trueman disposed of Kanhai and Pairadeau – nine for two – and then May called up Laker and Lock and pushed his fieldsmen closely around the bat. Weekes, never greater in his long-scoring extravagance than now, when the game was running against him, defended with tigerish endeavour. He made 33: otherwise, only Sobers reached double figures. In the last stages

Everton Weekes (Barbados) a tigerish batsman, gifted enough to invent and play strokes of his own

Goddard batted forty minutes for 0 and, 72 for seven at the finish, West Indies, so lately in an apparently winning position, were relieved to escape defeat.

On the third day of the series the initiative lay with the West Indies: they never held it again. At Lord's they brought back Valentine: Lock and Laker were unfit and England played Don Smith, a hard-hitting left-hand bat of Sussex. West Indies batted first on a wicket with some life in it. Bailey, bowling with remarkable precision to the length and line he wished for each batsman, took seven for 44. Against Gilchrist and Worrell with the new ball, England stood at 34 for three. At this point West Indies relinquished all grip on the series. Cowdrey and Close were dropped once each, and Evans five times. Cowdrey and Evans made 174 – a seventh wicket record for England – in less than two hours and England – 424 – were 227 on. Weekes, again with devoted tenacity, made 90

and Sobers 66: but the English seam bowling bit steadily through to a win by an innings and 36.

At Trent Bridge, Graveney made a lordly 258, Richardson 126 and May 104, in 619 for six – Ramadhin 0 for 95, Valentine 0 for 68, Gilchrist 0 for 118. Worrell went in first and, with superb poise, carried his bat through the collapse after Trueman bowled Weekes, for 191 out of 372. West Indies followed on and were 89 for five before 168 by Smith, 46 by Atkinson and 61 – in nearly four hours – by Goddard, won them time. England wanted 121 to win and were still 57 short, with one wicket down, at the end.

West Indies were now devoid of confidence. On a hard, fast pitch at Leeds, where they had first innings, Loader (six for 36) took the last three wickets in only the second Test hat trick performed by an English bowler in England. May, Cowdrey and Sheppard all reached the sixties in England's 279. Five English bowlers, their progress disputed only by Sobers and Walcott, bowled England to an innings win by the third afternoon. Lock unsettled the West Indian batting by some amazing fielding and Evans, when he caught Smith, took his two-hundredth wicket in Tests.

On a caked and turning wicket at The Oval, Ramadhin took four wickets for 107 while England, for whom Richardson and Graveney made centuries, scored 412. Then, as usual on their own killing-ground, Lock took eleven wickets and Laker five to bowl out West Indies twice: England won by an innings and 237.

Australia in South Africa, 1957–58

Early injuries to major batsmen seemed to cement rather than disturb the unity of Ian Craig's Australian side and they took the series 3–0. South Africa had the better only of the drawn Test at Durban, where McGlew and Waite made centuries and Adcock took six for 43 in the first Australian innings. The winners were at all points the stronger side. Australia, with an unusual quota of all-rounders for modern Test cricket, batted down to the end, Benaud, for instance, had a batting average of 54 and took 30 wickets at 21·93. A long and balanced hand of bowlers – the left-arm pace of Davidson and Meckiff, leg-breaks of Benaud and left-arm 'Chinaman' of Kline – threw the South African batsmen on to almost strokeless defence and then tumbled them out. Heine and Adcock were sometimes lively but Tayfield's wickets were expensive in face of the Australian determination to hit him off.

Pakistan in West Indies, 1957–58

The first Tests between the two countries, played on good batting wickets, duly produced batting records. West Indies won the series (by 3–1) in the last analysis because Gibbs, Eric Atkinson – brother of Dennis – and Gilchrist formed the sharper of the two attacks. For Pakistan, Nasim-ul-Ghani, at 16 years and 248 days, became the youngest Test cricketer and, steady, slow left-arm, was first in their bowling averages. When Pakistan followed on in the first Test, Hanif played the longest recorded innings – 16 hours, 13 minutes – to score 337 and save the match for Pakistan. In the third, Sobers set a new record for an individual Test score with 365*: he and Hunte (260) put on 446 for the second wicket. Pakistan were not easily beaten and they took the fifth Test through a long innings of 189 by Wazir Mohammad and the bowling of Fazal and Nasim, who took eight wickets each. Weekes announced his retirement from Test cricket, but the strength of the new generation of West Indian cricketers was already clear.

L. Gibbs

The tall, lean, passionate enthusiast, Lance Gibbs, succeeded Laker as the finest off-spinner in the world. His long, thin fingers give him immense purchase and he turns the off-break even on West Indian wickets. His length and line are good and he uses an accurate leg-break, a ball that goes with his arm, and a much faster one to add wide variety. He will bowl keenly through the longest spells and has accumulated much knowledge of batsmen and techniques in the course of his still short career.

C. C. Hunte

The Barbadian, Conrad Hunte, made three centuries in the series against Pakistan. When he started first-class cricket, he was an unusually aggressive opening batsman who took risks against the new ball and, because of his fine eye and physical quickness, often got away with them. In recent years he has changed his style, eschewing his former spectacular off-side strokes in favour of a safer, leg-side method, based on careful defence. His equable temperament and sound-

ness made him the type of sheet-anchor player West Indies have often lacked and his stability is often of as great value to his side as his scores. He is a fine field close to the wicket.

New Zealand in England, 1958

A wet summer and sorry lack of maturity or the bowling balance that such a slow stock bowler as Burtt of 1949 would have afforded, left the New Zealanders a struggling side. They were, as always, the most cheerful of tourists, generous and determined to enjoy themselves. They did well in May and beat MCC at Lord's – when Sutcliffe broke his wrist, which left the rest of the batting destitute. They had absorbed – presumably from the South Africans – the diehard approach, and few of them except the elders, Sutcliffe and Reid and, early on, Harford, ever made an attacking gesture. Such young players as Sparling, D'Arcy and Playle subordinated their batting gifts to strokeless defence, as if their innings were to be measured by time instead of runs. They died entrenched: each had the ability to have returned in 1965 if he had not feared his fate too much. MacGibbon, the tall fast-medium bowler who made an aggressive approach, took 20 wickets and, with an average of 19·44, was effectively the most successful *batsman* in Tests. Moir, a leg-spinner who really turned the ball, needed all his philosophic approach to survive the tour a happy man: but he could laugh that, with two not-outs in three innings, he was top of the Test batting averages with 74 – which was also his aggregate.

Lock – 34 wickets at 7·47 – was the destroying agent, but Laker, Bailey and Trueman also came by some cheap wickets. England neither learnt nor gained much from this series except the blossoming of Milton.

C. A. Milton

The last of the double – soccer and cricket – internationals – and likely to remain so in the present all-the-year-round football schedule, Arthur Milton of Gloucester is an undoubtedly talented batsman. He plays almost entirely off the back foot with an inborn sense of timing and tidy, unhurried footwork. A strong on-side player who sometimes surprises by the beauty of his cover and off driving, he is too often content to be patient. His gifts are such that he might take more risks than most first-class batsmen of today and succeed; yet he is content to drift with the tide. There have been few finer fieldsmen anywhere; fast and sure in the deep, he is remarkably quick in the close positions and, quite casually, he can deliver useful, medium pace, change bowling. Guaranteed ten Tests so long as he did not score at less than forty an hour, he might have made an outstanding player.

By August 1958, England were unbeaten in thirteen Test series since 1950–51 in Australia.

THE EASTERN THEATRE

Since Pakistan's first Test, in 1952, they and India, between them, have taken part in 25 Test series, meeting every other country except South Africa. Some of the rubbers have consisted of only a single Test and usually the visiting side has continued from one to the other in a single tour. Of these rubbers, 19 have been played in the sub-continent and, in addition, various Commonwealth and other privately organized teams have played representative matches there. It is lamentable that, in countries where such immense public support exists for the game, a point should have been reached where, of the 76 Tests played since 1951–52, 42 should have been drawn: in three series in India between 1960–61 and 1963–64, 13 out of 15 matches reached no decision.

The MCC team which Nigel Howard of Lancashire took to India, Pakistan and Ceylon in 1951–52 had only one of the players who had beaten South Africa in the previous summer. Sustained by Watkins, the Glamorgan all-rounder, Tattersall and Graveney, they tied the series with India 1–1. At Madras, India won a Test Match for the first time, when Pankaj Roy – a short, sturdy, opening bat, and tall 'Polly' Umrigar – a fine punisher of all but truly fast bowling – as batsmen, and the tireless Mankad, with twelve wickets, gave them an innings win.

Pakistan lost their 'inaugural' Test series with India in 1952–53 and, after tieing in the 1954 rubber in England, went home to draw all five games in their first home series with India. Ian Johnson's side, on their way home from the 1956 tour with England, beat India 2–0. In their only Pakistan Test, played on the matting wicket at Karachi, Fazal, with 13 wickets for 114, ran through their batting to beat them.

In that season's Indian cricket, P. Chatterjee, for Bengal against Assam, took all ten wickets for 20.

West Indies, in their tour of 1958–59, beat India 3–0. Eight West Indian batsmen averaged more than 30 and the two fast bowlers, Gilchrist and Hall, took 56 wickets between them. When they went on to Pakistan, Fazal's seven wickets in the first Test and 12 in the second gave Pakistan the rubber by 2–1: when West Indies won the third by an innings it was the first time Pakistan had been beaten in their own country. In this season, Hanif for Karachi v Bahawalpur made the record score – 499 – and was run out attempting the round figure!

Australia, in a separate tour of 1959–60, batted weightily and Benaud and Davidson were too much for almost all the batsmen they met except Hanif, Saeed Ahmed and Contractor, and they won both series. They lost a Test to India for the first time, however, when Patel, an off-spinner with a dubious action, took fourteen wickets in the second Test at Kanpur.

In their next home season – 1960–61 – India and Pakistan again met and drew all five matches. India went on to lose 2–0 in England; a year later, India, with a home and away series in the same season, were beaten 2–0 by England, and then lost all five Tests in a tour of the West Indies.

Dexter captained the MCC side of 1961–62 to the subcontinent. Without Statham or Trueman, the attack was not good enough, though Allen and Lock bowled with admirable stamina and application. Barrington, Pullar and Dexter all made runs – and if Cowdrey could have made the trip the batting might have been strong enough to counter Durani – slow left-arm – and Subhash Gupte. Gupte, a leg-spinner who was not afraid to give the ball air, bowled the leg-break and an unusually well hidden googly to a good length. Unfortunately he did not stand up well to the stresses of Test cricket. Many of his opponents thought him the best bowler of his type in the world, but heavy punishment – by batsmen who chanced their arms against him for fear he should master them – and some poor support from his own fieldsmen, discouraged him until he became a defensive – and lesser – bowler.

In this 1961–62 tour by MCC, India took their first series from England by 2–0: but Pakistan lost 3–1. Immediately the series with England was over, India left for the West Indies where, without Gupte, they were beaten by long batting and the well-blended attack of Hall, Gibbs and Sobers, skilfully handled by Worrell.

In the match between India and Barbados, Nari

Mohammed Hanif (Karachi) the neat and highly talented batsman who has submerged much of his potential brilliance to the breaking of records

Contractor, the Indian captain and opening bat, misjudging the rise of a ball from the fast-bowler, Charles Griffith, was struck on the head. For some time he was crucially ill and took no further part in the tour though he has since returned to play first-class cricket in India with some success. Later in the same match Griffith was no-balled for throwing. The Nawab of Pataudi, son of the Indian captain of 1946, took over the captaincy from Contractor. Pataudi, an Oxford Blue who also plays for Sussex, is a fine stroke-maker and among the best fieldsmen in the world. He made a remarkable recovery from an eye injury received in a car accident and now is as firmly established as an Indian cricket captain can be.

In the heavy-traffic season of 1964–65 – when eight separate series were played in six different countries –

Simpson's Australian side, on the way back from England, tied a three-match rubber with India, 1–1, and drew their only Test in Pakistan.

The pace-bowling of McKenzie, Hawke and Connolly and the off-spin of Veivers were the effective factors in the defeat of India. The Pakistan Test started with a first wicket partnership of 249 by Khalid Ibadullah (of Warwickshire) – 166 – and Abdul Kadir – 95. Simpson, with a century in each innings, made Australia safe.

Pakistan then set off on tour and drew their single Test with Australia – at Melbourne – largely through the 104 and 93 of Hanif. Continuing to New Zealand, they drew all three Tests. Hanif and Reid were the leading batsmen for the two sides. Collinge – five wickets in each Test – Motz and Cameron – all pace bowlers – and Yuile were the best bowlers for New Zealand; Asif Iqbul – 18 at 13·77 – for Pakistan.

Next in this shuttle-service of Tests, New Zealand, on their way to England, played a four-Test series in India: the first three matches were heavy-scoring draws; the fourth, in which Pataudi scored his second century of the rubber, was won for India by the off-spinner Venkataraghavan with 12 wickets for 152. At Calcutta, Richard Taylor, a late substitute for Sinclair, who fell ill on the morning of the match, scored 105 and took five wickets.

Pakistan won the three-match rubber on their own wickets by 2–0. The win at Rawalpindi was their first in a Test for six years. Reid, at Karachi, and Sinclair, in the draw at Lahore, resisted bravely for New Zealand, but the steady Pakistani slow-bowling turned the scale.

CLASHES AND CHARACTERS

As the balance of power between England, West Indies and Australia began to fluctuate, a series of absorbing clashes developed – between Benaud, May, and Dexter; the fast bowlers and May, Cowdrey, Smith, Barrington and O'Neill – and between bowlers suspected of throwing and an over-benevolent authority. Spectators wanted characters, and they were there. Dexter, O'Neill, Benaud, Trueman, Hall, Gilchrist, Kanhai, Mackay, Sobers, were men who made and met challenge in their individual fashions.

England in Australia, 1958–59

Holders of The Ashes and fancied by many critics to retain them, England were roundly beaten by 4–0 and had by no means the best of the drawn third Test. Certainly England suffered some misfortunes. Wardle, who had originally been selected, was left out after his dismissal by Yorkshire: Watson was injured on the voyage and had a cartilage operation on arrival in Australia: Statham and Loader were injured in a road accident before the fifth Test. Subba Row – who fractured his wrist quite early – Mortimore and Dexter were flown out as replacements, so that eighteen players took part in the tour.

Australia could attribute the shift in their favour to an access in batting strength through the maturing of McDonald and the emergence of O'Neill, and the penetrative opening bowling of Meckiff and Rorke in support of Davidson and Lindwall.

R. Subba Row

In an interrupted career, from his first appearance for Cambridge University in 1951 to his last, for Northants, in 1961 – when he was still only twenty-nine – Raman Subba Row played 400 innings for 14,009 runs at 41·69. A tall and strongly-built left-hander, he subordinated his hitting powers to a reliable defence; and he scored a century in both his first and last Tests against Australia. Steady in temperament, unperturbed by speed, a man of humour and wisdom, he made some long scores for Surrey before he went to Northants and became captain of that county. He did not always look a stylish player but he was hard to get out and his placing, quick running and generally busy approach kept his score moving. Unlike many players of his time, 'Subba' was first a leg-side player, who gradually extended his range through the off-side. He bowled slow right-arm leg-breaks with some amusement and was a good field anywhere – and quicker than he looked.

J. B. Mortimore

Gloucestershire's production of off-spinners is such that even good bowlers of that kind do not necessarily survive there. John Mortimore's progress has been steady, if not easy. With a studied action, his value is most apparent on wickets where the ball does not turn, when his control, flight and tactical sense set problems. This is not to say that he does not spin the ball; but that is only one of the several attributes that make him one of the most respected slow bowlers in English county cricket. He is a good close field and a batsman who, from correct defence, occasionally – and especially against off-spin – drives high and far. Quiet but observant and thoughtful, he has the qualifications of a sound, unobtrusive and unselfish captain.

E. R. Dexter

Only a few batsmen have refused to succumb to the tight bowling and restrictive field-setting of modern times and have had the ability to maintain their rebellion at Test level. Ted Dexter is among them – with Rohan Kanhai, Graeme Pollock, Garfield

Ted Dexter (Sussex) the only English batsman of his time to break the shackles of restrictive outcricket, and as hard a hitter as any in any age: Grout is the wicket-keeper, Simpson at slip

feelings throughout his career. He might have been outstanding as a golfer or a rugby player, but the challenge of cricket appealed to him. Virtually alone among current English batsmen he is capable of taking a Test Match in his hands and remoulding its shape. His once slapdash fielding has tightened considerably, at cover and close in. He does not often care to bowl, but his somewhat negligent-looking, fast-medium bowling sometimes swings dangerously late and, when he throws in full effort, he has marked pace from the pitch.

He remains the most memorable, if not the most consistent, English batsman of his generation and his improving defence makes it increasingly probable that he will one day play an even greater Test innings than he had so far done.

N. O'Neill

The Australian counterpart to Dexter, Norman O'Neill captured attention as soon as he came into the New South Wales side. His hitting may not be quite so hard as Dexter's, though it is little short of it and he has the same assertive streak and the same willingness to attack the bowler before the bowler can attack him. He has something of a right-hand bias and at times he has tended to play rather square-on but, when he is in touch, his stroke-play – particularly through the covers – is as fine and clean as any. There is a boyishness about him – he can be the picture of gaiety at one moment, distressed by an unnecessary dismissal at the next. His courage is unquestionable – he has come through some torrid tussles with True-man with eventual credit – and, if seam-movement in English conditions sometimes beats him, he buckled to finding out how to deal with it. The beauty of his batting is matched by that of his supremely athletic running, picking up and throwing in the deep field; and he has had some success with his leg-break and googly bowling. For all his bold approach, O'Neill has a genuine humility, and his diligence and study may yet lead him to a more consistent standard of brilliance.

I. Meckiff

A match-winner in 1958–59, Ian Meckiff was 'called' for throwing in the first Test of the Australia-South Africa series of 1963–64 and retired from first-class cricket. A tall, strong, left-arm fast bowler, he was erratic in both length and line but he made the ball swing awkwardly, frequently caused it to lift sharply

Sobers, Norman O'Neill, Roy McLean and – more briefly – Cammie Smith and the late Collie Smith.

Dexter's gifts were apparent from his first match for Cambridge University in 1956: but so, equally, to the eyes of experienced bowlers, were his faults, and his early batting was frequently brief. One technical flaw – as elementary as an open bat-face – was characteristically noticed and pointed out to him by John Mortimore after Dexter had become a Test player. Tall and wide-shouldered, his appearance is as imperious as his batting style. He will play any and every stroke and it is doubtful if anyone has ever driven a cricket ball harder than he does, with his long, pure bat-swing, strong wrists and inborn sense of timing. Fearless, and always willing to back his ability to attack any bowling, he has roused strong

Norman O'Neill (NSW) Test cricket has taken some of the joy from his batting but still, at his best, he is among the most handsome of modern batsmen

and, from time to time, he punctuated a series of wild deliveries with one that was all but unplayable. There was objection to his action, in some quarters, from the first, but his own pleasant character and his effectiveness carried him through six Test series before the final judgement was passed at Brisbane.

G. Rorke

A huge, fair-haired, fast-bowler, Gordon Rorke's action was also questioned – though it was less apparently illegal than Meckiff's – and his drag was so phenomenally long that one Test opponent said, seriously, that at his worst, Rorke actually bowled from eighteen yards. When his drag was stopped by the experimental rule in India and Pakistan in 1959–

60, he was far less effective and his pace ceased to be dangerous. He was flown home from that tour with hepatitis and, when he recovered, the earlier life had gone from his bowling, and he never recovered his Test place.

The Australian opening attack of 1958–59, picked from Lindwall, Davidson, Meckiff and Rorke – in the fifth Test all four of them – only once permitted the England batting to settle. In the first Test their score stood at 16 for two in the first innings, 34 for two in the next: in the second Test, seven for three and 27 for four: the third, 23 for two and 37 for two: the fourth, 11 for two and – through Richardson and Watson – 89 for the first wicket: the fifth, 13 for two and 12 for two. Richardson, Milton, Watson and Bailey all opened the innings at different times but none averaged as much as 21. So, in match after match, responsibility was thrust on May and Cowdrey and, though they were England's most successful batsmen, they did not win matches as they had done four years earlier. At Brisbane, the English batting was at times quite becalmed: Bailey batted over seven-and-a-half hours for 68. When Australia set about making 147 to win, Burke took more than four hours for 28 though this was partly offset by O'Neill's exuberant 71* in less than two hours. Davidson and Meckiff, with nine wickets each, were the match-winners at Melbourne: but Cowdrey's 100* drew the rain-affected third Test.

McDonald scored centuries in the last two Tests when Benaud, with nine and five wickets, backed the long hand of pace and Australia won by ten wickets at Adelaide and nine at Sydney.

Meckiff, Benaud, Davidson and Rorke all had better bowling averages than the first English bowler – Laker: and McDonald, O'Neill and Harvey had higher batting figures than anyone in the English side.

Benaud captained Australia alertly and, for all his good public relations, with ruthless efficiency. It was not a happy series, if only for the reason that the English players thought Meckiff, Rorke and Slater threw, and the Australians thought the same of Lock: many believed it of all four.

India in England, 1959

The touring side lost all five Tests, three of them by an innings: the pace of Trueman and Statham was altogether too much for them. A. A. Baig, the Oxford

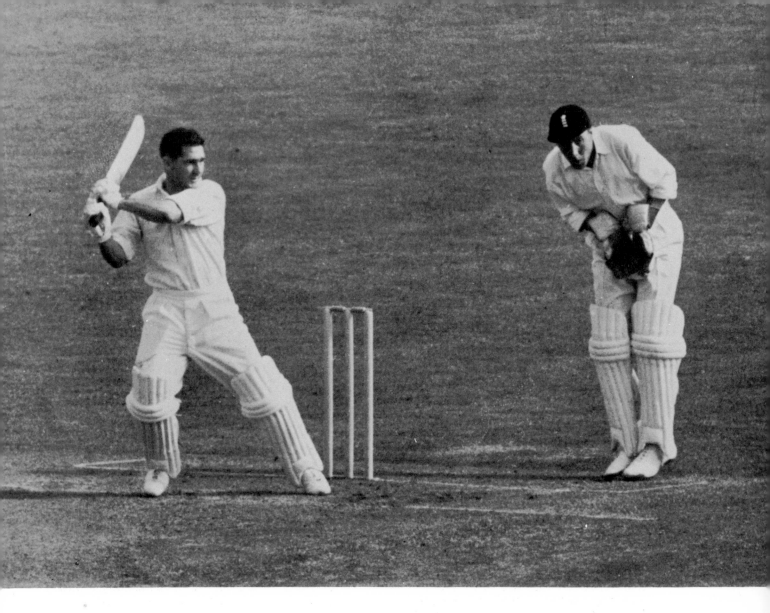

Neil Harvey (Victoria and NSW) the most graceful and adventurous left-hander in post-war cricket; his style is underlined by his figures: J. T. Murray (Middlesex) keeping wicket

Blue, joined the party after the University match, scored a century in his first match – against Middlesex – and, a week afterwards, another in his first Test. Umrigar made plenty of runs in other games but, despite a century at Old Trafford, only 230 altogether against England. Manjrekar, who looked their best batsman in the first two Tests, missed the last three through injury and an operation. Desai and Surendra Nath were persevering fast-medium bowlers: Borde, a leg-spinner who did not bowl enough, and a refreshingly aggressive batsman: Nadkarni, the thin, left-handed all-rounder, plugged away in some discouraging circumstances. India's cricket, apart from Borde and Baig, was completely defensive and, in defeat,

struck no sparks. The manager – the Gaekwar of Baroda – stated that the tour was largely educational: unhappily it was difficult to discern that any of their players had learnt much from the trip.

England, anxious to re-build against their imminent encounters with West Indies and Australia, used twenty-one players in the series. Some of these experiments merely confirmed what had been known already – that Roy Swetman of Surrey was one of several possible deputies for Evans as wicket-keeper; that Harold Rhodes of Derbyshire – whose action had been questioned – and Alan Moss of Middlesex were useful reserve fast-bowlers to Trueman and Statham; that Ray Illingworth of Yorkshire was a steady all-rounder but not likely to prove penetrative on Australian or West Indian wickets. The happiest discoveries – though success against such opposition did not guarantee adequacy against the major Test sides – were Subba Row, Smith, Pullar and Barrington.

M. J. K. Smith

One of the leading figures in English county cricket of the sixties, Mike Smith, of Oxford University, Leicester and now Warwickshire, is a heavy-scoring batsman of outstanding ability in on-side play; a superb field at short-leg; and a captain who thinks deeply on the game and runs his side in a manner at once friendly, perceptive, compelling of loyalty, and efficient. He plays in spectacles – without lag in vision or reaction at short-leg – but the Australians and the West Indians have always thrown pace at him as soon as he comes in and have often disposed of him quickly. It may be that, like many other useful batsmen whose eyesight is considered good, he simply is an uncertain starter against fast bowling. Once set, his range and control of strokes make him a capable batsman who can, at need, score fast runs without apparent risks. At Oxford he was an outstanding rugby half-back and, with Brace, originated some revolutionary tactics behind the scrum.

G. Pullar

In the fourth Test of 1959, Geoff Pullar became the first Lancashire batsman to score a century in a Test at Old Trafford – surprisingly, not Maclaren, Washbrook, J. T. – or Ernest – Tyldesley or Paynter ever did so on their own home ground. A tall, firmly-made left-hander, Pullar is a patient player with an easy style, an inclination to the front foot though sound also in back-play, strong in the off-drive and tidy in 'tucking away' the ball on or outside the leg stump. A diligent cricketer, he has been unlucky in the matter of injuries which interrupted his Test career at important junctures.

K. Barrington

An unfailingly run-hungry batsman of infinite patience, Ken Barrington was first chosen for England – against South Africa in 1955 – before he was ready for Test cricket. In 1959 he established his position and since then has gathered runs stolidly and prolifically all over the world. Chunkily built, he now uses an almost exaggeratedly square-on stance, which he believes serves him well when, as a major Test

Ken Barrington (Surrey) patient, dogged and run-hungry; not always attractive to watch but monumentally hard to get out

run-scorer, he is assailed with constant bouncers. He joined the Surrey staff in 1948 as, primarily, a leg-spin bowler and in that capacity he has had too little opportunity to demonstrate his ability. He can play attractively on the off-side but the facts of modern cricket enforce a large majority of his runs coming on the other side of the wicket. Highly professional, Ken Barrington considers his job is to make runs, and he does precisely that with undeviating thoroughness.

In the English domestic game, Yorkshire, under that cheerful personality, Ronnie Burnet, broke Surrey's long run as Champions. They needed to win their last match – against Sussex at Hove – to take the title and, set the apparently impossible task of making 215 in 105 minutes, they achieved it with seven minutes to spare after some of the finest attacking batting – by Stott and Padgett – that can be imagined. Five of their bowlers took more than fifty wickets and five batsmen scored over a thousand runs in the season.

188

England in the West Indies, 1959–60

The first English win in a Test rubber in the West Indies was achieved by spirit rather than markedly greater ability than that of their opponents. Their batsmen, all the way down, stood up firmly to a bouncer attack; their somewhat limited bowling, carefully handled, was manfully sustained against a long list of gifted West Indian batsmen; while the fielding reached a higher standard than at any time in the previous decade.

Of the fresh selections, Allen served England well and, when May fell out of the side through a recurrence of the ailment that had kept him out of the last two Tests against India in the previous English summer, Parks was brought into the side for the final match, as a wicket-keeper-batsman. Swetman, the first choice wicket-keeper, had not played well and it was unlucky for Keith Andrew – without doubt the best English wicket-keeper of the period – that his opportunity should coincide with May's absence and the consequent need to reinforce the batting. Parks – who was already in the West Indies on a coaching engagement – had played against Pakistan in 1954 as a batsman: he had subsequently kept wicket for Sussex.

The newest major figure in West Indies cricket was Hall who, though Ramadhin finished at the top of the bowling averages, took more wickets and was their chief striking force. Alexander, who captained the West Indies, equalled John Waite's record, for a wicket-keeper, of 23 wickets in a Test series.

D. A. Allen

No off-break bowler in English cricket of the moment turns the ball more than David Allen of Gloucester. From the briefest of runs, he bowls a good line with so much finger-spin as automatically imparts a puzzling flight and a tendency to float away from the batsman. Highly dangerous on turning wickets, he has the stamina and accuracy to keep batsmen quiet when the pitch gives him no help. On this tour of the West Indies his grimly defensive batting was often of considerable service.

J. M. Parks

Son of that J. H. Parks who, in 1939, scored 3,000 runs and took 100 wickets, 'Young Jim' Parks came into the Sussex side, in 1949, as a stroke-making batsman somewhat vulnerable to pace, a fine cover-point and an occasional leg-spin bowler. He tightened his defensive batting while retaining the ability to play freely in front of the wicket, began as a mere stopper wicket-keeper but devoted much attention to improving his standards there, and has now, for five series, been England's wicket-keeper batsman. He has been the most consistently effective bat in the Gillette Cup knock-out competition and has played in Tests with increasing assurance, particularly against the faster bowlers.

W. Hall

Latest in the line of 'the fastest in the world', Wesley Hall made the 1957 tour to England as a bowler of high potential who had not yet coordinated the mechanics of his action. By 1959 his bowling was one of the most stirring sights in the game. Tall and with a magnificent physique, he has a splendid, bounding run-up, a supremely fair and high action and a follow-through like the uncoiling of a giant spring. His bumper is an intimidating ball but he scrupulously does not employ the 'beamer'. Recently he has exploited late outswing and a break back, but on any pitch his pace alone can be menacing. A buoyant, generous man, he loves to bat – which he does extravagantly and sometimes with explosive success – he has a throw of amazing power, and all his cricket is whole-hearted and purely West Indian.

In Barbados, both sides batted slowly and 128 by Barrington and 136* by Dexter on one side, 226 by Sobers and 197* by Worrell on the other, ensured a draw.

In Trinidad, England won the only finished Test of the rubber. The time lost in a bottle-throwing 'incident' on the third day – 75 minutes – was made up by additions to the playing time on the subsequent three days of the match. Both Hall and the other West Indian fast-bowler, Watson, were warned by the umpire for intimidatory bowling. Barrington (121), Dexter (77) and Smith (108) built the England innings to 382 and then Trueman and Statham, in the major stroke of the series, put out the West Indies for 112. Instead of enforcing the follow-on, May batted again and eventually declared to set West Indies 501 in ten hours. Kanhai in a quite uncharacteristic innings took over six hours for 110, but no one else in the side scored as many as fifty, and England won by 256.

By the third Test, Cowdrey – who went in first against his inclination – and Pullar had become a

Wesley Hall (Barbados) whose pace, technique and heart place him unquestionably in the line of the great fast bowlers

capable opening pair of batsmen. Cowdrey's 114 (in face of fine bowling by Hall) and 97 left West Indies little more than six hours to make 230, and, after they lost a few quick wickets, they abandoned the attempt.

At Georgetown, Hall – six for 90 – and Sobers, with 145, left England 107 behind on the first innings. Then Subba Row and Dexter scored centuries which drew the match.

In Trinidad, needing only a draw to win the series, England won the toss for the fifth time in the series and a long team effort in which Cowdrey and Parks made hundreds kept West Indies far from the chance to win.

Meanwhile, in South Africa, at East London, Border scored 16 in their first innings and 18 in the second against Natal: the lowest recorded two-innings score in first-class cricket.

South Africa in England, 1960

This was one of the saddest of tours. Some errors made at home, and as much ill luck as can be imagined in England, left the South Africans with little of credit, profit or happiness to take back with them.

In the first place, the South African selectors sent a party of only fifteen players which, even in the normal course of cricketing accidents, was likely to be too few for the six-day-a-week cricket of an English tour. Secondly, they chose a bowler – Geoffrey Griffin – who had already been twice no-balled for throwing in Currie Cup matches in South Africa.

There was an anti-apartheid demonstration when the team arrived at London Airport and there were others at a number of grounds: on every occasion the touring players bore themselves with dignity.

English cricket was in no position to suffer further damage and it, not less than the South Africans, was injured by a dismally wet summer. Griffin was inevitably no-balled; South Africa lost the rubber outright when they were beaten in each of the first three Tests. The 1955 South African team made a profit of £36,000: that of 1960 did not cover its expenses. There was not even any apparent long-term gain, for none of their young players made any real advance.

Trueman, Statham and Moss took 61 wickets between them, more cheaply than the best South African bowler – Adcock – who, despite poor support, had 26 at 22·57. Tayfield, coming out of retirement, took 12 wickets but was less penetrative and less economic than before. Six English batsmen, but only three South African, had batting averages of more than thirty.

At Edgbaston, where England batted moderately, only O'Linn – the dogged left-hander who had previously played for Kent – Waite (twice) and McLean made more than forty in either South African innings, while Statham and Trueman, with Illingworth to mop up, bowled England to a win by 100 runs.

At Lord's, the England batting was more assertive: Subba Row made 90, Dexter 56, Smith 99 and Walker, the tall Glamorgan all-rounder, 52. Statham, bowling with unfailing accuracy at high speed and exploiting the fast pitch, took eleven wickets for 97 in the match. Trueman, Moss and Dexter were his assistants in giving England an innings win by the third afternoon.

Brian Statham (Lancashire) linked monumental accuracy to high pace and the classic break-back: a generous, unflagging cricketer

Griffin, a slightly built but wiry fast-medium bowler, was no-balled eleven times by the umpire Frank Lee for throwing in an innings when, by savage irony, he performed the first hat trick by any South African in a Test.

In the exhibition match which followed, he was put on to bowl opposite the other umpire – Sid Buller – who 'called' him four times in five balls. Griffin completed the over with lobs – the first of which was also no-balled because he had not declared his intention to bowl them – and thus, sadly, ended his Test career. Griffin was a mild, quiet young man who bore himself well in the midst of the controversy, and his team-mates stood by him loyally.

The whole issue of throwing was now being brought to a head. As in the 'purge' at the beginning of the

century, there was disagreement about the fairness of some actions but the players themselves knew perfectly well that there was an increasing amount of throwing. It is not difficult to make a list of more than twenty bowlers who have thrown in Test cricket since the second World War, and at least eight of them have been 'called' by umpires in their own countries.

There is a sentimental and understandable reluctance on the part of umpires to pass a decision on a player which is likely to end his career. Yet this attitude ignores those who suffer from unfair bowling – batsmen put out by it and fair bowlers who are kept out of teams – especially at Test level – by throwers. The most drastic solution remains that posed by F. R. Spofforth in 1897 – 'Legalize throwing and in one season it would bring about its own cure'.

At Trent Bridge, South African morale was understandably low. England made only 287 – and that was due almost entirely to Cowdrey and Barrington. South Africa, apart from the serious, game and generally under-estimated Jon Fellows-Smith, were bowled out by Trueman and Statham for the lowest completed Test innings at Trent Bridge – 88. When they followed on, McGlew – a captain who presented a bold front to all his problems – was at last batting well when he collided with the bowler, Moss, in midwicket and was run out. Cowdrey, the England captain, attempted to recall him, but the umpires, correctly if somewhat regrettably, ruled that their decision, once given, was irrevocable. O'Linn plodded his dutiful way to 98 and Waite, with an injured finger, made 60. Only rain delayed England's eight-wickets win – which settled the rubber – until Monday afternoon.

At Old Trafford, the first century of the series, by McLean – a spirited 109 in a total of 229 – and Adcock's seven wickets were bold gestures of South African revival, but the loss of two days to rain made a draw certain.

At the end, South Africa seized an advantage. Against Adcock (six for 65) and Pothecary, a burly fast-medium bowler (four for 58), England made only 155. South Africa, by steady batting – Goddard made the second 99 of the series – took a lead of 264. Their hopes of winning, however, faded before an opening partnership of 290 by Pullar (175) and Cowdrey (155) and their last flag was flown by McLean who, before the game became a draw, struck sixteen from a single over by Statham.

Dexter, McLean, Trueman and Statham had lifted

Bobby Simpson (NSW and Western Australia) who remained cool and poised under the weight of captaining Australia, opening the innings, bowling leg-breaks and establishing himself as the finest slip fieldsman in the world. Titmus is at short-leg

the cricket briefly out of the rut of niggardly bowling and slow-grinding batting – not, however, often enough to remove the impression of heaviness and lack of joy. Cricket needed an infusion of dash, risk and – adventure. Few people realized that it was at hand.

INSPIRATION FROM THE CARIBBEAN

West Indies in Australia, 1960–61

The leading players on both sides were now established. Australia brought in another pace bowler –

Misson – lean, fit, persevering, of the kind that used, years ago, to be called a 'trundler'; Kline, who bowled the 'Chinaman' with wide break; Johnnie Martin, the same type of left-arm wrist spinner, keen field and hard hitting bat; Les Favell, the stroke-making opener who never quite won a firm Test place; Simpson and Grout.

R. B. Simpson

In 1952–53, when he was sixteen, Bobby Simpson first appeared for New South Wales: four years later he went to work in Perth and played for Western Australia until 1960, when he returned to New South Wales.

Neat, quick on his feet, and well-balanced, he is a

sensitive, all-round batsman, who plays well off front or back foot, drives well through the complete arc from cover-point to mid-on, and cuts with considerable certainty. He is another cricketer who rarely hooks – not because he cannot, but because he considers the stroke uneconomic. Though he might well have become a regular Australian player before his five Tests against South Africa in 1957–58, he only played once against England in Australia, 1958–59. He made good his position as a Test opening bat in 1960–61 but, surprisingly, had not scored a century at that level until his 311 at Old Trafford in 1964.

He bowls slow leg-breaks, with a googly which some good batsmen find unusually hard to pick, and there is no better slip fieldsman in the world. He moves to catches with the quick assurance of one who watches unwinkingly, and his hands are extremely safe.

His captaincy in England in 1964 was cool, courteous, firm and astute; above all, his public relations were as good as those of any captain who has ever been to England.

A. W. T. Grout

In 1957–58 Wally Grout set the Test record for a wicket-keeper, of six catches in an innings: two seasons later, for Queensland v Western Australia, he created a record for all first-class cricket with eight dismissals in an innings.

Grout began first-class cricket in 1946–47, as understudy to Tallon, and did not come into the Australian side until eleven years afterwards. Since then he has been responsible for more dismissals in Tests than any other Australian wicket-keeper. Stockily built and strong-armed, he moves quickly and takes some extremely wide one-handed catches in long dives which allow first slip to stand wider than he might otherwise do. A quick, humorous man with a determined approach to cricket, he is a good batsman at a pinch, and hits the ball hard.

The West Indian Test side included Joe Solomon, a small, neat Guianese, solid batsman, occasional leg-spinner and quick fieldsman; Chester Watson, as fast-bowling support for Hall; Cammie Smith, a tall, lean, opening batsman who, with hardly any movement of his feet, throws his bat at the ball from the start, playing innings of precarious brilliance; Seymour Nurse, a tall Barbadian, strong striker of the ball on hard wickets; and Peter Lashley, another Barbadian, hard hitting left-hand bat and good close field.

Frank Worrell (Barbados and Jamaica) most relaxed and elegant of record-breaking batsmen; a cool and perceptive captain

The first Test, played at Brisbane, produced the first tie in the sequence of 498 Test Matches since 1877, and has been accorded a book to itself – *The Greatest Test of All* by J. H. Fingleton. The many thousands who must wish that they had seen the match may be grateful that Jack Fingleton, E. M. Wellings, A. G. Moyes and L. D. Roberts were there and have set down accounts of it. It is important to notice that, unusually in Tests on the Woolloongabba ground, this one suffered no rain – and that the two captains who allowed the game to run as it did were Richie Benaud and Frank Worrell.

West Indies won the toss and began their batting in such headlong fashion that, at the end of an hour, they had scored 65 and lost three wickets – all to

193

Davidson. At this dangerous juncture for West Indies, with little seasoned batting to come, Sobers played an innings which left a deep impression on everyone who saw it. Driving, cutting, and flicking to leg with his characteristic turn of the wrists, he made his century in only five minutes over two hours, 132 in under three hours. Meanwhile, Worrell (65) remained in calm control of the other end, giving his younger partner the strike whenever possible. Both were severe on Benaud, secure against Davidson, and their stand of 174 was made at 73 an hour. Solomon (65) closed an end, Alexander made a responsible 60 and Hall a hectic 50: so, from 65 for three, West Indies reached 453. McDonald (57) and Simpson (92) set the Australian innings in momentum, Favell, Mackay and Davidson all batted usefully, but the main innings was O'Neill's 181. He was twice missed in his fifties and, right hand low on the bat handle, he batted more cautiously and with greater on-side bias than formerly. Still, he struck the ball forcefully and rode out some extremely fast bowling from Hall with more courage than comfort. Ramadhin, Valentine and Worrell took only two wickets between them for 235 runs: Sobers – two for 115 – was the main support for Hall (four for 140).

Davidson followed his five for 135 of the first innings with six for 87 in the second: Kanhai, Worrell and Solomon bore the main burden of lifting West Indies to 184 and only a last wicket stand of 31, in forty valuable minutes, raised Australia's required run-rate to 45 an hour when they were set 233 to win. The immense and sustained pace of Hall brought the Australian innings down to 57 for five: Ramadhin bowled Mackay – 92 for six – and brought together Benaud and Davidson – the last two Australian batsmen capable of winning the match. They were still together – at 206 for six – with 27 needed in half-an-hour, when Hall took the new ball; and they had reached 226 – seven runs short – when they went for a quick single, Solomon hit the stumps from midwicket, and Davidson was run out. When Hall began the last (eight-ball) over, Australia, with three wickets left, needed six to win. The first ball ran off Grout's thigh for a leg-bye: from the second Benaud was caught at the wicket. Meckiff played his first ball back to Hall, missed the fourth and they scampered a run as the ball went through to the wicket-keeper. Grout skied the fifth, Hall ran to catch it, dropped it and the batsmen crossed again. Meckiff swung the sixth to leg; Hunte stopped it on the boundary as the batsmen turned for

the third run – which would have won the match – and, from the long accurate return, Grout was run out by a foot. With two balls to be bowled, the scores were level and Australia had one wicket left. Kline pushed the seventh ball to leg, Meckiff was already backing up, but Solomon, with only a single stump to aim at, again hit the wicket, Meckiff was run out, and the match was a tie.

Broadcasting had brought the match to every home in Australia and it kindled such an enthusiasm for the game as had not been known there since the great days of Bradman. The crowds came back.

In intense heat at Melbourne, the long Australian batting – based on Benaud's rare strength in all-rounders – made 348. West Indies were one for two, reached 124 for two through Kanhai and Nurse, and collapsed to 181 all out (Davidson six for 53). In their followed innings Hunte (110) and the invaluable Alexander (72) made all but 51 of their 233. Australia, with 67 to make, came through a fierce bumper attack to win by seven wickets.

At Sydney, West Indies rattled away at a rate almost forgotten in Test cricket – 303 for five by the end of the first day. They collapsed next morning, when Davidson and Benaud ended their innings for 339. But, after Hall had broken into the Australian innings, the spinners, Gibbs and Valentine, held up only by O'Neill, gave them a lead of 137. Davidson and Benaud brought West Indies to 166 for seven, only for Alexander, batting at number eight, to score 108. 464 was far beyond Australia on a turning wicket: Harvey and O'Neill made 108 for the third wicket before Valentine and Gibbs bowled West Indies to a win by 222 runs.

At Adelaide, where Kanhai made two centuries and there were seventeen scores of over forty, West Indies seemed to have carved out a winning position. In the second Australian innings, Gibbs did the hat trick and, when their ninth wicket fell, they were still 253 behind with one hour and forty minutes left for play. In tension as high as that at Brisbane, the West Indian bowlers sent down their overs, on the dead wicket, in almost unbalanced haste. Kline kept his bat straight and Mackay, in a situation made for him, chewed gum and batted for three-and-a-half hours. He took the last ball of the match – from Hall – on the body and was helped from the field, having denied West Indies the win they had so nearly gained.

With the rubber to be decided, the match at Melbourne was scheduled to be played to a finish. 90,800 people – the greatest number ever to attend a Test Match anywhere – were at the Melbourne Cricket Ground for the second day's play. West Indies left out Watson, and Benaud, when he won the toss, sent them to bat – which suggests that on one side or the other there was an error of judgement in 'reading' the pitch. With Misson, Sobers, Gibbs and Davidson all taking four or five wickets in one innings or the other, and eleven scores of forty or more – without a century – there was yet another close finish.

Alexander, after his 63* and 87* at Adelaide, now revived the second West Indies innings and they set Australia 258 to win. Simpson began with 24 from Hall's first ten balls, and Australia reached 154 before their third wicket fell. Then Worrell – bowling left-arm spinners – and Gibbs cut through to 200 for five: 236 for six: 248 for seven: ten wanted. At 254, Alexander appealed for 'bowled' against Grout, a bail being on the ground: the umpire gave him not-out, but two runs later Grout swung – perhaps deliberately – and was caught at cover: 266 for eight – it was like Brisbane all over again. This time, however, Martin and Mackay scrambled the three crucial singles to give Australia the game and the closest of Test rubbers, the story of which reverberated round the cricket world, rousing hope and envy in other countries.

Meanwhile, in India, Pakistan and India were playing a series of five draws.

Australia in England, 1961

This rubber, won by Australia, 2–1, was decided by character. At Old Trafford, England seemed twice to have the game won, only for first Davidson, and then Benaud, to establish their right to a place on the highest level of Test cricketers – those who turn and win matches.

The strength of the England side was known, and the introduction of Murray was the only real change from the established team. Australia, as usual, produced fresh players of ability – in Lawry, Booth and Mackenzie.

J. T. Murray

A typical Lord's-trained cricketer, trim, dutiful and competent, John Murray has been one of the most reliable wicket-keepers in the world for ten years and, when he scored 1,025 runs and made 104 dismissals in 1957, he became the second wicket-keeper to perform

the double: Leslie Ames was the first. Murray is a sound, wide-ranging wicket-keeper when standing back to pace; efficient and unfussy standing up to the stumps, and unfailingly keen in any circumstances. His batting is straightforward: he makes his runs by firm strokes, often at good pace, is strong against seam bowling, and a cool man in a crisis.

W. Lawry

A tall, gaunt, rather gangling left-hander, Bill Lawry is the most phlegmatic of batsmen, undisturbed when he plays and misses, strong on the leg-side, unruffled by any crowd and perfectly prepared to go without a run until the bowler proffers one. He made top score in three of the four innings of the two Tests won by Australia in 1961 and was the only batsman in the party to score 2,000 runs on the tour. Stolidly brave, conscious of his limitations and content to play within them, he is the type of stonewaller that has saddened crowds and relieved captains since cricket began.

B. C. Booth

Brian Booth first played for Australia in the fourth Test of 1961 in England, became a regular member of the side and scored 1,000 runs in his first eleven Tests. Slim and poised, a complete copy-book player, he has an upright stance, good wrists and a cool temperament. Modest and intelligent, he would make a good captain, for he is thoughtful about other men, quietly firm and a close student of cricket.

G. D. McKenzie

The youngest bowler to take a hundred wickets in Test cricket or fifty in England-Australia matches, Graham McKenzie is another in the line of superbly built Australian athletes. Over six feet tall and more than fourteen stone, he is a physical training instructor. His run-up is buoyant, his action high and pure, and, like all the great Australian pace-bowlers, he *hits* the pitch with the ball, hence the steep rise which is the most dangerous attribute of his bowling. His twentieth birthday fell in the middle of the second Test of 1961 – his first appearance for Australia – and he marked it by scoring a useful 34 in the first Australian innings, and taking six wickets. At that time he was not always accurate in either length or line, but he has since become steadier without losing his vital life from the pitch. His fitness is reflected in his ability to maintain precision and fire through long

Graham McKenzie (Western Australia) the finely athletic fast-bowler whose transcendent gift is to extort life from even the slowest pitches

spells in trying tropical heat, and he perseveres endlessly in the attempt to hammer life from a plumb pitch. A fine mover in the field and with the essentials of good batting in him, he has many years to develop into a major Test all-rounder.

While Australia were beating England in 1961, another Australian, the remarkable veteran, left-hand bat, Bill Alley – already, on his own admission, forty-two years old – was playing for Somerset, making 3,019 swashbuckling runs and, for good measure, taking 62 wickets with his right-arm medium swingers and making 29 catches: it made him laugh even more loudly than usual.

Peter May won the toss at Trent Bridge, but intermittent rain made first innings of little advantage to England. Mackay, with medium pace curves pitched just short of a length, first confined and then fretted out the main England batting: Benaud 'nipped in' with three late wickets and England were all out 195 – Subba Row 59. Australia, with the all-round strength that allowed Benaud to bat at number nine, made runs right down the order: Harvey's 114 was the highest score in their 516 for nine declared. Subba Row scored 112 – in his first Test against Australia – and Dexter 180, while England played with no other possible purpose than to draw the match.

The pitch at Lord's was fast and the pace bowlers could make the ball lift off what the players called 'The Ridge' but which expert survey later revealed to be a series of indentations. Davidson, McKenzie and Misson constantly made the England batsmen play at waist height or above: Mackay filled the gaps and Grout took eight catches in the match – only one short of Gil Langley's record nine in 1956. Subba Row – 48 – was again top scorer for England in a total of 206. Trueman, Statham and Dexter also exploited the pitch, but they were opposed by Lawry who, batting with what a Victorian cricketer-writer once called 'unflinching bottom', made 130 out of 340. Only Pullar (42) and Barrington (66) mounted effective resistance to Davidson, Misson and McKenzie as they thumped their way through the England batting again. Australia needed 69 to win and Statham and Trueman harried them to 19 for four. Then Lock, in a vast dive, narrowly failed to catch Burge who, with towering assertion, played through to a five-wickets win.

On a peculiar, piebald, chemical-ridden and shifting wicket at Leeds – for which official apologies were tendered – Trueman (11 for 88 in the match) twice bowled out Australia. Harvey – twice – and McDonald used every resource of skill in defensive innings, but Cowdrey's 93 was the finest batting performance of the match and England won, with slight qualms of conscience, by eight wickets.

Old Trafford was the scene of a magnificent Australian win. The four England pace-bowlers, Trueman, Statham, Dexter and Flavell (of Worcestershire) bowled them out for 190, which would have been much less but for the obdurate 74 of Lawry and Booth's meticulous 46. Pullar, May, Barrington and Allen took England to 358 for six before Simpson – four for two in 26 balls – finished off the innings for 367. Lawry – again – with 102, Simpson and O'Neill fought out the second Australian innings against the faster bowlers. Then Allen, finding some turn in the pitch on the last morning, reduced them to 334 for nine – only 157 ahead with most of the day left for England to make the runs. Allen had taken his last three wickets for no runs and Davidson, as a calculated risk, set out to hit him off before he could get at McKenzie. He struck him hard and high for twenty in an over. May whipped Allen off and, before Flavell bowled McKenzie (32), the last wicket partnership had added 98. England had now to aim altogether higher than they had anticipated – 256 in 230 minutes.

Pullar and Subba Row made forty level with the clock: then came Dexter to cut, pull and drive with lofty mastery. With a long, lazy six to long-on he carried his score to 76 and England to 150 for one made in 123 minutes – ahead of the clock. Benaud was now bowling himself with a hope which had no justification in the preceding cricket and, having started to bowl round the wicket, to pitch in the rough to the left-handed Subba Row, continued from that angle to Dexter who, hesitant for five balls of an over, cut at the last and was caught by Grout. Benaud continued round the wicket when May came in, pitched wide on the leg, and May, sweeping, was bowled behind his legs. Close, next, struck one six from Benaud and, after a series of huge mishits, was caught at backward short-leg. England were 163 for five at tea and afterwards, in a strange mixture of defence and attack, went down to defeat by 54 runs – beaten by Benaud's leg-breaks.

At the Oval, Gaunt – a lively fast-medium bowler only now match-fit after injury – and Davidson took seven English wickets in an innings for 256. Australia, for whom O'Neill made 117 and Burge 181, led by 238 on the first innings. Subba Row (137) who announced his retirement, May, Murray, Barrington and Allen could do no more than see England safe from defeat.

In this year, since South Africa had left the Commonwealth, her cricket authority was deemed to be no longer a member of the Imperial Cricket Conference. Therefore their international matches were not to be regarded as official Tests. In fact, cricket historians and record-keepers cannot, and do not, ignore matches played by full strength sides of other countries against South Africa. If only it could be contrived that South Africa played Tests against West Indies, India or Pakistan – as, surely, many of their cricketers would be prepared to do – the distinction

Richie Benaud (NSW) here bowling right-arm leg breaks, most unorthodoxly, round the wicket, in the spell that won the Old Trafford Test of 1961: a positive, assertive cricketer, a genuine all-rounder and an intuitive captain

would be abolished even now – and world relations would be happier.

In the same summer, Dennis Lindsay, son of Johnny Lindsay, wicket-keeper of the 1947 South African side – playing for the side of young South Africans touring England under the name 'Fezelas', against Essex – hit five sixes off five balls.

New Zealand in South Africa, 1961–62

This series of 'unofficial' Tests was played – as always between these two countries – in a spirit of keen but friendly competition. A 2–2 tie in the series lifted New Zealand to new heights and did not disgrace South Africa, for the performance of John Reid, the New Zealand captain, was of heroic quality. He was first in the New Zealand Test batting with an average of 60·64 and an aggregate greater than that of any other two of his batsmen put together; and top of the bowling table with 11 wickets at 19·72. The two seam-bowlers, Cameron and Motz, and the leg-spinner, Alabaster, were the mainstays of the New Zealand bowling. Lawrence, a six-feet-five Rhodesian pace-bowler who did not endure, took 28 wickets for South Africa, who made undoubted acquisitions in Barlow, Bland and Pollock.

E. J. Barlow

A busy cricketer, always in the game, Eddie Barlow plays in spectacles. He is thickset, a gritty opening batsman, predominantly a back-foot player, sound in method, strong off his legs and with a powerful square cut. He bowls useful right-arm medium, is a good close fieldsman and completely enthusiastic.

K. C. Bland

Many experienced observers of cricket consider Colin Bland the finest outfield in the history of the game. His anticipation, movement, catching, pick-up and throw cannot be faulted, and for spectators he is worth his place in any team for his fielding alone. Tall, relaxed, athletic, he is a positive cricketer. His batting strength lies off the front foot and is correct in technique: he is a powerful driver. A medium pace change-bowler, he is another thorough cricketer of genuine enthusiasm, likely to endure and win matches.

P. McC. Pollock

The elder of the two brothers, Peter Pollock, a fast

bowler, first played for Eastern Province when he was seventeen. Tall and strong, he bowls from a long run, at something less than the highest pace, but hostilely and with a genuine hatred of batsmen. Though he achieves occasional outswing, he does not move the ball to any great extent. His menace lies in the fact that he digs the ball in and makes it rear awkwardly. His accuracy has improved steadily and he has the stamina and purpose to come back and bowl hard in repeated spells against long batting on batsmen's wickets. He has, in short, all the essentials of the old-fashioned fast bowler and, because he never relents, he will take more wickets than lesser characters of greater technical resource.

The atmosphere and evenness of the series drew generous and enthusiastic crowds. New Zealand had a good chance to win the first Test. Though McGlew carried his bat for 127 in South Africa's 292, and the bowling of Pollock, Walter and Lawrence put New Zealand 47 behind on the first innings, the mixed attack of Motz, Cameron and Alabaster, halted only by Waite, left New Zealand a mere 197 runs to win, in nearly nine hours, on a good wicket. Pollock – who struck the decisive blow when he had Reid caught at the wicket – took six for 38, and New Zealand had failed to use their opportunity.

Time lost to rain on the first day made a draw at Johannesburg, where New Zealand's first innings was saved only by Dowling and Reid when Lawrence took eight for 53. But, set 278 to win, they were in no trouble and had made 165 for four at the end of time.

In the third Test, the batting of McGregor, Reid, Harris and Chapple in the first New Zealand innings created an advantage which was never lost. Six bowlers shared in bowling out South Africa twice and, despite McLean's defiant 113, New Zealand – by 72 – had, for the first time, won a Test in another country.

Reid – 60 and 142 – could not save New Zealand from an innings defeat in the fourth Test at Johannesburg, where McGlew (120) led the long South African batting and Lawrence took nine for 109 in the match.

New Zealand won the last Test – and tied the series – as a peak in John Reid's career. He scored 26 and 69, took two for 26 in the first innings of South Africa and then, in their second, when they were set 314 to win, bowled 45 overs to take four for 44: a magnificent effort for a 'change bowler'.

Waite, with 26 wickets (23 catches, 3 stumpings) set a new wicket-keeping record for a Test series.

Peter Pollock (Eastern Province) the hostilely fast South African bowler hits Ken Barrington with a bouncer: Varnals is at mid-on, Boycott is the other batsman and Kidson the umpire

Pakistan in England, 1962

This series was never a match. England, only once put out for less than 400, won by 4–0 without ever being extended. Hanif, troubled by an injured knee, averaged a sorry and surprising 17·7 in Tests, and batted with no enthusiasm. Two of the seam bowlers, Mahmood Hussain and Mohammad Farooq broke down, and Fazal was sent for, only, in his turn, to be over-worked. Burki, the captain and an Oxford Blue, batted bravely and so did Nasim and one of Hanif's

younger brothers, Mushtaq Mohammad. But, when seven England batsmen have averages of more than 70, and three bowlers share 51 wickets at less than 20, it is hard to regard the games as serious Test Matches.

It was a more salutary thought that the first batsman in the season's first-class averages was Reggie Simpson who, at the age of 42, played the pace-bowling of the day with mellow ease: and that the first bowler was 'Sam' Cook of Gloucester – forty-one – who played in few more than half his county's Championship matches but still, by length, line, flight and spin, took 58 wickets at 17.

England in Australia, 1962–63

Dexter's team to Australia faced two challenges. The first was to match the now well-trained and mobilized strength of Australia under Benaud; the second, to equal the public appeal of Worrell's West Indians of two years earlier. Contrary to general expectation they met the first demand and tied the series. They finished, however, to slow handclaps, having failed to take a risk, at the last, to win the rubber.

Australia's main strength did not change, though the thickset Western Australian left-hander, Barry Shepherd, was a useful stopgap batsman and Barry Jarman, for long a faithful reserve, replaced the injured Grout in three Tests.

England used Alan Smith, the Warwickshire wicket-keeper, on grounds of his batting ability; Parfitt, the Middlesex left-hander and fine close catcher; Knight of Essex, all-rounder; Coldwell the Worcester inswinger; and Illingworth – none of whom made any appreciable impact on the series; David Sheppard, who – taking time to adjust himself, especially in the field – made a century; and Titmus.

F. J. Titmus

In an age of somewhat intellectualized cricket, Fred Titmus is a perpetual reminder of the importance of the basic human and cricketing virtues. Diligent and unfaltering in approach, faithful to the established standards, he has become an England cricketer because he is inherently sound. His chief technical importance is as an off-spin bowler who may not turn the ball so sharply as some, but is always accurate, flights and 'seams' the ball on hard wickets, and studies to bowl to batsmen along a line and to a length which will be least convenient to them. His range of batting strokes is not wide but he will move down the pitch to drive slow bowling, go back to cut pace, play straight, with his head over the line, in defence. At gully, or wherever he is sent, he stops quickly and catches reliably. He would not expect to be included among the great match-winners of the game; but he is entitled to a place among its best craftsmen who, day in day out, demonstrated its cardinal virtues with professional pride.

Brisbane, in a spell of fine weather, saw the preliminary sparring, in which there were fourteen scores of over fifty. The twelve bowlers were steady, but Benaud's six for 115 in the first innings of England was the nearest approach to penetration. Neither side allowed the other a chance and they played a draw.

Dexter, head determinedly down, followed his 70 and 99 at Brisbane with 93 and 52 at Melbourne. Booth made his second century of the series, but Trueman with eight wickets, Titmus with five, left England 235 to win and Sheppard, coming into form, made a century: Cowdrey followed his first innings of 113 with a second of 58* and England were one up.

At Sydney, Davidson – nine wickets in the match – Simpson, five for 57 in the first England innings, and McKenzie, three for 26 in the second, decided the game. Pullar's 53 and Cowdrey's 85 were the chief scores in England's 279 when they batted first: but, in their second innings, they scored only 104, and Australia – winning by eight wickets – levelled the series.

At Adelaide, where Davidson bowled only three-and-a-half overs before he was injured, hundreds by Harvey, O'Neill and Barrington ensured a draw.

If the last Test was drawn, Australia would retain The Ashes. The onus was on England to force a win if they could. A slow wicket, slow batting and careful bowling made a draw, to the accompaniment of slow hand-clapping from a crowd persuaded by the West Indies visit of 1960–61 to expect dramatic Test cricket. Barrington made 101 and 94: Burge – recalled – 103 and 52*. But England, to whom a draw was all but useless, settled for a tied series. Davidson – who took a wicket with his last ball – and Harvey announced their retirement.

England won three Tests in New Zealand, two by an innings and the other by seven wickets. During the same New Zealand season Reid, in the course of an innings of 296 for Wellington v Northern Districts, hit fifteen sixes.

West Indies in England, 1963

The most important event of 1963 in cricket history was the abolition of the distinction between amateurs and professionals in the English first-class game: in future all would be simply 'cricketers', and the historic Gentlemen v Players fixture would never be played again.

As an experiment, the follow-on law was abolished: this was probably the most pointless piece of legislation ever introduced into cricket, and it was rescinded a year later. Much thought on bowling, especially in relation to 'drag', led to the trial law demanding that the front foot be grounded behind the popping crease.

Frank Worrell brought to England a side reinforced, since the last series with England, by Carew, a left-hand bat and leg-spinner; Rodriguez, potential opening bat and leg-spinner; McMorris, an opening bat from Jamaica who was a better player than his figures suggest; Allan, who came as first wicket-keeper and never played in a Test; Butcher, Murray and Griffith.

England, in the attempt to stiffen their batting after the retirement of Peter May and Subba Row, shuffled Richardson, Edrich, Stewart and Bolus as opening batsmen, brought back Close, and used Sharpe in three Tests; and, as a considered move to check the West Indian stroke-makers, included Shackleton as a bowler in four matches.

S. F. Butcher

The Guianese middle-order batsman, Basil Butcher, played consistently throughout the series. Short and wiry, he moved well on his feet, was quick to attack, watchful when the ball 'seamed' or turned. A late player of back foot attacking strokes, unhesitating in driving the over-pitched ball, he was by nature a fast scorer, but responsible and steady when an innings was in danger.

D. L. Murray

Only twenty years old when he came to England, Derryck Murray was regarded as the deputy wicket-keeper. When Allan fell ill early in the tour, Murray kept well enough to hold the position and ended with 24 wickets in the series – a record for a West Indian wicket-keeper. Murray grew up from day to day; small and adroit, he moved well when standing back to pace and, more impressively, learnt to take Sobers – when he bowled his left-arm wrist spin – and Gibbs confidently and close to the stumps. He proved, too, a useful tail-end batsman, correct and steady at difficult moments.

C. C. Griffith

Griffith, a massive and extremely strong Barbadian, bowled fast with an action to which some people took exception. There is no doubt that he bowled with his body square-on and his left foot pointing wide to the off in the delivery stride – the usual indications of an illegal delivery. The end-product of Griffith's bowling was undoubtedly entirely satisfactory to Worrell who, as captain of the side, must have been given the right

Charlie Griffith (Barbados) whose action might be questionable but about whose pace, or the efficacy of his bouncer and yorker, there can be no doubt

to decide whether or not his action was fair. Griffith broke every English partnership that ever threatened to take a match. His normal pace was high, his yorker deadly and his bouncer menacing. If he does not throw, he must rank among the half-dozen best fast-bowlers of all time. Yet it is difficult to believe that he is better, *as a true fast bowler*, than Wesley Hall, whose figures for this series are less impressive. Griffith does not seriously aspire to bat and in the field he is a steady picker-up.

P. J. Sharpe

A heavy scorer from his schooldays at Worksop, Philip Sharpe, of Yorkshire, is a short, stocky man, whose batting is thoughtful, devoted and correct. It may be that he takes too much thought about method, but he has the germ of batting in him and he strikes the bad ball strongly, with no great effort, because his timing is so good. He has, lately, reverted from a square-on stance to one sideways-on, and recovered some of his early off-side strokes. He has the attributes to become a steady player of courage, patience and measured aggression. His slip-fielding is quietly superb, his hands are good and his movement un-hurriedly quick.

J. H. Edrich

A sturdily built left-hander, with all the family courage, John Edrich, of Surrey, is a fighter, a realist and a run-maker. No pace is great enough to make him flinch and he watches the ball well. His bat gives an impression of width and he is quick to adjust his back defensive strokes. He drives and pulls with great power, and when he is in a 'run' he will go on scoring heavily for match after match.

M. J. Stewart

Lightly made, jaunty and an alert mover, Mickie Stewart is a militant opening bat who hooks more, and more securely, than most. A neat cutter and wristy driver, he has a lively approach to batting, is not easy to contain, and will always seize the slightest opportunity to take the initiative from the bowlers at the start of an innings. Fearless and quick at short-leg – he holds the record of seven catches in an innings – and, as captain of Surrey, never content with a static match, he is one of the liveliest characters in English cricket.

J. B. Bolus

A left-hand bat who was allowed to leave Yorkshire and joined Notts in 1963, Brian Bolus has twice changed his playing character. With Yorkshire he was a careful player, intent on fighting his way to a regular team place. Though he was capped in 1960 and scored 1,970 runs in 1961, he was not re-engaged at the end of the 1962 season. Moving to Notts, he scored more runs – 2,190 at 41·32 – than anyone else in England in 1963, by adventurous methods. Cutting, hooking, pulling and driving, he rode his luck, and his good eye saw him through. He could be given the main credit for Notts' rise from fifteenth in 1962 to ninth in 1963, and the county's entire cricket was lifted by his play. Picked twice against the West Indies in 1963 – an immense upward step for a man

whose county had not cared to keep him less than a year before – he seemed suddenly to lose confidence in his newly acquired aggressive methods. Chosen for the India tour of 1963–64, he batted slowly, as if convinced that grafted runs were safer, and he averaged 48·87 in Tests there. As a plodder, however, he reveals the flaws in technique, which may be covered for the moment by his good eye, for he is watchful and concentrates closely. There are those who feel that, taking chances, as he did in 1963, he is more effective than in any other style.

D. Shackleton

With 2,366 wickets – more than anyone else now playing – Derek Shackleton must be reckoned the most successful of all post-war county bowlers. Slim and of average height, he has a light-footed approach and an easy high swing. His pace is about medium – though faster than it looks – his length immaculate, and his movement through the air, and off any wicket with a remote amount of 'green' in it, is varied and sometimes quite surprising. No bowler in the history of the game can ever have been steadier, more impervious to punishment nor more certain of extracting retribution from the attacking batsman. Where the ball will move off the seam, no batsman in the world during the last seventeen years has been his master. He is completely tireless and, in many post-war seasons, he bowled more overs than anyone else in England.

Once again in 1963 it became apparent that the West Indies can strike sparks from England and Australia which those two can never produce from one another. A greater triumph for Worrell's team than their 3–1 winning of the series was their attraction to crowds and the stimulus they gave the game in England, which resulted in a re-vamping of the future tours-schedule to bring them back more frequently. Worrell wanted both these results and, by expert management, he achieved both. West Indies moved into the lead from the first Test, at Old Trafford, when Hunte, with a firm 182, and Kanhai, characteristically brilliant in making 90, laid the foundation for an innings of 501 for six declared. Hall made the first inroads on the English batting and, after that, only Dexter, with a handsomely defiant 73 in the first innings, and Stewart, with a quick-footed 87 in the second, played the difficult contrast of Sobers and Gibbs well enough to make the West Indies bat again – to score one run.

The second Test, at Lord's, lit up the English cricket season. The gates were closed from the start of play on Saturday and a vast television and wireless audience followed a game of absorbing and dramatic fluctuations.

Rain held up the start when West Indies batted hesitantly, for them, against Shackleton, who moved the ball disconcertingly, constantly beat the bat, and had two catches dropped. The West Indian innings grew steadily to 301. Dexter, standing up challengingly to the fast bowlers, swept to 70 at almost a run a minute: Barrington worked away for 80 and, in the lower half, Parks – 35 – and Titmus, with a stubborn 52, brought England to 297 – four behind on the first innings. Shackleton, immaculate in length and always keeping the batsmen on an economically tight rein, and Trueman, bowling with every scrap of resource and varied pace, were so effective against the remainder of the West Indian batting that only Butcher's 133 – in a total of 229 – saved both the innings and, as it proved, the match.

On the fourth day, England set about making 234 to win: at 64 for three, with Stewart, Edrich and Dexter out, they were in trouble. Cowdrey and Barrington were fighting to extricate them when a short ball from Hall fractured Cowdrey's wrist so severely that he did not play again that summer. Close and Barrington held on until rain and bad light ended play early on the fourth day and delayed the start of the fifth until 2.20, when England needed another 118, with seven wickets – including Cowdrey's – left.

In the first hour 18 runs were scored and Barrington was out. Close, taking savage punishment on the body from the bowling of Hall and Griffith, played the finest innings of his life. After tea England, with five wickets down, wanted 63 in 85 minutes. Hall whipped out Titmus and Trueman in two balls: 203 for seven – 31 wanted. Now Close, who had played bravely and soundly, driving the fast bowling with good judgement, decided to go down the wicket to Griffith and Hall, presumably in the hope of unsettling them. Before the tactic had shown any profit he tried to drive Griffith and edged a catch to Murray. Shackleton came in to Allen at 219 for eight – 15 wanted and 19 minutes left. Hall, who had bowled since the start of the day's play, maintained his thunderous pace with quite amazing heart and stamina. He began the last possible over with England wanting eight runs to win. Two of them came in singles: then Shackleton

was run out. The batsmen had crossed and, after a brief but dramatic pause, Cowdrey came out, with his broken wrist in plaster – to the non-striker's end. In an atmosphere of silent tension, Allen played the last two balls with a dead bat and the match was drawn.

At Edgbaston, where a huge and happy number of West Indians turned out to support their team, rain interrupted the play, but had little adverse effect on a true wicket which gained a little in pace as the game went on. Close, with a responsible 55, was top-scorer in the England innings when Sobers, bowling left-arm fast-medium with late movement and bounce sharp enough to hurry the stroke, took five early wickets for 60. England were all out for 216. Carew and Kanhai at the start of the West Indian innings, Murray and Hall later, worked hard for runs against Trueman and Dexter – nine wickets between them: West Indies, 186 – 30 behind. Stewart batted tenaciously against Griffith and Sobers until, at 69 for four, Dexter and Sharpe came together and slowly played themselves in. Once set, Dexter began to play strokes in an exciting hurry, until Gibbs beat him through the air and he was stumped. Three more wickets went quickly before Sharpe, driving shrewdly, and Lock – who played the fast bowlers with style and aplomb – put on 89 for the ninth wicket. Then Dexter declared, leaving West Indies 309 to win in 280 minutes. Hunte and Carew went to Trueman and Shackleton for ten and then, while Shackleton kept one end closed, Trueman went on to seven for 44 – a fine piece of controlled fast-medium bowling on a true pitch. West Indies, all out 91, were beaten by 217: and England still had not lost a Test at Edgbaston.

At Leeds, with the sun on their backs and taking first innings, West Indies won confidently. Kanhai (92 and 44), Sobers (102 and 52) and Butcher (23 and 78) all made strokes: Solomon jogged along for 62. Lock again batted with impressive assurance to make top score (53) and, with Titmus, to improve the England first innings from 93 for eight to 172 for nine. Bolus, Barrington, Close and Parks all held out in their own fashions in the second innings, but the varied, well-balanced and subtly handled attack of Hall, Griffith, Sobers and Gibbs moved relentlessly on, always winning the match; the final difference was 221.

The Oval Test – where England could still tie the series – ran evenly until the last stage. England batted first. Hall and Griffith mounted a bumper attack until

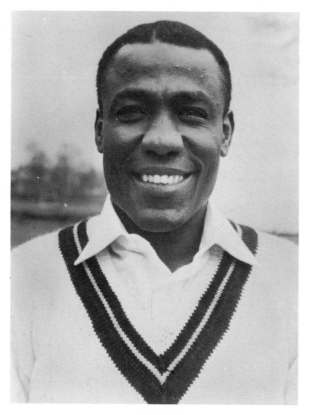

Conrad Hunte (Barbados) the formerly dashing stroke-maker who turned himself into the sheet-anchor of the West Indian batting

day, West Indies wanted 253 – seven more than they had made in the first innings – to win. Here, it seemed, was the making of another close finish. Trueman, however, had injured an ankle and bowled only one over. Without him, the English attack was loyal but no more. Hunte made certain of the West Indian win with an unhurried 108*: Kanhai, in a final flourish, made 77 at a run a minute. Butcher won the match with a boundary to long on, and a vast wave of West Indians flooded joyously across the pitch.

South Africa in Australia, 1963–64

South Africa, after more than a decade devoted to defence, suddenly emerged in a new character during this series, which they tied 1–1, and might well have won.

The touring side was captained by Goddard and included A. J. Pithey, still a batsman preoccupied with safety, but Barlow, Bland, R. G. Pollock and Lindsay gave the batting a bias towards attack. The bowling rested largely with Partridge – a steady fast-medium bowler of pronounced swing and considerable stamina; P. M. Pollock; Halse – fastish right-arm; Goddard; and the all-rounders Bland and Barlow; with only occasional spin from the two off-break bowlers, Seymour and D. B. Pithey.

Australia, still without adequate replacement for Davidson, brought in Connolly – fast-medium right-arm – and Hawke as pace bowlers, Veivers and Martin as spinners.

R. G. Pollock

The younger of the two brothers from Eastern Province, Graeme Pollock was only nineteen when he made this successful tour of Australia. A tall, graceful left-hander with a highly developed gift of timing, he is equally brilliant off the front or back foot, an elegant striker of the ball between cover and mid-off, and a certain and savage hooker. A quiet, pleasant person, he had proved himself, before he was twenty, to be one of the most handsome players in the world on hard wickets; and could face the test of less simple conditions in England with some confidence.

N. J. N. Hawke

His rather ugly – shoulderish – action is apt to create some prejudice against Neil Hawke's bowling at first

umpire Buller spoke to Worrell and, later, cautioned Griffith. The first eight batsmen all made some runs and Sharpe and Close capably and calmly put on 101 for the fifth wicket before Griffith – six for 71 – finally hammered his way through, and the innings ended at 275. Hunte, Kanhai and Butcher took West Indies to 152 and an apparently strong position before there were two run-outs. Then, while Shackleton bowled tight and had the steady Hunte caught at the wicket, Statham and Trueman took the remaining wickets and gave England an unexpected first innings lead of 29.

Worrell relied almost entirely on his faster bowlers in the second English innings, keeping Sobers on for most of the day and alternating Hall and Griffith in short spells: they shared the ten wickets. Dexter never settled in: Barrington hooked Griffith for 15 in one over, but the main England innings was that of Sharpe who, if crease-bound, played straight and unflinchingly and drove the pitched-up ball cleanly and hard: he made 83 out of 223. So, on the fourth

Graeme Pollock (Eastern Province) the rising star of South African batting, hitting assuredly against the spin. The other batsman is C. Bland; the wicket-keeper, J. Parks; the bowler D. Allen, and slip P. Parfitt

sight: bowlers of that kind usually suffer from torn muscles. Hawke, a tall, well-made man is, however, extremely strong and, swinging the new ball, cutting the old, he is a useful fast-medium bowler anywhere, and exceptionally useful in English conditions. He can bowl accurately for long spells and, unusually for one of his type, often bowls round the wicket. He can be employed as both shock bowler and stock bowler and his batting and catching are potentially good enough to make him into a Test class all-rounder.

T. R. Veivers

A sturdy – almost plump – and cheerful man, Tom

Veivers is an asset in any side. He made a marked advance as an off-break bowler on the English tour of 1964, when he extended his technique. His batting is straightforward but reliable in defence and, at need, he will hit quick runs. His catching near to the wicket is good and his pleasant manner and steady temperament make a considerable psychological contribution to his team.

The loss of a day to rain, and good batting by both sides, made the Brisbane Test a draw. In the second over of the South African innings, umpire Egar four times no-balled Meckiff for throwing. Meckiff was 'chaired' off the ground at the end of the day. Booth made a stylish 169 and, in opposition, Barlow a more aggressive 114. Peter Pollock bowled fast and well to take six for 95 in the first Australian innings; Benaud had five for 68 for Australia. After this match Benaud handed over the captaincy of Australia to Simpson, played to the end of the series under him, and then retired from the first-class game.

At Melbourne, Simpson won his first toss and sent in South Africa on a grassy wicket. Barlow made another century and Bland 50 but McKenzie, with four for 82, bowled well enough to justify Simpson's decision and South Africa were out for 274. Australia, in their turn, made 447. Lawry and his Victorian partner, Redpath, a tall, slim, cool batsman with a straight defence, scored 219 for the first wicket. Redpath made 97 in his first Test innings and Lawry went on to 157. Barlow, Pithey and Bland played steadily before the last seven South African wickets went down for 93 and, with Peter Pollock unable to bowl, Australia made 136 for two and won comfortably.

The third Test ran a fluctuating course. Again the pitch was grassy and Australia, batting first, were never comfortable against Pollock (five for 83) and Partridge (four for 88). Indeed, Simpson and Booth scored more than half the total of 260. Goddard played solidly as the South African anchor-man while Graeme Pollock made his first Test century: after playing steadily to fifty, he went to his hundred in seventeen scoring strokes. Bland scored 51 and South Africa led by 42. As the wicket lost its pace, Lawry, O'Neill, Benaud and McKenzie all made runs without undue trouble. Simpson's declaration left South Africa to make 409 at about 53 an hour and, at the end, they were only 83 short with five wickets left.

South Africa won the fourth Test by spirited cricket. Australia batted first and Goddard took five wickets for 60: after that his younger players settled the issue. Peter Pollock took five wickets – including Lawry's, twice – for 169, and his brother made 175. Barlow, after scoring 201 in the first innings, broke the middle of the Australian second innings with three for six and then made 47 of the 82 with which South Africa won by ten wickets. They might have imposed an innings defeat but for some dropped catches.

The fact that either side could win or lose the rubber in the last Test led both to go cautiously. Swinging the ball abruptly in a humid atmosphere, Partridge took seven for 91: only Booth (102*) and Burge (56) played him confidently. Goddard, Pithey and Bland – more than five hours for 126 – made a

slow way to 411 and a lead of 100. Burge, Booth and Veivers again batted responsibly but, when the ninth Australian wicket fell, they were only 125 ahead with 160 minutes left for play. Then, once more, Australians met a challenge resolutely: Veivers and Hawke scored 45 for the last wicket, leaving South Africa the impossible task of 171 in 85 minutes, and making a draw certain.

England in India, 1963–64

M. J. K. Smith took a side which did not include Trueman, Statham or Allen on an eight-week tour of India, in the course of which they drew all five Tests and four of their other five matches. The wickets were dead and neither side ever risked defeat. At one point of the tour, only ten of the fifteen members of the party were fit to play and Cowdrey – out of action since his injury at Lord's in the previous June – and Parfitt were flown out to make up the side. Despite the lack of match-results, Smith made his mark as an understanding captain, able to draw the best from his players in trying conditions. Still, too, the crowds rolled in – over a million saw the ten matches of the tour, and the profits were large. Nadkarni again was an industrious all-rounder; Jaisimha, Kunderam and Hanumant Singh all showed ability to bat attractively and at Delhi, Pataudi, the captain, scored 203 – the highest innings ever played for India against England. Titmus, still game and gay at the end of the tour, came near to bowling twice as many overs and taking twice as many wickets as any other bowler on either side, while Price laboured, not quite successfully, to flog some life from the uniformly dead pitches. It was, one of the players declared, good experience – adding, *quite* an experience.

Australia in England, 1964

Simpson's side was described in advance as the weakest ever to leave Australia. Certainly, by comparison with the team of 1961, it offered no convincing replacements for McDonald, Harvey, Mackay, Benaud and Davidson, the last three of whom had taken 54 of the 82 Test wickets in that series. But, unanswerably, Simpson's Australians retained The Ashes. Their main strengths, except Corling, were known; and Cowper, a left-hander Potter and

Redpath, all from Victoria, were accounted promising young batsmen.

England had high hopes of Boycott, who had made an impression as a new player in 1961, Cartwright, Parfitt and Barber: but there was anxiety – which proved well-founded – at the lack of obvious successors to Trueman and Statham as fast bowlers.

G. E. Corling

A lightweight fast-medium bowler from New South Wales with a light-footed approach to the wicket, Grahame Corling's main asset is his ability to make the new ball swing away from the right-hander late in flight. He is a fair field and no batsman, but his bowling several times disturbed the English batting of 1964.

G. Boycott

Of average size and wirily fit, Geoff Boycott squares his shoulders to the world and bends himself to cricket. There is no more dedicated player than this man who is, by nature, an opening batsman. By utter determination imposed on gifts which are not abnormal, he lifted himself, in a single year, from a beginner in county cricket to the position of England's opening batsman. He watches the ball tigerishly and, in the early stages of an innings, his care seems to cramp him. Like his predecessor, Herbert Sutcliffe, he is undisturbed by a narrow escape and a sequence of low scores merely makes him the more determined to make runs. He appears completely unaffected by the need to wear spectacles and fast bowling is to him no more than another technical problem to be solved. With his hands low on the bat handle, he keeps the ball down and does not care to risk the hook: he has most other back foot strokes and is careful to use them to the right ball. In a day of leg stump attack, he is adept at forcing away the ball on the leg stump, which he sometimes plays to the off side. He is a quick, dutiful fieldsman and occasionally bowls usefully at medium pace. His main aim, clearly, is to make his batting impregnable; and his application is such that he is more likely than anyone else in the game to succeed – if only he learns to play forward.

R. W. Barber

Since his move from Lancashire to Warwickshire, Bob Barber, the Oxford Blue, has changed in cricketing character. He was a somewhat pawky left-hand bat,

Geoff Boycott (*Yorkshire*) *the batsman of immense application and sharp cricketing brain who determinedly* made *himself England's opening batsman: Long (wicket-keeper) and Storey (slip) of Surrey.*

a fine athletic cover-point and a leg-spin bowler of obvious ability but all too little self-confidence. Much credit for his advance must be given to Mike Smith, humanly, as well as technically, a perceptive captain.

In a Warwickshire side where the batting runs deep, Barber now opens the innings on a basis of attack, and often makes fast runs which give his side a valuable early initiative. He now frequently fields close to the wicket, where he catches well.

Importantly, although he is by no means over-bowled in a team strong in seam-bowlers, his leg-spin is altogether steadier and more assured; his length is good for one of so much spin, and he hides his googly well enough to deceive the general run of batsmen. It is easy to believe that Barber may be on the verge of becoming one of the Test all-rounders of which England has so long stood in need.

T. W. Cartwright

Tall, adequately built and with plenty of stamina, Tom Cartwright is essentially a bowler for English conditions. From a short, easy, loping run-up, he bowls at medium pace, swinging both ways, deriving a little movement from the seam, occasionally experimenting with cut. The basis of his bowling, however, is accuracy. He will drop fractionally short of a length – according to the pace of the pitch and the method of the batsman – for as many hours as are asked of him. He belongs, with Derek Shackleton, among the born stock-bowlers.

P. H. Parfitt

A left-hand bat, Peter Parfitt is a brisk, jaunty enthusiast. Frequently a slow starter who needs time to play himself in, once set he is a natural striker of the ball, quick on his feet and fast in his reactions. He is an all-round batsman, somewhat addicted to a pulled drive and, in full confidence, a clean and daring hitter, capable of long, lively innings.

It may well be that Parfitt's off-break bowling has been neglected by both his county and his country, for he can certainly bowl a length and spin. He is one of the best catchers in England in the gully or at slip, and he plays cricket with an air of enjoyment.

Rain, which completely washed out Saturday's play for a large crowd, and cost a further eight hours of cricket on other days, made the Trent Bridge Test a sorry draw. Edrich injured his ankle at pre-match practice and Titmus moved up to open with Boycott when England took first innings. While Boycott was determinedly chiselling himself a niche in Test cricket, Titmus, going for a single, collided with the bowler – Hawke – and fell down. He was far from his crease when the ball was returned to Grout who refused to run him out – a gesture which made a marked and healthy impression on the feeling of the series.

Boycott's 48 was top score for England and, though Hawke with cut and Veivers with finger-spin, took three wickets each, Australia did not make the best use of the conditions, neither did they catch well. On Monday, with much time already lost to rain, Dexter declared at 216 for eight and his five bowlers put out Australia for 168 of which Simpson's 50 – at number six – was the top score. On the fourth evening, Dexter opened the England second innings in place of Boycott who had broken a finger in the field, and made 56 of 71 with Titmus by the close. After Dexter was out early next morning, Simpson's restrictive

field-setting – and perhaps their own inhibitions – prevented the remaining English batsmen from forcing the pace. Still, Dexter's second declaration set Australia 242 in 195 minutes. They lost two wickets for 25 and O'Neill, after hooking Trueman for four boundaries in an over, went off with his hand bruised by a ball from Flavell, before the rain put an end to it all.

At Lord's, the equivalent of two-and-a-half days was lost to bad light and weather. Dexter sent Australia in on the rain-damaged wicket where Trueman took five for 48 and Veivers, with a solid 54, was mainly responsible for their total reaching 176. England, in their turn, were unhappy against McKenzie, Hawke and Corling, but Edrich, playing with outstanding courage and judgement, scored a hundred in his first innings against Australia and, with Sharpe severe on some unusually inaccurate bowling by Simpson, England made 246. Australia had far to go when they batted again on Monday and lost Lawry. On the last day they were faced for an hour-and-a-half by pace bowling, and not until Gifford – the Worcester slow left-arm bowler – and Titmus were brought on did it appear that they were in trouble against spin. Redpath batted over three hours for 36 and went almost an hour without a run at the end of his innings. Burge was more aggressive, and Australia comfortably saved the game.

In what proved the deciding Test of the rubber, at Leeds, England batted first on an honest pitch. Dexter and Parks played freely enough and both reached the sixties but the remaining England batting was first contained and then dismissed by McKenzie and Hawke, backed by faultless catching. England's 268 seemed ordinary enough when Lawry and Simpson began the Australian innings with a stand of 50. But when Gifford bowled Simpson, Lawry – and, even more exaggeratedly, Redpath – fell on defence. At once, the two spinners, Titmus and Gifford, began to dominate the game. With one brief piece of assistance from Trueman, they bowled Australia to 178 for seven and they were still in command when, at 187, Dexter called for the new ball and gave it to Trueman and Flavell. From that moment Australia began to win the game. It may be that the change to pace bowling was less significant than the fact that Trueman bowled poorly and Flavell little better. Burge, who had played himself in with intense care, now stood up head and shoulders above everyone else in the match and hit the bowling in broad defiance. He hooked anything short – and there was much of it – with muscular severity, cut with heavy certainty and drove the full length ball with the full fling of his strong arms. In an hour and forty minutes, he and Hawke (37) made 105 for the eighth wicket; Burge reached his hundred moments before Hawke was out, and the day ended with Australia 283 for eight.

The next morning Grout comported himself with all the confidence of a Test batsman, hooking and cutting Trueman with unaffected confidence, while he and Burge made yet another 89 for the ninth wicket. Burge, in an innings fit to settle a Test or a rubber – mature, dominant, turning the course of a game by character as well as technique – made 160. Australia, out for 389, had come from their arrears and anxiety of the previous afternoon to a lead of 123.

Australia had now taken a mental as well as mathematical advantage. Though Edrich, Barrington and a determinedly subdued Dexter contested the issue, McKenzie – bowling far better than his figures – Corling and Veivers, with three wickets each, left Australia 109 to make. Titmus and Gifford could only slow their progress to a seven-wickets win.

Simpson, with his one-up situation to guard, took one look at a perfect Old Trafford wicket and hoped to win the toss and bat. He did that and, with Lawry, made 201 for the first wicket, a record for Australia against England. Lawry was run out for 106 but Simpson made his way, with calm assurance, beyond his first Test century, through the first and second days, with O'Neill, Booth and Burge, to a little bonfire of strokes on the third morning before he was out for 311 – in Australia's impregnable 656 for eight declared. Of the English seam bowlers, Rumsey – left-arm fast from Somerset – and Price, of Middlesex, took two for 99 and three for 183 respectively: Cartwright, unfailingly steady at lower pace, bowled 77 overs for 118 runs and two wickets. Rumsey and Cartwright were playing in their first Tests and Price his first in England: it was a harsh experience. Trueman must have been glad he was not there.

England's first problem was to avoid the follow-on: unless unexpectedly bad weather changed the character of the wicket, they had no chance to win. So they settled to making runs without hurry. Dexter (174) and Barrington (256) made the game safe. In their total of 611, McKenzie's figures of seven for 153 were magnificent and Veivers cheerfully bowled 95 steady overs and took three for 155. Too much of the match was spent in certainty of a draw for its last stages to be of more than statistical interest.

Rain interfered with the Oval Test, too, and slightly affected the wicket. More credit must go to Hawke – six for 47 – than blame to the pitch for the fact that, though England's first five batsmen all played themselves in, none reached fifty and they were all out for 182. Lawry, with a dishearteningly slow innings of 94 and steady support from the middle-order batting, put Australia reasonably safe at 379. The second England innings was more assured. Boycott scored the Test century he had promised himself; Dexter, Barber, Cowdrey, Barrington and Titmus all made runs, and, 381 at the end of the fourth day, England could see a distant possibility of forcing a win: but rain blotted out the last day and made another draw. McKenzie, with six wickets in the match, equalled Grimmett's record, for an Australian bowler, of 29 in a series in England. Trueman took his three-hundredth Test wicket.

Australia, if only narrowly the better equipped side by technical standards, were of stronger purpose, with Burge's great century at Leeds its high point.

If England had lost, however, there was junketing in the provinces when Glamorgan, Warwickshire and Essex all won their matches against the Australians.

England in South Africa, 1964–65

England, captained by M. J. K. Smith, won the only finished Test of a rubber so dominated by batting that thirteen batsmen on the two sides had averages of more than forty and no regular bowler one of less than 26. England, in their now almost feverish search for pace bowlers, took out David Brown of Warwickshire, the steady and resourceful Ian Thomson, and Price; the best of them on Test figures was Price with eight wickets at 52 each.

At Durban, Smith won the toss, Barber and Boycott opened the innings with 120, and Barrington and Parks scored centuries in 485 for five declared. Then, on a pitch yielding slight turn, Titmus and Allen, in some 130 overs, took thirteen wickets between them and bowled England to an innings win.

At Johannesburg, Dexter – who joined the team after the General Election – and Barrington made centuries and Barber 97 in a total of 531. All the South African batsmen made some runs – Bland 144 – but a match of 1,184 runs for 26 wickets could be little other than a draw.

Trevor Goddard (Natal) a major all-rounder of post-war cricket and a mainstay of South African sides for a decade. David Brown (Warwickshire) the fieldsman

So it was at Cape Town, where the two sides seemed in awe of one another's batting. This time Barlow, A. J. Pithey and Smith made the centuries and there were eleven other scores of forty or more: only 27 wickets fell.

In the fourth Test – Johannesburg again – the two first innings were even at 390 for six, to 384. But Goddard's hundred and runs from Barlow, Bland and Pithey and Graeme Pollock to a declaration at 307 for three, gave South Africa their best chance of a win. Boycott – 76* – saved England who were 153 for six at the end.

Centuries by Pollock and Boycott, 1,144 runs for 25 wickets, came in the fourth draw, at Port Elizabeth. Only a few months ahead lay the series between the two sides in England where bowlers would have a better opportunity to take wickets, and batsmen less to draw matches.

Australia in the West Indies, 1964–65

A series reasonably to be regarded as for the Championship of the cricket world was won, as had been expected, by West Indies (2–1). It was the first time Australia had lost a rubber to any country except England. But, in winning the last Test by ten wickets, they emphasized that their team-building is moving towards another high level.

It seemed that Simpson's side would be much weaker than in England for the absence of the mature and responsible Burge as a batsman, and Veivers, as an all-rounder and generally benevolent influence. In the event, Cowper went far towards becoming Burge's successor and Peter Philpott, a widely experienced leg-break bowler, took eighteen wickets.

The West Indies had still all their main strength of 1963 in England. Murray, the wicket-keeper, however, was in residence at Cambridge University and Jackie Hendriks, a tall Jamaican who bats capably and was unlucky to miss the 1963 tour, took his place with no weakening of the side. Bryan Davis, a stylish young Trinidadian batsman, made a promising opening partner for Hunte.

R. M. Cowper

Tall, powerful and of pleasantly fair-haired appearance, Bob Cowper is a left-handed batsman who was taken to England in 1964 as one of three young batsmen on trial: he was the one to win the vacant batting place. His batting in early 1964 looked a good-wicket product, with vulnerable gaps. During that summer he became altogether more solid and, in the West Indies, if less free than he had been, he batted with immense determination and dealt with the fast bowling of Hall and Griffith calmly and soundly. A useful catcher at slip and an occasional off-spin bowler, he should long remain a regular Australian player.

The West Indies won the first and third Tests. At Kingston, Mayne – a fast-medium bowler from Western Australia – Hawke and Philpott exploited some rather careless West Indian batting to dismiss them for 239, which might have been much less but for 57* by White, the Barbadian all-rounder coming in at number nine. Hall, bowling with splendid fire and occasional late movement, took five for 60 to give West Indies an unexpected first innings lead of 22. Hunte, Butcher and Solomon, by steady methods against more good bowling by Mayne and Philpott, set Australia 399 to win. That was more than enough manoeuvring space for Hall – four for 45 – and the five other bowlers who shared the remaining wickets, to win the game by 179.

On the easiest batting wicket in the world, at Port of Spain, Simpson put West Indies in and they made 429 (Butcher 117). Cowper's 143 and Booth's 117 were the chief Australian innings in a total of 516; West Indies batted through to the end of the match for 386 and the expected draw.

At Georgetown, West Indies brought in an extra batsman – the tall Barbadian, Seymour Nurse – for White and batted first on another good pitch. Hawke – quick to adapt his bowling methods to West Indian conditions as he had to English – bowled strongly under sharp direction by Simpson and took six for 72 in a West Indian total of 355 in which only Kanhai (89) made more than fifty. It appeared a towering score when Sobers, shuffling his four bowlers – Hall, Griffiths, Gibbs and himself – imaginatively, harried all the Australian batsmen: Cowper's 41 was top score in a total of 179. West Indies, batting again, made only 180; Sober's rapid 42 at a run a minute indicated his belief in the possibility of forcing a win. So it proved: the wicket began to respond to spin, Hall and Griffith bowled only seven overs before Gibbs – six for 29 – and Sobers ran through the Australian batting to 144, to give West Indies the match by 212.

West Indies needed now only one draw from the remaining two Tests to take the rubber. Sobers, in the manner of Test captains since Tests began, set out to confirm his side's victory. He had inherited a well-trained side from Frank Worrell and, though he had no previous experience of captaincy, he handled it well.

There were three double centuries at Bridgetown. When Australia took first innings, Lawry made 210, Simpson 201 and Cowper 102, and they had 522 before their second wicket fell. Simpson declared at 650 for six, whereupon West Indies – with 201 by Nurse and 129 by Kanhai – scored 573. Prepared to take a chance to win, Simpson declared Australia's second innings at 175 for four and set West Indies 253 in a little over four hours. An opening of 145, at almost a run a minute, by Hunte and Davis set West Indies on the way and only a mighty effort by Hawke and McKenzie with the second new ball kept them, at the last, eleven runs short of a third win. The rubber, however, now lay with West Indies. Hendriks,

while batting, was struck on the head by a bouncer, taken to hospital and found to be too severely injured to take part in the rest of the game, or in the fifth Test.

The pundits expected Port of Spain to produce another draw: they were proved wrong by superb Australian outcricket, vacillating West Indian batting and a pitch from which the ball turned, and sometimes crept.

West Indies batted: Hawke brought them down to 26 for three and Kanhai (121) made more than half their 224. The Australian innings was sustained by stands of 138 for the second wicket by Simpson and Cowper, and 55 for the fifth by Graham Thomas – a forcing bat from New South Wales – and Shepherd: 294 gave them a lead of 70. The second West Indian innings consisted of Hunte – who batted through for 60* – at one end, and collapse at the other. David Sincock, a left-arm wrist spinner, was erratic and took only two wickets, but Simpson gave him a long spell in which he seemed to unsettle all the West Indian batsmen except Hunte. Meanwhile, McKenzie (five for 33) and Hawke (three for 31) ripped through the innings. Simpson and Lawry undisturbedly made the 62 runs to win.

Hall, Gibbs, Griffith and Sobers again proved a fine bowling combination. Sobers, however, took his 12 wickets at 41 each; and he made only 352 runs, without a century, at 39·11: it would seem that the strain of captaincy reduced him – though surely only temporarily – to human level.

Australia, on the evidence of this series, have strengthened their batting with Cowper and Thomas; but are still short of one – even two – first-flight bowlers.

England, 1965

The re-shaped tours programme brought both New Zealand and South Africa to England – the only occasion on which two Test-playing countries have made the visit in the same summer apart from the Triangular Tournament of 1912. New Zealand, under John Reid – junior only to his team-mate Bert Sutcliffe among currently active Test cricketers – hold an impressive-looking hand of pace-bowling. South Africa, captained by Peter van der Merwe, presented their exciting young players – the two Pollocks, Bland, Barlow and Lindsay – for the first time

John Reid (Wellington) the major figure in New Zealand's cricket history, batsman, bowler, wicket-keeper and captain: a Test regular from 1949 *to* 1965*: chosen as captain of the World XI against England* 1965*. Cowdrey at slip, Parks keeping wicket*

in England at Test level.

When the first-class season ends, the most ambitious of the new – commercial patronage – ventures will take place. A World XI – chosen by the public through *The Radio Times* and subsidized by Rothmans – under the captaincy of John Reid will play two matches against England teams. There has never before been such a gathering of cricket talent at the same time on one cricket field and, released from the pressures of strict representative cricket, the players have the gifts and the freedom to mount an outstanding spectacle. By their success or failure, these games could make a deep impression on the future history of cricket – the ever-changing game.